YEAR

OF THE

PASSOVER

YEAR
OF THE
PASSOVER

Jesus
and the
Early Christians
in the
Roman Empire

JOHN HAGAN

Rauson Group LLC

ISBN 978-0-9820828-0-5

LCCN 2009925442

Proofreading services provided by Victoria Brouillette.
Acknowledgments to Peter Kirby, earlychristianwritings.com.
Contact: 2313 L-S, #138, San Antonio, Texas 78230

Cover: Rock of the Tomb of Jesus, Church of the Holy Sepulcher

Table of Contents

Graphics /Tables

Introduction

Year of the Passover is an investigation into history with the intent of establishing an accurate time line of early Christian events. In doing so, the reader will be taken on an extended journey through the ancient Roman and Jewish worlds of 2,000 years ago. As New Testament events take their place on the first century A.D. time line, many surprising and even astounding facts about Jesus and the early Christians will be discovered.

The people of antiquity were intelligent and competent—arguably more so than we are today. Technical advances make modern life easier, to be sure, but the human species hasn't changed significantly in 20,000 years. The ethical questions and moral dilemmas faced by all men are timeless. The stories of the ancients can give insights into our own lives, and we should learn from them.

As with any historical undertaking, *Year of the Passover* cannot be more accurate than the sources upon which it relies. Unfortunately, relatively few manuscripts written in the first century A.D. survive apart from the Christian. Additionally, in those remaining works some of the facts are clearly contradictory or in frank error–whether originally so or introduced later by well-intentioned copyists. In critical analysis a potential reference source is completely discarded if it is demonstrated to have any errors. But this luxury cannot be afforded in the study of ancient history, for provable errors occur in even in the "best" of source works.

So it is admitted at the outset that the conclusions drawn in *Year of the Passover* are unavoidably speculative—but not necessarily false. Even if, however, some conclusions are contentious, the reader should find the process of sifting through the ancient writings and fitting the pieces together a fascinating and worthwhile process in itself–as I have. As a warning, sections of *Year of the Passover* that are prefaced by "Interlude" go beyond the boundaries of reasonable speculation. I think you will find them enjoyable none-the-less.

When I began this project I had no idea where it would lead. The intent was to let the facts define the direction. Secondary and tertiary characters in the New Testament were followed in secular Roman historical works. My reference sources were very carefully chosen and I only rarely referred to works outside of them—a discipline which I feel gives *Year of the Passover* and its companion work, *Fires of Rome,* a unique integrity. Only after several years of research did the real politics of those times became clear. The two resulting books answer many of the questions behind not only Jesus' crucifixion but the saga of the early Christians over the first three decades of the religion's existence.

The first half of *Year of the Passover* sets the stage by outlining the history of the early first century A.D. eastern Roman Empire, which of necessity has its roots deep in the first century B.C. Early chapters include a review of the important secular sources, a description of the land and people of the Jewish East as seen through the eyes of contemporaneous writers, a brief and targeted history of the Roman Empire and other empires that arose around the Mediterranean Sea, and a biography of the Roman puppet ruler King Herod the Great. Later chapters move into Judaism and Christianity. The birth year of Jesus, the High Priesthood of the Jerusalem Second Temple, and the three major religious divisions of Jewish priests–one of them being the secretive sect of the Essenes — are all studied.

Biographies will prove to be an important source of chronological clues and so many of the stories of famous people of the Roman Empire will be told. Illustrious figures such as Emperor Tiberius Caesar, Agrippa the Great, Herod Antipas, and Queen Herodias, and others will be studied. *Year of the Passover* concludes on the eve of the fateful Passover of Jesus' crucifixion–with that year determined.

A limited index has been prepared for the convenience of the reader. It includes references made in the text proper and not the content in the reproduced selections from the ancient sources. All of the sources used in *Year of the Passover* are in the public domain and freely available online. The Bible source is the American Standard Version (ASV) unless otherwise noted.

Roman Events	12 B.C.- A.D. 34	Christian Events
	12 B.C. ?	Birth year of Jesus
Tiberius is in his fifteenth year of rule	A.D. 28	John the Baptist rises to fame as a prophet, possibly baptizes Jesus
Livia dies, the widow of Augustus Caesar and the protector of the Herod family in Rome	A.D. 29	
Attempted coup fails by Sejanus. Proscriptions and chaos reigns in Rome for years	Oct A.D. 31	
Herod Agrippa leaves Rome. Herodias weds Herod Antipas in Galilee. Pharaelis flees to Nabotea.	Spring A.D. 32	
Herod Philip marries Salome, Herodias' daughter	Summer A.D. 32	
Herod Philip dies. Tiberius delays award of his kingdom	Jan A.D. 34	
Pilate unveils aqueduct project, riots ensue.	Spring A.D. 34	Jesus drives out the merchants in the Second Temple at the Passover in Jerusalem
Parthia challenges Rome in Armenia. Parthian nobles approach Tiberius for help	Summer A.D. 34	

Roman Events	A.D. 34-36	Christian Events
Tiberius orders Vitellius to Syria to stop Parthian aggression, ? orders Herod Antipas to invade Nabotea.	Dec A.D. 34	
	Jan A.D. 35	John the Baptist is arrested by Herod Antipas as Antipas prepares for war
	Feb A.D. 35	John the Basptist is beheaded by Antipas, Jesus retreats north
	April A.D. 35	Jesus celebrates the Passover in the hills of the Decapolis
Vitellius successfully stops Parthia's attempted takeover of Armenia Herod Antipas continues to prepare his army for an invasion of Nabotea	Summer A.D. 35	Jesus introduces communion ceremony in Capernaum, loses many followers
Herod Antipas' army is defeated by Aretas'.	Late Summer A.D. 35	
Tiberius orders Vitellius to invade Nabotea and avenge Antipas' defeat	Fall A.D. 35	Jesus returns to Jerusalem for the feast of the Tabernacles
	Dec A.D. 35	Jesus revists John the Baptist's camp by the Jordan
Vitellius arrives in Jerusalem for the Passover after Jesus' crucifixion, Ciaiphas removed	Spring A.D. 36	Lazarus ressurrected Crucifixion of Jesus early in the Passover

Chapter 1   Herod's Golden Eagle

And that very night there was an eclipse of the moon. (*Antiq* XVII 6:4)

Ancient events could be dated using a relative scale of years and not an absolute one. Jesus' last Passover could be determined in terms of a particular year in the reign of Emperor Tiberius, for instance. All of the history and biographies and fascinating events of ancient times would still be there to be considered and mulled over, but without a link to modern times the history would lack impact and immediacy — as if it had taken place on another planet . Plus, parallel time lines in different cultures might not be able to be accurately synchronized which would be a great loss as well.

The continuity of the passage of years from ancient to modern times was broken sometime during the fall of the Roman Empire. Smaller kingdoms cared little about events of centuries ago, occupied with more immediate concerns. The final stroke might have been the Muslim destruction of the great library in Alexandria, Egypt, in A.D. 642. Very likely, until that time the priests of the Alexandrian library maintained an accurate chronology of historical events.

It was well into the Renaissance, a thousand years later, when a recrudescence of interest in ancient events made the repair of the time line desirable. But how was it possible to do so through the chronological fog of the Middle Ages? Where would one even begin?

As the informed reader knows, the broken continuum between the Roman age and the modern age has been repaired–the Medieval gap has, in fact, been bridged. How it came about lies in a story related by Jewish historian Flavius Josephus which took place in the last year in the reign of an evil king

King Herod the Great.

Herod was one of the great villains in history. He ruled over the Jewish lands by Roman proxy from 37 B.C. to 4 B.C. His most atrocious act was the mass slaughter of innocent babies in order to kill the one infant–Jesus–who he feared one day might challenge him or his descendants for power (Mt 2:16). For this and other instances of madness and brutality, Herod the Great was hated and feared by his Jewish subjects. Indeed, Herod was never considered a legitimate king at all in the eyes of most Jews. Not only was Herod appointed by Rome to the throne, but by blood Herod was far more Arabic than Hebrew.

Murder was no stranger to Herod and he committed it frequently and with little remorse. Herod killed his own wife, the famously beautiful Mariamne, in a jealous rage. He slaughtered three of his blood sons whom he suspected of plotting against him. Earlier in his reign, Herod eventually killed the entire 70-member Sanhedrin of Jerusalem after they had accused him of murder. Even the most innocuous of political enemies did not live long under Herod the Great. And when Herod ran short of funds, he would kill to gain the estates of wealthy subjects. It was Herod's murder of the Jewish scholar Matthias, however, that is relevant for our purposes here.

The execution of Matthias occurred in the last year of Herod's life and shortly before the Passover of that year which was a springtime festival. At that time, Herod was consumed by a painful and disfiguring disease — perhaps an appropriate end to his evil reign. His death was a long and lingering one. Herod would slip in and out of unconsciousness over the course of his final months. All the while, the Jewish nation waited nervously and expectantly as Herod lay dying in his palace at Jericho. Located on the cool bluffs overlooking the lush Jordan River delta, Jericho was only a day's journey east of Jerusalem.

During his deathbed watch and a few weeks before the Passover in that final year, Herod fell into an unconsciousness that was more catatonic than usual. Was he finally dead?!

There was one Judas, the son of Saripheus and Mattbias, the son of Margalothus, two of the most eloquent men among the Jews and the most celebrated interpreters of the Jewish laws..These men, when they found that the king's distemper was incurable, excited the young men that they would pull down all those works which the king had erected contrary to the law of their fathers.. for the king had erected over the great gate of the temple a large golden eagle, of great value and had dedicated it to the temple. Now the law forbids those that propose to live according to it, to erect images or representations of any living creature. So these wise men persuaded [their scholars] to pull down the golden eagle..

And with such discourses as this did these men excite the young men to this action; and a report being come to them that the king was dead, this was an addition to the wise men's persuasions; so, in the very middle of the day, they got upon the place, they pulled down the eagle and cut it into pieces with axes, while a great number of the people were in the temple. And now the king's captain, upon hearing what the undertaking was.. came up thither, having a great band of soldiers with him, such as was sufficient to put a stop to the multitude of those who pulled down what was dedicated to God; so he fell upon them unexpectedly and..so he caught no fewer than forty of the young men, who had the courage to stay behind when the rest ran away, together with the authors of this bold attempt, Judas and Matthius, who thought it an ignominious thing to retire upon his approach and led them to the king.. Herod deprived this Matthias of the high priesthood and burnt the other Matthias, who had raised the sedition, with his companions, alive. And that very night there was an eclipse of the moon. (*Antiq* XVII 6:2-4)

A rumor started that Herod had died. It was a rumor that people wanted to believe so it gained momentum and spread quickly. The false news was heard in Jerusalem and taken as fact. The rejoicing of the people began. One of the celebrants was Matthias, a learned man and a leader in the Jewish community. Matthias and his colleague Judas urged the young men under their tutelage to remove a large decorative golden eagle that Herod had placed over the tall bronze gates that led to the inner courtyards of the Second Temple. The gathered mob cheered Matthias and the perpetrators' bold actions!

Graven images were strictly forbidden within the holy city of Jerusalem. Any representation of a natural creature, man or beast, was considered a human challenge to the perfection of God. But Herod's dedication to Jewish law was halfhearted at best so he had set the eagle up over the Temple gates in order to spite the Jewish priesthood. To the Jews, the eagle was an abomination in itself, but also a symbol of hated Rome. So Matthias, believing that Herod had died, was driven to make the Temple pure again. The eagle had to be removed!

And it was. The perpetrators were captured by Herod's guard.

Unfortunately for them, back in Jericho, Herod recovered from his near-death swoon. Soon, he learned of the sedition in Jerusalem and the subsequent capture of the young men and Matthias by one of his loyal captains. After what passed for a trial in those days, Herod sentenced the men to be burned alive. A horrible punishment but not out of character for the barbarous and ruthless king. Most significantly for history, a lunar eclipse occurred on the evening of the execution which was documented by Josephus.

The eclipse was an evil portent for Herod, for he would die a hideous and lingering death less than seven months later. But for modern historians the eclipse was a godsend of epic proportions.

The Lunar Eclipse

We can do no better in explaining not only a lunar but a solar eclipse by referring to the third century A.D. Roman historian Dio, who not only had a surprisingly firm grasp of astronomy but knew that the earth was round 1,000 years before Columbus!

> The moon which revolves in its orbit (or so it is believed), either directly below it or perhaps with Mercury and Venus intervening, has a longitudinal motion, just as the sun has and a vertical motion, as the other perhaps likewise has, but it has also a latitudinal motion such as the sun never shows under any conditions. When, therefore, the moon gets in a direct line with the sun over our heads and passes under its blazing orb, it obscures the rays from that body that extend toward the earth. To some of the earth's inhabitants this obscuration lasts for a longer and to others for a shorter time, whereas to still others it does not

occur for even the briefest moment. For since the sun always has a light of its own, it is never deprived of it and consequently to all those between whom and the sun the moon does not pass, so as to throw a shadow over it, it always appears entire. This, then, is what happens to the sun and it was made public by Claudius at that time. But now that I have once touched upon this subject, it will not be out of place to give the explanation of a lunar eclipse also. Whenever, then, the moon gets directly opposite the sun (for it is eclipsed only at full moon, just as the sun is eclipsed at the time of new moon) and runs into the cone-shaped shadow of the earth, a thing that happens whenever it passes through the mean point in its latitudinal motion, it is then deprived of the sun's light and appears by itself as it really is. Such is the explanation of these phenomena. (Dio 60:26)

In analyzing the ancient and medieval documents available to modern scholars, the year of the death of King Herod can be roughly estimated to within 10 or 20 years. Using Newtonian equations and modern astronomy, the times of lunar eclipses and where they could have been seen on earth can be back-calculated. "Herod's" lunar eclipse was almost certainly the one that occurred over Jerusalem on the evening of the 13th of March, 4 B.C.

Assuming this, Herod the Great died in the fall of that year.

The establishment of this date is one of the great archaeological accomplishments of modern science. Using this famous date as a reference point, accurate dates can be assigned to most ancient events of importance. It can be determined, for instance, that that the city of Rome was founded in 753 B.C., that the first consul of Rome was elected in 153 B.C., and that Alexander the Great died in 323 B.C., and so on—all based on the lunar eclipse observed on the evening of the execution of the unfortunate Jewish scholar Matthias and his young charges.

The Passing of the Years

Most cultures keep track of the days and years in Calendars either based on the solar year or on the phasing of the moon. In a lunar-based Calendar, each new month must begin on a new moon (month—moonth). In a solar-based Calendar, the year is pegged to progression of the sun, and the months do not necessarily have to begin with a new moon. These two Calendars schemes can never quite be in phase as the earth rotating around the sun and the moon rotating around the earth are independent of each other.

In a lunar-based Calendar, the months are set in stone. The cycle of the moon's phasing is 29 ½ days long, so the months alternate between 29 and 30 days. But the solar cycle lasts for 365 ¼ days which means that a partial month of 11 days will have to be included or the year runs short. In the lunar Calendar of the Jews, that is still used to this day, and the ancient Roman Calendar that was also lunar-based, every three years an entire extra month was included to keep both cycles in synch.

In a solar Calendar, 12 months are inserted without regard to the phasing of the moon and can be of varying lengths. The error is much lower at only six hours per year. An extra day has to be added every four years as a result. Julius Caesar instituted this solar Calendar in the Roman Empire in 46 B.C.

What follows is an idealized table that correlates the Jewish months in their lunar year with the modern months in a solar year. The moon cycle is 29 ½ days.

Jewish Lunar	Modern Solar
Nissan 1 (30 days)	March 20
Iyar 1 (29)	April 19
Sivan 1 (30)	May 18
Tamuz 1 (29)	June 17
Ab 1 (30)	July 16
Elul 1 (29)	Aug 15
Tisri 1 (30)	Sept 13
Maychesvan 1 (29)	Oct 13
Casleu 1 (30)	Nov 11
Tebeth 1 (29)	Dec 10
Shebat 1 (30)	Jan 8
Adar 1 (29)	Feb 7
Nissan 1 (30)	March 8 (!)

To compensate in the Jewish Calendar, every three years a 13th month, Adar II, would be added after Adar I. Adar II would be of variable lengths depending upon the amount of error that had accumulated. It can be appreciated that the Jewish priests assigned Calendar duty did not have an easy time of it!

Tracking the moon closely was important in many pagan religions. Celestial bodies seen in the night sky were thought to be reflections of a divine force — windows into heaven — and their movements watched closely.

Calendar Schemes

The ancient Romans used a lunar based Calendar and numbered their years with the base year "1" being the year the city of Rome was founded. Roman historian Publius Tacitus followed another Roman convention, tracking the years according to the names of Senate consuls who were yearly elected, each pair taking office on the first day, or "Kalends," of January.

"Kalends" served the base root word for the modern word "Calendar." It always marked the new moon and was the first day of every month in the lunar Calendar. Likewise the "Ides" referred to the full moon and marked the 15th day of every month. "Nones" refers to the eighth day of the month or when the moon was in its half phase. In Rome, it was a market day, and every eighth day was so designated. When Rome adopted the solar Calendar, these names remained, though out of synch with the moon phases.

The ancient Jewish nation numbered years beginning with when the earth was supposedly created–several thousands of years before the time of Jesus. It is unknown if these years were counted off one by one as they were personally chronicled by the Jewish priests, or whether astrology or some other method was used to identify the year of creation in the distant past. Within the month, only the seven-day Sabbath cycle was observed.

Other noteworthy Calendar systems included the Greek. The Greeks counted their years with the first year of the first Olympiad being year "1." As the Olympic competition occurred every four years, the first Olympic year would be designated "1,1"–the first (1) year of the first (1) Olympiad. The third year after the year of the first Olympics was designated "1,4", with the next year, a year when the next Olympic games were held, was "2,1", or the first year of the second Olympic games.

The Babylonians had their own Calendar based on astrology, as did the Persians, as, in fact, did most other world cultures that had reached a level where the detailed tracking of time was essential.

Julius Caesar in A.D. 46 ordered that Rome adopt the solar-based Calendar which was then being used by the Egyptians. Queen Cleopatra might have convinced him of the advantages of it. This reflects the increasing importance of trade and economics within the empire. The solar Calendar tracks the growing season closely while the phasing of the moon does not. In Egypt, the all-important flooding of the Nile had nothing to do with the moon and everything to do with the seasons of the year. The lunar Calendar was designed for religion only and not for practical everyday considerations of commerce.

After the fall of Rome, the western world with its disparate feudal kingdoms stumbled its way through the Middle Ages with no common Calendar and no common culture. Recognizing this, Pope Gregory ordered the creation of a Calendar in the 16th century to be used by all of the Catholic world. This was called, fittingly enough, the Gregorian Calendar. Its base year was the birth of Jesus, but that determination was based on the Bible and conjecture.

Ancient Hours and Days

In ancient times the Jewish day was divided up into 12 hours of daylight and 12 hours of darkness, with each new "day" starting at sunset. The Jewish system of marking time was based on the Egyptian system which had 10 hours of daylight, two hours of twilight and 12 hours of night. The Jewish priests dispensed with the twilight and made the day and night both 12 hours long.

What determined the length of the hour? Astrology was a dominant force in those times, and the "science" was used to measure the passage of the hours as well as predict the future. The length of the hour was determined by the constellations in the night sky. As the horizon of the earth would arc across the identifiable star patterns, the length of the hour was determined. That time interval was standardized through sand or water-based hour-glasses of some sort and carried over into the day. Of course, in the daytime no constellations can be seen.

The hour itself was divided up into 60-minute intervals with each minute divided up into 60 seconds for practical reasons. The number 60 is evenly divided by 2, 3, 4, 5, 6, etc which makes for ease of calculation. Similarly, 12 is also an evenly divisible number. It is possible that sly early Egyptian priests fudged on the identification of the night sky constellations in order to come up with a number, 12, that would be the most practical in that respect. The Babylonians used 360 degrees when marking degrees on a circle for the same reason; the number is divided evenly by many other numbers.

As Judea is situated close to the earth's equator, each day throughout the year has roughly an equal amount of daylight and darkness hours–about 12 each. In modern terms, the first hour of the Jewish day would have been 6 a.m.; the sixth hour of the day corresponded to noon; the ninth hour to 3 p.m. Likewise, the first hour of the night would correlate to 6 p.m.

It should be noted that there was some variance as to when the sun set and when the Sabbath day was considered to begin. The Essenes began their holy day when the setting sun just touched the horizon. Alternatively, in starting the "night" clock and the beginning of the day, some Jewish religious authorities went by the appearance of three or four identifiable stars in the sky.

In the Jewish Calendar, the first five days of the week were not given individual names. The seventh, the holy day, was called the Sabbath. The sixth day of the week was called the day of

Preparation as it preceded the Sabbath day. During it, the Jews "prepared" for the Sabbath. In the modern Calendar, the Sabbath day is Saturday and the day of Preparation is Friday. On the day of Preparation all Jews would stop their regular labors at the ninth hour, or 3 p.m. The remaining three hours of daylight would be spent in the preparation of food, housecleaning, and the performance of other essential tasks that were forbidden during the Sabbath day itself.

In Jerusalem, the beginning and end of the Sabbath day was heralded by the sounding of a trumpet fanfare from high atop the Pastophoria which was a part of the Second Temple.

> ... where one of the priests stood of course and gave a signal beforehand, with a trumpet at the beginning of every seventh day, in the evening twilight, as also at the evening when that day was finished, as giving notice to the people when they were to leave off work and when they were to go to work again. (*Wars* IV 9:12)

Likely the larger Jewish towns had similar methods of audibly signaling the beginning of the holy day and the marking of other important days of the year.

The Year of the Crucifixion

Now that the ancient and modern years have been linked on a continuum, we will attempt to use Calendar-based information in the New Testament to mathematically back-calculate and find the year of Jesus' crucifixion—as was done with the "Herod's" lunar eclipse.

To do this, the ancient Jewish Passover must first be understood. The Passover meal, or Paschal meal, was celebrated on the 14th day of Nisan, after preparing for it the preceding four days (*Antiq* III 10:5). This commemorated the time in Egypt when, according to the Torah, God's Angels "passed over" the houses of the enslaved Hebrews who had marked their houses with sheep's blood. The angels then slew those first-born males in the unmarked homes of the Egyptians. This act of God finally convinced the Egyptian pharaoh to release the 13 enslaved tribes of Israel from captivity, allowing them to leave Egypt under the leadership of Moses.

In ancient Jewish times, after the day of the Paschal for the next seven days the feast of the unleavened bread was celebrated. Accordingly, this would run from the 15th day to the 21st day of Nisan (*Antiq* XI 4:8).

> ...and they offered the sacrifice which was called the Passover, on the fourteenth day of the same month and feasted seven days and spared for no cost, but offered whole burnt-offerings to God and performed sacrifices of thanksgiving, because God had led them again to the land of their fathers and to the laws thereto belonging and had rendered the mind of the king of Persia favorable to them. (*Antiq* XI 4:8)

The bread is unleavened to memorialize that the Hebrews left Egypt so quickly that they did not have time to put leaven in their bread. On the 16th day of Nisan, Jewish pilgrims would traditionally offer the first fruits of the field to the priests of the Jerusalem Second Temple. These specific days in Nisan were observed without exception every year according to a Calendar that was set yearly by the Jewish High Priesthood.

At least two of the Gospels–Matthew and Mark–provide important information on Jesus' last Passover. On the first day of the feast of the unleavened bread, the disciples were given instructions by Jesus as to the time and place of the so-called last supper.

> $^{26:17}$Now on the first *day* of unleavened bread the disciples came to Jesus, saying, Where wilt thou that we make ready for thee to eat the passover? $^{26:18}$And he said, Go into the city to such a man and say unto him, The Teacher saith, My time is at hand; I keep the passover at thy house with my disciples. $^{26:19}$And the disciples did as Jesus appointed them; and they made ready the passover. (Mt)

> $^{14:12}$And on the first day of unleavened bread, when they sacrificed the passover, his disciples say unto him, Where wilt thou that we go and make ready that thou mayest eat the passover? $^{14:13}$And he sendeth two of his disciples and saith unto them, Go into the city and there shall meet you a man bearing a pitcher of water: follow him; $^{14:14}$and wheresoever

he shall enter in, say to the master of the house, The Teacher saith, Where is my guest-chamber, where I shall eat the passover with my disciples? ^{14:15}And he will himself show you a large upper room furnished *and* ready: and there make ready for us. ^{14:16}And the disciples went forth and came into the city and found as he had said unto them: and they made ready the passover. ^{14:17}And when it was evening he cometh with the twelve. (Mk)

This last supper was held in Jerusalem on the second day of the feast of the unleavened bread, remembering that the Jewish day begins at sundown and runs 24 hours through to the next sundown. So Jesus was arrested late in the evening of the 16th of Nisan and was crucified later during the "same" day. According to the Gospels, in the year that Jesus was crucified the 16th day of Nisan had to be a Friday since it fell on the day of Preparation.

The month of Nisan by definition had to begin on a new moon. This would mean that the full moon would have been seen on the 15th day of Nisan, give or take twelve hours. It follows that Jesus would have been crucified roughly one day into the waning moon.

What can we now do with all this information? From the gospels, we know the day of the month, the month, the date within the year, and the phase of the moon when Jesus was crucified. Also, from the ancient writings, we have a rough 20-year idea within which the event had to occur.

In fact, computer back-calculations have been done using this data — with the year of Jesus' last Passover determined to be A.D. 34.

Should we now close our investigation and move on?

If we do, the reader will miss a lot of interesting history and biographies of the famous people of ancient times! But there are other reasons as well.

While A.D. 34 may indeed turn out be the correct year of Jesus' crucifixion, the time involved is simply too distant to rely what is related in the New Testament alone. After all, over 700,000 days have passed since Jesus was executed, and many civilizations and many Calendar schemes have come and gone over that time. Error could have easily crept in for any number of reasons — not the least of which is that the Gospels might be in error themselves on key points. Certainly, copying errors in ancient texts are well documented, and could effect how we interpret the New Testament scripture. So the journey is just beginning.

Leaving computers and astronomy behind (excepting for chapter 12!), we will now look at the eastern Roman world of 2,000 years ago in search for additional clues with which to build an accurate history-based Christian time line.

Chapter 2   Roman and Jewish Sources

..a most mischievous superstition...again broke out not only in Judaea, the first source of the evil, but even in Rome (*Annuls* XV 44)

The early Christian world was a Roman and Jewish world. The first step in understanding Christianity and the New Testament is to have a firm historical knowledge of the early first century A.D. Roman Empire. Fortunately, several such secular historical works survive — almost certainly because they were culled out of Roman libraries by the early Christians themselves and saved in Church repositories. All these manuscripts in some way either referenced Jesus himself, the Christians, or characters of importance from the New Testament.

Publius Tacitus

Publius Cornelius Tacitus (A.D. 56-120) is an invaluable source. Tacitus came from a wealthy and privileged Roman equestrian family. The equestrians comprised a powerful Roman order, also called "knights," that ranked just below the senators in power and prestige. In fact, most senators came from the ranks of the equestrians — who were entrusted with the handling of public monies.

Tacitus achieved the rank of Roman senator during the Flavian dynasty but higher honors were to come. Tacitus became consul in A.D. 97 and afterward was elected provincial governor of Asia for the years A.D. 112-113–a most powerful position.

I would not deny that my elevation was begun by Vespasian, augmented by Titus and still further advanced by Domitian; (Tacitus *Histories* 1:1)

Tacitus was also the name of a later emperor of the Roman Empire but a blood relationship to the historian Tacitus is questionable.

Tacitus championed the traditional Roman values of strength, loyalty, bravery and honor. Tacitus is most famous for his *Annuls of Imperial Rome* (*Annuls*), published in A.D. 117 which covers the successive reigns of the first four Roman emperors after Augustus: Tiberius, Caius, Claudius and Nero. Twelve of the original books still exist. Unfortunately, several of the middle books are missing. The first six books of *Annuls* deal with the ascension of Tiberius as emperor in A.D. 14 through to the succession of Caius Caesar in A.D. 37. The final books, 11-16, cover the late years of Claudius' reign and most of the reign of Nero ending with the events of A.D. 66. The earliest copy of *Annuls* (books 1-6) is dated to A.D. 850, while *Annuls* (books 11-16) date centuries later.

Histories is another major work of Tacitus which might originally have been a part of *Annuls*. *Histories* was written circa A.D. 105, with five books (I-V) extant, covering the years A.D. 69-70. The reason for their survival is apparent as they deal specifically with the Jews and the Jewish revolt. The early Christians believed that the destruction of Jerusalem and the leveling of the Second Temple was God's retribution against the Jews for the crucifixion of Jesus. Tacitus' *Histories* would be an important addition to any serious ancient Christian library of the time.

Tacitus and the Christians

Tacitus in his early books in *Annuls* covering the reign of Tiberius never mentions Jesus, the Jewish High Priests, or Judean Prefect Pontius Pilate. Only the territory of Judea itself is mentioned–and that only once.

The provinces too of Syria and Judaea, exhausted by their burdens, implored a reduction of tribute. (*Annuls* 2:42)

In book 15 of *Annuls* Tacitus does, however, refer to Jesus, the Christians and Pontius Pilate in a famous passage. The context of the reference is the devastating fires that occurred in Rome during the reign of Nero in July of A.D. 64.

Nero fastened the guilt and inflicted the most exquisite tortures on a class hated for their abominations, called Christians by the populace. Christus, from whom the name had its origin, suffered the extreme penalty during the reign of Tiberius at the hands of one of our procurators, Pontius Pilatus and a most mischievous superstition, thus checked for the moment, again broke out not only in Judaea, the first source of the evil, but even in Rome, where all things hideous and shameful from every part of the world find their centre and become popular. (*Annuls* 15: 44)

Tacitus shows his disgust for the Christian religion by calling it "hideous" and "shameful." Later, however, Tacitus shows sympathy for the sufferings of these same Christians — aghast at Nero's naked and cruel inhumanity.

Hence, even for criminals who deserved extreme and exemplary punishment, there arose a feeling of compassion; (*Annuls* 15: 44)

Tacitus and the Jews

Tacitus' negative opinion of the Jews was probably driven by the recent memory of the Jewish revolt of A.D. 66 where thousands of Roman soldiers had lost their lives. The revolt also represented a clear rejection by the Jews of the supposedly superior Roman culture. This had to have rankled the sensibilities of the ultra-patriotic Tacitus. The Jewish nation is described in *Histories* :

Moyses, wishing to secure for the future his authority over the nation, gave them a novel form of worship, opposed to all that is practised by other men. Things sacred with us, with them have no sanctity, while they allow what with us is forbidden. In their holy place they have consecrated an image of the animal by whose guidance they found deliverance from their long and thirsty wanderings. They slay the ram, seemingly in derision of Hammon and they sacrifice the ox, because the Egyptians worship it as Apis. ..We are told that the rest of the seventh day was adopted, because this day brought with it a termination of their toils; after a while the charm of indolence beguilded [sic] them into giving up the seventh year also to inaction.

This worship, however introduced, is upheld by its antiquity; all their other customs which are at once perverse and disgusting, owe their strength to their very badness. The most degraded out of other races, scorning their national beliefs, brought to them their contributions and presents. This augmented the wealth of the Jews, as also did the fact, that among themselves they are inflexibly honest and ever ready to shew compassion, though they regard the rest of mankind with all the hatred of enemies. They sit apart at meals, they sleep apart and though, as a nation, they are singularly prone to lust, they abstain from intercourse with foreign women; among themselves nothing is unlawful. Circumcision was adopted by them as a mark of difference from other men. Those who come over to their religion adopt the practice and have this lesson first instilled into them, to despise all gods, to disown their country and set at nought parents, children and brethren. (Tacitus *Histories* V 4-5))

Perhaps because of his bias Tacitus ignored events involving the interaction between Rome and Judea–events upon which Jewish historians like Flavius Josephus place great importance.

Suetonius

Gaius Suetonius Tranquillus lived about A.D. 70-130. Like Tacitus, he came from a patrician family and was the son of an equestrian. Suetonius held various high-ranking positions within the empire, most notably under Emperors Trajan and Hadrian. Suetonius' only surviving work is *Lives of the Caesars* or *The Twelve Caesars* (*Caesars*), written in A.D. 121. The work is a series of biographies of Julius Caesar and 11 other Roman emperors of the Cesarean era. Suetonius is considered a lesser historian compared to Tacitus as Suetonius tends to focus on the more racy and salacious aspects of these men–and is quick to relate rumors. To his credit, however, Suetonius always gave the

reader a physical description of the Caesar he was writing about–
rare in other surviving historical works.

Like Tacitus, Suetonius paid scant attention to the Jews and
Judea. However, unlike Tacitus, Suetonius' purpose was not to
write a complete history of those times, only biographies of the
ruling Caesars.

Suetonius and the Christians

In Suetonius' *Caesars*, there is a reference to Jesus which is one
of the earliest secular references to the Nazarene, superseded
only by Josephus and Tacitus.

> Since the Jews constantly made disturbances at the instigation of
> Chrestus, he (Claudius) expelled them from Rome (Sue *Claudius* XXV)

"Chrestus" presumably refers to "Christ." However, Jesus
himself was years dead before the reign of Claudius (A.D. 41-54)
and so could hardly have instigated anything. On this, Suetonius
is in error. Emperor Claudius' expulsion of the Christians as
alleged by Suetonius is lightly documented elsewhere but
probable.

As for the Christians, Suetonius notes their persecution during
Nero's reign but he doesn't express the moral indignation over
Nero's actions as Tacitus did. This is evident in the construct of
Caesars. In the biographies, Suetonius classifies the major actions
of the emperors as either commendable or not. The good deeds
are grouped together first and the bad deeds described later.

> These transactions, in part unexceptionable and in part highly
> commendable, I have brought into one view, in order to separate them
> from the scandalous and criminal part of his conduct, of which I shall
> now give an account. (Sue *Nero* XIX)

In Nero's biography, Suetonius placed the persecution of the
Christians in the commendable section.

Many severe regulations and new orders were made in his time. A sumptuary law was enacted. Public suppers were limited to the Sportulae; and victualling-houses restrained from selling any dressed victuals, except pulse and herbs, whereas before they sold all kinds of meat. He likewise inflicted punishments on the Christians, a sort of people who held a new and impious superstition.

He forbad the revels of the charioteers, who had long assumed a licence to stroll about and established for themselves a kind of prescriptive right to cheat and thieve, making a jest of it. The partisans of the rival theatrical performers were banished, as well as the actors themselves. (Sue *Nero* XVI)

Suetonius ranked the the persecution of the Christians between Nero's restrictions on butcher shop victuals and his stringent rules against the partying and casual thievery of strolling charioteers! Suetonius' negative view of the Christians is apparent.

Cassius Dio

Cassius Dio was born about A.D. 164 in Nicaea, Greece. He was the son of an aristocratic Roman senator of Greek heritage. Dio took to politics early and rose to become an important and influential man in the empire. He achieved the rank of senator, serving in several important foreign posts. His highest rank was Senate consul which he achieved twice–the last time in A.D. 229 under Emperor Alexander.

Dio retired to write a massive 80-book history of the Roman Empire. Many fragments of these volumes–some substantial–survive to this day. It took Dio over 20 years to produce the work which covers 1400 years of Roman history. Dio also wrote a history of the Roman Civil War of A.D. 193-197 (A.D. 193 being the so-called "Year of the Five Emperors").

Dio is considered an inferior historian to either Josephus or Tacitus in regards to first century A.D. events. Not only did Dio write a full century later but his narrative lacks the detail which is so important to modern researchers. This might not be all Dio's fault, however. Some of Dio's work — and perhaps all of it — was abridged by an 11th century monk copyist. But Dio is very useful in that he fills in many of the gaps left by the lost books of Tacitus in the Imperial age.

Flavius Josephus

The Jewish historian Flavius Josephus wrote about both Roman and Jewish history. Flavius Josephus, born Joseph bar Matthias in Jerusalem, was a Jewish priest, military leader and historian who lived A.D. 37-103. He wrote four major works that are essential to the understanding first century A.D. Jewish culture. Most other Roman historians paid scant attention to the Jewish East prior to the Jewish revolt of A.D. 66. The Books of the New Testament, while preserving important details of the life of Jesus and the early Christians, refer only tangentially to Jewish culture and politics. Flavius Josephus is the only source for information on many aspects of the first century A.D. Jewish world.

However, Josephus was more than just a dispassionate chronicler of the times. Jerusalem-born Josephus was an eyewitness and played a key role in many of the important events he documents. In fact, Flavius Josephus is a man of such consequence that the entire next chapter will devoted to him.

Wars of the Jews

The first of Josephus' major works, the seven-book *The Wars of the Jews* (*Wars*), was published in A.D. 78 in both the Greek and Hebrew languages. Josephus wrote it only five years after the last battle of the Jewish revolt which took place at Masada in A.D. 73. *Wars* begins with a history of the Jewish nation which takes up the first two books. Then, for the next five books, *Wars* plunges into a marvelous and thrilling recounting of the Jewish revolt itself. Josephus details the campaigns of Vespasian, Titus and the Jewish King Agrippa II which eventually resulted in Roman victory and the destruction of the Jerusalem and the Second Temple. Importantly, Josephus observed first-hand many of the events he documents.

Adding to its veracity, Emperors Vespasian and Titus, as well as King Agrippa II, read and endorsed Josephus' *Wars*. Emperor Titus ordered it placed in all the Royal libraries of the empire.

> offered my books to the emperors themselves, when the facts were almost under men's eyes; for I was conscious to myself, that I had observed the truth of the facts; and as I expected to have their attestation to them, so I was not deceived in such expectation. Moreover, I immediately presented my history to many other persons, some of whom were concerned in the war, as was king Agrippa and some of his kindred. Now the emperor Titus was so desirous that the knowledge of these affairs should be taken from these books alone, that he subscribed his own hand to them and ordered that they should be published; and for king Agrippa, he wrote me sixty-two letters and attested to the truth of what I had therein delivered; (*Life* 65)

Wars is also considered to be one of the finest stand-alone Roman historical works ever written. Josephus pays particular attention to Roman military organization and battle procedures in the work–subjects addressed in detail in no other surviving Roman manuscript.

Antiquities of the Jews

In A.D. 93 Josephus published his second major opus–the massive, 20-book *Antiquities of the Jews* (*Antiquities*). Josephus' intent was to educate the Roman intellectual elite on the specifics of the history of the Jewish nation. Josephus asserts that Jewish culture was then 5,000 years old and by far the most ancient of all the then-existing cultures. *Antiquities* was originally written in Greek, the universal scholarly language of the day. Josephus learned the language especially for this project.

> For those of my own nation freely acknowledge that I far exceed them in the learning belonging to Jews; I have also taken a great deal of pains to obtain the learning of the Greeks and understand the elements of the Greek language.. (*Antiq* XX 11:2)

Antiquities greatly expands upon the history of the Jews that Josephus sets down in the first two books of *Wars* and also corrects several of *Wars'* mistakes. *Antiquities* ends with the Jewish revolt of A.D. 66, where the third book of *Wars* begins.

> I have translated the Antiquities out of our sacred Books; which I easily could do, since I was a priest by my birth and have studied that philosophy which is contained in those writings.. (*Apion* 7)

Josephus follows closely many of the early books in the Old Testament and, among other works, the now-lost 144 volume history of Jews written by Nicolaus of Damascus. Nicolaus was part of Herod the Great's inner circle and at times served as a diplomat for Herod (*Antiq* XVI 1:3, 9:4, 10:8, 11:3; XVII 5:4-6), so Josephus' sections on Herod the Great have a special insight into the man. For other sources used in *Antiquities*, Josephus undoubtedly poured through the different library collections in Rome–most of them private–and probably traveled to the Alexandrian Library in Egypt as well.

Antiquities is an eclectic source of information on the entire ancient world and not just the Jewish nation. For instance, Josephus describes in detail the visit of Alexander the Great to Jerusalem (*Antiq* XXI 8:50) which is found nowhere else. Josephus also writes about Noah's ark (which Josephus says actually exists in the country of Carra (*Antiq* XX 2:2)) and Herod the Great's bold midnight robbery of the Tomb of David in Jerusalem (*Antiq* XVI 7:1), among many other interesting stories.

Critical to our own investigation is Book XVIII of *Antiquities* in which Josephus writes about the period from A.D. 6-39. These years cover the times of the ministries and deaths of both Jesus of Nazareth and John the Baptist. Unfortunately, that particular book is not nearly as detailed as much of the rest of *Antiquities* but it still has fascinating information not found elsewhere.

Josephus writes of the length of *Antiquities* at its conclusion.

> I shall put an end to these Antiquities which are contained in twenty Books and sixty thousand verses. (*Antiq* XX 11:3)

Other Works of Josephus

Josephus' third major historical project was his own autobiography, *Life of Flavius Josephus* (*Life*), published in A.D. 100. Josephus' motive in writing *Life* was to answer questions about his priestly lineage and the strength of his loyalty to the Jewish cause during the revolt of A.D. 66. In this amazing work, Josephus focuses on his tumultuous adventures in Galilee as a young Jewish general during an eight-month period from A.D. 66-67. This was just prior to the arrival of Vespasian's Roman army to put down the Jewish rebellion.

Josephus' fourth and last major work extant is *Against Apion* (*Apion*), a two-book treatise challenging the writings and opinions of Apion, an Egyptian writer. Apion and others had been critical of the Jews for various reasons and so Josephus decided to take them to task. The original works of Apion that so incensed Josephus are lost.

According to Eusebius the real name of *Antiquities* is *Ancient Jewish History*. The title *Antiquities of the Jews* (*Antiquities*) was meant for the Josephus work *Against Apion* (*Apion*). Somehow in the course of copying of these manuscripts over the centuries the titles were interchanged.

Eusebius tells of a fifth major work of Josephus, *The Supremacy of Reason*, or the *Maccabees*. In this writing, Josephus detailed the struggles of the Jews at different times in their history when their right to worship their God was challenged. Lost to modern scholars, Eusebius called it a work of "considerable merit" (Eusebius *History* III:10).

At the end of Book XX in *Antiquities*, Josephus promised to write four more books on the traditional beliefs of the Jews and their God. The aforementioned Maccabean treatise might have been one of those books. However, none of these works, if ever written, survives.

Philo Judaeus

Philo Judaeus is the our only source who actually lived during Jesus' lifetime. However, even though Philo was Jewish and wrote about Jewish history he never mentions Jesus in any of his voluminous writings. Philo's interests included not only history but also philosophy and religion.

Philo wrote most of his works in the Egyptian city of Alexandria. Born during the last years of Herod the Great's reign and dying about A.D. 50, Philo was part of a famous Jewish family that included his brother Alexander the alabarch and Tiberius Alexander—Alexander's son. Philo's rich and powerful family allowed him the freedom to concentrate on his writings. It is hard to imagine a more thoroughly Romanized Jewish family outside of the Herodian-Asamonean line.

Philo Judaeus knew first-hand many of the important people surrounding Emperor Tiberius, and he even spoke face-to-face with Emperor Caius (Caligula). The meeting with Caius occurred during an embassy to Rome in A.D. 40 to protest Caius' attempted placement of statues of himself in all of the Jewish temples.

The historian Philo would surely have known most of the powerful men in Jerusalem at the time, including Simon Ananus, Joseph Caiaphas, and others. Philo himself was important enough to be mentioned in the works of Jewish historian Flavius Josephus (*Antiq* XVIII 8:1). But no where does he mention Jesus or the early Christians.

Philo was an acknowledged leader of the Alexandrian Jewish community. Alexandrian Jews numbered an estimated 50,000 in the early first century A.D.–the largest Jewish population in the Roman Empire outside of Jerusalem. Alexandria itself was the second-largest city by population in the empire with Rome being first.

The Alexandrian Library, or Museum, was thriving during Philo's lifetime and was a center of study for every serious scholar of the age. Philo likely functioned as one of the great library's teacher-priests. In an important digression, a brief history of the library follows.

The Museum at Alexandria

No great culture can arise without a system of keeping written records and preserving them for the benefit of future generations. A few enlightened ancient rulers dedicated great efforts to the collection of important manuscripts from all over the world. To store and protect these works, special buildings were constructed. The most famous of these ancient libraries was at Alexandria in Egypt.

By the first century A.D. the ancient world had produced hundreds of thousands, if not millions, of manuscripts. Rome, Egypt, Greece, Babylon and other great centers of civilization all had contributed their share to the library. Many genres were represented, including the religious, technical, literary, historical, fictional, and mythological works. The writings were set down on either papyrus or animal skin and stored in scroll form. In eastern cities like Babylon, clay tablets were used for this purpose. The tablets were better able to withstand the ravages of time, but far more cumbersome.

The ancient Greek geographer Strabo (64 B.C.–A.D. 23) referred to the Alexandrian library as a Museum. This term derives from the Greek, meaning, roughly, "house of Muses," or "temple." Muses were Greek Goddesses or spirits that were thought to inspire men to create literature and other works of art. Greek was the intellectual language of the day throughout the Roman Empire and most of the important volumes were either written in Greek or translated into it.

The library of Alexandria became the forerunner of the modern university system. Great minds from all over the ancient world traveled to the Alexandrian library for study, research, and discourse among their peers. A community of ascetics dedicated to learning developed; some living within the Museum complex itself. As the decades turned into centuries, this group evolved into a semi-religious cult — even a high priest was appointed.

The Museum is also a part of the royal palaces; it has a public walk, an Exedra with seats and a large house in which is the common mess-hall of the men of learning who share the Museum. This group of men not only hold property in common, but also have a priest in charge of the Museum, who formerly was appointed by the kings, but is now appointed by Caesar. The Sema also as it is called, is a part of the royal palaces. This was the enclosure which contained the burial-places of the kings and that of Alexander; (Strabo *Geo* XVII:8)

The city of Alexandria in Egypt was founded by Alexander the Great in 334 B.C. After Alexander's death in 323 B.C., his Macedonian general and (likely) half-brother Ptolemy Soter assumed the rule of Egypt. Pharaoh Ptolemy started an Egyptian dynasty that would endure for 300 years, ending with the suicide of Queen Cleopatra in 30 B.C.

Ptolemy I was succeeded by his son Philadelphus who then became Ptolemy II. During his reign he established one of the finest manuscript collections of ancient times. He also spared no expense in constructing buildings to house it. Pharaoh Ptolemy II considered his Alexandrian library to be so important that it was built next to the Royal palace complex — in time becoming part of it. According to Josephus, Philadelphus' collection contained well over a half million scrolls (*Antiq* XII 2:1-2).

The city of Alexandria grew quickly with the best harbor in Egypt as Josephus describes:

The haven also of Alexandria is not entered by the mariners without difficulty, even in times of peace; for the passage inward is narrow, and full of rocks that lie under the water, which oblige the mariners to turn from a straight direction: its left side is blocked up by works made by men's hands on both sides; on its right side lies the island called Pharus, which is situated just before the entrance, and supports a very great tower, that affords the sight of a fire to such as sail within three hundred furlongs of it, that ships may cast anchor a great way off in the night time, by reason of the difficulty of sailing nearer. About this island are built very great piers, the handiwork of men, against which, when the sea dashes itself, and its waves are broken against those boundaries, the navigation becomes very troublesome, and the entrance through so narrow a passage is rendered dangerous; yet is the haven itself, when you are got into it, a very safe one, and of thirty furlongs in largeness; into which is brought what the country wants in order to its happiness, as also what abundance the country affords more than it wants itself is hence distributed into all the habitable earth. (Wars IV 10:5)

Trade between Egypt and the other cities of the Mediterranean was encouraged by the Greek Ptolemaic dynasty. Strategically located on the southern coast of the Mediterranean Sea, Alexandria became a popular stop-off point for travel between the city of Rome and the eastern empire. The city of Alexandria also became the home to the Egyptian Royal family and high-level military and administrative officials for much of the year. Enjoying cool breezes off the Mediterranean, Alexandria was a very pleasant place during the stifling summer months–the formal capital city of Memphis being located in the interior of Egypt on the Nile River. In time, over one-third of Alexandria was given over to either Royal palaces or public buildings.

The library reached its zenith during the reign of the Queen Cleopatra in the first century B.C. But the Alexandrian library was not without its tragedies. Queen Cleopatra herself had the unfortunate experience in 48 B.C. of seeing much of the library burned by the invading Roman armies of General Julius Caesar. While initially devastated by the loss, Cleopatra rebuilt and restocked the library to an even greater degree. Helpful in this regard was later Roman co-Emperor Marc Antony. To make amends for damage done by Julius Caesar's troops years before, Marc Antony donated 200,000 volumes from libraries in Rome, shipping them across the Mediterranean Sea to Alexandria.

The End of the Alexandrian Library

The libraries of antiquity have all suffered similar fates, whether located in Persepolis, Babylon, Rome, Athens, or lesser cities. Many were destroyed suddenly by conquering armies or natural disaster, with the rest dying slowly over the passing decades by neglect. Even Alexander the Great of Macedonia, considered a lover of books and learning and somewhat enlightened for a tyrant, burned down the huge library at

Babylon in a drunken lark shortly after conquering the Persian Empire in 331 B.C.

The Alexandrian library survived largely intact until A.D. 270, when a hoard of fanatical Christians burned most of the scrolls within it, considering the manuscripts heretical. However, the library recovered from this devastation and was restocked. The library then existed for another 400 years–almost a century after the generally accepted date for the fall of the Roman Empire. The ascetic order that lived in the Museum likely protected the collections with a fierce passion for as long as they could.

The finishing stroke came at the hands of the Muslim Caliph Omar in A.D. 642. The conqueror Omar ordered all manuscripts burned that were at odds with the philosophy of the Koran. Unfortunately, this was most of them. A subsequent earthquake turned the famous library complex into rubble. As the decades then passed, a Mosque was built over the site with much of the it constructed from materials taken from the destroyed Museum.

An ignominious end to be sure. But the library at Alexandria had served the ancient world well for the previous 800 years, bringing intellectuals together for study, research and collaboration — serving as a crucible for scientific and intellectual advancement as well as being a repository for the sum total of human knowledge then extant.

The Talmud

The Talmud is a compilation of written works and commentary on Jewish law, ethics, history and culture. These writings came into being as a unified concept after the Roman defeat of the second Jewish revolt in A.D. 132. Then, the center for Judaism was Tiberias, a city in Galilee.

After the second Jewish revolt the very survival of Judaism was in doubt. In order to guide future generations of Jews through an uncertain future, surviving Jewish writings were assembled and codified and oral traditions transcribed upon parchment or other durable materials. Through the centuries, these documents were added to and evolved into what was called the Talmud. Two written versions exist: the Talmud of the Babylonians which was produced in A.D. 600 and the Palestinian Talmud, produced in A.D. 400. As the authors are unknown and the works themselves are varied with little solid evidence that they reflected Jewish culture prior to A.D. 70, the Talmud will not be used as a source.

Historical Accuracy

In the first paragraph of *Annuls of Imperial Rome*, written in 117 A.D. and a half century after Nero's reign ended, historian Publius Tacitus acknowledges the problems he faced.

> The histories of Tiberius, Caius, Claudius and Nero, while they were in power, were falsified through terror and after their death were written under the irritation of a recent hatred. Hence my purpose is to relate a few facts about Augustus - more particularly his last acts, then the reign of Tiberius and all which follows, without either bitterness or partiality, from any motives to which I am far removed. (*Annuls* 1:1)

By the time of Tacitus, scores of historical works had been written in antiquity about the era of the Caesars. Tacitus read them all and considered most to be of low quality–laced with political innuendo and falsehoods.

Josephus will prove to be our major source. He acknowledges the same problem as Tacitus did.

> ..while some men who were not concerned in the affairs themselves have gotten together vain and contradictory stories by hearsay and have written them down after a sophistical manner; and while those that were there present have given false accounts of things and this either out of a humor of flattery to the Romans, or of hatred towards the Jews; and while their writings contain sometimes accusations and sometimes encomiums, but no where the accurate truth of the facts; (*Wars* Pref 1)

Fortunately, Josephus obligingly wrote an autobiography which is the subject of the next chapter. From a better understanding of Josephus, we can better determine his biases.

Chapter 3   Flavius Josephus

(I)..shall relate what hath happened to us Jews with great accuracy and shall not grudge our pains in giving an account both of the calamities we have suffered and of the crimes we have been guilty of. (*Antiq* XX 8:3)

Flavius Josephus is by far the most important source on early first century A.D. Jewish history. The world that Josephus knew was the world that Jesus knew–older only by two generations. Josephus conveniently wrote an autobiography (*Life*) which was published in A.D. 100.   A boon to researchers, the work documents important details about the first century A.D. Jewish East and also sheds light on the potential biases of Josephus as a historian.

Eastern Empire Politics

Flavius Josephus was born in A.D. 37, the first year of the reign of Emperor Caius (Caligula). At that time, the Jewish people had been under the subjugation of the Roman Empire for more than a century. For all practical purposes, however, the real rulers were the Jerusalem High Priesthood of the Second Temple. The Roman occupiers had little desire to get involved in the day-to-day minutia of the complicated and—to them—curious Jewish culture. This power proxy was gladly given over to the Jewish priests–as long as peace was reasonably maintained and Roman taxes were paid. The High Priesthood then delegated these powers to local Jewish councils—the Sanhedrin—to decide most civil and religious conflicts in Judea and Galilee.

The country of Samaria practiced a variant form of Judaism with its own Temple and High Priesthood based out of Sebaste.

The Romans made the same arrangements with Samaria for governance. In effect, the Jewish East was a Roman-sanctioned theocracy.

Both Judea and Samaria were technically under the control of a single Rome-appointed prefect (later termed a procurator). But the prefect and a large part of the Roman auxiliary army were based in Caesarea which was technically not a part of the Jewish East at all. The prefect was called in to settle disputes in Judea or Samaria only under the most unusual of circumstances.

In those days, there was hardly anyone in Jerusalem who wasn't in some way connected with the operation of the Second Temple. To support these priests and their families and pay for the massive religious infrastructure, Jewish law had a special system of mandatory tithes and "first fruit" donations required from all Jews. Money-generating festivals were also held in Jerusalem several times a year.

Early Life

Josephus was proud that he came from a long line of Jewish priests and possessed a measure of Royal Asamonean blood.

> The family from which I am derived is not an ignoble one, but hath descended all along from the priests; and as nobility among several people is of a different origin, so with us to be of the sacerdotal dignity, is an indication of the splendor of a family..by my mother I am of the royal blood; for the children of Asamoneus, from whom that family was derived, had both the office of the high priesthood and the dignity of a king, for a long time together. (*Life* 1)

Josephus describes himself as a child prodigy.

> I made mighty proficiency in the improvements of my learning and appeared to have both a great memory and understanding. Moreover, when I was a child and about fourteen years of age, I was commended by all for the love I had to learning; on which account the high priests and principal men of the city came then frequently to me together, in order to know my opinion about the accurate understanding of points of the law. (*Life* 2)

Early on, Josephus was on a track for a position of no small importance within the Second Temple priest hierarchy. In his training, Josephus was required to become familiar with all three disciplines of Judaism–the Sadducee, the Pharisee and the Essene.

In A.D. 53 at age 16 after learning what he could from the Jewish sects of the Pharisees and Sadducees, Josephus left Jerusalem for the nearby Judean desert. There, he studied under a religious ascetic named Banus, who was famous in his day and a decidedly John the Baptist-like figure. Arguably, Banus was an Essene.

> Banus.. lived in the desert and used no other clothing than grew upon trees and had no other food than what grew of its own accord and bathed himself in cold water frequently, both by night and by day, in order to preserve his chastity, I imitated him in those things and continued with him three years. (*Life* 2)

This decision for Josephus' three-year sojourn in the desert was probably made by Josephus' parents. They lived in Jerusalem and were likely alarmed at the unpredictable and brutal nature of the new Roman procurator, Antonius Felix. Felix had been appointed to that position by Emperor Claudius in A.D. 53, and perhaps Felix was revealing his true nature early in his tenure. Was Jerusalem becoming a dangerous place for a brilliant young man such as Josephus? Josephus documents that during those times, criminal elements were steadily gaining the upper hand (*Wars* II 13:5).

But now safely ensconced in the Judean desert in solitude, over the next three years Josephus learned the benefits of physical discipline and self-denial from the ascetic Banus, just as earlier he had mastered the particulars of Jewish law from the Pharisees. Meanwhile, the city of Jerusalem continued to suffer under the harsh administration of Procurator Felix and Judea sank further and further into the abyss of political violence and uncertainty.

Second Temple Murder

Josephus returned to Jerusalem from the desert in A.D. 56 when he was 19 years old. Perhaps he arrived in time for one of Procurator Felix's boldest actions. Felix had arranged for the murder of High Priest Jonathan, the son of Ananus. Jonathan had been a constant and relentless critic of Felix's quasi-criminal policies. This heinous act took place in the outer courtyard of the Second Temple (*Antiq* XX 8:5). Jonathan had been High Priest of the Second Temple for a single year, from A.D. 36 to A.D. 37. Likely it was Jonathan who unleashed a young Saul of Tarsus upon the early Christians, as well as being behind the stoning of Stephen the Apostle.

Josephus believed that that the murder of Jonathan was the beginning of God's turning of his countenance away from the Jewish people. The Temple-based Jews believed that the essence of God had an ethereal presence that required a physical domicile. The purpose of the inner Sanctuary of the Second Temple in Jerusalem was to provide God with a suitable place in which to dwell — a most-holy chamber filled with smoke and incense. After Jonathan's murder, Josephus writes that God abandoned not only this room, but the entire Jewish nation (*Antiq* XX 8:5).

Diplomacy and Revolt

In A.D. 63 when Josephus was 26 years old he traveled to Rome. His purpose was to broker the release of several Jewish priest prisoners sent there years earlier by now-former Procurator Felix. Josephus suggests that he was sent by his father but it is very possible that he was sent in late A.D. 62 on this mission–possibly illegally–by the Temple High Priesthood and the Sanhedrin. At that time Nero had been emperor for eight years. Josephus was fluent in Latin and well-suited for the job. After some difficulties, Josephus successfully negotiated their release in mid-to-late A.D. 63 (*Life* 3).

Returning to a turbulent Jerusalem on the brink of revolt, Josephus tried to talk some sense into the citizens of Jerusalem. In Rome, Josephus had seen first-hand the strength of the empire and knew that any revolt would be disastrous for the Jews. But his words had no effect and in A.D. 66 the rebellion began. Josephus did not forsake his Jewish roots, however. He decided to join the rebel forces even though he didn't agree with their course of action. Josephus was appointed the general of Galilee by a committee of the Temple priests and instructed to form an army, prepare for war, and to protect Jewish communities from not only the Romans but their Greek-Syrian neighbors.

The High Priesthood in Jerusalem had decided take control of the rebel nation whether the rest of the fractious towns in Judea and Galilee wanted them to or not. Dispatched to Galilee to organize the Jews, Josephus had soon assembled a force, according to him, of over 100,000 men. Josephus also put the Galilean people to work rebuilding their city walls in anticipation of a Roman invasion.

In those days siege warfare was the military order of the day. The best defense for a city was a strong wall impervious to the battering of war engines. Plenty of food and water would be stocked inside the city walls in case the action was protracted. Josephus knew the Roman forces would arrive either by sea or land and then mass at Ptolemais, so a priority was the reinforcement of the northern cities of Jotapata, Arbel, Gamala, Sepphoris, Tiberias, and others.

In A.D. 67, Rome responded with force to the Jewish rebellion. Emperor Nero sent General Vespasian and three Roman legions south from Syria into the Jewish lands. As Josephus had expected, Galilee was the point of first contact. In the mountaintop city of Jotapata, General Josephus and the Jewish rebels fought the Roman forces fiercely. Though Josephus wrote the only surviving account of this Alamo-like action (*Wars* III 7:2), there is no reason to doubt the particulars.

Jotapata eventually fell to the Romans, and Josephus was captured by General Vespasian in June of A.D. 67. Josephus, believing that it was God's will that the Romans triumphed, did not hesitate in offering his full assistance to the Romans. Josephus even changed his name from Joseph bar Matthias to Flavius Josephus at the suggestion of General Vespasian.

The Roman campaign in the Jewish East took six more years to complete. Two years into it, a lengthy hiatus occurred due to Emperor Nero's forced suicide. After the death of Nero, several generals and their armies fought for control of the Roman Empire. Three men gained the supreme power for a short period of time before losing out to Vespasian. In December A.D. 69, Vespasian was generally acknowledged as the new emperor of Rome. One of his first acts was to resume the subjugation of the rebelling Jewish nation. Emperor Vespasian remained in Alexandria while placing his son Titus in command of the Roman forces. Flavius Josephus was at Titus' side as an adviser, along with Tiberius Alexander and King Agrippa II, who were the most important Jews in the empire at that time. A young Trajan also served as general of the 10th legion under Vespasian. With some difficulty, Jerusalem was eventually captured.

So from a Jewish general Josephus found himself catapulted into the unlikely position as trusted adviser and confidant to four future Roman emperors, as well becoming friends with the powerful King Agrippa II, who headed up his own auxiliary army. Josephus' future in Rome was assured.

Retirement in Rome

For his services, Josephus achieved an honored position within the Flavian Royal court and was given income-producing land in Judea. Now a wealthy and famous man in his own time, Josephus began writing the books that would guarantee his fame throughout the ages. Third century A.D. Church historian Eusebius reports that a statue of Josephus was erected in Rome (Eus *History* 3:9). As the Jewish religion forbade graven images of any sort to be made, this could illustrate how far Josephus had fallen away from Judaism and his priestly origins. To be fair, however, the statue might have been erected without Josephus' approval after his death in A.D. 103.

Despite Josephus' scholarly dedication to Jewish culture most contemporary Jews held him in contempt for his perceived betrayal of the defeated rebel nation. Many Jews still do to this day. Josephus had to constantly defend himself against accusations of treason.

The Biases of Josephus

Josephus believed that the Jews, through their evil deeds, had lost the approbation of God. Because of the murder of High Priest Jonathan in the holy grounds of the Temple courtyard in A.D. 56, the Jews were no longer God's chosen people.

Also grating on the Jews was Josephus' continued support of the Roman rulers even after the war was over. Betrayal of the Jewish nation might have been understandable given the extreme conditions faced in wartime, but Josephus remained an enthusiastic member of the Roman Imperial court until he died during the reign of Trajan. Certainly Josephus owed his success and station in life to Vespasian and his sons–the Flavian dynasty of Rome.

Also, King Agrippa II became a personal friend of Josephus. For this reason, Josephus treated any topics in his writings that might reflect poorly on the families of Emperor Vespasian, or Agrippa II, with great tact.

The Testimonium Flavianum

During Josephus' life and through to the destruction of Jerusalem and the dispersion of the Jewish nation, the Christian religion was steadily gaining in numbers and power. Was there a bias either for or against the Christians in Josephus' writings? Or did Josephus consider the Christians so minor a factor that they barely deserved mention?

One verse of Josephus' *Antiquities* bears a special scrutiny in this regard–the so-called "Testimonium Flavianum" (testament of Flavius). Josephus appears to proclaim in it that Jesus of Nazareth was the Christ–no small declaration coming from our major non-Christian source. Was Josephus a crypto-Christian, or was his original text in *Antiquities* somehow corrupted?

> Now there was about this time Jesus, a wise man, if it be lawful to call him a man; for he was a doer of wonderful works, a teacher of such men as receive the truth with pleasure. He drew over to him both many of the Jews and many of the Gentiles. He was [the] Christ. And when Pilate, at the suggestion of the principal men amongst us, had condemned him to the cross, those that loved him at the first did not forsake him; for he appeared to them alive again the third day; as the divine prophets had foretold these and ten thousand other wonderful things concerning him. And the tribe of Christians, so named from him, are not extinct at this day. (*Antiq* XVIII 3:3)

A former Jewish priest declaring a belief in Jesus' divine origins would be an extraordinary thing it itself–even more so coming from Josephus. Does Josephus' other writings support this? Do the facts of Josephus' life suggest a later Christian conversion?

Josephus was born into an aristocratic family in Jerusalem. Like the Jewish historian Philo Judaeus, undoubtedly Josephus knew many of those principal men involved in Jesus' trial and crucifixion. Also, as Josephus grew up, he was probably aware of the activities of the early Christian sect in Jerusalem. Curiously, though, in Josephus' first work, *Wars*, published in A.D. 78, he did not mention Jesus or any of the early Christians. This suggests that Josephus, like Philo, thought at the time that Jesus and the Christians were either of little importance, or perhaps downright subversive. Josephus was a supporter of all things Roman and *Wars* was published only 14 years after Nero began his state-sanctioned persecution of the Christians in A.D. 64. At that time in Rome, Christianity was not a cause to be championed. That Josephus did not mention the Christians in *Wars* is understandable.

In *Antiquities*, however, published 15 years later in A.D. 93, Josephus referred to Jesus in the work not once but twice. After the Testimonium Flavianum in book XVIII, James the Just, the brother of Jesus, is referenced in book XX. Both references are from a 10th century copy of *Antiquities*, the oldest available to modern researchers.

Fortunately, the third century A.D. Church historian Eusebius, who was the bishop of the Caesarean Church, quotes the same passage from Josephus in a work of his own. Having available to him the Royal library resources of the great city of Caesarea, Eusebius had at his disposal a copy of *Antiquities* that could have been up to 500 years older.

> At this time appeared Jesus, a very gifted man–indeed if it is right to call him a man; for he was a worker of miracles, a teacher of such men as listened with pleasure to the truth and he won over many of the Jews and many of Gentile origin as well. This was the Christ; and when at the instigation of our leading men he had been condemned to the cross by Pilate, those who had loved him at the first did not cease to do so; for on the third day he appeared to them alive again, the inspired prophets having foretold this and countless other wonderful things about him. Even now the group of people called Christians after him has not died out. (Eusebius *History* 1:11)

While the "modern" version of the Testimonium Flavianum suggests that Josephus was a Christian himself ("He was (the) Christ."), Eusebius' copy does not completely support this, where "He was the Christ" becomes "This was the Christ"–a phrase that is a little less declarative. Also, the phrase "ten thousand other wonderful things" translates in Eusebius' older copy to "countless other wonderful things." The more recent copy–our "modern" copy–demonstrates a clear embellishment in this regard.

Even more fortunate for researchers, a third version of the Testimonium Flavianum is available–from an Arabic copy of *Antiquities* that is now lost. This particular version survived because it was quoted in another Arabic work.

> At this time there was a wise man who was called Jesus. And his conduct was good and he was known to be virtuous. And many people from among the Jews and the other nations became his disciples. Pilate condemned him to be crucified and to die. And those who had become his disciples did not abandon his discipleship. They reported that he had appeared to them after his crucifixion and that he was alive; accordingly,

he was perhaps the Messiah concerning whom the prophets have recounted wonders. (Arabic summary, presumably of *Antiquities* 18.63. From Agapios' Kitab al-'Unwan (*Book of the Title* 10th c.))

In this passage, Jesus is not called the Christ outright, but that he was "perhaps" the Messiah. A significant difference. Also, the numbers of "wonders" done by Jesus–in other copies "countless" and "ten thousand"–is not quantified at all.

How much weight should be placed on this third-hand Arabic version of *Antiquities*? The teachings of Mohammad revere Jesus as a great prophet but give him no divine status. Was there a Moslem "counter" influence at work? Is it possible that the original Greek text of *Antiquities* could have been altered by Moslem copyists?

Second Reference to Jesus

Josephus contains a second reference to Jesus in *Antiquities*.

..Ananus was of this disposition, he thought he had now a proper opportunity [to exercise his authority]. Festus was now dead and Albinus was but upon the road; so he assembled the sanhedrim of judges and brought before them the brother of Jesus, who was called Christ, whose name was James and some others, [or, some of his companions]; and when he had formed an accusation against them as breakers of the law, he delivered them to be stoned: (*Antiq* XX 9:1)

In late A.D. 62, James the Just was executed. In this passage, the reader should note that Josephus writes that Jesus was "called Christ" by some and not that Jesus "was" the Christ as was written in the Testimonium Flavianum.

Eusebius also quotes this passage from his older copy of *Antiquities*.

So he (Ananus) assembled a council of judges and brought it before James, the brother of Jesus, known as Christ and several others, on a charge of breaking the law and handed them over to be stoned. (Eusebius *History* 2:23 from *Antiq* XX 9:1)

There is not a significant difference between the two copies. The modern translation has the phrase "..called the Christ..", while Eusebius' has "..known as Christ.."

To bolster this view of Josephus as a non-Christian, in his autobiography written seven years later in A.D. 100, he does not refer to Jesus or the early Christians nor does he indicate that he embraced Christianity in any way. In all of his writings, except the controversial Testimonium Flavianum, Josephus does not suggest that he thought of the Christian Church as anything other than an offshoot sect of the Jewish religion.

Josephus and the Early Christians

The attitude of Josephus toward Jesus and the early Christians is a question that will become increasingly important to this investigation. Growing up in Jerusalem and being educated within the Temple priesthood, young Josephus almost certainly knew Ananus, Caiaphas and other members of that powerful Jewish family. Josephus also would have known the intellectual scholar Gamaliel. Josephus would have been too young to know Saul (Paul the Apostle) when Saul was a persecutor of the Christians and lived in Jerusalem, but probably knew of Saul's family, who continued to reside and work in Jerusalem for many years after Saul's conversion. An intelligent and inquisitive boy, Joseph would have also been aware of the odd band of Christians who would preach in the Second Temple outer courtyard always in the same spot, or who gathered together from time to time to chant and pray on the nearby slopes of the Mount of Olives. At times, these Christian evangelists would even gather around the busy gates of Jerusalem and preach to the passers-by–albeit unobtrusively (Acts 9:28). Did the inquisitive Josephus ever seek these early Christians out and engage them in a discussion of religion?

An exciting prospect to be sure, but likely it did not happen. The early Christians were poor, uneducated men and were mostly Galileans as well. This would place them far below the social class of the aristocratic young Josephus. Also, the Jewish establishment was repulsed by the cannibalistic overtones of the mysterious "communion" ceremony of these early Christians.

> [26:26] And as they were eating, Jesus took bread and blessed and brake it; and he gave to the disciples and said, Take, eat; this is my body. [26:27] And he took a cup and gave thanks and gave to them, saying, Drink ye all of it; [26:28] for this is my blood of the covenant which is poured out for many unto remission of sins. (Mt)

While the Jews had no problem with actual animal sacrifice, the thought of even symbolically drinking human blood or cannibalism would have been as repugnant to them as it was to the Romans. Was the missing body of Jesus used for that ghoulish purpose?. The connection was logical. The early Christians might have been considered pariahs, similar to the Untouchable class of the Indian Hindus.

Josephus documents several other men who led mobs of Jewish people into opposition against the Romans, including Theudas, whose leadership caused hundreds to be slain by Rome (*Antiq* XX 5:1); the mysterious Egyptian who was also mentioned in the New Testament Book Acts of the Apostles (*Antiq* XX 8:6; Acts 21:38); the charismatic Samaritan leader whom Pilate moved against with his soldiers late in his tenure (*Antiq* XVIII 4:1); and others. Josephus is uniformly critical of them all.

It is understandable, then, that Josephus did not include any mention of Jesus in *Wars* which was published in A.D. 78. However, *Antiquities*, with its controversial Testimonium Flavianum, was published in A.D. 93, 15 years after the publication of *Wars*. Josephus spent those years living the good life in Rome. With an open and intellectual mind, Josephus probably got to know some of the more prominent early Christians. Perhaps realizing that the communion ceremony was purely symbolic, or at least looking beyond it, Josephus might well have softened his view on Jesus and the new religion. To reflect this change, Josephus included two non-judgmental references to Jesus in his second major work, *Antiquities*.

In conclusion, the evidence is strong that the Testimonium Flavianum was originally written in a more secular fashion. The paragraph was likely later embellished by an over-enthusiastic early Christian copyist who worked on a seminal manuscript of *Antiquities*, or a marginal annotation was erroneously considered to be written by Josephus and transcribed in. The Arabic version of Josephus' famous passage was probably closer to Josephus' original writing.

Josephus' Reliability

Another criticism of Josephus is that he was a traitor to the Jewish nation and ended his life as an apologist for the Flavian Dynasty. If so, can any of his writings truly be believed? In this, there is little choice; Josephus is the one and only source for much of first century Jewish history.

Josephus has also been questioned on is his use of very large numbers. Critics say that either Josephus grossly exaggerated these himself, or that the numbers were erroneously amplified in translation by later copyists–and by a factor of at least ten. What evidence is there for these assertions?

Yodefat

Archaeologists are confident that a small mountain in Galilee, next to the modern Israeli settlement of Yodefat, is the site of the famous Jotapata where Josephus made a gallant stand against the Romans. Josephus stated that 40,000 Jews were killed during the 47 days of the siege.

> ..and went thus through every age, excepting the infants and the women and of these there were gathered together as captives twelve hundred; and as for those that were slain at the taking of the city and in the former fights, they were numbered to be forty thousand. So Vespasian gave order that the city should be entirely demolished and all the fortifications burnt down. (*Wars* 7:36)

Unless the dead were carried out and disposed of with regularity during the siege — which Josephus does not mention —, Josephus' number of Jewish dead is very contestable. The siege lasted for 47 days. Using the 40,000 figure, over 850 people a day would have had to have been killed to reach that number.

Land area is also a factor. Allowing for considerable erosion over 2,000 years, experts have estimated the size of Jotapata to have been no more than 13 acres. This would support a population of perhaps 2,000 people in times of peace and nowhere near 40,000.

The Galilean Army

In another example, Josephus, as a Galilean general, claims to have had an army of 100,000 men under his command. Was that an exaggeration? A Roman legion had 4,800 men. Vespasian's initial campaign against the Jews had three full legions plus auxiliaries.

> He (Josephus) also got together an army out of Galilee, of more than a hundred thousand young men, all of which he armed with the old weapons which he had collected together and prepared for them. (*Wars* II 20:6)

Did Josephus have the equivalent of 20 Roman legions under his command?

Second Temple

Josephus can be challenged on some of his building dimensions as well. He states that the walls of the Second Temple in Jerusalem were at least 300 cubits high. As a cubit is generally thought to be 18 inches, that would make the walls 450 feet tall-a mighty stack of blocks, indeed. Sections of the east wall might have approached that level but only if one includes the distance below the wall's base down to the lowest point of the Kidron Valley. Most experts place the height of the wall at no more than 130 feet from the base blocks to the top of the cloisters.

Other examples of numeric exaggeration in Josephus will be discussed as they arise. It is probably justifiable to reduce all very large numbers given by Josephus by a factor of ten.

The Death of Herod the Great

In dealing with written sources that are 2,000 years old, accuracy of transcription is always a question. Eusebius quotes at length from a copy of Josephus that is at least a half a millennium older than our modern reference copy. In fact, it is possible that Eusebius' copy was part of the "first–run" production that Emperor Titus himself ordered placed in the Caesarea Royal library. As noted in regard to the Testimonium Flavianum, there are differences between the accepted *Antiquities* of today and the older copy from which Eusebius quotes.

An interesting example of this error occurs in Josephus' description of the physical afflictions that led to Herod the Great's death.

> Nay, further, his privy-member was putrefied and produced worms; and when he sat upright, he had a difficulty of breathing which was very loathsome, on account of the stench of his breath and the quickness of its returns; (*Antiq* XVII 6:5)

In Eusebius, the passage is translated differently.

> The abdomen was in the same miserable state and in the genitals mortification set in, breeding worms. Breathing was constricted and only possible when sitting upright and it was most offensive because of the heavy stench and feverish respiration. (Eusebius *History* 1:8 from *Antiq* XVII 6:5)

Note that in the modern copy of *Antiquities*, Herod's breathing was difficult when he was sitting up, while in Eusebius' version it was the just the opposite–when sitting upright Herod breathed more easily. In this instance, modern medicine unequivocally supports the older Eusebius version.

Josephus describes Herod's terminal condition in *Wars*, but this time Herod's affliction is reported accurately in the "modern" copy.

> Besides which he had a difficulty of breathing upon him and could not breathe but when he sat upright, (*Wars* I 33:5)

Eusebius quotes the same passage differently, but the gist of it is accurate.

> ..as well as difficulty in breathing, especially when lying down, (Eusebius History 1:8 from *Wars* I 33:5)

Other Errors

Some errors in Josephus are translational and obvious. In several instances, in the spelling of proper names a single letter will be miscopied as two letters. "Cumanus,"for example, will later appear in the same paragraph as "Cureanus" (*Antiq* XX 5:3). In the same book of *Antiquities*, the name "Ananus" was written "Ananias" in the next paragraph–the "u" being split up into an "ia" (*Antiq* XX 9:1-2). In book XVII of *Antiquities*, "Simon" becomes "Simeon" (*Antiq* XVII 4:2). In another book, "Simon" becomes "Sireoh" (*Antiq* XVIII 5:1). If the misspelling is of a single occurrence of a name within a paragraph or section, the identification of the error becomes more problematic.

However, the purpose of this investigation is not to parse through the translations of Josephus and other ancient writers speculating on possible errors. It is admitted that we are at the mercy of the men who dedicated their lives to the copying of written works they believed to have been inspired by God. The competency of these great men will be trusted and it will be accepted that the writings of Josephus in use today are very close to Josephus' original intent of 2,000 years ago.

Chapter 4   Ancient Land

Their country and its limits are bounded on the east by Arabia, on the south by Egypt and on the west by Phoenicia and the sea; of the north they have a distant view on the side towards Syria. The health of the Jews is good and their physique sturdy. A dry climate and a fertile soil enable them to grow all the crops familiar to us.. (Tacitus *Histories* V:6)

The Jewish people, for much of their history, lived under the subjugation of foreign empires–the Greeks, the Egyptians, the Parthians, Medes, Assyrians, the Romans, and others. Despite this adversity, however, over its 5,000 year history prior to the Christian era, Jewish culture survived largely intact. Josephus theorizes as to why this was so.

As for ourselves, therefore, we neither inhabit a maritime country, nor do we delight in merchandise, nor in such a mixture with other men as arises from it; but the cities we dwell in are remote from the sea and having a fruitful country for our habitation, we take pains in cultivating that only. Our principal care of all is this, to educate our children well; and we think it to be the most necessary business of our whole life to observe the laws that have been given us and to keep those rules of piety that have been delivered down to us. Since, therefore, besides what we have already taken notice of, we have had a peculiar way of living of our own, there was no occasion offered us in ancient ages for intermixing among the Greeks, as they had for mixing among the Egyptians, by their intercourse of exporting and importing their several goods; as they also mixed with the Phoenicians, who lived by the sea-side, by means of their love of lucre in trade and merchandise. Nor did our forefathers betake themselves, as did some others, to robbery; nor did they, in order to gain more wealth, fall into foreign wars, although our country contained many ten thousands of men of courage sufficient for that purpose. (*Apion* 12)

While a core of Jews have always remained in Judea and sections of the "promised land" of the patriarch Moses, due to wars and cultural dislocations, many Jews found themselves scattered throughout the world. On this matter, Josephus quotes Strabo from a work that is now lost. Strabo was a Greek geographer and historian who lived from 63 B.C. to A.D. 23.

> Now these Jews are already gotten into all cities; and it is hard to find a place in the habitable earth that hath not admitted this tribe of men and is not possessed by them; and it hath come to pass that Egypt and Cyrene, as having the same governors and a great number of other nations, imitate their way of living and maintain great bodies of these Jews in a peculiar manner and grow up to greater prosperity with them and make use of the same laws with that nation also. Accordingly, the Jews have places assigned them in Egypt, wherein they inhabit, besides what is peculiarly allotted to this nation at Alexandria which is a large part of that city. There is also an ethnarch allowed them, who governs the nation and distributes justice to them and takes care of their contracts and of the laws to them belonging, as if he were the ruler of a free republic. In Egypt, therefore, this nation is powerful, because the Jews were originally Egyptians and because the land wherein they inhabit, since they went thence, is near to Egypt. They also removed into Cyrene, because that this land adjoined to the government of Egypt, as well as does Judea, or rather was formerly under the same government. (*Antiq* XIV 7:2)

Geology

The Jewish lands proper make up the northern portion of the Great Rift Valley, a geologically active zone formed by the meeting of two massive tectonic plates. The Rift Valley stretches from Syria in the north, southwards through the Jewish lands, and continuing into the Red Sea as an underwater canyon, finally to emerge in eastern Africa. Coursing through the center of the northern rift zone is the Jordan River system which includes Lake Gennesareth, Lake Asphaltitis, and the Aqaba River–the latter a seldom-flowing river that "empties" the briny Asphaltitis into the Red Sea. Lake Gennesareth today is called the

Sea of Galilee, Lake Asphaltitis is called the Dead Sea, while the Jordan retains its ancient name.

The massive Jordanian and Palestinian land plates shift position independently as they "float" on the surface of the earth's molten inner regions. Portions of the rift valley can suddenly shift several meters up, down, or sideways depending on the underground pressures involved. If the shifting is sudden, an earthquake occurs — which are numerous enough in the region. Slow shifting occurs constantly, and over the eons this causes mountains and occasionally volcanoes to form. The shifting can also cause geologic depressions. Indeed, both Lake Gennesareth and Lake Asphaltitis are hundreds of feet below sea level as a direct result of this natural action.

Geologists speculate that the Jordan River may have flowed into the Red Sea as recently as 3,000 years ago. Some have hypothesized that a powerful earthquake changed the course of the Jordan River and created the Dead Sea itself. In that cataclysmic event, there also might have been a huge volcanic explosion along the Rift Valley fault line — possibly accounting for the legends of the fiery destruction of the ancient cities of Sodom and Gomorrah.

The volcanic origins of the Great Rift Valley are also reflected in the number of hot springs that are noted in the ancient sources. Today, however, there are far fewer natural springs–hot or cold–in the Jewish lands. This is probably due to subsequent earthquakes that disrupted the natural underground aquifer system, along with a change in rainfall patterns.

The Jewish Land

Jewish historian Flavius Josephus described Galilee and other areas of the Jordan Rift Valley during the times of Jesus. The Galilean city of Nazareth was the boyhood home of Jesus and was located to the west of Lake Gennesareth. The rolling hills and blunted low mountains of Galilee provided good grazing for flocks of sheep and goats while the surrounding valleys and plains are well-suited for agriculture.

(The Galileans) have been always very numerous; nor hath the country been ever destitute of men of courage, or wanted a numerous set of them; for their soil is universally rich and fruitful and full of the plantations of trees of all sorts, insomuch that it invites the most slothful to take pains in its cultivation, by its fruitfulness; accordingly, it is all cultivated by its inhabitants and no part of it lies idle. Moreover, the cities lie here very thick and the very many villages there are here are every where so full of people, by the richness of their soil, that the very least of them contain above fifteen thousand inhabitants. (*Wars* III 3:2)

Perea, on the eastern side of the Jordan river south of the Decapolis, was also described by Josephus.

Perea which is indeed much larger in extent, the greater part of it is desert and rough and much less disposed for the production of the milder kinds of fruits; yet hath it a moist soil [in other parts] and produces all kinds of fruits and its plains are planted with trees of all sorts, while yet the olive tree, the vine and the palm tree are chiefly cultivated there. It is also sufficiently watered with torrents which issue out of the mountains and with springs that never fail to run, even when the torrents fail them, as they do in the dog-days. Now the length of Perea is from Macherus to Pella and its breadth from Philadelphia to Jordan; its northern parts are bounded by Pella, as we have already said, as well as its Western with Jordan; the land of Moab is its southern border and its eastern limits reach to Arabia and Silbonitis and besides to Philadelphene and Gerasa. (*Wars* III 3:3)

Samaria and Judea are next described.

Now as to the country of Samaria, it lies between Judea and Galilee; it begins at a village that is in the great plain called Ginea and ends at the Acrabbene toparchy and is entirely of the same nature with Judea; for both countries are made up of hills and valleys and are moist enough for agriculture and are very fruitful. They have abundance of trees and are full of autumnal fruit, both that which grows wild and that which is the effect of cultivation. They are not naturally watered by many rivers, but derive their chief moisture from rain-water, of which they have no want; and for those rivers which they have, all their waters are exceeding sweet: by reason also of the excellent grass they have, their cattle yield more milk than do those in other places; and, what is the greatest sign of excellency and of abundance, they each of them are very full of people. (*Wars* III 3:4)

Lake Gennesareth itself was a great fishery and generated much wealth for the surrounding towns. To the south in Judea and Samaria, small mountains and valleys predominated which were suitable for pasture land and small farms. Around Jerusalem itself the land is rocky and cut with deep chasms. To the southeast, the land eventually descends into Lake Asphaltitis five miles away. The city of Jerusalem was built on several small mountains and protected by rocky gorges on two of its three sides. Most importantly, and the prime reason for its location, was that Jerusalem was and is blessed with an unusual artesian water source that runs strong all year long.

Lake Gennesareth

Today, Lake Gennesareth remains substantially unchanged from ancient times. In the following excerpts from Josephus, note that one furlong is equal to about 700 feet.

> Now this lake of Gennesareth is so called from the country adjoining to it. Its breadth is forty furlongs and its length one hundred and forty; its waters are sweet and very agreeable for drinking, for they are finer than the thick waters of other fens; the lake is also pure and on every side ends directly at the shores and at the sand; it is also of a temperate nature when you draw it up and of a more gentle nature than river or fountain water and yet always cooler than one could expect in so diffuse a place as this is. Now when this water is kept in the open air, it is as cold as that snow which the country people are accustomed to make by night in summer. There are several kinds of fish in it, different both to the taste and the sight from those elsewhere. It is divided into two parts by the river Jordan. (*Wars* III 10:7)

The town of Capernaum, on the northwestern shores of the Gennesareth and where Jesus based his Ministry, has been rediscovered recently and completely excavated. Josephus comments on the land surrounding Capernaum which was also known as Gennesareth–the same name as the lake it adjoins.

> The country also that lies over against this lake hath the same name of Gennesareth; its nature is wonderful as well as its beauty; its soil is so fruitful that all sorts of trees can grow upon it and the inhabitants

accordingly plant all sorts of trees there; for the temper of the air is so well mixed, that it agrees very well with those several sorts, particularly walnuts which require the coldest air, flourish there in vast plenty; there are palm trees also which grow best in hot air; fig trees also and olives grow near them which yet require an air that is more temperate. One may call this place the ambition of nature, where it forces those plants that are naturally enemies to one another to agree together; it is a happy contention of the seasons, as if every one of them laid claim to this country; for it not only nourishes different sorts of autumnal fruit beyond men's expectation, but preserves them a great while; it supplies men with the principal fruits, with grapes and figs continually, during ten months of the year and the rest of the fruits as they become ripe together through the whole year; for besides the good temperature of the air, it is also watered from a most fertile fountain. The people of the country call it Capharnaum. Some have thought it to be a vein of the Nile, because it produces the Coracin fish as well as that lake does which is near to Alexandria. The length of this country extends itself along the banks of this lake that bears the same name for thirty furlongs and is in breadth twenty and this is the nature of that place. (*Wars* III 10:8)

The lake is fed by the Jordan River which was itself created by mountain rain and snow-pack runoff to the north. It is improbable that a fish species would have arisen in waters as cold as this. The Coracin fish was likely artificially introduced.

The Jordan River

One of the sources of the river Jordan is found 25 miles north of the Gennesareth at Mount Hebron. In ancient times, a prodigious flow of freshwater emerged from a cave at the southern base of this mountain to form the great river. Many temples were built close to this source as it was considered a sacred place–then called Banias (Panium). A severe earthquake later diverted this flow so that today the cold water flows out at a point just outside of the cave, but the formation carved in the rock wall is still an impressive and evocative site.

From Banias, the Jordan river then meanders 25 miles south through fertile land to finally reach Lake Gennesareth–dropping over 2,000 feet as it does so. Lake Gennesareth itself is 700 feet below sea level.

It (Lake Gennesareth) is divided into two parts by the river Jordan. Now Panium is thought to be the fountain of Jordan, but in reality it is carried thither after an occult manner from the place called Phiala: this place lies as you go up to Trachonitis and is a hundred and twenty furlongs from Cesarea and is not far out of the road on the right hand; and indeed it hath its name of Phiala [vial or bowl] very justly, from the roundness of its circumference, as being round like a wheel; its water continues always up to its edges, without either sinking or running over. And as this origin of Jordan was formerly not known, it was discovered so to be when Philip was tetrarch of Trachonitis; for he had chaff thrown into Phiala and it was found at Paninto, where the ancients thought the fountain-head of the river was, whither it had been therefore carried [by the waters]. As for Panium itself, its natural beauty had been improved by the royal liberality of Agrippa and adorned at his expenses. Now Jordan's visible stream arises from this cavern and divides the marshes and fens of the lake Semechonitis; when it hath run another hundred and twenty furlongs, it first passes by the city Julias and then passes through the middle of the lake Gennesareth; after which it runs a long way over a desert and then makes its exit into the lake Asphaltitis. (*Wars* III 10:7)

The Tetrarch Herod Philip was the son of Herod the Great and a Roman puppet ruler in his own right. Philip built his showcase city Caesarea Philippi near the source of the Jordan River at Banias. Decades later, King Agrippa II rebuilt Philip's palace in sumptuous fashion. The city of Julias is thought to be the ancient town of Bethsaida in Philip's old territory, located just east of the Jordan River and a few furlongs inland from the rocky north shore of Lake Gennesareth.

Now the region that lies in the middle between these ridges of mountains is called the Great Plain; it reaches from the village Ginnabris, as far as the lake Asphaltitis; its length is two hundred and thirty furlongs and its breadth a hundred and twenty and it is divided in the midst by Jordan. It hath two lakes in it, that of Asphaltitis and that of Tiberias, whose natures are opposite to each other; for the former is salt and unfruitful, but that of Tiberias is sweet and fruitful. This plain is much burnt up in summer time and, by reason of the extraordinary heat, contains a very unwholesome air; it is all destitute of water excepting the river Jordan which water of Jordan is the occasion why those plantations of palm trees that are near its banks are more flourishing and much more fruitful, as are those that are remote from it not so flourishing, or fruitful. (*Wars* IV 8:2)

The lake called Tiberius that Josephus refers to could mean the Gennesareth, or it could refer to a smaller lake south of the Gennesareth that has since disappeared.

Stretching from the east bank of the lower section of the Jordan River is a dry and desert-like country called Perea. This is where John the Baptist based his ministry. It is little wonder that the Jordan River was a magnet for religious ascetics. The Jordan's life-giving qualities was a stark contrast to much of the arid and parched country of Perea. Where the Jordan flowed, trees, lush green vegetation, and wildlife abounded. In the times of Jesus, after heavy rains the Jordan was not fordable in many places due to the deep and turbulent flow of water. In A.D. 68 during the Jewish revolt, Roman General Placidus pursued a group of zealots from Jericho east to the Jordan River where they were trapped and slain.

> But Placidus..followed them and slew all that he overtook, as far as Jordan; and when he had driven the whole multitude to the river-side, where they were stopped by the current, (for it had been augmented lately by rains and was not fordable,).. (*Wars* IV 7:5)

Today, in far too many places, the Jordan River is barely a trickle as most of its flow has been diverted for agricultural use.

Josephus describes the country of the Jordan River when devoting a section in *Wars* to the city of Jericho, the ancient city of renown and the capital of Herod the Great's kingdom.

> (Jericho)..is situated in a plain; but a naked and barren mountain, of a very great length, hangs over it which extends itself to the land about Scythopolis northward, but as far as the country of Sodom and the utmost limits of the lake Asphaltiris, southward. This mountain is all of it very uneven and uninhabited, by reason of its barrenness: there is an opposite mountain that is situated over against it, on the other side of Jordan; this last begins at Julias and the northern quarters and extends itself southward as far as Somorrhon which is the bounds of Petra, in Arabia. In this ridge of mountains there is one called the Iron Mountain, that runs in length as far as Moab. Now the region that lies in the middle between these ridges of mountains is called the Great Plain; it reaches from the village Ginnabris, as far as the lake Asphaltitis; its length is two hundred and thirty furlongs and its breadth a hundred and twenty and

it is divided in the midst by Jordan. It hath two lakes in it, that of Asphaltitis and that of Tiberias, whose natures are opposite to each other; for the former is salt and unfruitful, but that of Tiberias is sweet and fruitful. This plain is much burnt up in summer time and, by reason of the extraordinary heat, contains a very unwholesome air; it is all destitute of water excepting the river Jordan which water of Jordan is the occasion why those plantations of palm trees that are near its banks are more flourishing and much more fruitful, as are those that are remote from it not so flourishing, or fruitful. (*Wars* IV 8:2)

....there is a fountain by Jericho, that runs plentifully and is very fit for watering the ground; it arises near the old city which Joshua, the son of Naue, the general of the Hebrews, took the first of all the cities of the land of Canaan, by right of war. The report is, that this fountain, at the beginning, caused not only the blasting of the earth and the trees, but of the children born of women and that it was entirely of a sickly and corruptive nature to all things whatsoever; but that it was made gentle and very wholesome and fruitful, by the prophet Elisha...it waters a larger space of ground than any other waters do and passes along a plain of seventy furlongs long and twenty broad; wherein it affords nourishment to those most excellent gardens that are thick set with trees. There are in it many sorts of palm trees that are watered by it, different from each other in taste and name; the better sort of them, when they are pressed, yield an excellent kind of honey, not much inferior in sweetness to other honey. This country withal produces honey from bees; it also bears that balsam which is the most precious of all the fruits in that place, cypress trees also and those that bear myrobalanum; so that he who should pronounce this place to be divine would not be mistaken, wherein is such plenty of trees produced as are very rare and of the must excellent sort. And indeed, if we speak of those other fruits, it will not be easy to light on any climate in the habitable earth that can well be compared to it, - what is here sown comes up in such clusters; the cause of which seems to me to be the warmth of the air and the fertility of the waters; the warmth calling forth the sprouts and making them spread and the moisture making every one of them take root firmly and supplying that virtue which it stands in need of in summer time. Now this country is then so sadly burnt up, that nobody cares to come at it; and if the water be drawn up before sun-rising and after that exposed to the air, it becomes exceeding cold and becomes of a nature quite contrary to the ambient air; as in winter again it becomes warm; and if you go into it, it appears very gentle. The ambient air is here also of so good a temperature, that the people of the country are clothed in linen-only, even when snow covers the rest of Judea. This place is one hundred and fifty furlongs from Jerusalem and sixty from Jordan. The country, as far as Jerusalem, is desert and stony; but that as far as Jordan and the lake Asphaltitis lies lower indeed, though it be equally desert and barren. But so much shall suffice to have said about Jericho and of the great happiness of its situation. (*Wars* IV 8:3

Josephus also describes the Lake Asphaltitis which is fed by the Jordan River and located 80 miles south of Lake Gennesareth:

The nature of the lake Asphaltitis is also worth describing. It is, as I have said already, bitter and unfruitful. It is so light [or thick] that it bears up the heaviest things that are thrown into it; nor is it easy for any one to make things sink therein to the bottom, if he had a mind so to do. Accordingly, when Vespasian went to see it, he commanded that some who could not swim should have their hands tied behind them and be thrown into the deep, when it so happened that they all swam as if a wind had forced them upwards. Moreover, the change of the color of this lake is wonderful, for it changes its appearance thrice every day; and as the rays of the sun fall differently upon it, the light is variously reflected. However, it casts up black clods of bitumen in many parts of it; these swim at the top of the water and resemble both in shape and bigness headless bulls; and when the laborers that belong to the lake come to it and catch hold of it as it hangs together, they draw it into their ships; but when the ship is full, it is not easy to cut off the rest, for it is so tenacious as to make the ship hang upon its clods till they set it loose with the menstrual blood of women and with urine, to which alone it yields. This bitumen is not only useful for the caulking of ships, but for the cure of men's bodies; accordingly, it is mixed in a great many medicines. The length of this lake is five hundred and eighty furlongs, where it is extended as far as Zoar in Arabia; and its breadth is a hundred and fifty. The country of Sodom borders upon it. It was of old a most happy land, both for the fruits it bore and the riches of its cities, although it be now all burnt up. It is related how, for the impiety of its inhabitants, it was burnt by lightning; in consequence of which there are still the remainders of that Divine fire and the traces [or shadows] of the five cities are still to be seen, as well as the ashes growing in their fruits; which fruits have a color as if they were fit to be eaten, but if you pluck them with your hands, they dissolve into smoke and ashes. And thus what is related of this land of Sodom hath these marks of credibility which our very sight affords us. (*Wars* IV 8:4)

Today, Lake Asphaltitis is shrinking due to natural evaporation and a lack of replenishment from the Jordan River. It appears, too, that many of the natural springs around the Jordan mentioned in ancient sources–both cold and hot–are now gone.

So it is upon this fertile and productive landscape, and within an ancient nation governed by a Rome-sanctioned theocracy, that the drama of Jesus and the early Christians was to be played out.

Chapter 5   The Roman Empire

Rome at the beginning was ruled by kings. Freedom and the consulship were established by Lucius Brutus. Dictatorships were held for a temporary crisis...The despotisms of Cinna and Sulla were brief; the rule of Pompeius and of Crassus soon yielded before Caesar; the arms of Lepidus and Antonius before Augustus; who, when the world was wearied by civil strife, subjected it to empire under the title of "Prince." (*Annuls* 1:1)

The city of Rome was located on a strategic bend in the Tiber River. Legend has it that the defeated Prince Aeneas and his companions founded the city of Rome after escaping a burning and doomed Troy in Asia Minor. However, tribal migration from the north, as was the case with Greece, is a more plausible explanation.

Rome had to fight early and often in order to survive against its neighbors. The Etruscans were a loose confederation of cities that had also established themselves in the Italia peninsula along with Rome. Despite sharing sharing a common culture they found reason to war. The last Etruscans stronghold of Etruria was taken by Rome in 396 B.C.

Rome found success on the battlefield through a disciplined and innovative military. This tradition would reach its zenith a half a millennium later when the Roman Empire achieved its greatest expanse in the second century A.D. under Emperor Trajan.

Rome and Carthage

To the south of Italia on the large island of Sicily were several large cities belonging to the empire of Carthage. Conflicts arose between Rome and those cities and battles ensued. In the wake of this, the far-sighted leaders of Rome realized that for Rome and Italia to be truly secure the entire Mediterranean Sea had to be under their control. Rome had no choice but to expand or be conquered!

So eventually, the whole of the Carthaginian Empire was involved in what started out to be a local conflict. By that time, the fledgling Rome-based empire had discarded rule by king in favor of rule by aristocracy. Rome was now governed by a senate of noblemen from wealthy families–the Republican tradition had been born. By that time as well, Rome had developed an extensive set of written laws and a sophisticated system of administering justice to go along with their military traditions.

The Carthaginian Empire extended west into the Iberian peninsula (modern day Spain) and south into much of North Africa. The Carthaginians were also allied with several large Phoenician cities located on the eastern Mediterranean seacoast such as Tyre and Sidon. Earlier, Alexander the Great had conquered both cities—the island city of Tyre in a famous and prolonged siege. After Alexander's death, however, both these cities and others regained semi-autonomous status. Rome might have been encouraged to move against Carthage by Alexander's earlier military successes in those seemingly-impregnable eastern Mediterranean cities.

Rome's conflicts with Carthage were called the Punic Wars. Three of them were fought over more than a century from 260 B.C. to 146 B.C. Hundreds of thousands of soldiers from both Rome and Carthage died in the devastating and prolonged series of epic campaigns. A bleeding, battered, and reeling Rome ultimately became the last man standing and so claimed undisputed dominance over the Mediterranean Sea. Eschewing the concept of forgiveness, Rome in vengeance destroyed

Carthage so completely that little is known about this great early empire of the Mediterranean.

Battles with Carthage made the Romans realize the importance of the Italia peninsula. The scattered Samnite cities and others in Italia, while Roman allies (Socii), were absorbed or conquered into the empire. This included the southern walled city of Pompei, later to be buried under volcanic ash in the A.D. 79 eruption of Mount Vesuvius.

The Marian Reforms

Over the next 50 years, the Roman Empire evolved (or devolved!) greatly from the Rome that had existed at the end of the Punic Wars. Republican rule had given way to military rule by ambitious and dictatorial generals. This change was inadvertently brought about by the adoption of the so-called "Marian reforms" of 107 B.C.

After the last of the Punic Wars in 146 B.C., even though victorious, Rome spent decades recovering from the devastation. The assimilation of the defeated peoples of the Carthaginian Empire also required great attention and resources. During those years, the empire had to deal with recurrent invasions of its northern territories by the Gauls, as well as fending off a military adventure into Asia Minor and Greece by King Mithridates of Pontus. In the process of the successful management of these undertakings, the Roman generals gained an autonomy and power that would eventually prove to be fatal to Republican rule–as well as to the independent Jewish nation.

In the late second century B.C., Rome was under the clear control of the Republican Senate. But in response to continuing outside threats from Gaul, Consul Gaius Marius had convinced the senate in 107 B.C. to lower the standards for the enlistment of Roman soldiers. These "reforms" dramatically changed the nature of the Roman army. Previously, a soldier had to be of a certain class, have a set amount of money, and own land in order to qualify for service. The purpose of these requirements was to assure that the soldiers would be loyal to the Roman Republic and not to any individual Roman general.

But under Marius' plan, ultimately all these restrictions were abolished. Ambitious men of little means who had no property or real stake in Rome itself began to dominate the ranks of the Roman legions. The generals who commanded the soldiers also paid their wages, and thus the soldiers, did, in fact, identify far more with their generals than Rome.

The generation of Roman generals after Marius took full advantage of their new and powerful positions. Less than 20 years after the Marian reforms, in 88 B.C., a legion of Roman soldiers under the control of General Lucius Sulla marched into Rome itself under a pretext of protecting the city from a largely contrived civil sedition. Sulla then claimed supreme power as dictator in order to ostensibly keep the peace. Sulla's entrance into Rome with his army was hugely unpopular and his occupation was temporary. But the precedent had been set and the concept of the Roman Republic was irrecoverably compromised.

Well-trained, well-equipped and independent professional armies began to range across the known world loosely under the banner of the Roman Eagle. Their purpose was conquest and plunder and they were led by ambitious and avaricious generals. Gnaeus Pompey was the first of these daring and bold men and spent years subjugating the East. The Jewish nation was conquered by Pompey in 63 B.C., as will be seen. Later, Julius Caesar, following Pompey's example, would take his own legions and cut a bloody swath through Gaul and Germany in the north of Europe. None of these targeted foreign nations posed any real threat to Rome, but these countries did possess human resources–slaves!–and a few possessed some measure of wealth. Indeed, much of the impetus to conquest for these generals was the need to pay their soldiers. And in war, of course, nothing motivates a common soldier more than the promise of plunder.

While trying to maintain the facade of the Republic, the Roman Senate usually submitted to the demands of the generals under threat of the sword. Beginning with Marius and Sulla and continuing through to Julius Caesar, Pompey, Marcus Crassus and others, a progression of generals assumed dictatorial power in fact if not in name. The influence of the senate continued to erode. Worse, over the decades the civil wars that developed between competing generals ripped apart the empire and sapped the strength of the Roman people. The senate could do little more than helplessly look on.

Young General Octavian, the nephew of Julius Caesar, brought about the end of this unstable era. He recognized that the Marian reforms of 107 B.C. were the root cause of Roman civil unrest and a host of other problems. But the canny Octavian waited to reverse these reforms until after he himself had achieved the supreme power. This occurred in 31 B.C. with his defeat of rival Marc Antony. Octavian–soon to be known as the "divine" Emperor Augustus–then simply changed the way the soldiers were paid. Under the Octavian reform, payroll funds for all the soldiers were to come from the State treasury and not from the private wealth of the legions' commanding generals (Sue *Aug* XLIX). Instead of being tied to the pockets of the Roman generals–and by extension to their ambitions–the always-dangerous Roman army was now tethered to the Roman treasury. This reining in of the generals marked the beginning of the "Pax Romana," or the two-century period of relative peace and prosperity enjoyed by the Roman Empire.

The Assassination of Julius Caesar and the Second Civil War

When the senate of Rome voted Julius Caesar "Dictator for Life" in 44 B.C. after the conclusion of the First Civil War, it also guaranteed Rome a bloody future. Some historians mark senate's acquiescence as the official end of the Roman Republic.

The Roman Senate had ruled the empire for centuries but by 44 B.C. it was just a shell of its former powerful self. Over the years, the powers of the Roman Senate had been weakened by ruthless and contemptuous generals–either working alone or allied with other generals. Most of the senate members were cowed by the threats–implied or otherwise–of these ambitious men.

In the case of General Julius Caesar, he had initiated the first Roman Civil War by attacking his co-ruler Pompey and eventually defeating him. This will be gone into in more detail in the next chapter. Caesar's expectation for dictatorship was so bold that a handful of men from honored families, including Brutus and Cassius, decided to oppose him, forming a conspiracy for the purpose of assassination. They feared Caesar would next demand to be named king and dissolve the senate entirely. The assassination of Caesar occurred on the Ides (15th day) of March 44 B.C. in the Roman Forum soon after Caesar had been named "censor for life." But the conspirators underestimated the level of popular support that Caesar enjoyed, as well as the oratorical skills of Marc Antony, one of Caesar's generals. The population of Rome rose up against Brutus, Cassius, and the other conspirators and they had to flee the city.

The senate in those days was hardly a congress of the common man; it was a forum for the wealthy and elite of Rome. Julius Caesar was keenly aware of this and so intentionally had been free with his money for public purposes. Caesar was also popular with the masses for engineering a score of military victories–some of them brilliant and innovative. The supporters of the late Julius Caesar, led by Octavian, Marc Antony and Marcus Lepidus, picked up the fallen banner of Julius Caesar and opposed the conspirators. Rome was plunged into another civil war–her second in 10 years. Octavian, Antony and Lepidus soon defeated the republican alliance of Cassius and Brutus in battles that took place in scattered areas throughout the empire.

In 43 B.C. these three victorious men formed the "Second Triumvirate" which was then legally sanctioned by the senate to rule the empire for a 10-year period. Lepidus was given North Africa to rule, but the heart of the empire was split in two: Octavian ruled the West and Antony ruled the East.

The Roman Empire
Mid-First Century A.D.

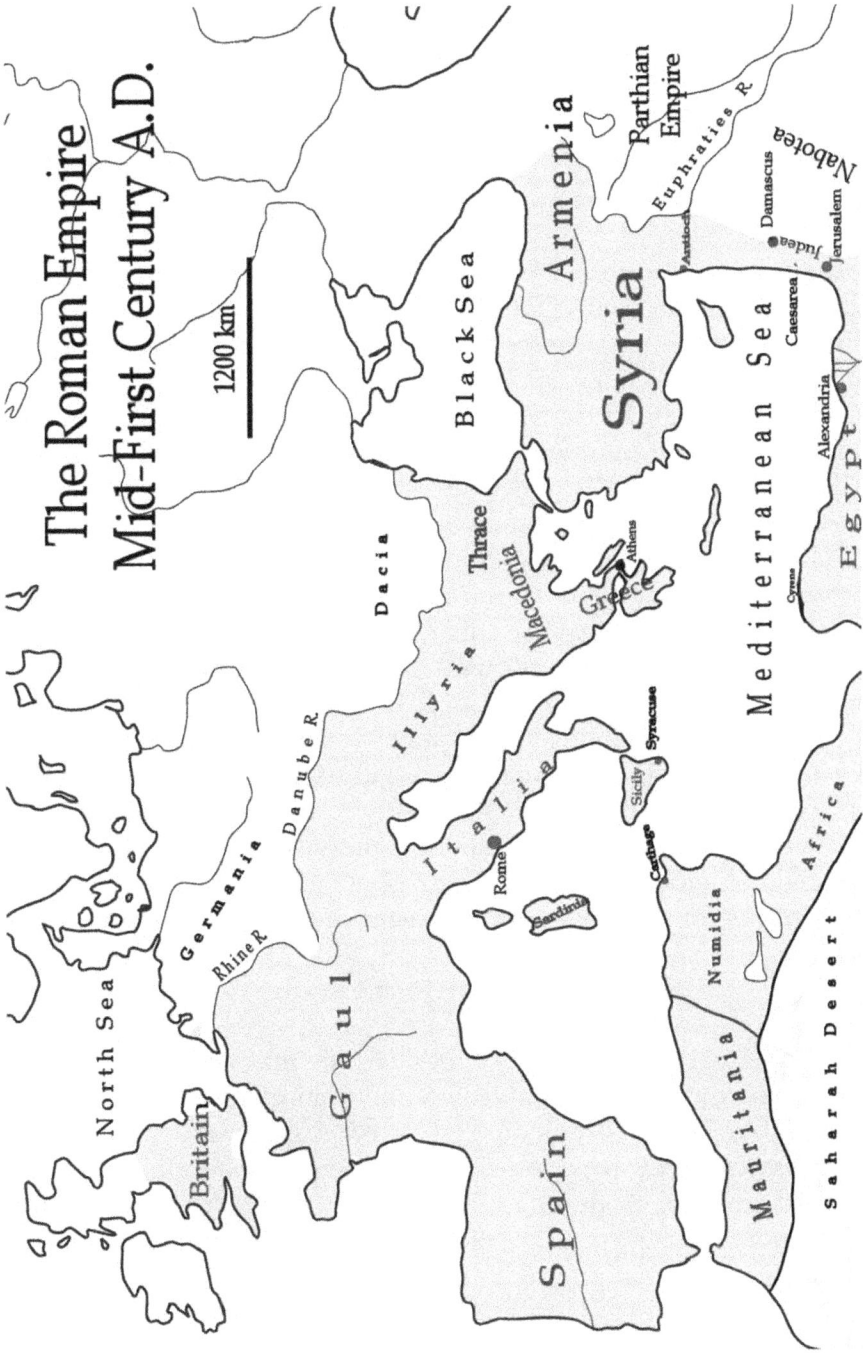

1200 km

North Sea

Britain

Germania

Rhine R.

Gaul

Danube R.

Dacia

Black Sea

Armenia

Parthian Empire

Euphraties R.

Illyria

Thrace

Macedonia

Greece

Athens

Syria

Antioch

Damascus

Judea

Jerusalem

Nabotea

Caesarea

Spain

Italia

Rome

Sardinia

Sicily

Syracuse

Carthage

Numidia

Mauritania

Africa

Saharah Desert

Mediterranean Sea

Cyrene

Alexandria

Egypt

The Rise of Octavian

In 33 B.C., the 10-year charter of the Second Triumvirate came up for renewal in the Roman Senate. Marc Antony and his supporters in Rome began political maneuvering designed to marginalize the power of the younger Octavian. Octavian responded strongly and surprised Antony with his unhesitating use of military force. Like Sulla and Caesar before him, Octavian marched his legions into Rome and seized control of the city. Rome was plunged into a third Civil War, although some historians view it as an extension of the second. The young Octavian was aided tremendously by the strategies developed by his able General Marcus Agrippa. At the end of 31 B.C. Octavian had defeated Marc Antony and his allies, and had his singular power affirmed by the Roman Senate.

Octavian allowed the Roman Senate to remain intact, but severely curtailed its powers. The deliberative body never again dared to oppose any of the edicts or proposals from the dictator. Octavian also had the Roman soldiers paid from the Royal treasury, thus deflecting their loyalties away from individual generals and stabilizing the empire. In 27 B.C. the senate voted Octavian powers that made him absolute ruler in fact and officially changed his name to Augustus. He ruled over the Roman Empire without challenge until his death in A.D. 14. Augustus' successor was his step-son Tiberius, who ruled over the empire for most of another quarter century.

Rome in the Early First Century A.D.

It was during the years of Tiberius' rule that Jesus of Nazareth and John the Baptist established their ministries in the Jewish East. Under the combined reigns of Augustus and Tiberius, perhaps 50 million people lived within the boundaries of the Roman Empire. Of those 50 million, only six million could claim Roman citizenship and enjoyed a measure of freedom and protection under Roman law (*Annuls* 11:25). Rome itself boasted a population of over a million inhabitants and at a density never before seen in the ancient world. This was made possible by aqueduct and sewer systems. Also in Rome, three-story buildings were the norm rather than the exception,

In contrast, the Jewish provinces were agrarian and held perhaps 3 million people in total–with very few Jews possessing Roman citizenship. Jerusalem, the largest Jewish city, had a population of about 50,000. A significant portion them were devoted to supporting the operation of the Second Temple in some capacity.

The Roman Legions

Rome controlled its empire through its legions and auxiliaries. At the end of the Second Civil War in 30 B.C. Octavian had or inherited by conquest 50 legions which he consolidated into 28. Three were cut to ribbons at the disastrous battle of Teutoburg Forest in A.D. 9 and never replaced.

A Roman legion was composed of approximately 4800 men, divided up as follows: a tent group, as the name suggests, was eight men who usually lived together in a tent; a century was composed of 10 tent groups or 80 men. A century was led by a Centurion; six centuries or 480 men made up a cohort; and a legion had 10 cohorts. The attendants, servants, women and other camp followers of any legion usually amounted to twice the size of the legion, or two people to each soldier on average.

Roman historian Publius Tacitus details the deployment of Roman military forces in A.D. 23, and in doing so also delineates the extent of the Roman Empire at that time.

> Italy on both seas was guarded by fleets, at Misenum and at Ravenna and the contiguous coast of Gaul by ships of war captured in the victory of Actium and sent by Augustus powerfully manned to the town of Forojulium. But chief strength was on the Rhine, as a defence alike against Germans and Gauls and numbered eight legions. Spain, lately subjugated, was held by three. Mauretania was king Juba's, who had received it as a gift from the Roman people. The rest of Africa was garrisoned by two legions and Egypt by the same number. Next, beginning with Syria, all within the entire tract of country stretching as far as the Euphrates, was kept in restraint by four legions and on this

frontier were Iberian, Albanian and other kings, to whom our greatness was a protection against any foreign power. Thrace was held by Rhoemetalces and the children of Cotys; the bank of the Danube by two legions in Pannonia, two in Moesia and two also were stationed in Dalmatia, which, from the situation of the country, were in the rear of the other four and, should Italy suddenly require aid, not to distant to be summoned. But the capital was garrisoned by its own special soldiery, three city, nine praetorian cohorts, levied for the most part in Etruria and Umbria, or ancient Latium and the old Roman colonies. There were besides, in commanding positions in the provinces, allied fleets, cavalry and light infantry, of but little inferior strength. But any detailed account of them would be misleading, since they moved from place to place as circumstances required and had their numbers increased and sometimes diminished. (*Annuls* 4.5)

Interesting in Tacitus' overview is that the Jewish lands of Judea, Galilee, Samaria, and Perea are not mentioned. Out of the 25 standing legions that made up the Roman army in A.D. 23, none was headquartered either in Judea or in Caesarea, the controlling Roman city for much of the Jewish East.

However, Tacitus does not mention that the Roman administrator of Judea had authority over several thousand auxiliary troops and horsemen stationed in Caesarea. In fact, auxiliary forces controlled by client kings, Roman legates, and administrators likely equaled the manpower in all 25 Roman legions. These auxiliaries were Rome's to deploy and command if need be. The appointed "kings" of Galilee and the area east of it who at that time in A.D. 23 were Herod Antipas and Herod Philip–both sons of Herod the Great–maintained their own armies, but they were technically considered auxiliary units of Rome.

On this same subject, it is interesting to note the variety of forces that Emperor Vespasian put at his son Titus' disposal to finalize the crushing of the Jewish revolt in A.D. 70.

Awaiting him in Judaea were three legions that had long served under Vespasian — the Fifth, Tenth and Fifteenth. The emperor also allotted him the Twelfth from Syria and the drafts from the Twenty-Second and the Third brought up from Alexandria. He was attended by twenty cohorts of allied infantry and eight regiments of cavalry, as well as by the two kings Agrippa and Sohaemus and the supporting forces offered by King Antiochus. Then there were strong levies of Arabs, who felt for the Jews the hatred common between neighbours and many individual adventurers from Rome and Italy who for various reasons hoped to ingratiate themselves with an emperor whose ear might still be gained. This then was the army with which Titus entered enemy territory. (Tacitus *Histories* V:1)

The new Emperor Vespasian was taking no chances that his son might suffer defeat at the hands of the Jews. Titus was given six full legions plus auxiliaries to complete the campaign–far more than what Vespasian had originally been given by Emperor Nero three years earlier in for the same purpose.

The Roman Navy

Rome is known today primarily as a land-based power. The roads that Rome built are still in use and stand as marvels of engineering for all to see. The shipbuilding skills of the Romans were also prodigious but under-appreciated in modern times. The reason is for this is simple: roads endure over time while ships disintegrate.

Tacitus describes a fleet of Roman ships that General Germanicus had constructed in A.D. 16. Their purpose was to move his Roman legions around the North Sea, specifically off the coast of what is now the Netherlands.

It seemed that a thousand vessels were required and they were speedily constructed, some of small draught with a narrow stem and stern and a broad centre, that they might bear the waves more easily; some flat-bottomed, that they might ground without being injured; several, furnished with a rudder at each end, so that by a sudden shifting of the oars they might be run into shore either way. Many were covered in with decks, on which engines for missiles might be conveyed and were also fit for the carrying of horses or supplies and being equipped with sails as well as rapidly moved by oars.. (*Annuls* 2.6)

It is very probable that the vaunted Scandinavian Viking longships of the late first millennium A.D. were not original to the Norse but based on Roman design.

Pax Romana

The rule of Augustus and the partial repeal of the Marian reforms had ushered in a golden age for the Roman Empire. The Mediterranean world was then solidly under the banner of the Roman Eagle. The oceans, seas and rivers were free from pirates. The major overland trade routes were studded with Roman military outposts and vastly safer for commerce. Peace reigned throughout the empire and the known world beyond it. Trade flourished, people prospered, and cities grew. This two century period of relative tranquility was called the Pax Romana–the Roman Peace. It would last through to the middle of the second century A.D.

Chapter 6   The Asamoneans

Then, since the Hellenistic rulers were weak and the Parthians had not yet developed into a great power (Rome, too, was still far away), the Jews established a dynasty of their own. (Tacitus *Histories* V:8)

The Jews were an ancient people who migrated from Egypt into the "promised land" of the Middle East a thousand years before the times of Jesus. Under the able leadership of a series of colorful and ruthless warrior-kings, the Jews eventually conquered the territories and cities that had been identified by their patriarch Moses as being given to them by God. The capital city became Jerusalem, where King Solomon built a large and ornate Temple to their God in partial thanks for their successful conquests.

The ancient independent nation of Israel lasted only a few hundred years. At different periods of time, the Jews were under subjugation by the Egyptians, the Assyrians, the Greek Syrians, and others. However, no matter which power was in control, the Jewish nation was usually allowed to practice its religion unimpeded and the people generally prospered under the facile leadership of the Jerusalem High Priesthood.

Legacy Kingdoms

In the mid-to-late fourth century B.C., Alexander the Great and his Greek armies stunned the known world by subjugating Egypt, the Jewish East, and Asia to include the Persian Empire and part of India. Introducing Greek ways and ideas into these vast foreign areas, the world was changed forever.

Interestingly, Jewish historian Flavius Josephus documents a visit that Alexander the Great made to Jerusalem early in his campaign. According to Josephus, Alexander had a favorable dream about the city and so approached it peacefully. He was met by Jewish priests dressed in their finest regalia and was escorted to the Temple where Alexander offered sacrifice and paid his respects to the Jewish God (*Antiq* XI 8:5-6). Alexander's armies then bypassed Jerusalem and the Jewish East–the "conquest" of the Jewish lands done without a single battle.

Alexander the Great died suddenly in Persia in 323 B.C. at the age of 32. It is suggested that he was poisoned by his Persian wife who was of noble birth, and resentful of being forced to marry the barbarian Alexander.

> Now when Alexander, king of Macedon, had put an end to the dominion of the Persians and had settled the affairs in Judea after the forementioned manner, he ended his life. And as his government fell among many, Antigonus obtained Asia, Seleucus Babylon; and of the other nations which were there, Lysimachus governed the Hellespont and Cassander possessed Macedonia; as did Ptolemy the son of Lagus seize upon Egypt. (*Antiq* XII 1:1)

Leaving no adult heir, Alexander's empire was fought over by his generals for the next 20 years. Eventually, four of these generals gained the lion's share of it–most notably General Ptolemy as the new Pharaoh of Egypt.

Ptolemy would start a Greek dynasty in Egypt that would last for 300 years. The most famous of his descendants would be Queen Cleopatra VII, the consort of both Julius Caesar and Marc Antony. The Greek General Seleucid received control of the Persian Empire and Antigonus controlled Greece. King Pontus received back the kingdom that Alexander had conquered from him and received more as well.

From Rome's perspective, the death of Alexander and the breakup of his empire was a fortunate development. Now, Rome could lay aside fears concerning Greek ambition. If he had not died, Alexander–only in his thirties–likely would have turned his eye and armies towards Rome and Carthage after returning to Greece in victory.

King Antiochus and the Maccabees

Alexander's legacy kingdoms continued to war amongst themselves for the next two centuries despite the fact that they were all ruled by Greeks and some of the ruling families were related to each other. These nations were termed "Hellenic" for their connection to Greek culture and the great Alexander.

The Greek-Syrian King Antiochus IV seized control of the Seleucid Empire by deceptive means in 173 B.C.. Antiochus subsequently led a successful conquest of parts of Egypt. In doing this, he marched his armies along the Mediterranean coastline and bypassed much of the more-inland Jewish East. The Roman Empire at that time was fighting the Punic Wars.

But even as it fought Carthage, Rome viewed with displeasure the ambition of Antiochus in the East. Rome then made it clear to Antiochus their concerns over any further expansion in Egypt. Daring not to cross Rome, King Antiochus aborted his plans for a complete conquest of the ancient Nile kingdom. But Rome had said nothing about Judea, so Antiochus turned his attention to the Middle East and overran the territory of the Jews in 169 B.C.

The Jews were used to being conquered. The victorious kingdom or empire would usually plunder the cities and countryside, seizing anything of value that they found. Citizens deemed desirable or useful would be enslaved. The wealthy would be ransomed for money. Lastly, the conquerors would leave a garrison in place to extort more money from the people should it become available and the main body of the army moved on. After the dust settled, the Jews were allowed to pick up the pieces of their lives and practice their religion without interference.

King Antiochus of the Greek-Syrians, however, was unusually intolerant. As a term of subjugation, Antiochus outlawed the practice of Judaism entirely. The king was a fanatical believer in all things Hellenic and was even so bold as to convert the great

Jewish Temple in Jerusalem into an exercise gymnasium (*Antiq* XII 5:4)!

Much of this information comes from the Books of the Maccabees in the Old Testament which Flavius Josephus also uses as a primary source. Some experts, however, suggest that the Old Testament is not completely accurate. Antiochus, it has been hypothesized, was actually intervening in a local war between two factions of Jews–one orthodox and one Hellenic. King Antiochus, being Greek, would have taken the side of the Hellenes. But whatever were the exact circumstances, the conquering Greek-Syrians turned the Temple courtyard into a pagan exercise arena and bath house. The traditional Jewish ways and rituals were outlawed.

For the Jews, to whom religion was life, this was a devastating development. The son of the Jewish priest Asamoneus, called Mattathias, organized a revolt against the powerful King Antiochus IV in 167 B.C. Mattathias died only a year later, but his five strong sons carried on the war. One of his sons was Judas Maccabeus.

That the Jewish rebels could defeat the mighty king of the Seleucid Empire is hard to think possible. At any other time Antiochus would have crushed the Jewish insurrectionists quickly, but, as luck would have it, the developing power of Parthia attacked Antiochus and his Seleucid Empire on its eastern flank at roughly the same time. The Seleucids were now forced to deal with a more formidable adversary on a second front. Thus hamstrung, after a few more years of frustration battling the guerrilla tactics of the Jewish nationalists, Antiochus abandoned the Jewish lands and retreated north. This was an astounding victory for the Jews and reestablished the independent Jewish nation.

The Asamoneans

One of Judas Maccabeus' first acts as the leader of the new nation was to send a delegation to Rome in hopes of making an alliance. This would serve to keep both Egypt and the Greek-

Syrians at bay. Rome agreed to it and so the "young" Jewish nation gained a measure of legitimacy in an otherwise hostile world (*Antiq* XII 10:6).

Rome, however, was over 1,500 miles away and occupied with battling the Carthaginians. So the Jewish nation still found itself involved in conflicts–albeit most of a minor nature–with Rome able to do little on their behalf. Despite this, the Jews were successful in defending their country and enjoyed an independent status for the next 100 years. The Jewish nation even became conquerors in their own right as they absorbed several smaller adjoining kingdoms.

Judas Maccabeus died in battle only a single year after the Roman alliance was established in 160 B.C. He was succeeded by his brother Jonathan Apphus, who led the Jewish nation until 143 B.C. During those early years, no formal king was recognized. Jonathan, however, did take the title of High Priest of the Temple in 152 B.C. which started a tradition of rule by priest-king. A third son of Mattathias, Simon Matthes, took the High Priest's position after Jonathan's death and ruled with religious authority until 135 B.C. Simon's son John Hyrcanus then became High Priest and ruled for another 31 years. This period by all accounts was a prosperous and expansive time for the nation. In fact, John Hyrcanus, or Hyrcanus I, is celebrated as being the ideal Jewish priest-king. Not only was he a just ruler and successful in battle but one whom God favored with prophetic dreams.

As the nation established itself over the decades the Maccabean rulers expanded its borders. The newly-subjugated people were expected to convert to Judaism. It was under Hyrcanus I that a kingdom to the south of Judea, Idumea, was conquered.

Hyrcanus took also Dora and Marissa, cities of Idumea and subdued all the Idumeans; and permitted them to stay in that country, if they would circumcise their genitals and make use of the laws of the Jews; and they were so desirous of living in the country of their forefathers, that they submitted to the use of circumcision and of the rest of the Jewish ways of living; at which time therefore this befell them, that they were hereafter no other than Jews. (*Antiq* XIII 9:1)

It was from Idumea, formerly a part of the Arab nation of Nabotea, that Herod the Great arose. It is important to note that Herod the Great's Jewish heritage went back just two or three generations–and that on his father's side only.

Hyrcanus I died in 105 B.C. and his son Aristobulos assumed control of the Jewish theocracy. Aristobulos then formally transformed the government into a monarchy, though he died after only a year in power as king. Aristobulos was succeeded by the second oldest son of Hyrcanus I, Alexander. King Alexander Jannaeus reigned for the next 27 years and assumed the harsh ways and absolute powers common and expected of kings in those ancient times. Alexander also had military success against the Egyptians, the Syrians and the Arabs, and so greatly extended the borders of the Jewish nation.

King Alexander was not popular among many in Jerusalem, however, especially the religious leaders of the Temple. Fully aware of this, when Alexander was dying in 76 B.C., he developed a strategy with his wife, Queen Salome Alexandra. After his death, she boldly carried out those plans. Alexandra approached the powerful Pharisees of the Sanhedrin. She promised the priests that if they supported her in power, as was Alexander's desire, that she would defer to their wishes on important matters. The Temple priests agreed, seeing value in keeping her as a figurehead. The arrangement worked successfully. Alexandra ruled well and wisely for nine years, dying in 67 B.C.

The Warring Brothers

Before her death, Alexandra appointed her eldest son, John Hyrcanus, to the High Priesthood. Under the agreement with the Temple priests that meant that Hyrcanus would succeed her as ruler when she died. Alexandra, however, also had another son, Aristobulos, who passionately coveted the crown.

Descendants of Asamoneus

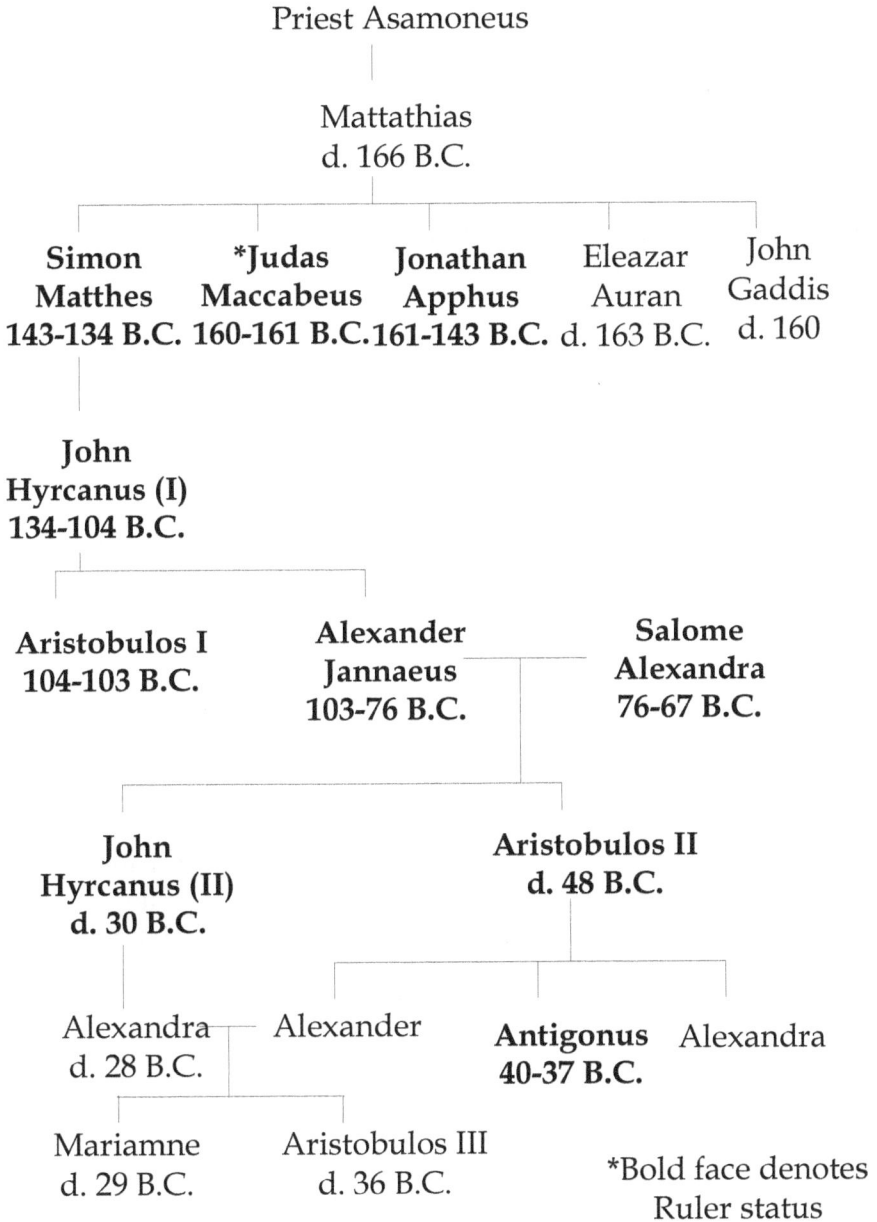

Priest Asamoneus

Mattathias
d. 166 B.C.

Simon Matthes 143-134 B.C.   ***Judas Maccabeus** 160-161 B.C.*   **Jonathan Apphus** 161-143 B.C.   Eleazar Auran d. 163 B.C.   John Gaddis d. 160

John Hyrcanus (I) 134-104 B.C.

Aristobulos I 104-103 B.C.   **Alexander Jannaeus** 103-76 B.C.   **Salome Alexandra** 76-67 B.C.

John Hyrcanus (II) d. 30 B.C.   **Aristobulos II** d. 48 B.C.

Alexandra d. 28 B.C.   Alexander   **Antigonus** 40-37 B.C.   Alexandra

Mariamne d. 29 B.C.   Aristobulos III d. 36 B.C.

*Bold face denotes
Ruler status

Aristobulos, an energetic man with a devious nature, had nothing but contempt for his older brother–the docile and slothful John Hyrcanus II. Even before Queen Alexandra had died, Aristobulos was making alliances with his father's old friends and assembling an army in the countryside. Aristobulos' ill-disguised intent was the eventual takeover of the entire Jewish nation.

After Alexandra's death in 67 B.C. there was, in fact, a fierce battle for the throne between the two brothers. The more popular older brother Hyrcanus eventually lost and was forced to name Aristobulos as king. Aristobulos allowed Hyrcanus to continue on as High Priest–the duties of which little interested Aristobulos anyway. In return, the defeated Hyrcanus promised to stay out of Aristobulos' way and live quietly in the Jerusalem Temple.

The chief military adviser to John Hyrcanus II was a man called Antipater, a general of wealth and ambition who was from a long line of Idumean kings. Antipater did not like the settlement Hyrcanus had made with Aristobulos. Antipater suspected–and not without justification–that Aristobulos planned to kill his popular brother Hyrcanus at the first opportunity. General Antipater eventually convinced the gentle-natured Hyrcanus of Aristobulos' true intention, and the two men escaped from Jerusalem and sought refuge in the neighboring Arabic Kingdom of Nabotea.

Antipater was on good terms with King Aretas III of Nabotea. Promising Aretas money and land concessions if he helped defeat Aristobulos, soon an invasion force of 50,000 men had been assembled in the Arab nation. In 66 B.C. Hyrcanus, Aretas III, and Antipater led this army into Judea and defeated Aristobulos decisively in their first open battle. Aristobulos was forced to retreat into his stronghold city of Jerusalem. The army of Aretas and Hyrcanus surrounded the walled city and lay siege to it.

While the preceding Asamonean history is largely taken from Josephus, Tacitus also gives a capsule summary of this century-long period of absolute rule by the Asamoneans. It is quoted for the sake of completeness. Tacitus wrote only decades after a war

Rome had with the rebel Jewish nation, so this might partially explain his negative view of the Asamonean rulers.

> In the Hellenistic period, King Antiochus made an effort to get rid of their primitive cult and Hellenize them, but his would-be reform of this degraded nation was foiled by the outbreak of war with Parthia, for this was the moment of Arsaces' insurrection. Then, since the Hellenistic rulers were weak and the Parthians had not yet developed into a great power (Rome, too, was still far away), the Jews established a dynasty of their own. These kings were expelled by the fickle mob, but regained control by force, setting up a reign of terror which embraced, among other typical acts of despotism, the banishment of fellow-citizens, the destruction of cities and the murder of brothers, wives and parents. The kings encouraged the superstitious Jewish religion, for they assumed the office of High Priest in order to buttress their regime. (Tacitus *Histories* V:8)

Enter Pompey

While the siege of Jerusalem was underway, the Roman General Gnaeus Pompey, co-dictator of the empire, and his legions were active to the north in Syria and Armenia. Pompey's long-term objective was to "settle the affairs" of the remnants of the old Seleucid Empire. In this he was spectacularly successful; Pompey and his disciplined legions conquered all that they challenged with Pompey becoming the wealthiest man in the empire in the process.

The brothers Hyrcanus and Aristobulos were well aware of the near-invincible power of Rome and the ambition of Pompey. They also knew that it was only a matter of time before the Roman general turned his avaricious eyes southward to the Jewish lands. Realizing that their future interests now lay with Rome, both Hyrcanus and Aristobulos suspended their war and traveled to Celesyria to meet with Pompey. There, talks were held and substantial brides offered by both men in an effort to gain Pompey's support.

Along with Gaius Marius and Lucius Sulla, Gnaeus Pompey was one of the first and most successful of the Roman military dictator-generals. In 70 B.C. Pompey controlled the Roman Empire in an uneasy alliance with Marcus Crassus who was a lesser general but then the richest man in Rome. For the next few years an ambitious Pompey moved his Roman legions to the eastern Mediterranean area seeking riches and conquests, which he found in great abundance.

While each of the Royal Asamonean brothers offered similar bribes to General Pompey, Pompey decided to support John Hyrcanus II. Perhaps Pompey was impressed with Hyrcanus' able and energetic military commander, Antipater–the father of the future Herod the Great.

Pompey and Hyrcanus

Now allied with the forces of Hyrcanus and Antipater, Pompey fought against King Aristobulos and joined the siege of Jerusalem in 63 B.C. Jerusalem was soon taken and King Aristobulos captured. The next year, in A.D. 62, Pompey brought the former King Aristobulos and his family to Rome in triumph and paraded them about as war trophies to the cheers of the Roman mob.

King Aristobulos would prove to be the last true independent Asamonean king. The conqueror was the Roman Empire in alliance with Aristobulos' brother, Hyrcanus. As a reward to Hyrcanus, Pompey kept the Asamonean in his position as High Priest of the Temple in Jerusalem. To administer the Jewish lands, Pompey appointed General Antipater, the Idumean. While the Asamoneans lost, the Idumean Antipater gained greatly.

In his eight years in the East from 70-62 B.C., Pompey had conquered many of the pieces of Alexander the Great's crumbled empire and had also forged an alliance with Parthia. Those eastern nations that had been formerly joined to Rome by alliance were now either provinces or client kingdoms, with Pompey establishing within them a regular system of tribute and taxation. Pompey's conquests in the East brought him another benefit–he became a richer man than his rival and co-ruler, Lucius Crassus.

Julius Caesar

When Pompey returned to Rome in 62 B.C. after his successful conquests, competition for absolute power flared up between him and the jealous Crassus. Mediating a truce between the two men was a young and opportunistic general named Julius Caesar who himself had no small stature as the nephew of Gaius Marius. Beginning as Senate consul in 59 B.C. Caesar became the weaker third member of the "First Triumvirate," ruling Rome along with Crassus and Pompey.

The young Julius Caesar was well mindful of the riches and power Pompey had gained through his conquests in the East and the already established wealth of Lucius Crassus. To remedy these deficiencies, Caesar turned his attention to the northern territories of Gaul, Germany, and the island of Britain seeking fortune and power. Successful military campaigns soon followed. Julius Caesar's efficient and disciplined legions were no match for the loose collection of tribes that were Caesar's usual battlefield opponents. Merciless in war, Caesar bragged in his memoirs that in a single military campaign his armies had killed over a million Gauls! But these northern territories, though vast, were of no real strategic value to Rome. Additionally, they had little economic use, except to provide a Rome with a steady supply of Teutonic slaves and soldiers to replenish the ranks of the Roman legions. Interestingly, in later years, the best of the Roman Imperial soldiers were mercenaries of Teutonic origin.

In 53 B.C., Lucius Crassus, jealous of the victories and glories won by his fellow Triumvirs Julius Caesar and Pompey, mounted his own military expedition to Parthia–this despite the fact that Parthia was ostensibly an ally of Rome. Crassus stopped en route to ransack the Temple in Jerusalem–something Pompey had never considered doing. Crassus then marched beyond the Euphrates River into Parthia with the intent of subjugation. There, two-thirds of his men were lost and Crassus himself killed in one of the great disasters of Roman history.

The First Civil War

With Crassus' destruction on foreign soil, General Julius Caesar sensed opportunity. He promptly moved against co-dictator General Pompey for complete control of the now-vast Roman Empire. This was the beginning of the first Roman Civil War.

The legions of Julius Caesar defeated those of Pompey in a series of battles and Pompey was driven to seek refuge in the East. But Pompey was treacherously killed on command of the 15-year-old Egyptian Pharaoh Ptolemy XIII–with whom he had sought sanctuary. Ptolemy XIII recognized Caesar's superior strength and thought he could retain control of Egypt by presenting Caesar with the head of Pompey, Caesar's greatest rival. At that time, Ptolemy himself was vying for control of Egypt against his older sister Queen Cleopatra.

From the relative safety of the Jewish East, Antipater and Hyrcanus observed the fall of Pompey with apprehension. Formerly solidly aligned with Pompey, now they had no patron. The two men had little choice but to throw themselves upon the mercy of Julius Caesar. Fortunately for them, Caesar was a practical man. He accepted their pledges of loyalty and in fact allowed Antipater and Hyrcanus to organize their own army in order to aid his designs upon Egypt.

As a testament to Antipater's political power and organizational skill, the 5,000-man mongrel army he eventually recruited was not only made up of Jews but also Arabs and even a number of hated Greek Syrians. The army performed admirably well in a key battle against the Egyptians. As a reward, in 47 B.C. Caesar made Antipater an official Roman citizen and released him from paying Roman taxes. Caesar also affirmed Antipater as the Roman governor of the Jewish lands. In turn, Antipater made his young son Herod the governor of Galilee. To reward Hyrcanus II, who also played a role in the battle, Caesar continued the appointment of the former Jewish king as High Priest of the Jerusalem Temple.

Antigonus and the Parthians

But Antipater and Hyrcanus were not without rivals. Antigonus was the son of Aristobulos, the brother of Hyrcanus II whom Pompey had captured in 63 B.C. Aristobulos and his family had been sent to Rome in chains and put on display, but the son, Antigonus, had managed to escape. He then returned to the East to lead the loyalist Jews against the Roman occupiers. Years later, after disposing of Pompey, Julius Caesar had planned to free the Jewish King Aristobulos and send him with two legions to settle Pompey's previous conquests in the East. But Aristobulos was poisoned in Rome by agents of Hyrcanus II. This made Antigonus hate the Romans even more, to the point of seeking the support of the Parthian Empire in getting rid of them.

During the aftermath of the assassination of Julius Caesar in 44 B.C., the Parthian Empire would, indeed, accept the offer of Antigonus, who had widespread support within Judea. Antigonus and his loyalists became a part of the Parthian force that drove Herod the Great out of much of the Jewish lands in 41 B.C. Antigonus thus became the last of the "true" Asamonean kings, though he was hardly independent.

King Antigonus ruled for only a few years. He and his allied forces were defeated by a rejuvenated Herod the Great and the Roman army in 37 B.C.

Chapter 7 Herod the Great

A man he was of great barbarity towards all men equally.
(*Antiq* XVII8:1)

Herod the Great ruled the Jewish East under Roman authority from 37-4 B.C. Amazingly, Herod maintained power through five Roman dictators, two Roman Civil Wars, and a successful invasion by the Parthian Empire (which was beaten back by Herod four years later). Though Herod the Great died almost 40 years before Jesus' crucifixion, his influence endured well beyond the times of Jesus and the destruction of the Second Temple.

The story of Herod is largely drawn from Books XIV-XVII of Josephus' *Antiquities*. Josephus based much of these writings on a now-lost 144-volume treatise on Jewish history by Nicolaus of Damascus. Nicolaus was a friend and confidant of Herod, however, so his impartiality must be questioned. Josephus was well aware of the potential biases in Nicolaus, and Josephus likely confirmed the stories from Nicolaus with other sources whenever possible.

But the principal scope that authors ought to aim at above all the rest, is to speak accurately and to speak truly, for the satisfaction of those that are otherwise unacquainted with such transactions and obliged to believe what these writers inform them of. (*Antiq* XIV 1:1)

Antipater the Politician

Herod the Great was born in 73 B.C. in Idumea, an Arab-dominated land to the south of Judea. He was the son of Antipater, a general and adviser to the Asamonean Priest-King John Hyrcanus II. General Antipater played a key role during the long, protracted Jewish civil war that pitted Hyrcanus against his brother Aristobulos. Both men were sons of the great King Alexander Jannaeus, who was himself the son of Hyrcanus I.

> But there was a certain friend of Hyrcanus, an Idumean, called Antipater, who was very rich and in his nature an active and a seditious man; who was at enmity with Aristobulus and had differences with him on account of his good-will to Hyrcanus. (*Antiq* XIV 1:3)

Antipater and Hyrcanus allied themselves with General Pompey of Rome. King Aristobulos was defeated after a lengthy siege of Jerusalem in 63 B.C. Pompey subsequently allowed Hyrcanus II to retain the position of High Priest in the now-subjugated Jewish kingdom. The real power Pompey gave to the shrewd Idumean General Antipater, Herod the Great's father. Impressing Pompey with his strength, Antipater became the *de facto* ruler of the Jewish lands by Roman authority.

> And both Antipater and Herod came to their greatness by reason of his (Hyrcanus') mildness; (*Antiq* XV 6:4)

In 49 B.C., Julius Caesar made a bid for complete control of the Roman Empire and started the First Civil War against the forces of Pompey. Caesar led his legions across the Rubicon and into the "demilitarized zone" of southern Italia. Pompey was eventually defeated and killed.

Without the protection of Pompey in the Jewish East, Antipater and Hyrcanus found themselves vulnerable. They had no choice but to pledge their support for the dictator Julius Caesar and hope that he accepted. In 47 B.C., Caesar, with some reservations, did, in fact, reaffirm Antipater and Hyrcanus in their positions.

Soon afterward, Caesar was planning an invasion of Egypt, a country that was aligned with Rome by an alliance that Caesar was more than willing to abrogate. To aid Caesar, Antipater and Hyrcanus II assembled a large army composed of soldiers from Syria, Arabia, and the Jewish lands. The army performed heroically in battle and was an essential element in a key victory for Caesar. The grateful dictator then granted Antipater full Roman citizenship, freedom from Roman taxes and the unquestioned governorship over all the Jewish lands. Hyrcanus, the former Asamonean King, also earned his reward and was affirmed in the position of Jerusalem High Priest. It was not long afterward that the now-Governor Antipater appointed his eldest son Phasaelus to administer Jerusalem and his 25-year-old son Herod to administer the territory of Galilee. Antipater himself ruled over the rest of the Jewish East (*Antiq* XIV 8).

The Idumeans

The High Priest John Hyrcanus II remained a strong supporter of Antipater and his sons, but many in the Jerusalem priesthood and the principal men of the Jerusalem Sanhedrin resented the rule of the Idumeans. Antipater's claim to being Jewish and his dedication to religious ritual were superficial at best. The country of Idumea had been conquered by the Maccabean King John Hyrcanus I just a few generations before. The Idumeans had been forced convert to Judaism and become circumcised under threat of banishment or slavery. The family of Antipater had accepted the terms of Judaism.

The Idumeans previously had worshiped a pagan god called Koze, and Idumea itself had been an integral part of the Arabic nation of Nabotea before revolting.

It is true that Nicolaus of Damascus says, that Antipater was of the stock of the principal Jews who came out of Babylon into Judea; but that assertion of his was to gratify Herod, who was his son..However, this Antipater was at first called Antipas and that was his father's name also; of whom they relate this: That king Alexander and his wife made him general of all Idumea and that he made a league of friendship with those

Arabians and Gazites and Ascalonites, that were of his own party, (*Antiq* XIV 1:3)

The wife of Antipater and the mother of Herod the Great was also not of Jewish blood. She was an Arabian woman named Cypros and a Nabotean princess. Since the ethnicity of the mother traditionally determines "Jewishness" of an individual, Herod found himself in a difficult position. When Herod gained power in the East, he became murderously jealous of those of the Royal Asamonean line. When Herod's power was confirmed as absolute by the Romans in 40 B.C., Herod wasted little time in marrying into the Jewish Royal family and having sons to secure his legitimacy. However, for all of his reign Herod maintained a paranoid suspicion of the Asamoneans, even if they were his fervent supporters and a part of his own family.

Governor of Galilee

The young Herod displayed great energy and innovation in his position as governor of Galilee. He personally routed out several bands of robbers that were afflicting the people—not only in Galilee but in parts of southern Syria as well. His father Antipater and and his older brother Phasaelus, seeing Herod's political success, also began to place a priority on subduing criminals, resulting in an increase in their own popularity.

This alarmed the Jerusalem Sanhedrin, who had hoped that the rogue Idumean family would only serve as temporary rulers. Seeing Herod as the greater threat, the Jewish deliberative body began to look for ways to get rid of him. Their chance soon came. In the course of capturing a band of Galilean robbers, Herod personally killed their Jewish ringleader, a man called Hezekiah. However bad Hezekiah might have been, it was unlawful for any Jew to kill another Jew–even a robber–without the prior approval of the Sanhedrin. The High Priest John Hyrcanus II was forced by the Pharisees to call Antipater's son to task. Herod was summoned from Galilee to Jerusalem to answer charges of murder. Herod, furious, showed up in Jerusalem for the trial, but with a large number of armed soldiers. He had them stand by threateningly in the council chamber as he answered the charges. The Sanhedrin, in fear for their lives, quickly dismissed the issue (*Antiq* XIV 9).

Hotheaded and a man to hold a grudge if there ever was one, Herod returned to Galilee and plotted revenge. He purchased the command of a Roman auxiliary force based out of Celesyria, a nearby country located in the southern part of Syria. Herod then marched his mercenary army through Judea with the intent of capturing Jerusalem and slaughtering all in the Sanhedrin who had challenged him. He was only stopped from doing so by the entreaties of his father and brother. However, years later, when Herod had attained absolute power, he found a reason to execute every single person of the 70-member Sanhedrin that had indicted him for murder, including John Hyrcanus II, the affable former king and his erstwhile ally.

Patricide to Gain a Kingdom?

Julius Caesar's assassination in 44 B.C. again turned the Roman world upside down. Gaius Cassius and other Republican conspirators gathered in the East and took control of the Roman legions headquartered there. These were the former legions of Pompey, and Cassius hoped to use them in the fight against the combined forces of Octavian and Marc Antony.

At that time, Herod was 29 years old and the governor of the Galilee. Ever the astute politician, Herod quickly ingratiated himself to this new set of Roman generals. Herod paid whatever tax they demanded and more besides, and provided them with all men and supplies they needed.

Cassius was impressed. He placed Herod in complete charge of the military force that had been assembled so far–including a fleet of ships and an army of horsemen and footmen. Cassius also promised Herod that the entire kingdom of Judea would be his if he and his Republican co-conspirators prevailed against Octavian and Antony (*Antiq* XIV 11).

Interlude: Patricide to Gain a Kingdom?

Interestingly, shortly after Cassius' promise to Herod, Herod's father Antipater was poisoned. Josephus suggests this was done by a servant at the instigation of an Asamonean loyalist, but the evidence supporting this was contentious and the murder was never solved.

Can it be speculated that Herod, smitten with the possibility of his own kingdom in the East, either planned or was at least complicit in the death of his own father Antipater? If Gnaeus Cassius and the conspirators had won the empire, Antipater would have a greater natural claim to rule–despite Cassius' promise to Herod. And even if Antipater was ready to retire and cede rights to the throne, it would rightfully go to his older brother Phasaelus, not to Herod. If Herod did commit patricide, this would go a long way in explaining his paranoid fear of being poisoned by his own sons decades later.

Octavian and Antony in Power

Cassius and the other conspirators did not prevail. They were defeated in late 43 B.C. by the forces of Octavian and Marc Antony. The two victors then divided up the Roman Empire along with Marcus Lepidus–an older and wealthier man who received a token amount of land in North Africa. Antony gained control of Greece and the eastern half of the empire and Octavian the western half. Italy and Rome were common to all three. The Second Triumvirate had been formed!

Co-Emperor Marc Antony then came to the East to settle its affairs. Soon Antony had taken up with the avaricious Queen Cleopatra of Egypt. Antony was so smitten with her that Cleopatra sat at Antony's side as he considered all the petitioners who sought to rule in the Jewish lands. Among these petitioners was Governor Herod of Galilee. Now with his father Antipater dead and Cassius and the conspirators defeated, Herod had to throw himself upon the mercy of Antony–and Cleopatra (*Antiq* XIV 13)!

In this open forum, many representatives from the Jewish nation decried the rule of the now-deceased Antipater and his still-living sons. Many of these Jews wanted the Asamoneans to regain control, favoring Antigonus, the son of former King Aristobulos. Queen Cleopatra also coveted the lands of the Jews and wanted them for Egypt, claiming them as a traditional possession of her country. In her favor, Cleopatra had been a strong supporter of Julius Caesar from the outset. In fact, she had bore Caesar a son.

But Herod had his own advantage. Marc Antony had gotten to know the late Antipater and his sons well 10 years ago when he served as a Roman staff officer in the East. Antony and Herod had fought in several military actions together. So Antony already liked and trusted Herod as a fellow warrior, and knew Herod was more than competent in military affairs. To further gain favor, Herod and his brother Phasaelus showered Antony with huge sums of money and promised him even more besides if they could remain in power. John Hyrcanus II, the former Asamonean King and the current High Priest of the Jerusalem Temple, was also there supporting Herod. Antony weighed all the pertinent factors and then made his decision. He appointed Herod and Phasaelus as rulers over the Jewish lands, with Hyrcanus remaining in the High Priest's position. This was much to the disappointment of Queen Cleopatra.

Herod Defeated

Antigonus, the late King Aristobulos' son, was stung by Marc Antony's rebuff of his Asamonean claim to power. He successfully sought out an ally in the Parthians. The Parthians had seen weakness in Rome during the Second Civil War and acted quickly. Through military actions, they had already gained back much of the Roman province of Syria. The Parthians had further ambitions in the Jewish lands, but they needed their own puppet Asamonean ruler to smooth out the road of conquest. Antigonus, the son of the poisoned King Aristobulos, pledged his support to them and a deal was struck.

For his loyalty, Antigonus wanted Herod put to death if Parthia was victorious. He also wanted Parthia to declare him   king over all of the Jewish lands, as well as appoint him the High Priest of the Temple in Jerusalem. In return, Antigonus promised to give the Parthian king a thousand talents of gold and to provide five hundred Jewish women of good family to the king and nobles (*Antiq* XIV 13:3).

In 41 B.C., the Parthians invaded Judea and quickly secured the country, capturing Phasaelus and Hyrcanus II by ruse. Herod was defeated, but he managed to escape capture and retreated into his secure southern provinces near the Nabotean border. Herod stationed a number of his troops in the mountain-top fortress of Masada near the shores of the Asphar (Asphaltitis) in southern Judea. There he also placed his betrothed Mariamne (I) and the other women of his entourage.

True to their word, the victorious Parthians set up Antigonus as king and High Priest of the Temple. Antigonus promptly ordered the ears of his uncle Hyrcanus II cut off, knowing that such a mutilation would preclude Hyrcanus from ever serving as High Priest again. Hyrcanus was then sent as a prisoner to Babylon to be out of the way. Phasaelus, in order to avoid a torturous death,   dashed his head against a rock and killed himself. As for the money and Jewish women promised to the Parthians, the Parthians ransacked the Temple for money, but Antigonus never supplied the women as he had promised.

Malchus was the king of Arabian Nabotea at that time, and he was one for whom Herod had done many favors in the past. Before his brother Phasaelus committed suicide in prison, Herod had planned to borrow 300 talents of gold from Malchus for Phasaelus' ransom. Herod had also planned to leave Phasaelus' seven-year-old son with King Malchus as a surety for repayment. But Malthus sent his messengers into Perea to tell Herod not to enter his country. The reason given was that the Parthians were threatening Malthus if he should harbor Herod as a fugitive. This, however, was a lie.

Rebuffed by Nabotea, without a kingdom, and with his family in hiding, Herod left Arabia accompanied by a small detachment of soldiers and traveled to Egypt. There, Herod stayed with

Queen Cleopatra in Alexandria for a time and then found a ship to take him to Rome.

In Rome, Herod told of his plight to a sympathetic Marc Antony. The Roman Senate was convened to consider options in the East. Certainly, Parthia posed a considerable threat to the Roman Empire and traitorous Antigonus had to be dealt with. After due consideration and many speeches, the Senate declared Herod the sole king of the Jewish lands and gave him authority over more land besides. Herod, surprised at the unexpected honor, left the Senate House to standing applause from the senators. Preceded by the Roman consuls and magistrates and walked, Herod walked out of the Senate house between Antony and Octavian. Outside, he was hailed by the awaiting Roman mob as a hero. The year was 40 B.C. (*Antiq* XIV 14).

Herod the Warrior-King

With the firm backing of Antony and Octavian, Herod had soon formed an army of mercenaries and Roman regulars and sailed across the Mediterranean to Celesyria. With barely a pause, Herod and his army began to make war on the Parthians and the Jewish Asamonean loyalists (*Antiq* XIV 15).

Herod and his Roman forces fought for four years, from 40 to 37 B.C., before the Jewish East was finally wrested from the Parthian-Asamonean alliance. The culmination of the campaign was the capitulation of Jerusalem and the subsequent capture of King Antigonus. At the same time, Marc Antony was in Syria and also battling the Parthians–pushing them back across the Euphrates River.

Herod sent the captured King Antigonus north to Marc Antony, where Antony ordered Antigonus beheaded. This was an extraordinary event for the times. It was thought that even a deposed king had at one time been favored by God and no mortal man had the right to end his life. But Antigonus had been a thorn in the side of Rome for too long and so Antony ignored this convention.

Now when Antony had received Antigonus as his captive, he determined to keep him against his triumph; but when he heard that the nation grew seditious and that, out of their hatred to Herod, they continued to bear good-will to Antigonus, he resolved to behead him at Antioch, for otherwise the Jews could no way be brought to be quiet. (*Antiq* XV 1:2)

Thus ended the government of the Asamoneans–the Maccabees!–126 years after it began. And with the death of Antigonus, the formal reign of Herod "the Great" began.

Earlier in that same year Herod had married Mariamne, a tall and elegant beauty of the Royal Asamonean line. She was the daughter of Alexandros and Alexandra and the niece of the soon-to-be-deposed King Antigonus. Her grandfather was John Hyrcanus II, now earless and still held captive in Babylon (*Antiq* XIV 16).

At the end of 37 B.C., the Parthians had been defeated and Antigonus executed. Herod had regained complete control of the Jewish lands and had a beautiful new wife besides. Herod quickly fathered two sons by the Royal Jewish Princess Mariamne I–now his queen.

Herod the Tyrant

With scant oversight from Roman co-dictator Antony and the armies of Parthia well beyond the Euphrates and in disarray, Herod could relax and enjoy life as a puppet monarch. With this idle time, Herod's true nature surfaced. He began to extract large sums of money from the Jewish wealthy under various pretenses. Most of this money Herod would send on to Antony in order to remain in his favor–Herod knew what the Roman co-ruler liked! The Jews chaffed under this harshness, but the overtly seditious were dealt with promptly and brutally. For devices of torture, Herod was partial to the rack and he used it liberally and for any reason. If torture failed to produce the desired results, execution usually followed.

Even though Herod had married into the Asamonean line and had Royal sons, most Jews did not fully accept his right to rule.

The people did not dare to overtly challenge Herod, but Herod could easily sense this hatred. In an attempt to gain their favor, Herod arranged with the Parthians to bring back Hyrcanus II, who was still held as a prisoner in Babylon. The king of Parthia had treated Hyrcanus well. The former king and High Priest was living in relative luxury in Babylon amongst the large Jewish community there, though he was still technically a captive (*Antiq* XV 2).

Despite the warnings of many Jews who suspected Herod's motives, the affable and guileless Hyrcanus did return. Herod gave Hyrcanus II a high position within his government, but since Hyrcanus had been mutilated by his nephew Antigonus, Hyrcanus could never again be High Priest. Herod, instead, appointed as High Priest another captive priest who had just been released from Babylon, an old friend named Ananelus.

This appointment infuriated both Herod's wife Mariamne and Mariamne's mother Alexandra. They wanted Aristobulos, Alexandra's son and Mariamne's brother, to get the honor. Eventually, Herod succumbed to the pressure from the two women and in 36 B.C. appointed the 17-year-old Aristobulos to the High Priest's position.

Aristobulos was young, tall, and good-looking. He quickly became very popular with the people. Sensing competition and a possible rival for the throne, Herod regretted his appointment. To remedy his error, Herod had the young High Priest drowned in the Royal pool at his palace in Jericho. Aristobulos had not yet served out a full year in the position.

Herod on Trial

Unfortunately for Herod, his mother-in-law Alexandra, the mother of the slain High Priest Aristobulos, was on good terms with Cleopatra. Alexandra was incensed over the murder of her son. She wrote to Queen Cleopatra and Cleopatra was very sympathetic. Cleopatra also saw an opportunity to finally get rid of Herod and gain control of his kingdom which in her mind rightfully belonged to Egypt anyway. Cleopatra pestered Marc

Antony about it to the point where Antony finally gave in and summoned Herod before him for trial. The charge: murder!

Herod feared the wrath of Cleopatra and knew he might well be executed by Antony if found guilty–which he certainly was. Before he left Jerusalem in late 36 B.C. to face Antony, Herod placed control of the kingdom in the hands of his uncle Joseph. Herod also told Joseph that if he were to be killed by Antony, that Joseph should have his wife Mariamne executed as well. This was a shocking order, but Herod gave this reason for it: if he was executed by Antony, Antony would surely summon his wife Mariamne, a great beauty, and have his way with her. Herod, having such a great passion for his wife, could not bear the thought of that happening. In Herod's mind, it was better that Mariamne suffer death than wind up abused by the co-emperor of Rome! Herod made Joseph swear an oath to secrecy over the order.

But when Herod was away defending himself before Antony, Joseph let slip Herod's order to Mariamne concerning her. A fiery and proud woman, she was understandably frightened and angry and immediately told her mother Alexandra.

> But the women, as was natural, did not take this to be an instance of Herod's strong affection for them, but of his severe usage of them, that they could not escape destruction, nor a tyrannical death, even when he was dead himself. And this saying [of Joseph] was a foundation for the women's severe suspicions about him afterwards. (*Antiq* XV 3:6)

The meeting between Herod and Antony went quite well despite the antagonistic pleadings of Cleopatra. Herod put on an able defense–and gave Antony many gifts besides. Satisfied, Antony reaffirmed his affection and trust for his old friend and ally, Herod. He then gently chided Cleopatra for the role she had played in this trial.

> for Antony said that it was not good to require an account of a king, as to the affairs of his government, for at this rate he could be no king at all, but that those who had given him that authority ought to permit him to make use of it. He also said the same things to Cleopatra, that it would

be best for her not busily to meddle with the acts of the king's government. (*Antiq* XV 3:8)

To placate his lover Cleopatra, Antony gave the Egyptian Queen the territory of Celesyria. Antony also included in the gift several Phoenician cities along the eastern Mediterranean coast.

After Herod returned home to Jerusalem, he placed his mother-in-law Alexandra, who had started all the trouble in the first place, under virtual house arrest. It wasn't long before Herod found out that his uncle Joseph had betrayed his confidence and told Mariamne about his conditional instructions for her death. Herod had Joseph executed for this betrayal, and Herod's relationship was never the same afterward with Mariamne.

Queen Cleopatra

Josephus paints a dark picture of the famous Egyptian Queen.

Now at this time the affairs of Syria were in confusion by Cleopatra's constant persuasions to Antony to make an attempt upon every body's dominions; for she persuaded him to take those dominions away from their several princes and bestow them upon her; and she had a mighty influence upon him, by reason of his being enslaved to her by his affections. She was also by nature very covetous and stuck at no wickedness. She had already poisoned her brother, because she knew that he was to be king of Egypt and this when he was but fifteen years old; and she got her sister Arsinoe to be slain, by the means of Antony, when she was a supplicant at Diana's temple at Ephesus; for if there were but any hopes of getting money, she would violate both temples and sepulchers. Nor was there any holy place that was esteemed the most inviolable, from which she would not fetch the ornaments it had in it; nor any place so profane, but was to suffer the most flagitious treatment possible from her, if it could but contribute somewhat to the covetous humor of this wicked creature: yet did not all this suffice so extravagant a woman, who was a slave to her lusts, but she still imagined that she wanted every thing she could think of and did her utmost to gain it; for which reason she hurried Antony on perpetually to deprive others of their dominions and give them to her. And as she went over Syria with him, she contrived to get it into her possession; so he slew Lysanias, the son of Ptolemy, accusing him of his bringing the

Parthians upon those countries. She also petitioned Antony to give her Judea and Arabia; and, in order thereto, desired him to take these countries away from their present governors. As for Antony, he was so entirely overcome by this woman, that one would not think her conversation only could do it, but that he was some way or other bewitched to do whatsoever she would have him; yet did the grossest parts of her injustice make him so ashamed, that he would not always hearken to her to do those flagrant enormities she would have persuaded him to. (*Antiq* XV 4:1)

While Herod was fighting the Parthians in the Jewish East during the years 40-37 B.C., Cleopatra accompanied Marc Antony as his legions also battled the Parthians to the north in Syria. When Antony was successful in battle and gained back a particular country or small kingdom, Cleopatra was right there to request it be given to her.

Realizing the avariciousness of Cleopatra and being a diplomat, Herod had given Cleopatra several small tracts of income-producing land in Judea, most notably in the fertile delta of the Jordan River close to Jericho. Later, she had visited Herod several times in Judea at his large palace in Jericho to inspect her land. Then, she apparently made it clear to Herod that she would welcome his amorous advances. Cleopatra's overtures to Herod occurred after she had escorted Antony to Armenia circa 34 B.C., where Antony was planning a military campaign.

But Herod felt that Cleopatra was only pretending to be in love with him, hoping to trap him in a compromising situation in order to extort more concessions from Antony–or perhaps to have Antony kill him. When it came to protecting his power and his life, Herod had no emotion. Herod even considered killing Cleopatra himself.

> However, he refused to comply with her proposals and called a counsel of his friends to consult with them whether he should not kill her, now he had her in his power; for that he should thereby deliver all those from a multitude of evils to whom she was already become irksome and was expected to be still so for the time to come; and that this very thing would be much for the advantage of Antony himself, since she would certainly not be faithful to him, in case any such season or necessity should come upon him as that he should stand in need of her fidelity.

But when he thought to follow this advice, his friends would not let him; and told him that, in the first place, it was not right to attempt so great a thing and run himself thereby into the utmost danger; and they laid hard at him and begged of him to undertake nothing rashly, for that Antony would never bear it, no, not though any one should evidently lay before his eyes that it was for his own advantage; and that the appearance of depriving him of her conversation, by this violent and treacherous method, would probably set his affections more on a flame than before. (*Antiq* XV 4:2)

In the end, Herod treated Cleopatra with kindness and gave her many presents, just as he always did with powerful people of influence.

Octavian Battles Antony

In 33 B.C., the rift between Octavian and Antony widened to the point of open conflict. Most experts consider this a continuation of the Second Roman Civil War that had begun with the assassination of Julius Caesar in 44 B.C.

Herod was in full support of his friend and benefactor Antony. He gathered together a large army and readied it for battle. But Antony told Herod that his help was not needed. Herod's exclusion was probably at the request of Queen Cleopatra. Likely Queen Cleopatra anticipated victory and did not want Herod to share the spoils. Antony instead suggested that Herod use his army to attack Nabotea and gain that kingdom for himself and Rome. Antony knew that Herod bore a grudge against Malchus of Arabia and would welcome his suggestion. The Arab king had turned Herod away years before when he had been fleeing from the Parthians and sought refuge in Nabotea.

Cleopatra would also benefit from a war between Herod and Malthus. If the battles were ruinous enough, she could pick up territories on both sides, perhaps gaining Judea as well as Arabia. Upon those instructions from Antony, Herod did go to war with the hated Malchus and the kingdom of Nabotea (*Antiq* XV 5).

During a major battle, it appeared that Herod's forces would prevail and gain decisive victory over the Naboteans. However, one of Cleopatra's own armies was stationed nearby on Egyptian land on the Jordan River delta. Cleopatra had given her generals secret orders to make sure Herod was unsuccessful against Nabotea. Seeing the Naboteans almost defeated, the Egyptian army intervened on behalf of the Arabs. The tide was turned against Herod and the Jews, resulting in a disastrous defeat for them.

Soon afterward, another calamity befell Herod's army. It was caught up in a massive earthquake and was devastated. After these two calamities, Herod thought it best to sue for peace with Malthus. However, the Arabian king showed no mercy to Herod's ambassadors and had them killed.

Despite these disasters and setbacks, in time Herod managed to gather together the remains of his forces and eventually defeated Malthus and the Naboteans. According to Josephus, Herod then became the king of Arabia by popular acclamation.

> so for the future they yielded and made him ruler of their nation; whereupon he was greatly elevated at so seasonable a success and returned home, taking great authority upon him, on account of so bold and glorious an expedition as he had made. (*Antiq* XV 5:5)

The Defeat of Antony

At about the same time of Herod's victory in Arabia, in late 31 B.C. the combined naval forces of Antony and Cleopatra were defeated by Octavian's navy in the waters off Actium in Greece. The puzzling retreat of Cleopatra's fleet, upon her personal order, was considered the turning point in the loss. Marc Antony had survived the debacle and was now hiding out in Alexandria along with Queen Cleopatra and the remnants of his armies. With his benefactor Antony out of power, once again Herod feared for his kingdom (*Antiq* XV 6:1). Herod had little choice but to humbly petition Octavian to retain his throne.

Octavian, instead of sailing straight to Alexandria in pursuit of Antony and Cleopatra, wisely decided to take his time before making the final stroke against them. Octavian marched with his armies through the lands of the eastern empire making sure that

Antony had no more allies. Herod was the most formidable of them, as he now controlled Arabia as well as the Jewish lands.

Herod prepared for the worst. The only Royal Asamonean alive who had any claim to power was his old friend and ally, Hyrcanus II, who was the grandfather of his wife, Mariamne. To give Octavian fewer options, Herod ruthlessly had Hyrcanus executed.

> As for Herod himself he saw that there was no one of royal dignity left but Hyrcanus and therefore he thought it would be for his advantage not to suffer him to be an obstacle in his way any longer; (*Antiq* XV 6:1)

Herod also again sequestered much of his family, a number of troops and his treasury at his southern fortress Masada and stocked it with enough provisions to withstand a lengthy siege. Herod had done this 10 years before when he had been defeated by the Parthians. Herod would not give up his kingdom without a fight! Herod placed his wife, Mariamne and his mother-in-law Alexandra, both potential troublemakers, under house arrest in another of his fortresses at Alexandrium, north of Jerusalem. Then, in the spring of 30 B.C., Herod traveled to Rhodes to meet with Octavian who as sole ruler of the Roman Empire held his fate in his hands.

Facilitated by paying 800 talents of gold to Octavian, Herod impressed the young Octavian with his candor. Speaking without a diadem on his head, Herod boldly stated that he should have done more to aid Antony, as Antony was his friend and benefactor and that was what friends and allies do. Herod humbly offered to transfer his allegiance wholly and completely to Octavian as ruler of the empire. Herod then went on to blame Antony's downfall on Cleopatra.

> I have not deserted him upon his defeat at Actium; nor upon the evident change of his fortune have I transferred my hopes from him to another, but have preserved myself, though not as a valuable fellow soldier, yet certainly as a faithful counselor, to Antony, when I demonstrated to him that the only way that he had to save himself and not to lose all his authority, was to slay Cleopatra; for when she was once dead, there would be room for him to retain his authority and rather to bring thee to

make a composition with him, than to continue at enmity any longer. (*Antiq* XV 6:6)

Octavian probably had a similar opinion about Cleopatra. Certainly Marcus Agrippa, Octavian's adviser and lead general, did. Octavian also knew that the East was a troublesome part of the empire. A replacement of Herod's caliber would be hard to find. Octavian had trusted Herod before the split with Antony and decided to trust him again. This was made easier by the fact that none of Herod's armies had actually engaged any of Octavian's forces.

So in Rhodes, Octavian affirmed Herod as king and gave him even more eastern territory to rule over besides. Later, Octavian would give Herod most of Cleopatra's holdings in Judea and surrounding areas as well. So it was a jubilant Herod who, along with his army, escorted Octavian and his forces from Rhodes on a land route through the eastern Mediterranean coastline and into Egypt.

Deaths of Antony and Cleopatra

Only a few months later, in the fall of A.D. 30, Cleopatra died in Alexandria, as did Antony. The accepted story is that Cleopatra committed suicide instead of allowing herself to be captured. However, at the time of her alleged suicide, Octavian and his men were in Alexandria camped only a few hundred yards away. Octavian knew that Cleopatra was potential trouble, as her amorous relationships with both Julius Caesar and Marc Antony attested. If Cleopatra was captured, as a queen of Royal blood, execution by Roman order was out of the question.

Octavian's master strategist and general, Marcus Agrippa, might have played a secret role. Cleopatra was in her thirties and Octavian only a few years younger. Agrippa might have wanted to eliminate temptation for the now-most powerful man in the empire.

Marc Antony had committed suicide only days earlier in Alexandria by falling on his sword, apparently believing that

Cleopatra had already died. Did Octavian, remembering Herod's words against Cleopatra, arrange to surreptitiously kill the woman after Antony's death and make it look like suicide? Or did Octavian execute both Antony and Cleopatra, making the killings look like suicide to preserve what was left of the shattered honor of Rome? Or was it Agrippa who masterminded both deaths on his own in order to protect the young Octavian?

Whatever the real story behind the deaths of the famous couple, once again, Herod survived another leadership change in Rome and with even more power than he had before.

The Execution of Mariamne I

Now secure again in his kingdom with the full support of Rome and Octavian–soon to be known as the "divine Augustus"–Herod returned to administering his lands. Mariamne and her mother Alexandra were not happy to see Herod return triumphant.

This was taken advantage of by Herod's mother Cypros and sister Salome, both of whom were not of Asamonean Royal blood. Mariamne and her mother Alexandra were targeted by them. Herod loved Mariamne with a passion, but Mariamne grew cold to him, even contemptuous. Herod's murders of members of her family became to much for her to ignore, and she remembered when Herod ordered her own execution, albeit under "special" circumstances.

At one point, when Mariamne expressed venomous anger to Herod over this, Herod decided to act. He brought Mariamne to trial over one of her love potions for him which he suspected might actually have been a poison. The "jurors" in the trial knew what was best for them and Mariamne was found guilty and sentenced to death. She was quickly executed in 29 B.C.

And thus died Mariamne, a woman of an excellent character, both for chastity and greatness of soul; but she wanted moderation and had too much of contention in her nature; yet had she all that can be said in the beauty of her body and her majestic appearance in conversation; and thence arose the greatest part of the occasions why she did not prove so agreeable to the king, nor live so pleasantly with him, as she might otherwise have done; for while she was most indulgently used by the king, out of his fondness for her and did not expect that he could do any hard thing to her, she took too unbounded a liberty. Moreover, that which most afflicted her was, what he had done to her relations and she ventured to speak of all they had suffered by him and at last greatly provoked both the king's mother and sister, till they became enemies to her; and even he himself also did the same, on whom alone she depended for her expectations of escaping the last of punishments. (*Antiq* XV 7:6)

Herod immediately regretted her death. The howls of his laments for Mariamne echoed through the halls of his great palace for some time afterward and Herod was constantly haunted by her visage. While always paranoid and vengeful at heart, Herod now became even more so. At about the same time, a devastating plague swept through Judea. The Jews believed it was God's revenge on Herod for having killed his Royal wife.

Despite his personal problems, the following years were boon ones for Herod. Agrippa had been appointed by Octavian to serve a 10-year term as president of Asia. Herod spent much time with him.

(Caesar) also made (Herod) one of the procurators of Syria and commanded that they should do every thing with his approbation; and, in short, he arrived at that pitch of felicity, that whereas there were but two men that governed the vast Roman empire, first Caesar and then Agrippa, who was his principal favorite, Caesar preferred no one to Herod besides Agrippa and Agrippa made no one his greater friend than Herod besides Caesar. (*Antiq* XV 10:3)

Herod's Building Projects

Herod was a man of great and restless energy. With his kingdom peaceful and secure after Octavian's affirmation of him in 30 B.C., Herod embarked on several ambitious building programs. After first constructing a palace for himself and the beautiful Mariamne II in Jerusalem and rebuilding the tower of Antonia of the great Temple, he built sumptuous fortress-cities in Sebaste, Alexandria, Herodium and other places. On craggy mountains that overlooked Lake Asphaltitis, the old Jewish southern fortresses of Masada and Macherus were made battle-ready and filled with supplies. Herod also rebuilt the Roman seaport city of Caesarea on the east coast of the Mediterranean. In the course of it, Herod constructed a harbor that was a marvel of the ancient world and its sunken remains still amaze experts.

> (Herod)..laid out such a compass towards the land as might be sufficient for a haven, wherein the great ships might lie in safety; and this he effected by letting down vast stones of above fifty feet in length, not less than eighteen in breadth and nine in depth, into twenty fathom deep; and as some were lesser, so were others bigger than those dimensions. This mole which he built by the sea-side was two hundred feet wide, the half of which was opposed to the current of the waves, so as to keep off those waves which were to break upon them, (*Antiq* XV 9:6)

Herod the Great did not limit his largess to his own country. He built impressive structures throughout the East.

> ..but what was the greatest and most illustrious of all his works, he erected Apollo's temple at Rhodes, at his own expenses and gave them a great number of talents of silver for the repair of their fleet. He also built the greatest part of the public edifices for the inhabitants of Nicopolis, at Actium; and for the Antiochinus, the inhabitants of the principal city of Syria, where a broad street cuts through the place lengthways, he built cloisters along it on both sides and laid the open road with polished stone and was of very great advantage to the inhabitants. (*Antiq* XVI 5:3)

Herod's renovation of great Temple at Jerusalem was also impressive and some experts consider it a wonder of the ancient world.

In financing these projects, Herod drove the country he ruled to near-bankruptcy. And in the end, for all his efforts he never received the adulation from his subjects that he sought. In fact, the Jewish people hated Herod as much for his wasting the wealth of their nation in constructions as much as for his murderous ways.

Caesarea, formerly Strato's Tower, was finished around 10 B.C. after ten years of work. For the occasion, Herod sponsored a traditional Greek festival with music, plays and athletic contests. He also held horse and chariot races at the newly-built circus that lay close to the seashore. Dedicating the games to Caesar Augustus, Herod commanded that they be held every five years. These games have been revived in modern times. Curiously, today they are called the Maccabean Games which is ironic given the fact that Herod the Great executed so many of the Royal Asamoneans (*Antiq* XV 9:6).

Herod generosity in foreign countries was in stark contrast to his cruelty toward his subjects.

Now some there are who stand amazed at the diversity of Herod's nature and purposes; for when we have respect to his magnificence and the benefits which he bestowed on all mankind, there is no possibility for even those that had the least respect for him to deny, or not openly to confess, that he had a nature vastly beneficent; but when any one looks upon the punishments he inflicted and the injuries he did, not only to his subjects, but to his nearest relations and takes notice of his severe and unrelenting disposition there, he will be forced to allow that he was brutish and a stranger to all humanity; insomuch that these men suppose his nature to be different and sometimes at contradiction with itself; but I am myself of another opinion and imagine that the occasion of both these sort of actions was one and the same; for being a man ambitious of honor and quite overcome by that passion, he was induced to be magnificent, wherever there appeared any hopes of a future memorial, or of reputation at present; and as his expenses were beyond his abilities, he was necessitated to be harsh to his subjects; for the persons on whom he expended his money were so many, that they made him a very bad procurer of it; and because he was conscious that he was hated by those under him, for the injuries he did them, he thought it not an easy thing to amend his offenses, for that it was inconvenient for his revenue; he therefore strove on the other side to make their ill-will an occasion of his gains. As to his own court, therefore, if any one was not very obsequious to him in his language and would not confess himself to be his slave, or but seemed to think of any innovation in his government, he was not able to contain himself, but prosecuted his very kindred and friends and punished them as if they were enemies and this wickedness he undertook out of a desire that he might be himself alone honored. Now for this, my assertion about that passion of his, we have the greatest evidence, by what he did to honor Caesar and Agrippa and his other friends; for with what honors he paid his respects to them who were his superiors, the same did he desire to be paid to himself; and what he thought the most excellent present he could make another, he discovered an inclination to have the like presented to himself. But now the Jewish nation is by their law a stranger to all such things and accustomed to prefer righteousness to glory; for which reason that nation was not agreeable to him, because it was out of their power to flatter the king's ambition with statues or temples, or any other such performances; And this seems to me to have been at once the occasion of Herod's crimes as to his own courtiers and counselors and of his benefactions as to foreigners and those that had no relation to him. (*Antiq* XVI 5:4)

Herod constantly needed money to fund his various projects and would scheme to get funding by any means possible. Herod taxed whatever and whoever he could as a matter of course. Another of Herod's methods was to simply murder prominent people–executing them on false charges and then seizing their estates. Herod's low point in this respect was the midnight robbery of the tomb of King David and King Solomon in Jerusalem (*Antiq* XVI 7:1), something that Hyrcanus I had partially accomplished a century before. Josephus suggests that Herod's complete loss of sanity, culminating with the execution of his Royal sons in 7 B.C., began with this desecration of the ancient Royal tombs. King Herod was cursed by the ghost of King David!

Herod's Roman Ways

As the years passed, Herod began increasingly to adopt Greek and Roman customs. The religious Jews whom he ruled were concerned and distressed. In emulation of the Romans, Herod sponsored gladiator games and grisly spectacles where the condemned were eaten alive by wild beasts, or the beasts themselves would fight to the death. Herod also instituted the Maccabean Games which were patterned along the lines of the Greek Olympic Games which Herod also financially sponsored. Herod the Great built a large theater near Jerusalem for the exhibition of plays, even though plays–like athletic contests–were antithetical to Judaic law.

In defending himself against his Jewish critics, Herod falsely claimed that these events were ordered by Augustus. Josephus describes an unsuccessful attempt to assassinate Herod by zealot Jews when he attended a theater competition. The conspirators wanted to preserve Jewish traditions and thought that the only way to do so would be through Herod's own death (*Antiq* XV 8).

The Children of Herod

The children of Herod to the third generation were of great consequence in the Jewish lands. Through to the destruction of the Second Temple in A.D. 70 and beyond, they occupied places of honor in the Roman hierarchy and ruled the Jewish East at various times.

Herod had five children by Mariamne I, two of whom he executed.

> Now of the five children which Herod had by Mariamne, two of them were daughters and three were sons; and the youngest of these sons was educated at Rome and there died; but the two eldest he treated as those of royal blood, on account of the nobility of their mother and because they were not born till he was king. (*Wars* I 22:2)

During the years shortly after Mariamne's execution, Herod the Great married several other wives and had royal issue from three of them.

> Now the king had nine wives and children by seven of them; Antipater was himself born of Doris and Herod Philip of Mariamne, the high priest's daughter; Antipas also and Archelaus were by Malthace, the Samaritan, as was his daughter Olympias which his brother Joseph's son had married. By Cleopatra of Jerusalem he had Herod and Philip; and by Pallas, Phasaelus; he had also two daughters, Roxana and Salome, the one by Phedra and the other by Elpis; he had also two wives that had no children, the one his first cousin and the other his niece; and besides these he had two daughters, the sisters of Alexander and Aristobulus, by Mariamne. (*Wars* I 28:4)

Of particular later importance is that Malthace, a Samaritan, was the mother of Archelaus an Antipas, while Cleopatra of Jerusalem was the mother of son named Herod Philip. All three sons would share in Herod's kingdom upon his death.

In a later generation, grandchildren of Herod the Great and Mariamne I through their Royal son Aristobulos would become rulers–most notably Agrippa I.

Famine

During the years 24-23 B.C., a tremendous famine gripped Judea and the Jewish lands. Early in the famine in 24 B.C., Herod accepted the invitation of Emperor Augustus and sent his two Royal sons, Alexander and Aristobulos, to Rome for study. Their ages were perhaps 11 and 10, respectively. Herod may have feared for their safety as the famine grew more intense and the Jews more seditious against him.

To partially fight the effects of the drought, Herod gathered together much of his Royal furniture, most made of gold and transported it to Egypt, where it was given to the Roman Prefect Petronius in exchange for corn. The corn was given to the Jewish people to alleviate the burden of the drought and so Herod was partially redeemed in the eyes of the people (*Antiq* XV 9).

Mariamne II

During the same time, Herod removed the High Priest Jesus from his position and appointed a man named Simon in his place. This was a remarkable act, for the Temple High Priest usually held the position for life or until resignation. But Herod had an ulterior purpose. Simon had a beautiful daughter called Mariamne (Mariamne II) and Herod wanted to marry her. But Mariamne was not of the proper station to be a Royal wife. However, after Herod had elevated her father Simon to the High Priest's position, she was. Mariamne II had a son named Herod Philip by Herod the Great. To avoid confusion, he is referred to as Herod Philip of Rome. This Herod Philip was to become the first husband of Herodias, who would bring about the death of John the Baptist.

Herod the Great- First Generation

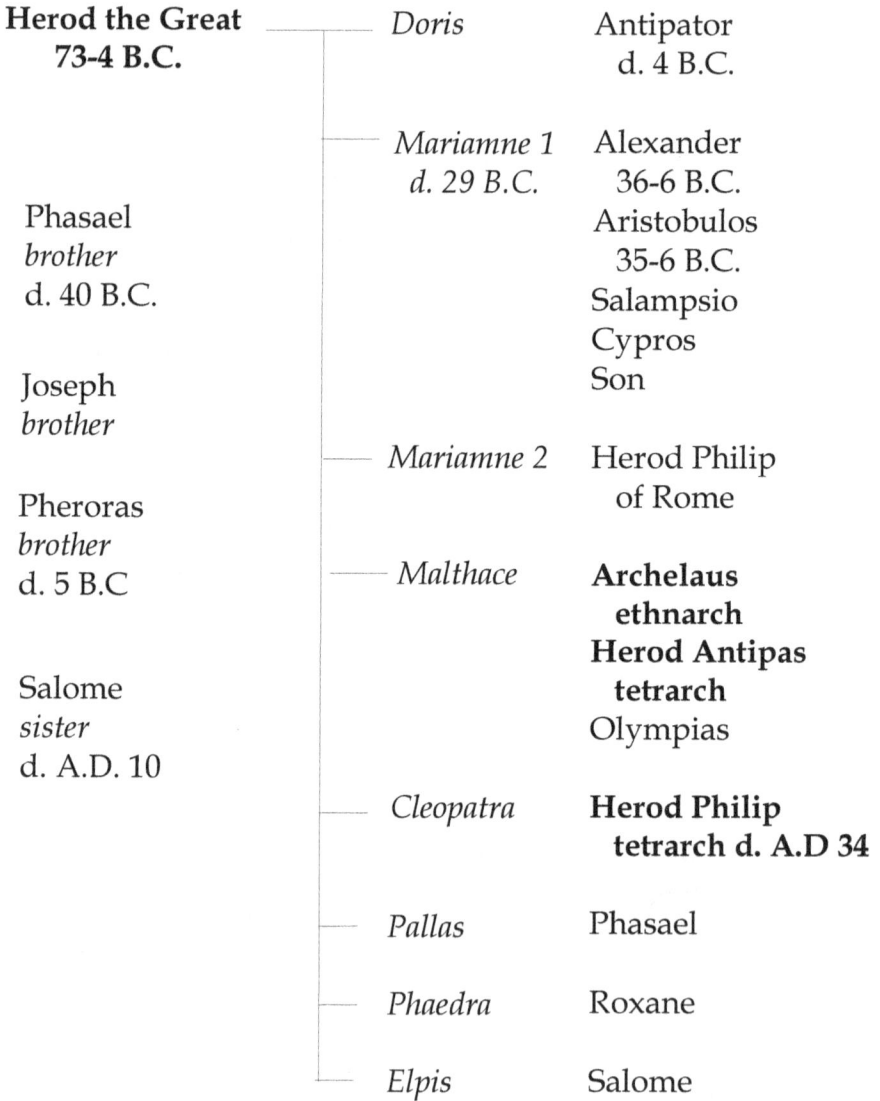

| **Herod the Great** | *Doris* | Antipator |
| **73-4 B.C.** | | d. 4 B.C. |

	Mariamne 1	Alexander
	d. 29 B.C.	36-6 B.C.
Phasael		Aristobulos
brother		35-6 B.C.
d. 40 B.C.		Salampsio
		Cypros
Joseph		Son
brother		
	Mariamne 2	Herod Philip
Pheroras		of Rome
brother		
d. 5 B.C	*Malthace*	**Archelaus**
		ethnarch
		Herod Antipas
Salome		**tetrarch**
sister		Olympias
d. A.D. 10		
	Cleopatra	**Herod Philip**
		tetrarch d. A.D 34
	Pallas	Phasael
	Phaedra	Roxane
	Elpis	Salome

Royal Executions

In 18 B.C. Emperor Augustus released Herod's Royal sons Alexander and Aristobulos from Rome after six years of education and training. Since they were of age, Augustus adjudged them fit to rule and returned them to Judea to the care of their father. In Judea, the people rallied around these two young men excitedly because they were of the Royal Asamonean blood line. Aristobulos and Alexander had both grown up to be tall, strong, and handsome men.

However, Herod's sister Salome and brother Phasaelus, both of common birth, together started a sustained campaign against the Royal sons by spreading rumors of their sedition against Herod. Herod, who was naturally inclined to paranoia anyway, over the years began to believe that his sons were indeed plotting against him.

Seeking to put the young men in their places, Herod brought into the Royal "fold" his oldest son Antipater. Herod had married Antipater's mother Doris before he was declared a king. Thus, she and her son Antipater had no Royal standing. When Herod assumed a Royal position and married Mariamne I, Doris and Antipater were benevolently banished as a matter of course.

Herod held his non-Royal son Antipater out over his Royal sons Alexander and Aristobulos. Antipater, for his part, was pleased and surprised at this turn of events. He might yet gain a kingdom! Now a member of Herod's Royal court, Antipater and his mother Doris soon joined Herod's sister Salome and brother Phasaelus in plotting against Herod's Royal sons.

Alexander and Aristobulos were alarmed and dismayed at their father's suspicions and tried to defend themselves, but with little success. Herod's paranoia over the years increased to the point where he brought his two sons before Augustus in Rome and had the emperor sit in judgment as Herod accused them of sedition (*Antiq* XVI 4:1). Augustus resolved the matter with insight and wisdom. Herod accepted, at least temporarily, that his sons bore him no ill will. Caesar Augustus then reaffirmed to Herod that he could name his own heir. Herod took that opportunity to publicly announced that Antipater would succeed him first with Alexander and Aristobulos next in line. So all left Rome happy in this resolution. But Emperor Augustus suspected that nothing good could come from Herod's paranoia. He was later to famously remark that he would rather be Herod's pig than Herod's son.

Despite the harmonious end to this trial, Herod's sister and brother were not to be denied. Antipater was first in line of succession, yes, but they feared that if the Royal sons were still living at the time of Herod's death, it would be the worse for him!

Herod finally succumbed plotting by his "common" family. In 7 B.C., he had both Aristobulos and Antipater executed, along with 300 of his Royal sons' closest friends and supporters.

> As for Herod, if he had before any doubt about the slaughter of his sons, there was now no longer any room left in his soul for it; but he had banished away whatsoever might afford him the least suggestion of reasoning better about this matter, so he already made haste to bring his purpose to a conclusion. He also brought out three hundred of the officers that were under an accusation, as also Tero and his son and the barber that accused them before an assembly and brought an accusation against them all; whom the multitude stoned with whatsoever came to hand and thereby slew them. Alexander also and Aristobulus were brought to Sebaste, by their father's command and there strangled; but their dead bodies were in the night time carried to Alexandraum, where their uncle by the mother's side and the greatest part of their ancestors, had been deposited. (*Antiq* XVI 11:7)

> .. it..was the action of a murderous mind and such as was not easily moved from that which is evil. (*Antiq* XVI 11:8)

Final Years

Herod's last years after the executions were tumultuous–and a dark period for the Jewish East. Over the next three years, Herod changed his will and testament four times. Initially, his Royal sons by Mariamne I, Aristobulos and Alexander, were to be second in line of succession after his eldest son Antipater. After the execution of his Royal sons, Herod chose to still favor Antipater as first heir, but he placed Herod Philip, his son by the high priest's daughter, Mariamne II, second in line.

In time, however, Herod discovered a supposed plot to poison him created by his eldest son Antipater, who apparently could not wait for Herod to die naturally. Through the torture of a suspected conspirator, the mother of Herod Philip of Rome was also implicated–albeit peripherally. Both Antipater and Herod Philip of Rome were removed from his will. Herod then left his entire kingdom to Herod Antipas, the youngest son of his Samaritan wife Malthace. This might have been at the suggestion of Herod's sister Salome and Phasaelus, Herod's brother. At that time, Antipas was perhaps 22 years of age. Did Antipas truly have the stuff of kings, or did Salome and Phasaelus feel that Antipas would be the easiest of Herod's sons to manipulate?!

Antipater, after a trial in front of the president of Syria Quintilius Varus in 5 B.C., was placed in chains. Herod apparently did not have the heart to execute Antipater as he did his two Royal sons only two years earlier. But Antipater did not have long to live. While in prison, Antipater received a false report that Herod had died and he rejoiced at the news. But unfortunately for Antipater, Herod had just lapsed into a temporary coma–one of many in his final months. Recovered, Herod learned of Antipater's premature jubilation and had him executed. This occurred just days before Herod's actual death.

Herod the Great had two other sons of quality, apart from Herod Antipas, who had also been educated in the court of Rome: Archelaus, also Malthace's son, and Herod Philip, the son of Cleopatra of Jerusalem. The devious Antipater had previously turned Herod against these two sons and they were never seriously considered for succession.

In his final will, however, made after executing his eldest son Antipater, Herod divided his kingdom between Herod Antipas, Archelaus and Herod Philip. Herod's sister Salome also received a small measure of land for her unwavering loyalty to him. Herod wrote this last will only four days before his death, so there was reason to question whether Herod at that time possessed a rational state of mind.

Herod's Death

In his last months, Herod was possessed of a lingering disease that would kill him in hideous fashion.

> But now Herod's distemper greatly increased upon him after a severe manner and this by God's judgment upon him for his sins; for a fire glowed in him slowly which did not so much appear to the touch outwardly, as it augmented his pains inwardly; for it brought upon him a vehement appetite to eating which he could not avoid to supply with one sort of food or other. His entrails were also ex-ulcerated and the chief violence of his pain lay on his colon; an aqueous and transparent liquor also had settled itself about his feet and a like matter afflicted him at the bottom of his belly. Nay, further, his privy-member was putrefied and produced worms; and when he sat upright, he had a difficulty of breathing which was very loathsome, on account of the stench of his breath and the quickness of its returns; he had also convulsions in all parts of his body which increased his strength to an insufferable degree. It was said by those who pretended to divine and who were endued with wisdom to foretell such things, that God inflicted this punishment on the king on account of his great impiety; yet was he still in hopes of recovering, though his afflictions seemed greater than any one could bear. (*Antiq* XVII 6:5)

It can be concluded from these symptoms that a large contributor to his death was liver failure, or cirrhosis. Perhaps a lifetime of drinking had taken its toll.

> an aqueous and transparent liquor also had settled itself about his feet and a like matter afflicted him at the bottom of his belly...And when the physicians once thought fit to have him bathed in a vessel full of oil, it was supposed that he was just dying; but upon the lamentable cries of his domestics, he revived (*Antiq* XVII 6:5)

That Herod recovered somewhat when immersed in oil is also consistent with end-stage cirrhosis.

Herod knew that the end was near. For his last atrocity, Herod ordered that all the principal Jews be gathered together and held in the hippodrome in Jerusalem. No one dared defy Herod the Great, not even on his deathbed. These wealthy and important Jews probably thought that Herod was going to make a deathbed pronouncement of some importance.

But when all were assembled in the hippodrome, Herod the Great gave a secret order that they were to be slain at the time of his own death (*Antiq* XVII 6:5). Also, Herod ordered that one member from every family in the Jewish nation be slain. The purpose? That everyone in the Jewish nation should shed real tears on the day of his funeral. If the citizens did not weep for him, they would certainly weep for their own loved ones! Salome, Herod's sister, a woman not known for her compassion, rescinded those orders upon Herod's death.

Herod's Funeral Procession

Herod the Great died in the fall of 4 B.C. His son Archelaus assumed power and directed the funeral of his father. A procession was made from Jericho to Herodium, where a tomb had been prepared. Herodium was built out of a small mountain five miles south of Jerusalem.

> The body was carried upon a golden bier, embroidered with very precious stones of great variety and it was covered over with purple, as well as the body itself; he had a diadem upon his head and above it a crown of gold: he also had a scepter in his right hand. About the bier were his sons and his numerous relations; next to these was the soldiery, distinguished according to their several countries and denominations; and they were put into the following order: First of all went his guards, then the band of Thracians and after them the Germans; and next the band of Galatians, every one in their habiliments of war; and behind these marched the whole army in the same manner as they used to go out to war and as they used to be put in array by their muster-masters and centurions; these were followed by five hundred of his domestics carrying spices. So they went eight furlongs to Herodium; for there by his own command he was to be buried. And thus did Herod end his life. (*Antiq* XVII 8:3)

Assuming that Herod died in Jericho, Josephus probably meant to say that the procession traveled eight furlongs per day which meant that it took a little under a month for Herod's body to reach Herodium. Recently, excavations at Herodium revealed evidence of a large tomb that was likely Herod's. Little of value was found and it is suggested that the tomb was broken into and desecrated very soon after Herod's final interment. Indeed, in 3 B.C., as Herod's will was being adjudicated in Rome, a major insurrection erupted in the Jewish East. Tens of thousands of Jews turned to violence as they rebelled against any further rule by the Herod family–or Rome. It took a full year before General Quintilius Varus quelled the uprising. Thousands were slain and Varus was forced to crucify over 1,000 Jewish captives.

Will and Testament

Herod's final testament was contested by his son, Herod Antipas, who wanted the entire kingdom for himself. Herod's second-to-last will did just that and Antipas wanted it to take precedence. But after a lengthy period of Roman-style probate, Herod's last will was affirmed by Emperor Augustus. A major consideration for Augustus was to have the kingdom divided up in such a way that provided the most support for the many descendants of Herod the Great.

Thus, the sons of Herod and the sons of the sons of Herod carried on the rule of the Jewish nation under Roman proxy, even unto the times of Jesus. But the family line of Herod the Great itself almost died out completely within a century of his death (*Antiq* XVIII 5:3). Josephus blames it upon a curse from God for their evil ways, but more likely it was due to the consequences of genetic inbreeding.

Josephus sums up the life of Herod the Great in a famous passage:

> A man he was of great barbarity towards all men equally and a slave to his passion; but above the consideration of what was right; yet was he favored by fortune as much as any man ever was, for from a private man he became a king; and though he were encompassed with ten thousand dangers, he got clear of them all and continued his life till a very old age. (*Antiq* XVII 8:1)

Chapter 8   The High Priests

..we have the names of our high priests from father to son set down in our records for the interval of two thousand years; (*Apion* 7)

The Jewish High Priest represented the perfect man–created by God in his own image — whole and without deformity. As a perfect creation, the High Priest served as a link between the natural and the divine. The Jews believed that God would make his wishes for man and the natural universe known only through the High Priest. Likewise, it was only the High Priest who could communicate natural concerns back to God through ceremony and ritual.

For this purpose a special chamber existed deep within the Sanctuary building of the Jerusalem Second Temple — where God supposedly "lived." Only the High Priest was allowed to enter this room–and then only once a year.

For there are, as it seems, two temples belonging to God; one being this world, in which the high priest is the divine word, his own firstborn son. The other is the rational soul, the priest of which is the real true man, the copy of whom, perceptible to the senses, is he who performs his paternal vows and sacrifices, (Philo *Special Laws* 1.215)

To be considered for the High Priest position, the candidate had to have no physical flaws.

Now these are the laws which relate to the priests. It is enjoined that the priest shall be entire and unmutilated, having no blemish on his body, no part being deficient, either naturally or through mutilation; and on the other hand, nothing having been superfluous either from his birth or having grown out subsequently from disease; his skin, also, must never have changed from leprosy, or wild lichen, or scab, or any other eruption or breaking out; all which things appear to me to be designed to be symbols of the purity of his soul. (81) For if it was necessary to examine the mortal body of the priest that it ought not be imperfect through any misfortune, much more was it necessary to look into his immortal soul, which they say is fashioned in the form of the living God. Now the image of God is the Word, by which all the world was made. (Philo *Special Laws* 80-81)

According to Josephus, continuous records existed of the Jewish High Priests going back 2,000 years, which is more than 1,000 years earlier than the accepted date for the Jewish exodus out of Egypt. To the Jews, chronicling the succession of the High Priests was just as important as chronicling the Jewish kings. There were many periods when the Jewish nation had no king, but never a time when the ancient Jews didn't have a High Priest.

The High Priest usually held that position until his death or incapacitation. This line of succession ended in A.D. 70, when the Romans did away with the High Priesthood entirely and destroyed the great Temple.

Romans and the High Priesthood

A century before the arrival of the Romans, the Maccabeans started their own dynasty of High Priests after their successful revolt against the Syrian Greeks. During much of the reign of the early Maccabeans, the nation was content to have no king at all; the High Priesthood served that function ably. This dynasty of priest-kings were called the Asamoneans, named after the priest grandfather of Judas Maccabeus and his brothers.

Gnaeus Pompey conquered Jerusalem and the surrounding Jewish territories in 63 B.C. His ally was the Jewish Asamonean deposed king, John Hyrcanus II, who also held the position of High Priest of the Jerusalem Temple. Together, Pompey and Hyrcanus II defeated Hyrcanus' younger brother, Aristobulos, who had previously usurped Hyrcanus from the Jewish throne.

Although the Jewish nation had lost its independence, and Hyrcanus II lost his Royal position, Pompey decided to keep the theocracy of the Jewish nation intact. Hyrcanus remained as High Priest and the operations of the Temple continued as before.

This decision by Pompey, which was later confirmed by Julius Caesar, was not unusual. Rome usually let subjugated nations retain their own religious ways as long as the native rituals were not too outrageous or destabilizing. The Romans only cared about peace, commerce, and the payment of tribute. If the Jewish priests could guarantee those three things, then Rome would support them.

For this reason, the High Priesthood flourished for the next 142 years under Roman authority. It evolved into a powerful aristocracy dominated by several families. Elaborate ritual sacrifices and feasts continued to be centered around the Jerusalem Temple, and these families, however wealthy they had been before the Romans, became far more so.

However, with the Romans came one important change—the High Priest would now serve at the pleasure of the Roman authorities. Herod the Great was the first to dismiss and appoint High Priests as political expediency dictated.

Herod was then made king by the Romans, but did no longer appoint high priests out of the family of Asamoneus; but made certain men to be so that were of no eminent families, but barely of those that were priests, excepting that he gave that dignity to Aristobulus; for when he had made this Aristobulus, the grandson of that Hyrcanus who was then taken by the Parthians, and had taken his sister Mariamne to wife, he thereby aimed to win the good-will of the people, who had a kind remembrance of Hyrcanus [his grandfather]. Yet did he afterward, out of his fear lest they should all bend their inclinations to Aristobulus, put him to death, and that by contriving how to have him suffocated as he was swimming at Jericho, as we have already related that matter; but after this man he never intrusted the priesthood to the posterity of the sons of Asamoneus. Archelaus also, Herod's son, did like his father in the appointment of the high priests, as did the Romans also, who took the government over the Jews into their hands afterward. Accordingly, the number of the high priests, from the days of Herod until the day when Titus took the temple and the City, and burnt them, were in all twenty-eight; the time also that belonged to them was a hundred and seven years. Some of these were the political governors of the people under the reign of Herod, and under the reign of Archelaus his son, although, after their death, the government became an aristocracy, and the high priests were intrusted with a dominion over the nation. (*Antiq* XX 10:1)

Herod the Great even murdered a High Priest–the brother of his Royal wife, Mariamne I (*Antiq* XV 3:3). This act turned Mariamne against Herod and indirectly resulted in her own execution ordered by Herod several years later.

After Herod the Great's death, his son King Archelaus found it advantageous to keep only a single High Priest in power, Joazar, during the nine years of his reign. When Archelaus was removed in A.D. 6 by Augustus, Archelaus' ethnarchy was turned into a Roman province. After an evaluation by Syrian President Cyrenius, it was decided to remove Joazar as High Priest. Cyrenius appointed a young priest named Simon Ananus bar Seth to that position. Ananus was to remain in power for the next 15 years (though a case can be made for only an eight-year tenure).

To the Romans, the Jews were a difficult nation to understand. The Jewish culture was complicated by religious rituals based on the phases of the moon, astrology, the results of animal sacrifice, and written laws that predated Rome's by hundreds of years. But as long as peace reigned and taxes were paid, Rome was willing to leave the High Priesthood and the Sanhedrin alone in running the theocracy. Crimes of a political nature went before the appointed Roman governor, but those were relatively few.

As the decades passed under Roman protection, the Second Temple became a huge money-maker. Safe passage on Roman-patrolled roads was likely a large factor as well as a Mediterranean free of pirates. Travel was safe. With the peace brought by the Roman Empire, people became wealthier and so would travel for their pleasure to Jewish festivals and others. Not all visitors to the Temple were Jews.

In the times of Jesus, according to Josephus millions of Jews would come to the Temple for the major festivals–along with a significant number of non-Jews. The Temple money that had in previous years been paid in graft to Archelaus and Herod the Great was now passed on to the Roman prefect. Much of the profits were also likely retained by the families of the High Priesthood, making them richer still.

Simon Ananus bar Seth

Ananus bar Seth was the first High Priest under the new Judean prefecture system, beginning his term in A.D. 7, appointed by the Roman Governor Cyrenius.

> When Cyrenius had now disposed of Archelaus's money, and when the taxings were come to a conclusion, which were made in the thirty-seventh year of Caesar's victory over Antony at Actium, he deprived Joazar of the high priesthood, which dignity had been conferred on him by the multitude, and he appointed Ananus, the son of Seth, to be high priest (*Antiq* XVIII 2:1)

Ananus recognized the unique opportunity given to him and took full advantage of it. Through the prosperity of the Second Temple, Simon Ananus and his family would become extremely wealthy and powerful–kings in all but name only.

> the report goes that this eldest Ananus proved a most fortunate man (*Antiq* XX 9:1)

Ananus was of the Sadducee sect of the Jews. Sadducees do not believe in personal salvation or an afterlife, and moral judgment, when it exists, is harsh. The Sadducees believe that an individual determines his own destiny in life with little direction from God. Ananus was certainly a stern and practical man who believed not in fate or astrology, but in shaping his own future. Like Herod the Great, Ananus recognized early that the way to wealth, power, and security was to tirelessly serve the interests of the Roman Empire.

Ananus remained as a favorite of Rome for more than a half century. According to Josephus, Ananus served as High Priest for either eight or 15 years, starting in A.D. 7 (*Antiq* XVIII 2:2). After giving up the exalted position, Ananus retained much his power and authority functioning as a Second Temple elder and power broker until his violent death in A.D. 68 during the Jewish revolt. He was killed not by the Romans, but by Idumeans. They had been let into the city of Jerusalem ostensibly to help the Jews defend it.

Ananus is also mentioned several times in the New Testament, and he is most famous for initially questioning Jesus of Nazareth after Jesus' arrest (Jn 18:13-24). Ananus' son-in-law, Joseph Caiaphas, was the actual High Priest at the time, but Ananus could well have been the driving force behind Jesus' arrest. Ananus was also involved in the questioning of the arrested Disciple Peter in the months after Jesus' crucifixion (Acts 4:5-22).

Ananus had many natural sons—several of whom attained High Priest status. The most infamous of the Second Temple High Priests was Joseph Caiaphas, a man who married Ananus' daughter. Another son, Ananus, after gaining the High Priest's position in A.D. 62, would orchestrate the execution of Jesus' brother, James the Just.

Joseph Caiaphas

Caiaphas served for at least 11 Passovers and possibly as many as 18. One interpretation of Josephus' writings has Caiaphas becoming High Priest in A.D. 26 and being removed by Syrian President Lucius Vitellius in either A.D. 35 or 36. But Caiaphas' appointment could have come eight years earlier, giving him a tenure of either 17 or 18 years as High Priest (*Antiq* XVIII 2:2).

This is an extraordinary amount of time for a Roman-era High Priest and serves as a testament to Caiaphas' capabilities. It must have been a cruel and unexpected blow to proud Caiaphas to lose the High Priest's position after being in power for so long!

The Christian-inspired image of Caiaphas as an ugly and wretched man is a false one. In all likelihood, Caiaphas was one of the handsomest, most intelligent, and physically attractive men in Jerusalem. The High Priest had to reflect the perfect man, and crafty Ananus knew that the most effective High Priest also had to have "star" qualities. And Caiaphas married Ananus' daughter, after all!

The Sons of Ananus

When the young Simon Ananus tired of the High Priest's position after 15 years of duty, he had great sway with the Roman Prefect Valerius Gratus concerning who should succeed him. In fact, most of the later prefects or procurators who were appointed by Rome deferred to Ananus' opinion. Whenever possible, Ananus used this influence to place his own sons in the High Priest's position. Sometimes, however, Ananus let the sons of other powerful "old guard" priest families attain that prestigious position as well. The Sanhedrin might have also had some input as to who was appointed High Priest, but clearly Ananus had the ear of Rome and held the true religious power in the East.

> Now the report goes that this eldest Ananus proved a most fortunate man; for he had five sons who had all performed the office of a high priest to God, and who had himself enjoyed that dignity a long time formerly, which had never happened to any other of our high priests. (*Antiq* XX 9:1)

The first son of Ananus, Eleazar, served as High Priest for a single year before Caiaphas' appointment. Caiaphas served through to the Passover of either A.D. 35 or 36. Then Jonathan, Theophilis, and Matthias–all blood sons of Ananus–became High Priests in rough succession. Jonathan served for one or two years before Lucius Vitellius, the president of Syria, removed him in A.D. 37. Theophilis served next for four years with his term ending in A.D. 41. Simon, the son of Boethus, served for two years before another of Ananus' sons, Matthias, was appointed High Priest for the year of A.D. 43. Lastly, Ananus, a son of Ananus, served for a few months in late A.D. 62. If sons-in-law are also counted, six "sons" of Ananus served as Second Temple High Priests over a 50-year period.

End of a Dynasty

In the revolt of A.D. 66, according to Josephus both the elder Ananus and his son played key roles early in the defense of Jerusalem. Zealots from the countryside had sought haven in Jerusalem and wound up taking over the walled Second Temple complex and using it as a stronghold. There, they preyed upon the citizens of the city. The zealots also invited the armies of Idumea to come to Jerusalem to help defend it against the advancing Romans.

In trying to root out these zealots, the former High Priest Ananus, the son of Ananus, organized a citizen army which was only temporarily successful. Eventually, the zealots and their Idumean allies prevailed, with both Ananus and his father being killed in early A.D. 68. Josephus wrote a eulogy for the elder Ananus, who was was at least in his mid-eighties at the time of his death.

> ..the death of Ananus was the beginning of the destruction of the city, and that from this very day may be dated the overthrow of her wall, and the ruin of her affairs, whereon they saw their high priest, and the procurer of their preservation, slain in the midst of their city. He was on other accounts also a venerable, and a very just man; and besides the grandeur of that nobility, and dignity, and honor of which he was possessed, he had been a lover of a kind of parity, even with regard to the meanest of the people; he was a prodigious lover of liberty, and an admirer of a democracy in government; and did ever prefer the public welfare before his own advantage, and preferred peace above all things; for he was thoroughly sensible that the Romans were not to be conquered. He also foresaw that of necessity a war would follow, and that unless the Jews made up matters with them very dexterously, they would be destroyed; to say all in a word, if Ananus had survived, they had certainly compounded matters; for he was a shrewd man in speaking and persuading the people, and had already gotten the mastery of those that opposed his designs, or were for the war. (*Wars* IV 5:2)

The infamous and illustrious family of Ananus was lost to history after the destruction of Jerusalem and the Second Temple in A.D. 70. The historian Flavius Josephus was an eyewitness to the final devastation, and he personally reviewed the prisoners and captives after the fighting ended. General Titus told Josephus that he could save from slavery any of the captured Jews. Josephus protected many friends, but he did not document any member of the Ananus family among them.

Josephus makes reference to a monument to the Ananus family outside the city wall of Jerusalem. Apparently, it survived the devastation of the Jewish revolt undamaged (*Wars* V 12:2).

The Business of the Priesthood

In Jesus' time, Ananus bar Seth was in charge of the operation of the Second Temple with nominal oversight by the Romans and the Sanhedrin. According to Josephus, the Temple employed a hierarchy of over 20,000 priests, but even a tenth of that number (the Josephus adjustment factor for very large numbers) would be a huge amount (*Apion* II 8).

All Jews were expected to tithe yearly in support of the Temple. Male Jews over the age of 20 were supposed to give a half shekel, preferably in person, during the Jerusalem Passover celebration. A shekel was a measure of weight of silver thought to be ten grams in Jesus' times. Ancient records indicate that in those days a skilled craftsman, or a Roman soldier, would earn about five grams of silver a day, so this tax was not onerous.

Another tax was called "first fruits" which was the first portion of that year's harvest and a portion of the livestock. These were brought in to Jerusalem and laid up in the Temple or sacrificed as the case may be. Also, over the decades, the Temple came to own quite a bit of land on its own, probably from being named a beneficiary in the probate of wealthy estates.

> But the temple has for its revenues not only portions of land, but also other possessions of much greater extent and importance, which will never be destroyed or diminished; for as long as the race of mankind shall last, the revenues likewise of the temple will always be preserved, being coeval in their duration with the universal world. (77) For it is commanded that all men shall every year bring their first fruits to the temple, from twenty years old and upwards; and this contribution is

called their ransom. On which account they bring in the first fruits with exceeding cheerfulness, being joyful and delighted, inasmuch as simultaneously with their making the offering they are sure to find either a relaxation from slavery, or a relief from disease, and to receive in all respects a most sure freedom and safety for the future. (78) And since the nation is the most numerous of all peoples, it follows naturally that the first fruits contributed by them must also be most abundant. Accordingly there is in almost every city a storehouse for the sacred things to which it is customary for the people to come and there to deposit their first fruits, and at certain seasons there are sacred ambassadors selected on account of their virtue, who convey the offerings to the temple. And the most eminent men of each tribe are elected to this office, that they may conduct the hopes of each individual safe to their destination; for in the lawful offering of the first fruits are the hopes of the pious. (Philo *Special Laws* 76-78)

(141) After this he also appointed another source of revenue of no insignificant importance for the priests, bidding them to take the first fruits of every one of the revenues of the nation namely, the first fruits of the corn, and wine, and oil, and even of the produce of all the cattle, of the flocks of sheep, and herds of oxen, and flocks of goats, and of all other animals of all kinds; and how great an abundance of these animals there must be, any one may conjecture from the vast populousness of the nation; (142) from all which circumstances it is plain that the law invests the priests with the dignity and honour that belongs to kings; since he commands contributions from every description of possession to be given to them as to rulers; (143) and they are accordingly given to them in a manner quite contrary to that in which cities usually furnish them to their rulers; for cities usually furnish them under compulsion, and with great unwillingness and lamentation, looking upon the collectors of the taxes as common enemies and destroyers, and making all kinds of different excuses at different times, and neglecting all laws and ordinances, and with all this jumbling and evasion do they contribute the taxes and payments which are levied on them. (144) But the men of this nation contribute their payments to the priests with joy and cheerfulness, anticipating the collectors, and cutting short the time allowed for making the contributions, and thinking that they are themselves receiving rather than giving; and so with words of blessing and thankfulness, they all, both men and women, bring their offerings at each of the seasons of the year, with a spontaneous cheerfulness, and readiness, and zeal, beyond all description. (Ibid 141-144)

The priests probably also took a percentage of the income that the local merchants earned off the religious pilgrims. Sacrificial stock such as white birds or paschal lambs were a big business. Also, the priests had their own "holy" coin that was especially blessed. It was the only type of money accepted by by the Temple, hence the necessity for Temple-based "moneychangers." Additionally, a portion of every animal that was sacrificed was given to the priesthood as well as the skin of the slain beast.

Even Philo admitted that the priestly class could live very well from these offerings if the people truly gave the "first fruits" as they were commanded to by law.

> For if we were to obey the commands which we have received, and if we were to take care to give the first fruits as we are commanded, they would not only have abundance of all necessary things, but would also be filled with all kinds of supplies calculated for enabling them to live in refinement and luxury. (Ibid 153)

The amount of money flowing into the coffers of the priests during the major festivals must have been enormous. In the times of Jesus, with hundreds of thousands of pilgrims, the festival "business" of Jerusalem was probably as sophisticated and as logistically complex as any Roman military campaign. The Roman prefects likely shared in the profits from the operation of the Second Temple–a form of bribery. In turn, the Roman administrators allowed Ananus' family and other favored Jewish families to run the lucrative operation without interference.

Duties and Rituals

The High Priesthood set the Calendar which was a very important task done by priests who specialized in astronomy. Every month also had to begin on a waxing moon, a very important consideration. The monthly waxing and waning of the moon was considered a manifestation of a great mystical power. In fact, it was an accepted practice in most ancient civilizations to plant the spring crops and even start military campaigns only at the time of a new moon.

Certain of the Jewish priests were experts in astrology, and were able to chart every possible aspect of human life. No treatises on Jewish astrology have survived to the present day, although many undoubtedly existed in ancient times. Similarly, the "art" of animal sacrifice was one that the Jewish Priests knew well. Whether that included the examination of the entrails of the sacrificed for prophetic signs–as the Greeks would do–is not known.

A large part of the duties of the High Priest was the performance of ritual ceremonies within the Second Temple. The Priests followed a strict routine during the day.

> Now there is so great caution used about these offices of religion, that the priests are appointed to go into the temple but at certain hours; for in the morning, at the opening of the inner temple, those that are to officiate receive the sacrifices, as they do again at noon, till the doors are shut. Lastly, it is not so much as lawful to carry any vessel into the holy house; nor is there any thing therein, but the altar [of incense], the table [of shew-bread], the censer, and the candlestick, which are all written in the law; for there is nothing further there, nor are there any mysteries performed that may not be spoken of; nor is there any feasting within the place. For what I have now said is publicly known, and supported by the testimony of the whole people, and their operations are very manifest; for although there be four courses of the priests, and every one of them have above five thousand men in them, yet do they officiate on certain days only; and when those days are over, other priests succeed in the performance of their sacrifices, and assemble together at mid-day, and receive the keys of the temple, and the vessels by tale, without any thing relating to food or drink being carried into the temple; nay, we are not allowed to offer such things at the altar, excepting what is prepared for the sacrifices. (*Apion* II 8)

Much of this ritual was based on the 1,000-year-old writings of Moses. For these ceremonies, special jewel-encrusted vestments were worn, as Josephus describes:

> The high priest did also go up with them; not always indeed, but on the seventh days and new moons, and if any festivals belonging to our nation, which we celebrate every year, happened. When he officiated, he had on a pair of breeches that reached beneath his privy parts to his thighs, and had on an inner garment of linen, together with a blue

garment, round, without seam, with fringe work, and reaching to the feet. There were also golden bells that hung upon the fringes, and pomegranates intermixed among them. The bells signified thunder, and the pomegranates lightning. But that girdle that tied the garment to the breast was embroidered with five rows of various colors, of gold, and purple, and scarlet, as also of fine linen and blue, with which colors we told you before the veils of the temple were embroidered also. The like embroidery was upon the ephod; but the quantity of gold therein was greater. Its figure was that of a stomacher for the breast. There were upon it two golden buttons like small shields, which buttoned the ephod to the garment; in these buttons were enclosed two very large and very excellent sardonyxes, having the names of the tribes of that nation engraved upon them: on the other part there hung twelve stones, three in a row one way, and four in the other; a sardius, a topaz, and an emerald; a carbuncle, a jasper, and a sapphire; an agate, an amethyst, and a ligure; an onyx, a beryl, and a chrysolite; upon every one of which was again engraved one of the forementioned names of the tribes. A mitre also of fine linen encompassed his head, which was tied by a blue ribbon, about which there was another golden crown, in which was engraven the sacred name [of God]: it consists of four vowels. However, the high priest did not wear these garments at other times, but a more plain habit; he only did it when he went into the most sacred part of the temple, which he did but once in a year, on that day when our custom is for all of us to keep a fast to God. (*Wars* V 5:7)

Philo also writes about the highly symbolic attire of the High Priest in Second Temple ceremonies.

And after enjoining that the priest is to be of pure blood, and sprung from fathers of noble birth, and that he must be perfect in body and soul, laws are enacted also respecting the garments which the priest must wear when he is about to offer the sacred sacrifices and to perform the sacred ceremonies. (83) And this dress is a linen tunic and a girdle, the latter to cover those parts which must not be displayed in their nakedness near the altar of sacrifice. And the tunic is for the sake of promptness in performing the requisite ministrations; for they are but lightly clad, only in their tunics, when they bring their victims, and the libations, and the other requisite offerings for sacrifice, being apparelled so as to admit of unhesitating celerity. (84) But the high priest is commanded to wear a similar dress when he goes into the holy of holies to offer incense, because linen is not made of any animal that dies, as woollen garments are. He is also commanded to wear another robe also, having very beautiful embroidery and ornament upon it, so that it may seem to be a copy and representation of the world. And the description of the ornament is a clear proof of this; (85) for in the first place the whole of the round robe is of hyacinthine colour, a tunic reaching to the feet, being an emblem of the air, since the air also is by nature black, and in a manner may be said to be reaching to the feet, as it is extended from above from the regions about the moon, to the lowest places of the earth. (86) Next there was a woven garment in the form of a breastplate upon it, and this was a symbol of the heaven; for on the points of the shoulders are two emerald stones of most exceeding value, one on one side and one on the other, each perfectly round and single on each side, as emblems of the hemispheres, one of which is above the earth and the other under the earth. (87) Then on his chest there are twelve precious stones of different colours, arranged in four rows of three stones in each row, being fashioned so as an emblem of the zodiac. For the zodiac also consists of twelve animals, and so divides the four seasons of the year, allotting three animals to each season. (88) And the whole place is very correctly called the logeum (logeion), since every thing in heaven has been created and arranged in accordance with right reason (logois) and proportion; for there is absolutely nothing there which is devoid of reason. And on the logeum he embroiders two woven pieces of cloth, calling the one manifestation and the other truth. (89) And by the one which he calls truth he expresses figuratively that it is absolutely impossible for falsehood to enter any part of heaven, but that it is entirely banished to the parts around the earth, dwelling among the souls of impious men. And by that which he calls manifestation he implies that the natures in heaven make manifest every thing that takes place among us, which of themselves would be perfectly and universally unknown. (90) And the clearest proof of this is that if there were no light, and if the sun did not shine, it would be impossible for the indescribable variety of qualities of bodies to be seen, and for all the manifold differences of colours and forms to be distinguished from one another. And what else could exhibit to us the days and the nights, and the months and the years, and in short the divisions of time, but the harmonious and inconceivable revolutions of the sun, and moon, and other stars? (91) And what could exhibit the true nature of number, except those same bodies just mentioned in accordance with the observation of the combination of the parts of time? And what else could have cut the paths through the ocean and through such numerous and vast seas, and shown them to navigators, except the changes and periodical appearances of the stars? And wise men have observed, (92) also, an innumerable quantity of other circumstances, and have recorded them, conjecturing from the heavenly bodies the advent of calm weather and of violent storms, and the fertility or barrenness of crops, and the mild or violently hot summers, and whether the winters will be severe or spring-like, whether there will be droughts or abundance of rain, whether the flocks and trees will be fruitful, or on the contrary barren, and all such matters as these. For the signs of every thing on earth are engraved and firmly fixed in heaven.(93) And besides this, golden pomegranates are attached to the lower parts of the tunic, reaching to the feet, and bells and borders embroidered with flowers. And these things are the emblems of earth and of water; the flowers are the emblems of the earth, inasmuch as it is out of it that they all rise and derive strength to bloom. And the Pomegranates as above mentioned are the emblems of water, being so named from the flowing of the stream. And the harmony, and concord, and unison of sound of the different parts of the world is betokened by the bells. (94) And the arrangement is a very excellent one; for the upper garment, on which the stones are placed, which is called the breast-plate, is a representation of heaven, because the heaven also is the highest of all things. And the tunic that reaches to the feet is in every part of a hyacinthine colour, since the air also is black, and is placed in the second classification next in honour to the heaven. And the embroidered flowers and pomegranates are on the hem, because the earth and water have been assigned the lowest situation in the universe. (95) This is the arrangement of the sacred dress of the high priest, being a representation of the universe, a marvellous work to be beheld or to be contemplated. For it has an appearance thoroughly calculated to excite astonishment, such as no embroidered work conceived by man ever was for variety and costly magnificence; (96) and it also attracts the intellect of philosophers to examine its different parts. For God intends that the high priest should in the first place have a visible representation of the universe about him, in order that from the continual sight of it he may be reminded to make his own life worthy of the nature of the universe, and secondly, in order that the whole world may co-operate with him in the performance of his sacred rites. And it is exceedingly becoming that the man who is consecrated to the service of the Father of the world should also bring his son to the service of him who has begotten him. (97) There is also a third symbol contained in this sacred dress, which it is important not to pass over in silence. For the priests of other deities are accustomed to offer up prayers and sacrifices solely for their own relations, and friends, and fellow citizens. But the high priest of the Jews offers them up not only on behalf of the whole race of mankind, but also on behalf of the different parts of nature, of the earth, of water, of air, and of fire; and pours forth his prayers and thanksgivings for them all, looking upon the world (as indeed it really is) as his country, for which, therefore, he is accustomed to implore and propitiate its governor by supplications and prayers, beseeching him to give a portion of his own merciful and humane nature to the things which he has created (98) After he has given these precepts, he issues additional commandments, and orders him, whenever he approaches the altar and touches the sacrifices, at the time when it is appointed for him to perform his sacred ministrations, not to drink wine or any other strong drink, on account of four most important reasons, hesitation, and forgetfulness, and sleep, and folly. (Philo *Special Laws* 82-98)

The Romans thought that the robe was such a powerful symbol that it potentially could serve as a rallying point for insurrection. For that reason, the robes were kept locked up for most of the year by the Romans—released to the priests only for the Passover celebration—and even then kept under close supervision.

The End of the High Priesthood

During the Jewish revolt against Rome from A.D. 66-73, the Jerusalem priests initially assumed control of the Jewish nation, giving the charge to certain men to raise armies and provide for the nation's common defense and protection. But the Jewish revolt was eventually crushed and Jerusalem and the Second Temple razed to their foundations. The Jews were then forbidden to live in Jerusalem by the victorious Romans. The city was subsequently renamed Aelia Capitolina. Most Jewish survivors were forced into slavery and scattered throughout the empire or sold to foreign countries.

The Romans also banned the High Priesthood and its rituals. On the site of the devastated Second Temple a Roman temple was erected.

Later historians began to refer to the Jewish East after the revolt as Palestine instead of Judea. A center for Judaism grew up over the decades in the northern city of Tiberias on Lake Gennesareth, but without being under the authority of a High Priest.

Chapter 9   The Essenes

For their doctrine is this:.. that the souls are immortal, and continue for
ever; and that they come out of the most subtile air, and are united to
their bodies as to prisons, into which they are drawn by a certain natural
enticement; but that when they are set free from the bonds of the flesh,
they then, as released from a long bondage, rejoice and mount upward.
(*Wars* II 8:11)

The Essenes were an ancient Jewish religious sect that practiced
a form of monastic Judaism about which few details are known.
The Essenes lived communally in dedicated houses in many of
the larger cities and villages of the Jewish East. If Jesus wasn't an
Essene himself, he certainly knew of them. Jesus' own teachings
are reflective of the Essenic philosophy and a strong connection
between the Essenes and Jesus is tempting to make.

The sources of information on the ancient Essenes are limited.
Josephus writes about the sect at some length, while Philo
mentions them in two different selections. One of them is a lost
writing that comes down to us second-hand from Bishop
Eusebius, a third century Christian scholar. Pliny the Elder, a first
century Roman natural historian, also documents the presence of
an Essenic colony in Judea. Pliny actually visited the sect which
was located in a small mountain-top village outside of Jerusalem
and near the northwest shore of Lake Asphaltitis. This site could
have been what is known today as Qumran which is close to
where the Dead Sea Scrolls were found.

While Josephus writes that the Essenes were a third major
priestly sect of the Jews, the Essenes are never mentioned in the
Bible. Despite this, many scholars and interested Christians have
tacitly assumed that Jesus was, in fact, an Essene–and for good

reason. The Essenic philosophy was one of peace, understanding, and the forgiveness of sins. Many of the Essenes labored as shepherds or worked in agriculture–settings commonly found in Jesus' parables. For this reason, artists throughout the ages have traditionally shown Jesus wearing a white robe even though this attire is never described in the New Testament. A white robe is, however, the accepted garb for the Essenes.

But all the Essenes were not pacifists. Josephus writes of an Essene named John who served as a general in the Jewish revolt. In A.D. 66, John and others led a guerrilla action hoping to take the lightly defended city of Ascalon. This is the modern-day city of Ashkelon which is located on the Mediterranean coast north of Gaza. John was wounded in the action, and Josephus reports no more about him (*Wars* III 2:1).

Josephus argued that the famous cult society of the Greek Pythagoreans was actually an offshoot of the more ancient Essenic sect.

> Pythagoras, therefore, of Samos, lived in very ancient times, and was esteemed a person superior to all philosophers in wisdom and piety towards God. Now it is plain that he did not only know our doctrines, but was in very great measure a follower and admirer of them. (*Apion* 1:22)

The Essenic Way

All Jews, including the Essenes, strictly followed the law of Moses as was written in the five holy Books of the Torah. In fact, that was a prerequisite, along with male circumcision, to claim to be Jewish. However, even with the Torah as a common base, distinct philosophical and practical differences developed that separated Judaism into three sects.

The Sadducees were the sect to which the High Priests Ananus and Caiaphas belonged. The Sadducees did not amplify upon the laws of Moses. They followed these laws without amendment or supplement. The Sadducees did not believe in an afterlife-believing that the soul died with the body. The Sadducees also believed that the individual man was the maker of his own destiny. Fate played no role in the affairs of men, and God rarely took an interest in them. While astrology and its predictive power played a large role in Jewish religious life in ancient times, the Sadducees apparently placed little importance on it.

The Pharisees, like the Sadducees, also followed the laws of Moses strictly but developed an intricate and all-encompassing set of sub-laws and by-laws to additionally govern Jewish behavior. The Pharisees were fatalistic and believed in the immortality of the soul and in both a heaven and a hell.

The Essenes were also fatalistic like the Pharisees and believed in a heaven and hell. However, unlike both the Pharisees and Sadducees, the Essenes were strict ascetics and denied their natural inclinations as much as was possible. The Essenes believed that God was a part of every natural man. To know God, the individual had to deny their natural passions and desires.

Due to the Essenes' acknowledged capacity for discipline and self-denial, these men were assumed to be closer to God than other men. As a result, the Essenes were respected–and even feared–among all in the ancient Jewish world. Unsullied by earthly desires, the nighttime dreams of the Essenes were thought to be visions from God–direct windows into heaven! And, indeed, the Essenes were known for their ability to foretell the future (*Wars* I 3:5; *Antiq* XV 10:5, XVII 13:3).

> This now is the enviable system of life of these Essenes, so that not only private individuals but even mighty kings, admiring the men, venerate their sect, and increase their dignity and majesty in a still higher degree by their approbation and by the honours which they confer on them. (Philo *Hypothetica* 11:1-18)

When Herod the Great was demanding all of his subjects declare an oath of fidelity to him, he specifically exempted the Essenes. It was understood that the Essenes swore allegiance only to God (*Antiq* XV 10:5).

The Essenes did not believe in animal sacrifice which set them at odds with both the Pharisees and the Sadducees. For that reason, the Essenes were rarely seen at the Jerusalem Temple, though they did pay their half-shekel taxes every year. Despite their monastic ways, the Essenes worked in the local community as laborers. And it was common to see them in attendance at the local synagogues.

According to Josephus, many of the Essenes lived to be over a hundred years old.

> (The Essenes)..are long-lived also, insomuch that many of them live above a hundred years, by means of the simplicity of their diet; nay, as I think, by means of the regular course of life they observe also. (*Wars* II 8:10).

Both Philo and Josephus were in agreement that, in their time, only about 4,000 men were practicing members in this sect.

The Three Jewish Sects

Josephus discusses the Essenes, the Sadducees and the Pharisees, in *Antiquities*.

> The Jews had for a great while had three sects of philosophy peculiar to themselves; the sect of the Essens, and the sect of the Sadducees, and the third sort of opinions was that of those called Pharisees; of which sects, although I have already spoken in the second Book of the Jewish War, yet will I a little touch upon them now.
> Now, for the Pharisees, they live meanly, and despise delicacies in diet; and they follow the conduct of reason; and what that prescribes to them as good for them they do; and they think they ought earnestly to strive to observe reason's dictates for practice. They also pay a respect to such as are in years; nor are they so bold as to contradict them in any thing which they have introduced; and when they determine that all things are done by fate, they do not take away the freedom from men of acting as they think fit; since their notion is, that it hath pleased God to make a temperament, whereby what he wills is done, but so that the will of man can act virtuously or viciously. They also believe that souls have an immortal rigor in them, and that under the earth there will be rewards or punishments, according as they have lived virtuously or viciously in this life; and the latter are to be detained in an everlasting prison, but that the former shall have power to revive and live again; on account of which doctrines they are able greatly to persuade the body of the people;

and whatsoever they do about Divine worship, prayers, and sacrifices, they perform them according to their direction; insomuch that the cities give great attestations to them on account of their entire virtuous conduct, both in the actions of their lives and their discourses also.

But the doctrine of the Sadducees is this: That souls die with the bodies; nor do they regard the observation of any thing besides what the law enjoins them; for they think it an instance of virtue to dispute with those teachers of philosophy whom they frequent: but this doctrine is received but by a few, yet by those still of the greatest dignity. But they are able to do almost nothing of themselves; for when they become magistrates, as they are unwillingly and by force sometimes obliged to be, they addict themselves to the notions of the Pharisees, because the multitude would not otherwise bear them.

The doctrine of the Essens is this: That all things are best ascribed to God. They teach the immortality of souls, and esteem that the rewards of righteousness are to be earnestly striven for; and when they send what they have dedicated to God into the temple, they do not offer sacrifices because they have more pure lustrations of their own; on which account they are excluded from the common court of the temple, but offer their sacrifices themselves; yet is their course of life better than that of other men; and they entirely addict themselves to husbandry. It also deserves our admiration, how much they exceed all other men that addict themselves to virtue, and this in righteousness; and indeed to such a degree, that as it hath never appeared among any other men, neither Greeks nor barbarians, no, not for a little time, so hath it endured a long while among them. This is demonstrated by that institution of theirs which will not suffer any thing to hinder them from having all things in common; so that a rich man enjoys no more of his own wealth than he who hath nothing at all. There are about four thousand men that live in this way, and neither marry wives, nor are desirous to keep servants; as thinking the latter tempts men to be unjust, and the former gives the handle to domestic quarrels; but as they live by themselves, they minister one to another. They also appoint certain stewards to receive the incomes of their revenues, and of the fruits of the ground; such as are good men and priests, who are to get their corn and their food ready for them. They none of them differ from others of the Essens in their way of living, but do the most resemble those Dacae who are called Polistae [dwellers in cities]. (*Antiq* XVIII 1:2-5)

Josephus also writes about the Pharisees and Sadducees in *Wars*.

But then as to the two other orders at first mentioned, the Pharisees are those who are esteemed most skillful in the exact explication of their laws, and introduce the first sect. These ascribe all to fate [or providence], and to God, and yet allow, that to act what is right, or the contrary, is principally in the power of men, although fate does co-operate in every action. They say that all souls are incorruptible, but that the souls of good men only are removed into other bodies, –but that the souls of bad men are subject to eternal punishment. But the Sadducees are those that compose the second order, and take away fate entirely, and suppose that God is not concerned in our doing or not doing what is evil; and they say, that to act what is good, or what is evil, is at men's own choice, and that the one or the other belongs so to every one, that they may act as they please. They also take away the belief of the immortal duration of the soul, and the punishments and rewards in Hades. Moreover, the Pharisees are friendly to one another, and are for the exercise of concord, and regard for the public; but the behavior of the Sadducees one towards another is in some degree wild, and their conversation with those that are of their own party is as barbarous as if they were strangers to them. And this is what I had to say concerning the philosophic sects among the Jews. (*Wars* II 8:14)

The Fourth Jewish Sect–the Zealots

Interestingly, a man called Judas, from Galilee, is identified as starting a fourth religious sect. This sect was much like the Pharisees but with a penchant for political activism. Not surprisingly, it arose to prominence around the time of the death of Herod the Great. From this sect came the zealots–a group to which Caiaphas accused Jesus of belonging. In fact, it is probable that more than a few of Jesus' followers leaned toward zealotry.

But of the fourth sect of Jewish philosophy, Judas the Galilean was the author. These men agree in all other things with the Pharisaic notions; but they have an inviolable attachment to liberty, and say that God is to be their only Ruler and Lord. They also do not value dying any kinds of death, nor indeed do they heed the deaths of their relations and friends, nor can any such fear make them call any man lord. And since this immovable resolution of theirs is well known to a great many, I shall speak no further about that matter; nor am I afraid that any thing I have said of them should be disbelieved, but rather fear, that what I have said is beneath the resolution they show when they undergo pain. And it was in Gessius Florus's time that the nation began to grow mad with this distemper, who was our procurator, and who occasioned the Jews to go wild with it by the abuse of his authority, and to make them revolt from the Romans. And these are the sects of Jewish philosophy. (*Antiq* XVIII 1:6)

It should be noted that late in Herod the Great's reign, the sect of the Pharisees also had a reputation for antagonism against Herod and the Romans. This was very bold because Herod was ruthlessly unforgiving when it came to the seditious. Josephus gives their numbers as 6,000, while the numbering the Essenes at 4,000.

> For there was a certain sect of men that were Jews, who valued themselves highly upon the exact skill they had in the law of their fathers, and made men believe they were highly favored by God, by whom this set of women were inveigled. These are those that are called the sect of the Pharisees, who were in a capacity of greatly opposing kings. A cunning sect they were, and soon elevated to a pitch of open fighting and doing mischief. Accordingly, when all the people of the Jews gave assurance of their good-will to Caesar, and to the king's government, these very men did not swear, being above six thousand; (*Antiq* XVII 2:4).

The Essenes in Josephus

No better description of the Essenes exists than in the eighth chapter of the second book of *Wars* which deals in detail with this extraordinary group of men.

> For there are three philosophical sects among the Jews. The followers of the first of which are the Pharisees; of the second, the Sadducees; and the third sect which pretends to a severer discipline, are called Essens. These last are Jews by birth, and seem to have a greater affection for one another than the other sects have. These Essens reject pleasures as an evil, but esteem continence, and the conquest over our passions, to be virtue. They neglect wedlock, but choose out other persons children, while they are pliable, and fit for learning, and esteem them to be of their kindred, and form them according to their own manners. They do not absolutely deny the fitness of marriage, and the succession of mankind thereby continued; but they guard against the lascivious behavior of women, and are persuaded that none of them preserve their fidelity to one man.

These men are despisers of riches, and so very communicative as raises our admiration. Nor is there any one to be found among them who hath more than another; for it is a law among them, that those who come to them must let what they have be common to the whole order, – insomuch that among them all there is no appearance of poverty, or excess of riches, but every one's possessions are intermingled with every other's possessions; and so there is, as it were, one patrimony among all the brethren. They think that oil is a defilement; and if any one of them be anointed without his own approbation, it is wiped off his body; for they think to be sweaty is a good thing, as they do also to be clothed in white garments. They also have stewards appointed to take care of their common affairs, who every one of them have no separate business for any, but what is for the uses of them all.

They have no one certain city, but many of them dwell in every city; and if any of their sect come from other places, what they have lies open for them, just as if it were their own; and they go in to such as they never knew before, as if they had been ever so long acquainted with them. For which reason they carry nothing at all with them when they travel into remote parts, though still they take their weapons with them, for fear of thieves. Accordingly, there is, in every city where they live, one appointed particularly to take care of strangers, and to provide garments and other necessaries for them. But the habit and management of their bodies is such as children use who are in fear of their masters. Nor do they allow of the change of or of shoes till be first torn to pieces, or worn out by time. Nor do they either buy or sell any thing to one another; but every one of them gives what he hath to him that wanteth it, and receives from him again in lieu of it what may be convenient for himself; and although there be no requital made, they are fully allowed to take what they want of whomsoever they please.

And as for their piety towards God, it is very extraordinary; for before sun-rising they speak not a word about profane matters, but put up certain prayers which they have received from their forefathers, as if they made a supplication for its rising. After this every one of them are sent away by their curators, to exercise some of those arts wherein they are skilled, in which they labor with great diligence till the fifth hour. After which they assemble themselves together again into one place; and when they have clothed themselves in white veils, they then bathe their bodies in cold water. And after this purification is over, they every one meet together in an apartment of their own, into which it is not permitted to any of another sect to enter; while they go, after a pure manner, into the dining-room, as into a certain holy temple, and quietly set themselves down; upon which the baker lays them loaves in order; the cook also brings a single plate of one sort of food, and sets it before every one of them; but a priest says grace before meat; and it is unlawful for any one to taste of the food before grace be said. The same priest, when he hath dined, says grace again after meat; and when they begin, and when they end, they praise God, as he that bestows their food upon them; after which they lay aside their [white] garments, and betake themselves to their labors again till the evening; then they return home to supper, after the same manner; and if there be any strangers there, they sit down with them. Nor is there ever any clamor or disturbance to pollute their house, but they give every one leave to speak in their turn; which silence thus kept in their house appears to foreigners like some tremendous mystery; the cause of which is that perpetual sobriety they exercise, and the same settled measure of meat and drink that is allotted them, and that such as is abundantly sufficient for them.

And truly, as for other things, they do nothing but according to the injunctions of their curators; only these two things are done among them at everyone's own free-will which are to assist those that want it, and to show mercy; for they are permitted of their own accord to afford succor to such as deserve it, when they stand in need of it, and to bestow food on those that are in distress; but they cannot give any thing to their kindred without the curators. They dispense their anger after a just manner, and restrain their passion. They are eminent for fidelity, and are the ministers of peace; whatsoever they say also is firmer than an oath; but swearing is avoided by them, and they esteem it worse than perjury for they say that he who cannot be believed without [swearing by] God is already condemned. They also take great pains in studying the writings of the ancients, and choose out of them what is most for the advantage of their soul and body; and they inquire after such roots and medicinal stones as may cure their distempers.

But now if any one hath a mind to come over to their sect, he is not immediately admitted, but he is prescribed the same method of living which they use for a year, while he continues excluded'; and they give him also a small hatchet, and the fore-mentioned girdle, and the white garment. And when he hath given evidence, during that time, that he can observe their continence, he approaches nearer to their way of living, and is made a partaker of the waters of purification; yet is he not even now admitted to live with them; for after this demonstration of his fortitude, his temper is tried two more years; and if he appear to be worthy, they then admit him into their society. And before he is allowed to touch their common food, he is obliged to take tremendous oaths, that, in the first place, he will exercise piety towards God, and then that he will observe justice towards men, and that he will do no harm to any one, either of his own accord, or by the command of others; that he will always hate the wicked, and be assistant to the righteous; that he will ever show fidelity to all men, and especially to those in authority, because no one obtains the government without God's assistance; and that if he be in authority, he will at no time whatever abuse his authority, nor endeavor to outshine his subjects either in his garments, or any other finery; that he will be perpetually a lover of truth, and propose to himself to reprove those that tell lies; that he will keep his hands clear from theft, and his soul from unlawful gains; and that he will neither conceal any thing from those of his own sect, nor discover any of their doctrines to others, no, not though anyone should compel him so to do at the hazard of his life. Moreover, he swears to communicate their doctrines to no one any otherwise than as he received them himself; that he will abstain from robbery, and will equally preserve the Books belonging to their sect, and the names of the angels [or messengers]. These are the oaths by which they secure their proselytes to themselves.

But for those that are caught in any heinous sins, they cast them out of their society; and he who is thus separated from them does often die after a miserable manner; for as he is bound by the oath he hath taken, and by the customs he hath been engaged in, he is not at liberty to partake of that food that he meets with elsewhere, but is forced to eat grass, and to famish his body with hunger, till he perish; for which reason they receive many of them again when they are at their last gasp, out of compassion to them, as thinking the miseries they have endured till they came to the very brink of death to be a sufficient punishment for the sins they had been guilty of.

But in the judgments they exercise they are most accurate and just, nor do they pass sentence by the votes of a court that is fewer than a hundred. And as to what is once determined by that number, it is unalterable. What they most of all honor, after God himself, is the name of their legislator [Moses], whom if any one blaspheme he is punished capitally. They also think it a good thing to obey their elders, and the major part. Accordingly, if ten of them be sitting together, no one of them will speak while the other nine are against it. They also avoid spitting in the midst of them, or on the right side. Moreover, they are stricter than any other of the Jews in resting from their labors on the seventh day; for they not only get their food ready the day before, that they may not be obliged to kindle a fire on that day, but they will not remove any vessel out of its place, nor go to stool thereon. Nay, on other days they dig a small pit, a foot deep, with a paddle (which kind of hatchet is given them when they are first admitted among them); and covering themselves round with their garment, that they may not affront the Divine rays of light, they ease themselves into that pit, after which they put the earth that was dug out again into the pit; and even this they do only in the more lonely places which they choose out for this purpose; and although this easement of the body be natural, yet it is a rule with them to wash themselves after it, as if it were a defilement to them.

Now after the time of their preparatory trial is over, they are parted into four classes; and so far are the juniors inferior to the seniors, that if the seniors should be touched by the juniors, they must wash themselves, as if they had intermixed themselves with the company of a foreigner. They are long-lived also, insomuch that many of them live above a hundred years, by means of the simplicity of their diet; nay, as I think, by means of the regular course of life they observe also. They contemn the miseries of life, and are above pain, by the generosity of their mind. And as for death, if it will be for their glory, they esteem it better than living always; and indeed our war with the Romans gave abundant evidence what great souls they had in their trials, wherein, although they were tortured and distorted, burnt and torn to pieces, and went through all kinds of instruments of torment, that they might be forced either to blaspheme their legislator, or to eat what was forbidden them, yet could they not be made to do either of them, no, nor once to flatter their tormentors, or to shed a tear; but they smiled in their very pains, and laughed those to scorn who inflicted the torments upon them, and resigned up their souls with great alacrity, as expecting to receive them again.

For their doctrine is this: That bodies are corruptible, and that the matter they are made of is not permanent; but that the souls are immortal, and continue for ever; and that they come out of the most subtile air, and are united to their bodies as to prisons, into which they are drawn by a certain natural enticement; but that when they are set free from the bonds of the flesh, they then, as released from a long bondage, rejoice and mount upward. And this is like the opinions of the Greeks, that good souls have their habitations beyond the ocean, in a region that is neither oppressed with storms of rain or snow, or with intense heat, but that this place is such as is refreshed by the gentle breathing of a west wind, that is perpetually blowing from the ocean; while they allot to bad souls a dark and tempestuous den, full of never-ceasing punishments. And indeed the Greeks seem to me to have followed the same notion, when they allot the islands of the blessed to their brave men, whom they call heroes and demi-gods; and to the souls of the wicked, the region of the ungodly, in Hades, where their fables relate that certain persons, such as Sisyphus, and Tantalus, and Ixion, and Tityus, are punished; which is built on this first supposition, that souls are immortal; and thence are those exhortations to virtue and dehortations from wickedness collected; whereby good men are bettered in the conduct of their life by the hope they have of reward after their death; and whereby the vehement inclinations of bad men to vice are restrained, by the fear and expectation they are in, that although they should lie concealed in this life, they should suffer immortal punishment after their death. These are the Divine doctrines of the Essens about the soul which lay an unavoidable bait for such as have once had a taste of their philosophy.

There are also those among them who undertake to foretell things to come, by reading the holy Books, and using several sorts of purifications, and being perpetually conversant in the discourses of the prophets; and it is but seldom that they miss in their predictions. (*Wars* II 8:2-12)

This last sub-chapter is most interesting as it describes an offshoot of the Essenes whose members were allowed to marry, albeit under very strict rules.

Moreover, there is another order of Essens, who agree with the rest as to their way of living, and customs, and laws, but differ from them in the point of marriage, as thinking that by not marrying they cut off the principal part of human life which is the prospect of succession; nay, rather, that if all men should be of the same opinion, the whole race of mankind would fail. However, they try their spouses for three years; and if they find that they have their natural purgations thrice, as trials that they are likely to be fruitful, they then actually marry them. But they do not use to accompany with their wives when they are with child, as a demonstration that they do not many out of regard to pleasure, but for the sake of posterity. Now the women go into the baths with some of their garments on, as the men do with somewhat girded about them. And these are the customs of this order of Essens. (*Wars* II 8:13)

Philo on the Essenes

Philo also references the Essenic community.

But our lawgiver trained an innumerable body of his pupils to partake in those things, who are called Essenes, being, as I imagine, honoured with this appellation because of their exceeding holiness. And they dwell in many cities of Judaea, and in many villages, and in great and populous communities. (11.2) And this sect of them is not an hereditary of family connexion; for family ties are not spoken of with reference to acts voluntarily performed; but it is adopted because of their admiration for virtue and love of gentleness and humanity. (11.3) At all events, there are no children among the Essenes, no, nor any youths or persons only just entering upon manhood; since the dispositions of all such persons are unstable and liable to change, from the imperfections incident to their age, but they are all full-grown men, and even already declining towards old age, such as are no longer carried away by the impetuosity of their bodily passions, and are not under the influence of the appetites, but such as enjoy a genuine freedom, the only true and real liberty. (11.4) And a proof of this is to be found in their life of perfect freedom; no one among them ventures at all to acquire any property whatever of his own, neither house, nor slave, nor farm, nor flocks and herds, nor any thing of any sort which can be looked upon as the fountain or provision of riches; but they bring them together into the middle as a common stock, and enjoy one common general benefit from it all. (11.5) And they all dwell in the same place, making clubs, and societies, and combinations, and unions with one another, and doing every thing throughout their whole lives with reference to the general advantage; (11.6) but the different members of this body have different employments in which they occupy themselves, and labour without hesitation and without cessation, making no mention of either cold, or heat, or any changes of weather or temperature as an excuse for desisting from their tasks. But before the sun rises they betake themselves to their daily work, and they do not quit it till some time after it has set, when they return home rejoicing no less than those who have been exercising themselves in gymnastic contests; (11.7) for they imagine that whatever they devote themselves to as a practice is a sort of gymnastic exercise of more advantage to life, and more pleasant both to soul and body, and of more enduring benefit and equability, than mere athletic labours, inasmuch as such toil does not cease to be practised with delight when the age of vigour of body is passed; (11.8) for there are some of them who are devoted to the practice of agriculture, being skilful in such things as pertain to the sowing and cultivation of lands; others again are shepherds, or cowherds, and experienced in the management of every kind of animal; some are cunning in what relates to swarms of bees; (11.9) others again are artisans and handicraftsmen, in order to guard against suffering from the want of anything of which there is at times an actual need; and these men omit and delay nothing which is requisite for the innocent supply of the necessaries of life. (11.10) Accordingly, each of these men, who differ so widely in their respective employments, when they have received their wages give them up to one person who is appointed as the universal steward and general manager; and he, when he has received the money, immediately goes and purchases what is necessary and furnishes them with food in abundance, and all other things of which the life of mankind stands in need. (11.11) And those who live together and eat at the same table are day after day contented with the same things, being lovers of frugality and moderation, and averse to all sumptuousness and extravagance as a disease of both mind and body. (11.12) And not only are their tables in common but also their dress; for in the winter there are thick cloaks found, and in the summer light cheap mantles, so that whoever wants one is at liberty without restraint to go and take whichever kind he chooses; since what belongs to one belongs to all, and on the other hand whatever belongs to the whole body belongs to each individual. (11.13) And again, if any one of them is sick he is cured from the common resources, being attended to by the general care and anxiety of the whole body. Accordingly the old men, even if they happen to be childless, as if they were not only the fathers of many children but were even also particularly happy in an affectionate offspring, are accustomed to end their lives in a most happy and prosperous and carefully attended old age, being looked upon by such a number of people as worthy of so much honour and provident regard that they think themselves bound to care for them even more from inclination than from any tie of natural affection. (11.14) Again, perceiving with more than ordinary acuteness and accuracy, what is alone or at least above all other things calculated to dissolve such associations, they repudiate marriage; and at the same time they practise continence in an eminent degree; for no one of the Essenes ever marries a wife, because woman is a selfish creature and one addicted to jealousy in an immoderate degree, and terribly calculated to agitate and overturn the natural inclinations of a man, and to mislead him by her continual tricks; (11.15) for as she is always studying deceitful speeches and all other kinds of hypocrisy, like an actress on the stage, when she is alluring the eyes and ears of her husband, she proceeds to cajole his predominant mind after the servants have been deceived. (11.16) And again, if there are children she becomes full of pride and all kinds of license in her speech, and all the obscure sayings which she previously meditated in irony in a disguised manner she now begins to utter with audacious confidence; and becoming utterly shameless she proceeds to acts of violence, and does numbers of actions of which every one is hostile to such associations; (11.17) for the man who is bound under the influence of the charms of a woman, or of children, by the necessary ties of nature, being overwhelmed by the impulses of affection, is no longer the same person towards others, but is entirely changed, having, without being aware of it, become a slave instead of a free man. (11.18) This now is the enviable system of life of these Essenes, so that not only private individuals but even mighty kings, admiring the men, venerate their sect, and increase their dignity and majesty in a still higher degree by their approbation and by the honours which they confer on them. (*Hypothetica* 11:1-18 from Eusebius)

Philo comments on the Essenes in his *Quod omnis probus liber.*

Moreover Palestine and Syria too are not barren of exemplary wisdom and virtue which countries no slight portion of that most populous nation of the Jews inhabits. There is a portion of those people called Essenes, in number something more than four thousand in my opinion, who derive their name from their piety, though not according to any accurate form of the Grecian dialect, because they are above all men devoted to the service of God, not sacrificing living animals, but studying rather to preserve their own minds in a state of holiness and purity. (76) These men, in the first place, live in villages, avoiding all cities on account of the habitual lawlessness of those who inhabit them, well knowing that such a moral disease is contracted from associations with wicked men, just as a real disease might be from an impure atmosphere, and that this would stamp an incurable evil on their souls. Of these men, some cultivating the earth, and others devoting themselves to those arts which are the result of peace, benefit both themselves and all those who come in contact with them, not storing up treasures of silver and of gold, nor acquiring vast sections of the earth out of a desire for ample revenues, but providing all things which are requisite for the natural purposes of life; (77) for they alone of almost all men having been originally poor and destitute, and that too rather from their own habits and ways of life than from any real deficiency of good fortune, are nevertheless accounted very rich, judging contentment and frugality to be great abundance, as in truth they are. (78) Among those men you will find no makers of arrows, or javelins, or swords, or helmets, or breastplates, or shields; no makers of arms or of military engines; no one, in short, attending to any employment whatever connected with war, or even to any of those occupations even in peace which are easily perverted to wicked purposes; for they are utterly ignorant of all traffic, and of all commercial dealings, and of all navigation, but they repudiate and keep aloof from everything which can possibly afford any inducement to covetousness; (79) and there is not a single slave among them, but they are all free, aiding one another with a reciprocal interchange of good offices; and they condemn masters, not only as unjust, inasmuch as they corrupt the very princepal of equality, but likewise as impious, because they destroy the ordinances of nature which generated them all equally, and brought them up like a mother, as if they were all legitimate brethren, not in name only, but in reality and truth. But in their view this natural relationship of all men to one another has been thrown into disorder by designing covetousness, continually wishing to surpass others in good fortune, and which has therefore engendered alienation instead of affection, and hatred instead of friendship; (80) and leaving the logical part of philosophy, as in no respect necessary for the acquisition of virtue, to the word-catchers, and the natural part, as being too sublime for human nature to master, to those who love to converse about high objects (except indeed so far as such a study takes in the contemplation of the existence of God and of the creation of the universe), they devote all their attention to the moral part of philosophy, using as instructors the laws of their country which it would have been impossible for the human mind to devise without divine inspiration. (81) Now these laws they are taught at other times, indeed, but most especially on the seventh day, for the seventh day is accounted sacred, on which they abstain from all other employments, and frequent the sacred places which are called synagogues, and there they sit according to their age in classes, the younger sitting under the elder, and listening with eager attention in becoming order. (82) Then one, indeed, takes up the holy volume and reads it, and another of the men of the greatest experience comes forward and explains what is not very intelligible, for a great many precepts are delivered in enigmatical modes of expression, and allegorically, as the old fashion was; (83) and thus the people are taught piety, and holiness, and justice, and economy, and the science of regulating the state, and the knowledge of such things as are naturally good, or bad, or indifferent, and to choose what is right and to avoid what is wrong, using a threefold variety of definitions, and rules, and criteria, namely, the love of God, and the love of virtue, and the love of mankind. (84) Accordingly, the sacred volumes present an infinite number of instances of the disposition devoted to the love of God, and of a continued and uninterrupted purity throughout the whole of life, of a careful avoidance of oaths and of falsehood, and of a strict adherence to the princepal of looking on the Deity as the cause of everything which is good and of nothing which is evil. They also furnish us with many proofs of a love of virtue, such as abstinence from all covetousness of money, from ambition, from indulgence in pleasures, temperance, endurance, and also moderation, simplicity, good temper, the absence of pride, obedience to the laws, steadiness, and everything of that kind; and, lastly, they bring forward as proofs of the love of mankind, goodwill, equality beyond all power of description, and fellowship, about which it is not unreasonable to say a few words. (85) In the first place, then, there is no one who has a house so absolutely his own private property, that it does not in some sense also belong to every one: for besides that they all dwell together in companies, the house is open to all those of the same notions, who come to them from other quarters; (86) then there is one magazine among them all; their expenses are all in common; their garments belong to them all in common; their food is common, since they all eat in messes; for there is no other people among which you can find a common use of the same house, a common adoption of one mode of living, and a common use of the same table more thoroughly established in fact than among this tribe: and is not this very natural? For whatever they, after having been working during the day, receive for their wages, that they do not retain as their own, but bring it into the common stock, and give any advantage that is to be derived from it to all who desire to avail themselves of it; (87) and those who are sick are not neglected because they are unable to contribute to the common stock, inasmuch as the tribe have in their public stock a means of supplying their necessities and aiding their weakness, so that from their ample means they support them liberally and abundantly; and they cherish respect for their elders, and honour them and care for them, just as parents are honoured and cared for by their lawful children: being supported by them in all abundance both by their personal exertions, and by innumerable contrivances. (Philo *Quod omnis probus liber* 75-87)

Pliny the Elder and the Essenes

Pliny the Elder was a Roman writer and former Roman army officer who in his later years wrote extensively about natural history. He was born in A.D. 23 and died in A.D. 79 in the eruption of Mount Vesuvius. Pliny mentions the Essenes in *Natural History*.

To the west (of the Dead Sea) the Essenes have put the necessary distance between themselves and the insalubrious shore. They are a people unique of its kind and admirable beyond all others in the whole world; without women and renouncing love entirely, without money and having for company only palm trees. Owing to the throng of newcomers, this people is daily reborn in equal number; indeed, those whom, wearied by the fluctuations of fortune, life leads to adopt their customs, stream in in great numbers. Thus, unbeleivable though this may seem, for thousands of centuries a people has existed which is eternal yet into which no one is born: so fruitful for them is the repentance which others feel for their past lives! (Pliny *Natural History*)

In modern times, this quote has been taken to mean that the Essenes formerly populated the archaeological site at Qumran, which is large enough to hold a great many people and is close to the Dead Sea. The location of Qumran is also nearby to the caves where the Dead Sea Scrolls were found. Many have postulated a connection between the hiding of these ancient scrolls, the Essenes, and the Jewish revolt of A.D. 66; all of these theories are controversial. The Essenes had their own writings but nothing specifically linked to the sect have been identified among the Dead Sea Scrolls.

Was Jesus an Essene?

Jesus embraced parts of the Essenic philosophy but did he take the vows and join the Essenic order at some point in his life? Looking strictly at Jesus' actions in the Gospels, he probably did not. At the very least, if Jesus did live with the Essenes for a time, he left the movement after his baptism by John the Baptist and the starting of his own Ministry. Several reasons justify this conclusion.

As a true Essene, Jesus would not have been as confrontational as he was toward the Second Temple High Priesthood and the Romans; aggression and conflict were were generally antithetical to the Essenic way of life. Also, a core Essenic belief was that no man came into authority over other men without the blessing of God. By this reasoning, it follows that the Romans–and the priests–came into their power because it served some unknowable divine purpose. Opposing Roman power would be like opposing God himself.

The Essenes would also look with disfavor upon the working of miracles. Fatalists in the extreme, the Essenes believed that all people must bear their physical burdens with stoicism. Physical and mental afflictions were God-given and served a divine purpose–as awful and debilitating as those afflictions might be. Jesus, however, healed the sick frequently and was not apologetic about doing so.

The Essenes were repulsed by ritual animal sacrifice which was central to Temple-based Judaism. For this reason, the Essenes never frequented the Second Temple. In contrast to this, Jesus was not shy about preaching in the Second Temple–where the smell of freshly slaughtered and burnt animal flesh had to be ever-present — and at times overwhelming.

Another argument against Jesus being an Essene was that he actively preached to the masses and sought out converts. The Essenic community was closed to all but other members, initiates, and their stewards. A three-year period of initiation was required before a new member was accepted. The Essenes only rarely sought out members.

The Nazorites

At this point, the Nazorites should be mentioned. The Nazorites were a group of ascetics that had their roots in the times of Moses, and are described in the Book of Numbers in the Old Testament. The Nazorites took strict vows and followed rigorous rituals, but only for a set period of time–usually at least three months. In effect, every male Jew could become an ascetic Nazorite and enjoy the benefits of such, but also be safe in knowledge that the discipline and self-denial was only temporary. Usually, the individual shaved his head and agreed to follow certain laws and perform certain sacrifices.

6:1 And Jehovah spake unto Moses, saying,
6:2 Speak unto the children of Israel, and say unto them, When either man or woman shall make a special vow, the vow of a Nazirite, to separate himself unto Jehovah,
6:3 he shall separate himself from wine and strong drink; he shall drink no vinegar of wine, or vinegar of strong drink, neither shall he drink any juice of grapes, nor eat fresh grapes or dried.
6:4 All the days of his separation shall he eat nothing that is made of the grape-vine, from the kernels even to the husk.
6:5 All the days of his vow of separation there shall no razor come upon his head: until the days be fulfilled, in which he separateth himself unto Jehovah, he shall be holy; he shall let the locks of the hair of his head grow long.
6:6 All the days that he separateth himself unto Jehovah he shall not come near to a dead body.
6:7 He shall not make himself unclean for his father, or for his mother, for his brother, or for his sister, when they die; because his separation unto God is upon his head. 6:8 All the days of his separation he is holy unto Jehovah.
6:9 And if any man die very suddenly beside him, and he defile the head of his separation; then he shall shave his head in the day of his cleansing, on the seventh day shall he shave it.
6:10 And on the eighth day he shall bring two turtle-doves, or two young pigeons, to the priest, to the door of the tent of meeting:

6:11 and the priest shall offer one for a sin-offering, and the other for a burnt-offering, and make atonement for him, for that he sinned by reason of the dead, and shall hallow his head that same day.

6:12 And he shall separate unto Jehovah the days of his separation, and shall bring a he-lamb a year old for a trespass-offering; but the former days shall be void, because his separation was defiled.

6:13 And this is the law of the Nazirite, when the days of his separation are fulfilled: he shall be brought unto the door of the tent of meeting:

6:14 and he shall offer his oblation unto Jehovah, one he-lamb a year old without blemish for a burnt-offering, and one ewe-lamb a year old without blemish for a sin-offering, and one ram without blemish for peace-offerings,

6:15 and a basket of unleavened bread, cakes of fine flour mingled with oil, and unleavened wafers anointed with oil, and their meal-offering, and their drink-offerings.

6:16 And the priest shall present them before Jehovah, and shall offer his sin-offering, and his burnt-offering:

6:17 and he shall offer the ram for a sacrifice of peace-offerings unto Jehovah, with the basket of unleavened bread: the priest shall offer also the meal-offering thereof, and the drink-offering thereof.

6:18 And the Nazirite shall shave the head of his separation at the door of the tent of meeting, and shall take the hair of the head of his separation, and put it on the fire which is under the sacrifice of peace-offerings.

6:19 And the priest shall take the boiled shoulder of the ram, and one unleavened cake out of the basket, and one unleavened wafer, and shall put them upon the hands of the Nazirite, after he hath shaven *the head of* his separation;

6:20 and the priest shall wave them for a wave-offering before Jehovah; this is holy for the priest, together with the wave-breast and heave-thigh: and after that the Nazirite may drink wine.

6:21 This is the law of the Nazirite who voweth, *and of* his oblation unto Jehovah for his separation, besides that which he is able to get: according to his vow which he voweth, so he must do after the law of his separation. (Nm)

Some debate has arisen that instead of references to Jesus the Nazareth, the proper term should be Jesus the Nazorite. But while Jesus certainly was an ascetic in many facets of his life, he drank wine freely–indeed, Jesus' own communion ceremony was based on wine. That is not to say that Jesus did not take the Nazorite vows upon occasion in his religious life prior to his baptism by John the Baptist.

But Jesus cannot be fitted into any of the popular sub-groups of Judaism extant in the first century A.D. as we understand them to be. Jesus' teachings borrow from all three of the major sects, though most heavily from the Essenic philosophy. The zealot philosophy of Judas the Galilean probably had some influence on Jesus, but to what degree is speculative.

Chapter 10   Unrest in Judea

a certain Galilean, whose name was Judas, prevailed with his
countrymen to revolt, and said they were cowards if they would endure
to pay a tax to the Romans (*Wars* II 8:1)

Under the Romans in the early first century A.D., unrest in Judea
was a constant problem. Insurrections would flare up frequently
and for any reason. Fanning the flames, the religion of Judaism
predicted the coming of a unique type of revolutionary leader.
The Old Testament prophets called this man the Messiah, or
"anointed one." Most Jews thought that this leader–if he came–
would lead them to independence from the hated Romans.

The Messiah

The concept of the Messiah was one of the most resonant
ancient Jewish religious and cultural beliefs, and some Jews
believe in his eventual coming even to this day. Details about the
Messiah can be found laced throughout many Books of the Old
Testament. According to these writings, the Messiah would be a
philosopher-king in the truest sense of the word. His ultimate
mission would be to establish God's kingdom on earth.

The earliest reference to the Messiah is found in the Torah–the
first five Books of the Old Testament that were written by Moses
himself.

18: I will raise them up a Prophet from among their brethren, like unto
thee, and will put my words in his mouth; and he shall speak unto them
all that I shall command him.

19: And it shall come to pass, that whosoever will not hearken unto my words which he shall speak in my name, I will require it of him. (KJV Deut 18)

And from the Book of the Psalms of David.

Yea, all the kings shall fall down before him: all nations shall serve him. For he shall deliver the needy when he crieth; the poor also, and him that hath no helper... His name shall endure forever, his name shall be continued as long as the sun, and men shall be blessed in him, all nations shall call him blessed" (KJV Psalms 72:11-12, 17).

Writing 700 years before the times of Jesus, the prophet Isaiah also envisioned a god-like warrior-king arising out of the House of David. Israel's enemies would be destroyed as the Messiah smote the wicked and lifted up the meek and downtrodden.

Therefore the Lord Himself shall give you a sign; Behold, a Virgin shall conceive, and bear a Son, and shall call his name Immanuel, (KJV Isaiah 7:14)

For unto us a child is born, unto us a son is given: and the government shall be upon his shoulder: and his name shall be called Wonderful, Counseller, The mighty God, The everlasting Father, The Prince of Peace.
Of the increase of his government and peace there shall be no end, upon the throne of David, and upon his kingdom, to order it, and to establish it with judgment and with justice from henceforth even for ever. The zeal of the LORD of hosts will perform this. (KJV Isaiah 9:6-7)

The prophet Isaiah also predicted the deeds and destiny of the Messiah.

Then the eyes of the blind shall be opened, and the ears of the deaf shall be unstopped. Then shall the lame man leap as an hart, and the tongue of the dumb sing: for in the wilderness shall waters break out, and streams in the desert ..(KJV Isaiah 35:5-6)

And he said, It is a light thing that thou shouldest be My servant to raise up the tribes of Jacob, and to restore the preserved of Israel: I will also give Thee for a light to the Gentiles, that Thou mayest be My salvation unto the end of the earth (KJV Isaiah 49:6).

A lengthy section from Isaiah provides a virtual template for the life of Jesus to come. Many of these phrases and allusions are found echoed throughout the New Testament.

Who has believed our report? And to whom has the arm of the LORD been revealed? For He shall grow up before Him as a tender plant, And as a root out of dry ground. He has no form or comeliness; And when we see Him, There is no beauty that we should desire Him. He is despised and rejected by men, A Man of sorrows and acquainted with grief. And we hid, as it were, our faces from Him; He was despised, and we did not esteem Him. Surely He has borne our griefs And carried our sorrows; Yet we esteemed Him stricken, Smitten by God, and afflicted. But He was wounded for our transgressions, He was bruised for our iniquities; The chastisement for our peace was upon Him, And by His stripes we are healed. All we like sheep have gone astray; We have turned, every one, to his own way; And the LORD has laid on Him the iniquity of us all. He was oppressed and He was afflicted, Yet He opened not His mouth; He was led as a lamb to the slaughter, And as a sheep before its shearers is silent, So He opened not His mouth. He was taken from prison and from judgment, And who will declare His generation? For He was cut off from the land of the living; For the transgressions of My people He was stricken. And they made His grave with the wicked; But with the rich at His death, Because He had done no violence, Nor was any deceit in His mouth. Yet it pleased the LORD to bruise Him; He has put Him to grief. When You make His soul an offering for sin, He shall see His seed, He shall prolong His days, And the pleasure of the LORD shall prosper in His hand. He shall see the labor of His soul, and be satisfied. By His knowledge My righteous Servant shall justify many, For He shall bear their iniquities. Therefore I will divide Him a portion with the great, And He shall divide the spoil with the strong, Because He poured out His soul unto death, And He was numbered with the transgressors, And He bore the sin of many, And made intercession for the transgressors" (Isaiah 53:1-12).

These powerful prophecies in the Old Testament provided a potent fuel for Jewish demagogues throughout the subsequent generations. Frequently, bold men with energy and a desire for innovation and power claimed the name of Messiah. Their promise to the Jews was freedom from whatever subjugating nation happened to be in power at that particular time. If the Jewish nation happened to be enjoying a period of independence, then the God-given mission of the Messiah would be the overthrow a bad Jewish king, perhaps, or a corrupt High Priest. When the Caesars dominated the Jewish East, they and their puppet rulers and administrators automatically became targets.

The Jerusalem High Priesthood recognized the susceptibility of the common Jews to fall prey to such religious charlatans, and so strict laws were made: all those who claimed to be the Messiah were to be stoned to death. But false Messiahs found fertile grounds in the countryside where Temple oversight was slight and so many Jews were led astray. The most charismatic of them led their followers to destruction as well. Jesus of Nazareth even warned his followers against them.

> .. there shall arise false Christs and false prophets, and shall show signs and wonders, that they may lead astray, if possible, the elect. (Mk 13:21-22)

Many of these bold pretenders were, in fact, stoned. If in Jerusalem, traditionally they were thrown to their deaths off the southeast corner of the Temple.

Roman Occupation

Roman General Pompey in 62 B.C. correctly assumed that the Jews would fight to the death if their religion was compromised by Roman edict. For that reason, Pompey left the High Priesthood hierarchy and Temple ritual intact. The great riches that were laid up within the Jerusalem Temple, called the Corban, Pompey also did not touch. For most of the next 70 years the Jewish East was ruled through Roman proxy by either Herod the Great, his father, or his sons. In that time, Judaism was allowed to be practiced as it had been for 2,000 years.

Roman Emperor Octavian (Augustus) released a proclamation concerning the Jews early in his reign, around 29 B.C.

> Caesar Augustus, high priest and tribune of the people, ordains thus: Since the nation of the Jews hath been found grateful to the Roman people, not only at this time, but in time past also, and chiefly Hyrcanus the high priest, under my father Caesar the emperor, it seemed good to

me and my counselors, according to the sentence and oath of the people of Rome, that the Jews have liberty to make use of their own customs, according to the law of their forefathers, as they made use of them under Hyrcanus the high priest of the Almighty God; and that their sacred money be not touched, but be sent to Jerusalem, and that it be committed to the care of the receivers at Jerusalem; and that they be not obliged to go before any judge on the sabbath day, nor on the day of the preparation to it, after the ninth hour. (*Antiq* XVI 6:2)

This accommodating attitude towards the Jews was extraordinary in itself and an acknowledgment by the Romans of the high level of culture the Jews possessed. But despite this apparent magnanimity, most Jews wanted a return to rule by the Royal Asamonean family.

Insurrection after Herod

As Herod the Great neared death after 33 years of oppressive rule, men of innovation saw opportunity. Many organized their own small armies and prepared to establish local kingdoms after Herod was finally gone. In fact, when Herod did die in late 4 B.C., widespread rebellion occurred. The president of Syria, Roman General Quintilius Varus, was forced to bring down his legions from the north to battle the rebel Jews. Eventually, the country was settled, but it took an entire year and resulted in the deaths of tens of thousands of insurrectionists.

For the next 75 years, until the destruction of the Second Temple in A.D. 70, there were other sporadic outbreaks of violence. At the center of many were charismatic men who bore striking resemblances to the predicted Old Testament figure of the Messiah. The religious movements generated by these crypto-Messiahs were usually thwarted by the Jerusalem High Priesthood and the priests' own small army of Temple guards. Sometimes the Jewish people themselves would take matters into their own hands and run off an obvious charlatan. If a seditious, quasi-religious movement became large and threatening enough, the priesthood would petition the Roman army for relief–which would usually be provided with little questioning.

King Archelaus

In 4 B.C., after Herod's death, many Jews openly and violently rebelled against Rome–something they never dared to do when Herod was alive. Archelaus, Herod the Great's son and heir to Judea and Samaria, was faced with a difficult situation. Initially, Judea enjoyed several months of peace when Herod's death was ostensibly mourned and during which Archelaus assumed control of his father's army. During the Passover celebration of 3 B.C., however, along with the usual peaceful supplicants came thousands of Jews from the countryside intent on revolution. Only a year before, two Temple scholars, Judas and Matthias, and several of their followers, had been burned alive by Herod the Great (*Antiq* XVII 6:4; chapter 1) for their sedition. They had become martyrs for the cause of Jewish independence.

Archelaus organized an action to confront the rebels. In the course of that civil battle, Archelaus' men killed 3,000 allegedly seditious Jews who had been encamped around Jerusalem.

> Now, upon the approach of that feast of unleavened bread which the law of their fathers had appointed for the Jews at this time which feast is called the Passover and is a memorial of their deliverance out of Egypt, when they offer sacrifices with great alacrity; and when they are required to slay more sacrifices in number than at any other festival; and when an innumerable multitude came thither out of the country, nay, from beyond its limits also, in order to worship God, the seditious lamented Judas and Matthias, those teachers of the laws, and kept together in the temple, and had plenty of food, because these seditious persons were not ashamed to beg it. And as Archelaus was afraid lest some terrible thing should spring up by means of these men's madness, he sent a regiment of armed men, and with them a captain of a thousand, to suppress the violent efforts of the seditious before the whole multitude should be infected with the like madness; and gave them this charge, that if they found any much more openly seditious than others, and more busy in tumultuous practices, they should bring them to him. (*Antiq* XVII 9:3)

Early First Century A.D. Roman East

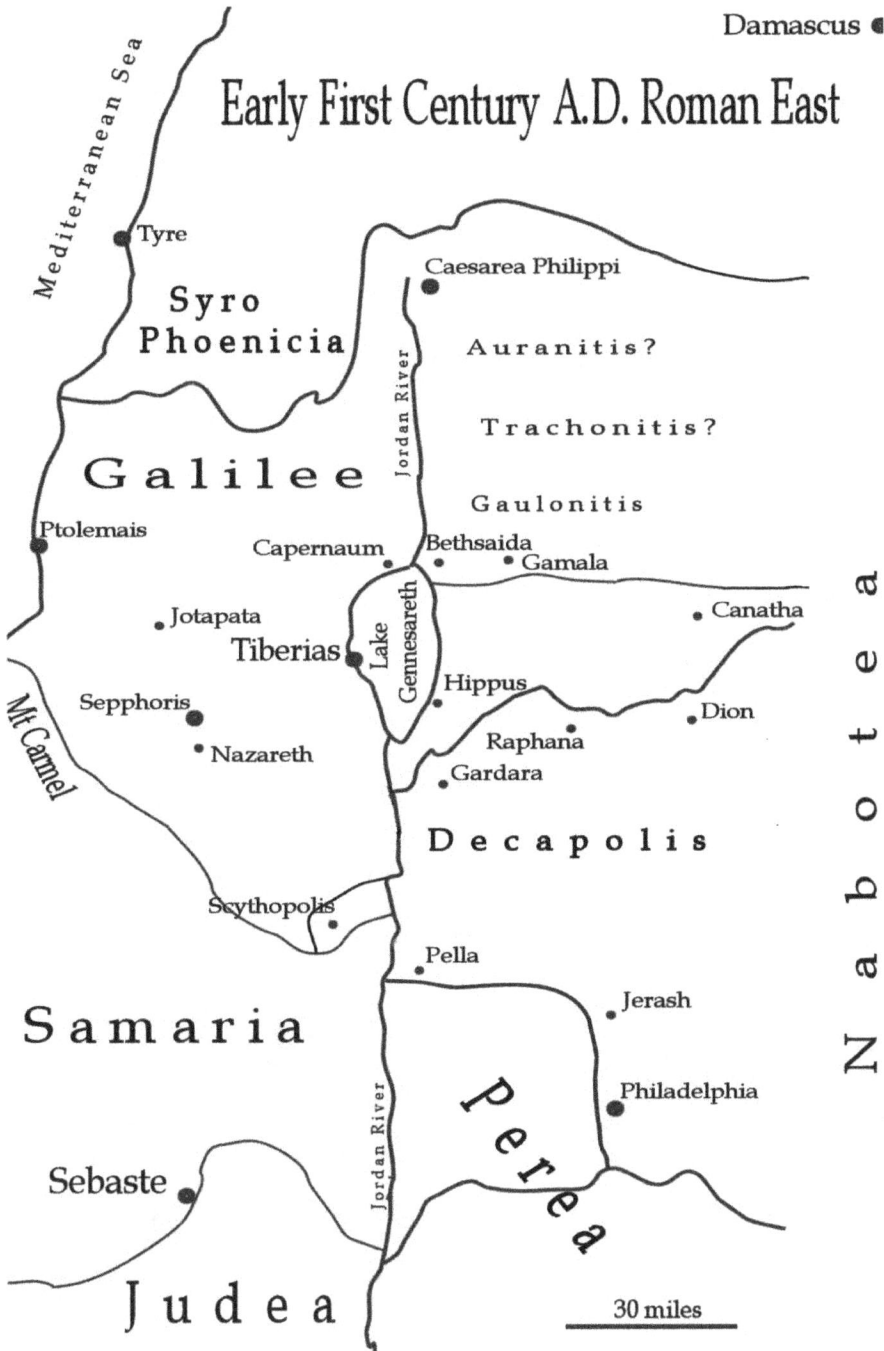

Damascus

Mediterranean Sea

Tyre

Caesarea Philippi

Syro Phoenicia

Auranitis?

Jordan River

Trachonitis?

Gaulonitis

Galilee

Ptolemais

Capernaum Bethsaida Gamala

Jotapata

Canatha

Tiberias Lake Gennesareth

Sepphoris

Hippus

Dion

Nazareth

Raphana

Gardara

Decapolis

Mt Carmel

Scythopolis

Pella

Jerash

Samaria

Perea

Philadelphia

Jordan River

N a b o t e a

Sebaste

Judea

30 miles

Archelaus continued to fight vigorously against the insurgents even before Emperor Augustus had officially confirmed him as king. In that regard, questions had been raised about the legality of Herod's last testament, for in his final year, Herod had changed his will four separate times—the last one being sealed only days before his death.

So even as the East erupted in violence, Emperor Augustus called Archelaus and other members of Herod's family to Rome in the spring of 3 B.C. to determine the final disposition of Herod's kingdom. Augustus even welcomed a group of important Jewish leaders to speak before him on the matter. These principal men of Judea wanted a Roman prefect to rule over them and not someone from the family of Herod the Great —boldly stating as such before Augustus.

> when he (Herod the Great) took the kingdom, it was in an extraordinary flourishing condition, he had filled the nation with the utmost degree of poverty; (*Antiq* XVII 11:2)

While Archelaus was away in Rome, the Judean garrison under General Sabinus was attacked by Jerusalem rebels. The Roman forces won. In their zeal they burned a large part of the Second Temple and absconded with the Corban. Sabinus himself stole 400 talents from the Temple treasury.

Archelaus was confirmed in principle by Emperor Augustus, but he returned to Judea in late 3 B.C. to find not accolades from the Jews but continued insurrection.

> Now at this time there were ten thousand other disorders in Judea which were like tumults, because a great number put themselves into a warlike posture, either out of hopes of gain to themselves, or out of enmity to the Jews. In particular, two thousand of Herod's old soldiers, who had been already disbanded, got together in Judea itself, and fought against the king's troops, (*Antiq* XVII 10:4)

> And thus did a great and wild fury spread itself over the nation, because they had no king to keep the multitude in good order, and because those foreigners who came to reduce the seditious to sobriety did, on the

contrary, set them more in a flame, because of the injuries they offered them, and the avaricious management of their affairs. (*Antiq* XVII 10:6)

Thousands of people were killed in these actions. Josephus estimates that 2,000 more were crucified after capture by General Varus.

> Upon this, Varus sent a part of his army into the country, to seek out those that had been the authors of the revolt; and when they were discovered, he punished some of them that were most guilty, and some he dismissed: now the number of those that were crucified on this account were two thousand. (*Antiq* XVII 10:10)

Interestingly, Varus was the same Roman General who 12 years later would be responsible for one of the empire's worst military defeats. The disaster occurred in the northern province of Germany in A.D. 9. The principal battle took place in the Teutoburg forest. In that battle, three Roman legions–15,000 men plus auxiliaries–were destroyed (Dio 56 18-23). Varus' beheaded and burned body was recovered in the aftermath of the carnage.

Surprisingly, some of Herod the Great's own relatives led uprisings against Archelaus and Rome in hope of gaining their own kingdoms. All eventually were defeated. Roman historian Tacitus writes that the major rebel leader was a man named Simon, but documents little else about the Jewish rebellion of 3 B.C.

> On Herod's death, one Simon, without waiting for the approbation of the Emperor, usurped the title of king. (Tacitus *Histories* 5:9)

Meanwhile, Emperor Augustus considered the disposition of Herod the Great's kingdom for several months after sending the petitioning sons of Herod back to the East. Archelaus assumed he would be confirmed, and went to work helping Generals Varus and Sabinus quell the myriad of seditious disturbances in the country.

Archelaus' assumption was proven correct, and after a period of time Augustus made public his decision to accept the last will of Herod. Archelaus would keep power in Judea and Samaria, with the remaining northern half of Herod the Great's kingdom being split apart between two other sons of Herod–Herod Antipas and Herod Philip.

King Archelaus had a rough time in Jerusalem and Judea despite the successful campaign against the insurrectionists. Over the years of his reign, Archelaus was forced to resort to the same heavy-handedness for which his father had been famous in order to keep the peace. Over the years of his reign, Archelaus alienated his two brother rulers as well. Eventually, both Tetrarchs Herod Antipas and Herod Philip petitioned to Augustus to have him removed. In A.D. 6, Augustus decided to remove Archelaus from power and banish him to Gaul. In Archelaus' place, Augustus appointed a Roman of the equestrian order. The kingdoms of Herod Antipas and Herod Philip were unaffected.

Judas the Galilean

The most dedicated and organized of these seditious Jews that arose after the death of Herod the Great were called zealots. The zealots had a long and violent history in the first century A.D. Jewish East. Eventually they swayed enough of the population over to their way of thinking to ignite a nationwide revolt in A.D. 66. The first "official" zealot was a man named Judas. He formed a separate religious sect of Judaism for the express purpose of opposing the enrollment instituted by Augustus after the removal of Archelaus.

Judas, from Galilee, was outwardly incensed over this Roman accounting, knowing that it would inevitably lead to further Roman assimilation of the Jewish nation. Judas determined that the best way to incite a revolt was through religion, and so he started up a separate Jewish sect. A central tenet would be the refusal to pay Roman taxes. The Jews, Judas argued, should pay taxes only to God. Judas knew that the Jews would not hesitate to die for their religious beliefs–thus, if he could get enough Jews to believe in his interpretation of the scripture, a revolt against Rome would be assured.

Caesarea

Samaria

Pella

Sebaste

Jerash

Decapolis

Jordan River

Jabbok R.

Philadelphia

Jericho

Jerusalem

Bethany-by-the-Jordan

Qumran

Herodium

Madaba

Bethlehem

Ashkelon

Judea

Idumea

Lake Asphaltitis

Perea

Macherus

Arnon R.

Masada

Nabotea

Mediterranean Sea

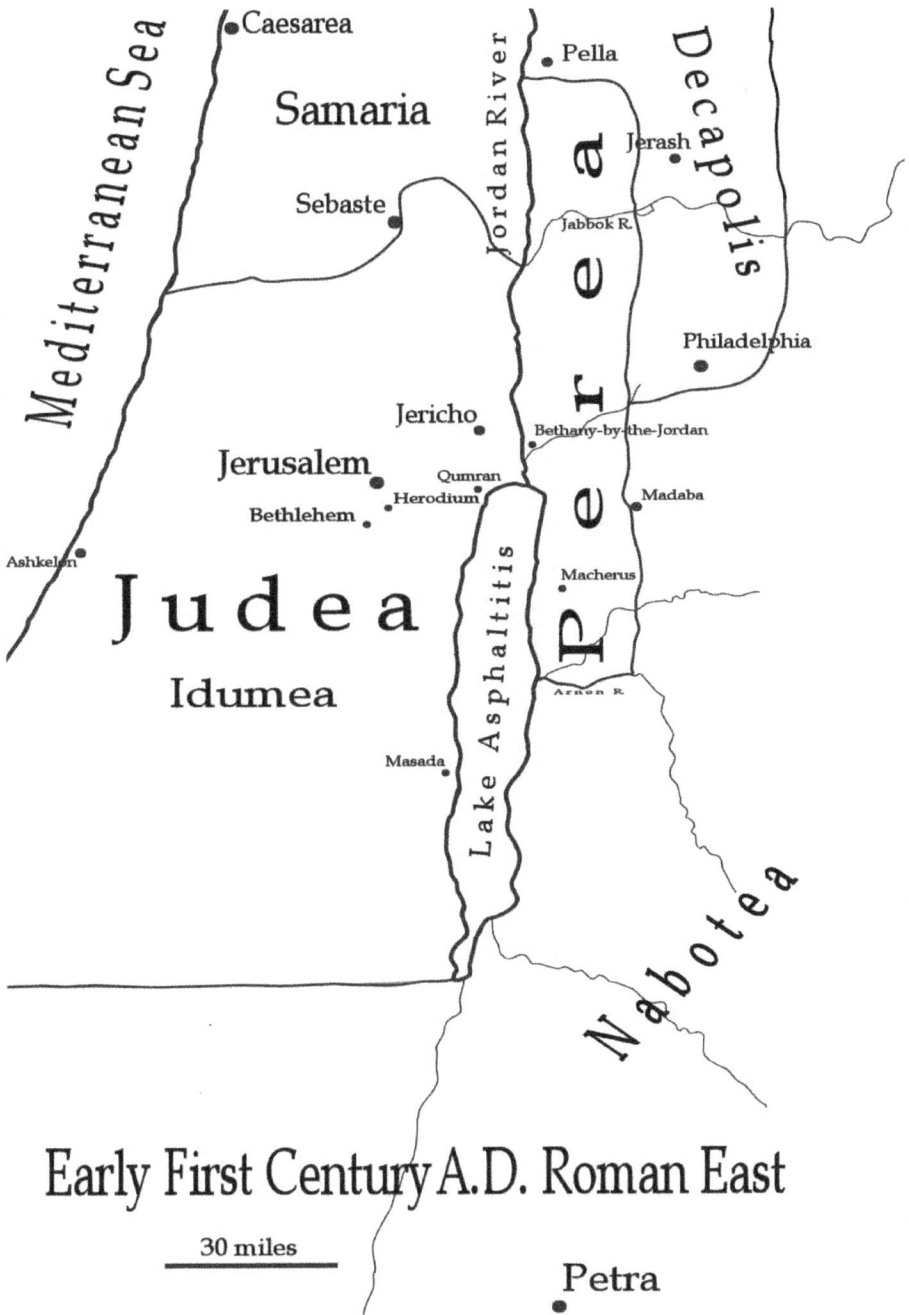

Early First Century A.D. Roman East

30 miles

Petra

Judas' "new" religious philosophy was in marked contrast to that of the Pharisees, the Sadducees, and the Essenes, the three main sects of the Jews at that time. These sects all held that God approved of any men in a position of power–even if those men were clearly ungodly. For this reason, Roman rule was accepted and Roman taxes paid.

Judas the Galilean is referred to in the Book of Acts of the Apostles by Gamaliel, a Sanhedrin elder and intellectual. In the New Testament passage, Gamaliel states that Judas was killed for his beliefs.

> After this man rose up Judas of Galilee in the days of the enrolment, and drew away some of the people after him: he also perished; and all, as many as obeyed him, were scattered abroad. (Acts 5:37)

In *Wars*, Josephus also mentions Judas the Galilean.

> And now Archelaus's part of Judea was reduced into a province, and Coponius, one of the equestrian order among the Romans, was sent as a procurator, having the power of [life and] death put into his hands by Caesar. Under his administration it was that a certain Galilean, whose name was Judas, prevailed with his countrymen to revolt, and said they were cowards if they would endure to pay a tax to the Romans and would after God submit to mortal men as their lords. This man was a teacher of a peculiar sect of his own, and was not at all like the rest of those their leaders. (*Wars* II 8:1)

Josephus refers to Judas at different times as being from Galilee or the city of Gamala in the Gaulonitis–the same man in either case. Josephus also asserts that a large criminal element operated under the cover of Judas' zealotry. The worst of these unlawful zealots would freely rob their fellow Jews, rationalizing that their victims' wealth was fair game because it was gained through collaboration with the hated Romans.

> Yet was there one Judas, a Gaulonite, of a city whose name was Gamala, who, taking with him Sadduc, a Pharisee, became zealous to draw them to a revolt, who both said that this taxation was no better than an introduction to slavery, and exhorted the nation to assert their liberty; as if they could procure them happiness and security for what they

possessed, and an assured enjoyment of a still greater good which was that of the honor and glory they would thereby acquire for magnanimity. They also said that God would not otherwise be assisting to them, than upon their joining with one another in such councils as might be successful, and for their own advantage; and this especially, if they would set about great exploits, and not grow weary in executing the same; so men received what they said with pleasure, and this bold attempt proceeded to a great height. All sorts of misfortunes also sprang from these men, and the nation was infected with this doctrine to an incredible degree; one violent war came upon us after another, and we lost our friends which used to alleviate our pains; there were also very great robberies and murder of our principal men. This was done in pretense indeed for the public welfare, but in reality for the hopes of gain to themselves; whence arose seditions, and from them murders of men which sometimes fell on those of their own people, (by the madness of these men towards one another, while their desire was that none of the adverse party might be left,) and sometimes on their enemies; a famine also coming upon us, reduced us to the last degree of despair, as did also the taking and demolishing of cities; nay, the sedition at last increased so high, that the very temple of God was burnt down by their enemies' fire.

..for Judas and Sadduc, who excited a fourth philosophic sect among us, and had a great many followers therein, filled our civil government with tumults at present, and laid the foundations of our future miseries, by this system of philosophy which we were before unacquainted withal, concerning which I will discourse a little, and this the rather because the infection which spread thence among the younger sort, who were zealous for it, brought the public to destruction. (*Antiq* XVIII 1:1)

But of the fourth sect of Jewish philosophy, Judas the Galilean was the author. These men agree in all other things with the Pharisaic notions; but they have an inviolable attachment to liberty, and say that God is to be their only Ruler and Lord. They also do not value dying any kinds of death, nor indeed do they heed the deaths of their relations and friends, nor can any such fear make them call any man lord. And since this immovable resolution of theirs is well known to a great many, I shall speak no further about that matter; nor am I afraid that any thing I have said of them should be disbelieved, but rather fear, that what I have said is beneath the resolution they show when they undergo pain. (*Antiq* XVII 1:6)

Decades later, the sons of Judas the Galilean would cause trouble in Galilee that would lead up to the revolt of in A.D. 66. From his writings, it is clear that Josephus had little regard for these zealots whom he thought were no more than opportunistic religious impostors–and dangerous ones at that.

The Rise of the Priesthood

Under the prefecture system established by Emperor Augustus in A.D. 6, the level of prosperity gradually but undeniably rose in Judea, despite the criminal nature of many Judean governors. Benefiting most from the change was the merchant class, of course, but also gaining was the class of the High Priesthood. The Second Temple in Jerusalem generated huge amounts of money through various means.

The Judean prefect was far more a military commander than a civilian administrator and cared little for the details of Jewish law or custom; the High Priesthood was expected to deal with those issues. The Judean prefect lived in Herod the Great's opulent palace in the insular seacoast city of Caesarea–technically not a part of Judea at all. The prefect enjoyed the good life in this pleasant place while the High Priesthood did the day-to-day work of administering the land and people. Roman garrisons were stationed in various strategic places in the Jewish East as deemed necessary to keep the peace and collect taxes. But the Jewish High Priest and his small army of Second Temple guards, and the thousands of other Second Temple Priests, were generally left to their own devices for purposes of civilian control.

High Priest Simon Ananus and his family benefited in particular, and they kept a firm control of the operation of the Second Temple until their violent deaths by Jewish rebels in A.D. 68. In time, High Priest elder Ananus became a virtual king. He and other important members of the Jerusalem High Priesthood learned to give little quarter to those seditious Jews who sought to challenge Rome under the guise of Messiah or some other type of innovative religious prophet.

Beginning of the Christian Era

It was in this charged and incendiary political atmosphere that both John the Baptist and Jesus of Nazareth lived and had their ministries, and into which the early Christian Church was born and grew. We will now turn to the beginning of the Christian era, and the development of an accurate time line of events. First, the Christian source material to be used will be defined and reviewed.

Chapter 11   Christian Sources

Forasmuch as many have taken in hand to draw up a narrative concerning those matters which have been fulfilled among us, even as they delivered them unto us, who from the beginning were eyewitnesses and ministers of the word, it seemed good to me also, having traced the course of all things accurately from the first, to write unto thee in order, most excellent Theophilus; that thou mightest know the certainty concerning the things wherein thou wast instructed. (Lk 1:1-4)

While virtually all manuscripts from antiquity have been lost through neglect or deliberate destruction, likely every significant writing about Jesus of Nazareth has survived into modern times. The final collapse of Rome in the early seventh century saw the disappearance of the Imperial libraries and many of the empire's great private manuscript collections. Those scrolls that survived did so through chance, or had been carefully culled out of ancient collections by Christians and stored in churches or monasteries. Some ancient works that were not obviously Christian but referred to New Testament figures — such as Emperor Tiberius or Pontius Pilate–were also saved. The assumption made by these early Christians was that even a peripheral reference to New Testament characters meant the works had been touched by God and so were worthy of preservation. In their zeal to propagate these "Christian" works, Monk copyists would sometimes cannibalize less interesting secular writings if papyrus or animal skin was scarce. This practice was a great loss for mankind on the whole, but most fortunate for Christianity and Christian researchers.

The New Testament

The New Testament, of course, is our major Christian source, containing 27 different books and letters that relate to either Jesus, the early Christians, or the early Christian Church. Today there are extant over 250 complete copies of the New Testament that were produced before A.D. 600. In contrast, Tacitus' historical work *Annuls of Imperial Rome* (*Annuls*) has only a single copy dating older than A.D. 900.

Individually, these works of the New Testament were well known by the middle of the second century A.D.

> Matthew also issued a written Gospel among the Hebrews in their own dialect, while Peter and Paul were preaching at Rome, and laying the foundations of the Church. After their departure, Mark, the disciple and interpreter of Peter, did also hand down to us in writing what had been preached by Peter. Luke also, the companion of Paul, recorded in a Book the Gospel preached by him. Afterwards, John, the disciple of the Lord, who also had leaned upon His breast, did himself publish a Gospel during his residence at Ephesus in Asia. (Irenaeus Book III-1:1)

Irenaeus was a second century Church Father and historian. He makes assertions as to the origins of the four Gospels, but gives little supporting evidence. Two centuries later, the Church Fathers constructed the New Testament largely based on the above quotation. In this collection, the Book of Matthew was placed first, Mark second, Luke third, and John fourth.

The fifth Book of the New Testament, Acts of the Apostles (Acts), details the journeys and ministries of the disciples of the crucified Jesus and also those of the early Christian converts. Following Acts is a series of 21 letters written by early Church Apostles—17 of them are by Paul the Apostle who was one of the most important early Christians. Placed last in the New Testament is the Book of Revelation–technically a letter but was probably considered a book by the Church Fathers due to the weighty nature of its subject matter.

The Christian Fathers

While the early Church Fathers wrote hundreds of years after the actual crucifixion of Jesus, but they lived before the fall of the Roman Empire. The Christian Fathers enjoyed access to the voluminous libraries of ancient Rome, Alexandria, and Caesarea as well as access to the religious manuscript collections that were kept in Christian Churches and monasteries, so their writings are important. Christianity then was well established and not much later would become the official religion of the Roman Empire. This hallmark occurred during the reign of Emperor Constantine in the early fourth century A.D.

Irenaeus became the Bishop of Lyons in Gaul in A.D. 177. He was born early in the second century A.D. and originally was from Asia Minor. As a boy, Irenaeus listened to Polycarp, the Bishop of Smyrna, who was a Church Father who died in A.D. 155. Polycarp himself was a disciple of John the Evangelist, who was reputedly a Disciple of Jesus' and present at many of the important events of Jesus' Ministry. John is the presumed author of the Gospel of John and other works in the New Testament. Polycarp also claimed to have talked with other eyewitness participants in Jesus' Ministry.

> I (Irenaeus) remember how he (Polycarp) spoke of his intercourse with John (the Evangelist) and with the others who had seen the Lord; how he repeated their words from memory; and how the things that he had heard them say about the Lord, His miracles and His teachings, things that he had heard direct from the eye-witnesses of the Word of Life, were proclaimed by Polycarp in complete harmony with Scripture. (Eusebius *History* 5:20 from Irenaeus Florinus)

While the link is tenuous and somewhat non-specific, that is probably the best outside confirmatory evidence of the Gospels that can be expected for a story that was played out nearly 2,000 years ago—Irenaeus personally knew Polycarp, and Polycarp personally knew John the Evangelist and other people who themselves personally knew Jesus of Nazareth—witnessing key events of Jesus' Ministry.

Irenaeus' many writings include the five-book *Adversus Haereses*, or *Detection and Overthrow of the False Knowledge* which has been dated between A.D. 175-185. Much of this work was concerned with countering the influence of several heretical quasi-Christian groups that were gaining traction within the Roman Empire at that time.

Eusebius (A.D. 263-339) was an early Christian Bishop of Caesarea. Among his surviving works is *The History of the Christian Church* (*History*) that he wrote in the early fourth century A.D. Though a controversial figure at times, Eusebius ultimately became the favorite of Roman Emperor Constantine. Constantine reigned from A.D. 306 until his death in A.D. 337. It was under Constantine that Rome adopted Christianity as its state religion. Eusebius was also the driving force behind a group of Christian elders who met at Nicaea in Bithynia (modern day Iznik, Turkey) early in the fourth century A.D. This group reviewed all the Christian writings extant at that time and determined what would constitute the "true" books of the New Testament. It is widely believed that Eusebius was also the author of the Nicene Creed.

> The Divine Scriptures that are accepted and those that are not. Since we are dealing with this subject it is proper to sum up the writings of the New Testament which have been already mentioned. First then must be put the holy quaternion of the Gospels; following them the Acts of the Apostles. After this must be reckoned the Epistles of Paul; next in order the extant former Epistle of John, and likewise the Epistle of Peter, must be maintained. After them is to be placed, if it really seem proper, the Apocalypse of John, concerning which we shall give the different opinions at the proper time. These then belong among the accepted writings. Among the disputed writings which are nevertheless recognized by many, are extant the so–called Epistle of James and that of Jude, also the second Epistle of Peter,, and those that are called the second or third of John, whether they belong to the evangelist or to another person of the same name. (Eusebius *History* 3:25)

Eusebius' assertions have to be taken at face value. Like Irenaeus, he gives few attributions. But also like Irenaeus, Eusebius had access to the vast libraries of Rome before the fall of the empire. He was also familiar with the various heretical

Christian groups who might have been producing false or self-serving manuscripts. Certainly, if there were credible works about Jesus that had been lost through the ensuing centuries, they would have been referenced by the early Christian Fathers like Eusebius.

The belief of Eusebius as expressed in his *History*, and undoubtedly the belief of all of the early Christians, was that the Roman destruction of Jerusalem and the Second Temple in A.D. 70 was a direct result of God's wrath over the crucifixion of Jesus. Eusebius assumes that the Gospel of Luke was written before the Jewish revolt and quotes from it several apparently prescient passages: Lk 19:42-44, 21:23-4, and 21:20 (Eus *History* III 7:6).

Eusebius' *History* is especially useful in that he quotes extensively from the works of Josephus. Since the earliest modern copy of Josephus' *Antiquities of the Jews* (*Antiquities*) dates 500 years after Eusebius' time, comparisons in translations of the same passages of *Antiquities* between modern copies and Eusebius' are enlightening. In fact, it is very possible that Eusebius might have used an original Greek copy of Josephus' *Antiquities* that Emperor Titus ordered placed in the Caesarea library.

Eusebius also proves to be a valuable source for several other important Christian historians. Hegesippus wrote in the second century A.D. during the papacy of St. Eleuterus, who served from A.D. 174-189. Hegesippus produced the five-volume *Memoirs* from which Eusebius quotes extensively. This work was known to exist until the 16th century, when it became lost. Hegesippus was a Jewish convert to Christianity and originally came from Palestine.

Justin Martyr is another early Christian writer of note who is known primarily through Eusebius. Originally from Samaria and likely of Greek descent, Justin was born a pagan and later converted to Christianity. He was martyred in Rome in A.D. 165. An important theologian and writer, Justin Martyr created *Apologies* I and II.

Tertullian is also quoted and referenced by Eusebius. Born in Carthage in 160 A.D., Tertullian was the son of a Roman centurion. Tertullian converted to Christianity around A.D. 197 and died in A.D. 220. He was a prolific Christian writer and most famous for his *Apology*. Some have suggested that professionally he was a Roman lawyer but this has come into doubt. Tertullian is credited with first developing the Trinity concept of the Christian faith (Father-Son-Holy Ghost).

Clement of Alexandria is also quoted by Eusebius, largely from Clement's work *Outlines*. Clement was an educated man for his day and had been born in Athens to wealthy parents. He died in Alexandria in A.D. 215 where he had been the leader of the Christian Church. Outside of quotes in Eusebius' works, only a single letter from Clement's writings survives.

These Christian Fathers did modern researchers a great service by identifying clearly fraudulent Christian written works—many manuscripts of which have recently been discovered.

First Writings

The accepted Canon of the New Testament was declared early in fourth century A.D. with the five main Books of New Testament extant in assembled form dating from early in the second century A.D.

As the years passed after Jesus' crucifixion, many of the early believers were coming to the realization that Jesus might not return to earth anytime soon, despite his promise to the contrary. Written documents were then deemed necessary by Church leaders as the original eyewitnesses to Jesus' ministry were either dead, dying, or getting forgetful. The Gospels were set down and became the central focus for the Christian Church.

Because three of the Gospels—Matthew, Mark, Luke—have remarkably similar passages, they are collectively termed the "Synoptic" Gospels (syn-same).

The following chart delineates the similarities that the three Gospels have to each other. It can be seen that even within the Synoptic Gospels there are unexplained differences. From the chart, it can also be argued that Mark is the earliest Gospel, as almost all of it is found in either Luke or Matthew.

Synoptic Gospel Commonality

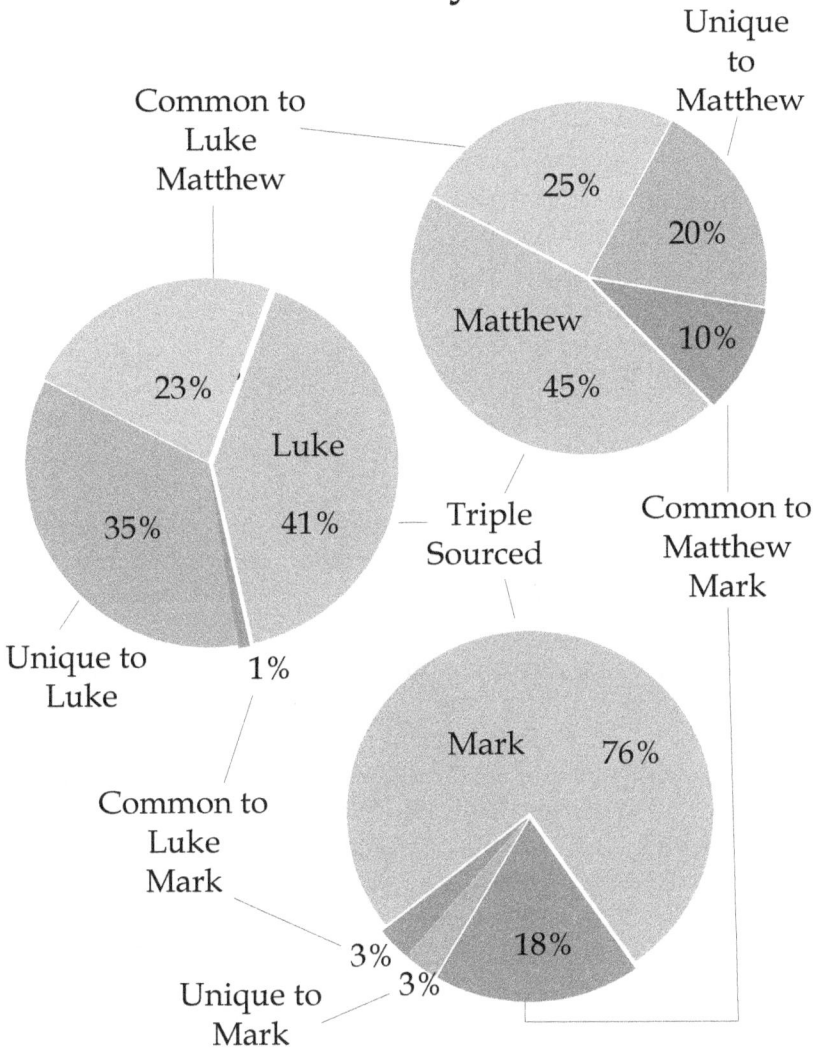

Unique to Matthew

Common to Luke Matthew

25%

20%

Matthew 45%

10%

Common to Matthew Mark

Triple Sourced

23%

Luke

35%

41%

Unique to Luke

1%

Common to Luke Mark

Mark 76%

18%

3%

3%

Unique to Mark

Interlude: The Earliest Gospel?

Most of the New Testament authors did not know Jesus when he was alive. The lone exception to this might have been John the Evangelist, the presumed author of the Gospel of John, the Book of Revelation, and the Epistle (Letter) of John. John, however, wrote or dictated his remembrances of Jesus' Ministry well after the Roman destruction of Jerusalem in A.D. 70.

Most experts place the crucifixion early in the fourth decade of first century A.D. with A.D. 33 being the usually accepted year. The earliest Gospel was probably the Book of Mark but even it was written well over a quarter century later. Why the delay? Different theories have been advanced.

One argument holds that Jesus was much less of a religious force than the Gospels suggest. It was only many years after Jesus' crucifixion that his legacy gained enough momentum and followers to merit a written doctrine–with perhaps much of that doctrine being fabricated. In support of this, the historian Flavius Josephus documents that many Messiah-like evangelists were preaching in Judea and Galilee during those years. Josephus and the Jerusalem High Priesthood were uniformly suspicious of them all.

Another theory argues the contrary. Jesus was, in fact, a very famous man, but nothing was written in the years after Jesus' crucifixion out of a fear of repercussions from the High Priesthood. In support of this, on the day of his crucifixion, Jesus was interrogated by not only the Second Temple High Priest Joseph Caiaphas, but also by Caiaphas' father-in-law–the former High Priest Simon Ananus, the Roman Prefect Pontius Pilate, and even (according to the Gospel of Luke) Herod Antipas, who was the son of Herod the Great. These were the most powerful men in the East at that time and does suggest that Jesus was a famous man; certainly Jesus was perceived as being a very dangerous one!

The most reasonable explanation is the simplest. The early disciples fully expected Jesus to soon return from heaven along with God's Angels with the purpose of establishing God's kingdom in earth. Why would the disciples bother to document Jesus' past history in writing when future events would be so spectacular and overshadowing? Most, of course, were uneducated men, like Jesus himself, and could neither read or write in any case (Jn 7:13).

The Gospel of Matthew

The authorship of the Book of Matthew is unknown. Tradition holds that the Book of Matthew was written by the tax-collecting Apostle.

> [9:9]And as Jesus passed by from thence, he saw a man, called Matthew, sitting at the place of toll: and he saith unto him, Follow me. And he arose, and followed him. (Mt)

Eusebius recounts that tradition (Eusebius *History* 3:24) also stating that the Book of Matthew was written in Hebrew for the Jews and originated in Judea. Both Irenaeus and Eusebius assert that Matthew was written earlier than the other Gospels. Conservative scholars argue that the book had to have been written by at least A.D. 66 as there was no direct reference to either the destruction of the Second Temple (A.D. 70) or the Jewish revolt (A.D. 66). But none of the Gospels reference the Jewish rebellion or the Temple destruction, including the Book of John which even the Christian Fathers admit was written well after both events.

The earliest copies of Matthew are in Greek. Matthew dwells on sections of the Old Testament that seem to be prescient of New Testament events–an indication that Jews were indeed the intended target audience for Matthew.

The earliest known fragment of the Book of Matthew is the Magdalen Papyrus which contains portions of chapter 26. These fragments demonstrate a similar style of other Greek manuscripts that can be dated before A.D. 66. This date would be consistent with Irenaeus' assertions. Other scholars do not agree, however, and date the Magdalen Papyrus to around A.D. 200.

The Gospel of Mark

The early Church Fathers believed the author of the Book of Mark was the same John Mark who is referenced several times in the Acts of the Apostles (Acts). This John Mark was a disciple of the Apostle Peter, a companion to the Apostle Paul, and later founded the Christian Church in Alexandria, Egypt.

According to tradition, John Mark set down in writing Peter's recollections of the events of Jesus and his Ministry. Because certain phrases in the Book of Mark are Latin based, experts have argued that this is further evidence that the Gospel was written in Rome.

John Mark is a minor figure in Acts. The Apostle Peter took refuge in John Mark's family house in Jerusalem after his escape from prison. Peter had been imprisoned by King Agrippa I for his Christian activities.

> 12:12And when he had considered *the thing*, he came to the house of Mary the mother of John whose surname was Mark; where many were gathered together and were praying. (Acts)

The author of the Book of Mark is supposedly referred to by Peter in his first Epistle–a letter generally considered to be authentic.

> She that is in Babylon, elect together with *you*, saluteth you; and *so doth* Mark my son. (1Pt 5:13)

Apparently, John Mark traveled with the Apostle Paul–and sometimes the Apostle Barnabas–between his times spent traveling with the Apostle Peter and serving as Peter's disciple.

> 12:25And Barnabas and Saul returned from Jerusalem, when they had fulfilled their ministration, taking with them John whose surname was Mark. (Acts)

> 15:37And Barnabas was minded to take with them John also, who was called Mark. 15:38But Paul thought not good to take with them him who

withdrew from them from Pamphylia, and went not with them to the work. [15:39]And there arose a sharp contention, so that they parted asunder one from the other, and Barnabas took Mark with him, and sailed away unto Cyprus; (Acts)

Eusebius (Eusebius *History* 2-14) relates a story from Clement (*Outlines* Book VI–now lost) that John Mark traveled with the Apostle Peter to Rome during the reign of Emperor Claudius in order to fight the evil influence of Simon the Magician. Simon was a "holy" man whom Peter had probably met earlier while proselytizing in Samaria (Acts 8:9–10). Simon had since traveled on to Rome, where he was honored as a god–even to the point of having his statue erected in a public place (Justin Martyr I *Apology* I–26). In Rome, according to Eusebius, Peter was so galvanizing an evangelist that the Christians there asked John Mark to write down all that Peter was telling them about about Jesus because the Apostle Peter, a Galilean fisherman, was illiterate. John Mark did so and the eponymous Book of Mark was created. Afterward, according to Clement, John Mark went on to establish the Christian Church in Alexandria, Egypt.

In the eighth year of Nero's reign Annianus was the first after Mark the evangelist to take charge of the see of Alexandria. (Eusebius *History* II:24)

The eighth year of Nero's reign would have been A.D. 62. It would be most helpful if Clement would have documented the number of years John Mark spent as a leader of the Church in Alexandria. As it is, relying on Eusebius and the Church Fathers, and assuming that Annianus took over the Church of Alexandria because Mark had died, it can be concluded that the Gospel of Mark had to have been written at least before A.D. 62, and probably before A.D. 54 which was the year when Emperor Claudius' reign ended.

The earliest full copies of Mark date to around A.D. 200. There are, however, fragments of Mark deciphered from the Dead Sea Scrolls found in Qumran Cave Seven in 1946. The Dead Sea Scrolls are thought to have been hidden away by devout Jews before Roman army overran the area by at least late A.D. 70. If this is true, it would support a date of authorship earlier.

The Gospel of Luke

Luke is thought to be written by a Christian physician from the city of Antiochene in Macedonia, Greece (Eusebius *History* 3:4). Luke was a companion of the Apostle Paul and lived perhaps into the second century A.D. This Luke is presumed to be the same person mentioned in the Epistles (Letters) of II Timothy and Philemon in the New Testament; both Epistles were written by Paul.

> Only Luke is with me. (II Tim 4:11)

> Epaphras, my fellow-prisoner in Christ Jesus, saluteth thee; and so do Mark, Aristarchus, Demas, Luke, my fellow-workers. (Phile 1:23-24)

Irenaeus first made the case that the author of the Gospel of Luke was this companion of Paul (Irenaeus III-XIV-1) and asserted that Luke's Gospel was written after the death of Paul in Rome in late A.D. 64.

Both the Book of Luke and the following book, Acts of the Apostles (Acts), are addressed to an individual named Theophilus (Lk 1:3; Acts 1:1). It can be assumed that this man either commissioned both works or supported Luke in their research and production in some fashion. Acts documents events up to A.D. 63, so of necessity both Acts and the Gospel of Luke had to have been written after that year.

The earliest manuscript of Luke is written in Greek and is dated around A.D. 200. However, in the same cave in Qumran that contained a fragment of the Book of Mark there also was a fragment from the Acts of the Apostles. If these manuscripts were hidden to prevent their destruction by the Romans in A.D. 70, the Book of Luke could be considerably older.

The Gospel of John

The Book of John differs from the other three Gospels in many ways, and introduces characters–such as Nicodemus and Lazarus–who are not mentioned anywhere else. The time line of Jesus' ministry also departs significantly from that of the three Synoptic Gospels.

The author of the Book of John claims to be a disciple and an eyewitness to all the events he describes.

> This is the disciple that beareth witness of these things, and wrote these things: and we know that his witness is true. (Jn 21:24)

This author may well be the "beloved disciple" who is mentioned during the crucifixion.

> 19:25These things therefore the soldiers did. But there were standing by the cross of Jesus his mother, and his mother's sister, Mary the wife of Clopas, and Mary Magdalene. 19:26When Jesus therefore saw his mother, and the disciple standing by whom he loved, he saith unto his mother, Woman, behold thy son! 19:27Then saith he to the disciple, Behold, thy mother! And from that hour the disciple took her unto his own home. (Jn)

The early Christians asserted that the author of the Book of John was a man called John the Evangelist who was, indeed, the beloved disciple. If so, John the Evangelist lived an extraordinarily long life before dying in Ephesus in Syria during the reign of Emperor Trajan (A.D. 98–117). Banished for a number of years to the island of Patmos by Emperor Domitian, John the Evangelist was also the author of the first Epistle of John and possibly the Book of Revelation.

Eusebius gives the reason for John deciding to write his Gospel.

> The three Gospels already written were in general circulation and copies had come into John's hands. He welcomed them, we are told, and confirmed their accuracy, but remarked that the narrative only lacked

the story of what the Christ had done first of all at the beginning of His mission (Eusebius *History* III 24)

The oldest fragmented copy of the Book of John was found in Egypt and has been dated to about A.D. 125. The earliest complete copy dates to around A.D. 200.

Acts of the Apostles

The Acts of the Apostles (Acts) was written by the author of the Book of Luke, who has been determined to be Luke, a physician from Macedonia. These two works were probably separated due to considerations of length based on the size of the standard scroll in those days. (Even after being split away from Acts, however, Luke is by far the longest of the four Gospels.) Experts date the writing of Acts between A.D. 70-80. The earliest known fragment is from Qumran Cave Seven–as has been previously discussed–with the earliest full copy written in Greek and dated around A.D. 200.

Other clues suggest an earlier date. Acts ends with Paul the Apostle in Rome in the year A.D. 63. According to Christian legend, Paul was executed during the Christian persecutions that were initiated by Emperor Nero in the late summer of A.D. 64. Acts spends considerable time documenting the Apostle Paul's Christian adventures. If Acts had been written after Paul's execution, it certainly would included a section referencing it.

Scholars argue that Luke's story of Jesus as a boy in the Temple (Lk 2:41-49) was borrowed from a similar story in Josephus' autobiography (*Life* 1) that was written around A.D. 100, pushing far back the date for Luke's work. But, as will be seen, in A.D. 63 both Luke and Josephus were in Rome, providing a possible link through which Luke learned of Josephus' story — which he misinterpreted.

For these reasons, it can be speculated that both the Book of Luke and Acts were written after A.D. 63, but before the persecutions of A.D. 64. The author Luke was either killed along with Paul during the Christian executions, or survived but somehow lost control of his unfinished manuscript.

The Epistles

In the last years of his life, the Apostle Paul wrote many letters to the different Christian Churches scattered across Italia, Greece, Syria, and Asia Minor. Irenaeus believed that only 12 true letters from Paul existed–along with the first Epistle (letter) of John (the author of the Gospel), and the first Epistle of the Apostle Peter. When the New Testament was assembled by Eusebius and others, these letters were included. Some of these Epistles will be important in determining a time line of early Christian events. Indeed, in correlating the New Testament with known Roman history some of the Epistles of Paul can be reasonably dated to A.D. 58, making them arguably the most ancient of Christian manuscripts.

The Apocrypha

The term "Apocrypha" (Greek for "those having been hidden away") technically refers to any texts or writings outside of the accepted Canon of the New Testament. There is an Old Testament Apocrypha as well. The writings of the early Church Fathers that are not included in the New Testament are apocryphal by definition.

The first five Books of the New Testament are regarded as the only veracious sources on the life and teachings of Jesus of Nazareth. Other books about the life of Jesus were written about the same time but were adjudged to be fraudulent by the Christian Fathers. These works included the Book of Mary, the Book of Judas, the Book of Thomas, the Acts of John, and others. Among these fraudulent books, Eusebius even places the NT Book of Revelation.

> ...Among the rejected writings must be reckoned also the Acts of Paul, and the so-called Shepherd, and the Apocalypse of Peter, and in

addition to these the extant Epistle of Barnabas, and the so-called Teachings of the Apostles; and besides, as I said, the Apocalypse of John, if it seem proper which some, as I said, reject, but which others class with the accepted Books. And among these some have placed also the Gospel according to the Hebrews, with which those of the Hebrews that have accepted Christ are especially delighted. And all these may be reckoned among the disputed Books. (Eusebius *History* 3:25)

As Christianity grew, so grew the number of these questionable Gospels and religious writings. In the early fourth century A.D., Eusebius and others decided to do a rigorous evaluation of all of these works. After much consideration, the New Testament was assembled–a series of books and letters thought to be true and divinely inspired based on the best evidence the Church elders had available to them. The other gospels and false writings were ordered burned, but a few of these ancient works escaped destruction.

In 1945, 52 of these manuscripts, printed on fourth century papyrus, were dug up in Egypt near the village of Nag Hammadi. The texts were written upon 13 codices–sheets of papyri–that had been rolled up, wrapped in leather, placed in a large clay jar and buried. How did they get there? Almost certainly they were deliberately buried by a Christian monk in the fourth century. He had likely received an order from his controlling Church, probably in Alexandria, to burn them. But the monk couldn't bring himself to destroy them, for he thought they were God-inspired. Instead of burning them, he had the manuscripts buried so they could be found at some future date– if God so ordained it.

As interesting as these books might be, none of the Apocryphal "Gospels" will be used as source material. The considered opinion of early Christian authorities 1600 years closer to the time of Jesus was that all of the works are fraudulent. On what basis can modern researchers argue that they are not?!

Chapter 12   The Birth Year of Jesus

Where is he that is born King of the Jews? for we saw his star in the east
and are come to worship him (Mt 2:1)

The birth of Jesus traditionally marks the beginning of the Christian era. In a perfect world, that year would be A.D. 1 as it is defined by the Gregorian Calendar of 1582 and based on previous assumptions taken by the Council of Nicaea in A.D. 325. Unfortunately, that year is probably not even close to the real one. Finding the birth year of Jesus is another challenge we will undertake, for solving it will add an interesting dimension to the year of Jesus' crucifixion–which will be determined later.

Direct references are limited to the Books of Luke and Matthew. However, using Jewish and Roman historical sources–and modern science–a date for Jesus' birth can, in fact, be derived with some degree of assurance.

Season of the Year

The traditional placement of Jesus' birth in late December is probably incorrect as well. That particular date was established by the Church at the Council of Nicaea, too. The Church's purpose then was to provide the Christians with a counterpoint holiday to the pagan festivals that centered around the winter solstice — December 21. After that date, the days would become longer, symbolizing a rebirth of sorts and worthy of celebration. This was especially important in the northern climes where the winter days are very short. The lengthening of the winter days can be compared to the waxing of the new moon as a manifestation of a divine power.

The Book of Luke, however, suggests that the nativity actually occurred in the spring.

> "And there were shepherds in the same country abiding in the field and keeping watch by night over their flock." (Lk 2:8)

Why were the shepherds staying awake at night? Because it was in the spring when the ewes of the flock were giving birth–a very critical time of the year. During this period, the shepherds would stay up at night in order to help the ewes through difficult births or to protect the vulnerable new-born lambs from predators or even thieves. That Jesus was born in the spring–not the winter–is now generally accepted.

Birth of John the Baptist

Important clues about Jesus' birth year are indirectly given when Luke writes about the birth of John the Baptist.

> There was in the days of Herod, king of Judaea, a certain priest named Zacharias, of the course of Abijah: and he had a wife of the daughters of Aaron and her name was Elisabeth. (Lk 5:1)

Zacharias was a Jerusalem Temple priest of no small importance. His job was to keep the incense altar stocked and burning in the Second Temple's inner Sanctuary building. This special incense altar was in the antechamber of the most-holy room where God himself was thought to dwell. The incense altar was placed near 80-foot-high purple Babylonian curtains which shielded an equally tall set of golden double doors. These ornate doors led into to the "God" chamber. The chamber was entered only once a year and then only by the current High Priest–the perfect man–after he had been properly purified and robed.

The Angel Gabriel came to Zacharias in the Temple Sanctuary antechamber one day when Zacharias was tending to his duties. The Angel told Zacharias that his wife would bear him a son who would become a great and good man. Zacharias, after getting over his initial shock at the Angel's appearance, expressed doubt about that possibility for his wife Elisabeth was well past her child-bearing years. Irritated at Zacharias' lack of faith, Gabriel struck Zacharias dumb.

> 1:22And when he came out, he could not speak unto them: and they perceived that he had seen a vision in the temple: and he continued making signs unto them and remained dumb. 1:23And it came to pass, when the days of his ministration were fulfilled, he departed unto his house. 1:24And after these days Elisabeth his wife conceived; and she hid herself five months, saying, 1:25Thus hath the Lord done unto me in the days wherein he looked upon *me*, to take away my reproach among men. (Lk)

After the newly mute Zacharias ended his "ministration"–probably a work shift of a few days where he stayed overnight in the Sanctuary building–he left the Temple complex. Zacharias then made his way across the upper city of Jerusalem and passed through one of the city gates and arrived at his home town of Judah, a suburb of Jerusalem.

Zacharias could not speak, but as an important priest he probably knew how to write and could still communicate to others. How much about the Angel and the Angel's prediction did Zacharias relate to his wife?! As time passed, much to Zacharias' surprise his aged wife Elisabeth did, in fact, conceive. Moreover, in the sixth month of Elisabeth's pregnancy, Gabriel visited Elisabeth's cousin, Mary, as well–who was a virgin.

> 1:26Now in the sixth month the angel Gabriel was sent from God unto a city of Galilee, named Nazareth, 1:27to a virgin betrothed to a man whose name was Joseph, of the house of David; and the virgin's name was Mary. 1:28And he came in unto her and said, Hail, thou that art highly favored, the Lord *is* with thee. 1:29But she was greatly troubled at the saying and cast in her mind what manner of salutation this might be. 1:30And the angel said unto her, Fear not, Mary: for thou hast found favor with God. 1:31And behold, thou shalt conceive in thy womb and bring forth a son and shalt call his name JESUS. (Lk)

When did all this occur? Knowing who the Judean ruler was when either woman conceived would be useful. It is assumed that the "Herod, King of Judaea" referred to in Luke is the actual Herod the Great and not any of his sons. Herod's son Archelaus ruled Judea after Herod's death, granted, but was never referred to as Herod–only Archelaus. A king sometimes referred to as simply "Herod" would rule Judea later, but that would be Herod's grandson Herod Agrippa (Agrippa I), and he wouldn't begin his reign for almost 50 years.

What time frame can we put these events in? Presumably, after Gabriel appeared to Zacharias, only a matter of days or weeks passed before Elisabeth conceived the son who would be called John. It is possible that at some time in the nine-month period of Elisabeth's pregnancy Herod the Great died. Therefore, the time of Herod's death in October of 4 B.C. would have been the latest date for John the Baptist's conception. Adding nine months would make John's birth no later than mid 3 B.C. It would follow that with Jesus' conception being six months after John's, the latest date for Jesus' birth would have been at the end of 3 B.C.

But it has been previously determined that Jesus was born in the springtime. If so, then his birth date would have to be moved back a several months to the spring of 3 B.C., with John the future Baptizer being born in the fall of 4 B.C. at the latest. If this is accurate, John's birth so close to the time of Herod's death might have been seen as very symbolic and portentous by the Jewish people, especially with Elisabeth being well beyond normal child-bearing years.

At any rate, happily for Zacharias, on the day of his newborn son's circumcision, and after Elisabeth affirmed before God that indeed the baby's name would be John, Zacharias' tongue was loosened by the Angel Gabriel. Zacharias had been mute for more than nine months!

Ministry of John the Baptist

The Gospels say little about John's youth. Since his father Zacharias was a Temple priest, it can be assumed that John grew to manhood following strict Jewish law if not training for the priesthood itself. At some point in time, however, John left Judah for the wilds of Perea. There he started his own ministry.

In a seminal and crucial passage, the Book of Luke gives the date when this occurred.

> 3:1Now in the fifteenth year of the reign of Tiberius Caesar, Pontius Pilate being governor of Judaea and Herod being tetrarch of Galilee and his brother Philip tetrarch of the region of Ituraea and Trachonitis and Lysanias tetrarch of Abilene, 3:2in the highpriesthood of Annas and Caiaphas, the word of God came unto John the son of Zacharias in the wilderness. (Lk)

The 15th year of Tiberius' reign would be A.D. 28.

According to Luke, Jesus was afterward baptized by John (or by one of John's disciples) and began his own Ministry at 30 years of age.

> 3:21Now it came to pass, when all the people were baptized, that, Jesus also having been baptized and praying, the heaven was opened, 3:22and the Holy Spirit descended in a bodily form, as a dove, upon him and a voice came out of heaven, Thou art my beloved Son; in thee I am well pleased. 3:23And Jesus himself, when he began *to teach*, was about thirty years of age, being the son (as was supposed) of Joseph, the *son* of Heli, (Lk)

With the beginning of John the Baptist's ministry in A.D. 28, two questions need to be answered. The first is how long was it after John started his ministry that Jesus was baptized? The second is how long after Jesus was baptized did Jesus begin his own Ministry?

Using the earliest possible dates allowed by the Book of Luke, John the Baptist would have begun his ministry in early A.D. 28. If John immediately baptized Jesus and Jesus immediately began his own Ministry, Jesus would have been thirty years of age by early A.D. 28–and just prior to his thirty-first birthday in the spring of that year. This would fit with a 3 B.C. spring birth date for Jesus, making John the Baptist's birth in mid-to-late 4 B.C.

and is consistent with the earlier information in the Book of Luke.

Of course, any amount of time could have elapsed between the beginning of John's ministry and Jesus' baptism, and from Jesus' baptism to the beginning of Jesus' own Ministry. Besides, in the Book of Luke, the term used is "about" thirty years of age. The only limiting factor would be the year of Jesus' crucifixion which has yet to be determined.

So far in the Book of Luke, using information provided about John the Baptist, a birth date can be determined that fits for Jesus–3 B.C. However, in deriving that number, the most extreme parameters must be used for both John the Baptist's birth and the start of both John's and Jesus' ministries.

Census of Augustus

Aside from information about Jesus' birth date inferred from the story of John the Baptist, Luke also gives considerable direct information about the nativity. Unfortunately, much of this information is contradictory to what has already been presented.

> [2:1]Now it came to pass in those days, there went out a decree from Caesar Augustus, that all the world should be enrolled. [2:2]This was the first enrolment made when Quirinius was governor of Syria. [2:3]And all went to enrol themselves, every one to his own city. [2:4]And Joseph also went up from Galilee, out of the city of Nazareth, into Judaea, to the city of David which is called Bethlehem, because he was of the house and family of David; [2:5]to enrol himself with Mary, who was betrothed to him, being great with child. [2:6]And it came to pass, while they were there, the days were fulfilled that she should be delivered. [2:7]And she brought forth her firstborn son; and she wrapped him in swaddling clothes and laid him in a manger, because there was no room for them in the inn. (Lk)

In previous chapters, we have gone over the circumstances of the A.D. 6 census ordered by Augustus. Briefly, Herod's son Archelaus was being removed as ethnarch over Judea and Samaria and those lands were being turned into a Roman province. Previously, Augustus had accepted what Herod the Great, and then his son Archelaus, reported on the wealth of those territories. Now he had to find out the real data for administration purposes.

In those days, throughout the empire Rome would predetermine the amount of taxes that each province had to pay yearly. The "king" or "tetrarch" in the case of Herod and his sons, or the prefect in the case of a Roman civil appointee, would dutifully send the proper tax to Rome. The local governors would collect money over and above the Rome-required amount and make a profit.

What exactly was the population and wealth of the Jewish East? What should the new level of tax be? And what type of treasures had the Herods had amassed in Judea and Samaria over the family's more than 45 years of rule?

Josephus and the Census

Flavius Josephus, the first century A.D. Jewish historian, writes about this period:

> So Archelaus's country was laid to the province of Syria; and Cyrenius, one that had been consul, was sent by Caesar to take account of people's effects in Syria and to sell the house of Archelaus. (*Antiq* XVII 13:5)

> Now Cyrenius, a Roman senator and one who had gone through other magistracies and had passed through them till he had been consul and one who, on other accounts, was of great dignity, came at this time into Syria, with a few others, being sent by Caesar to he a judge of that nation and to take an account of their substance. Coponius also, a man of the equestrian order, was sent together with him, to have the supreme power over the Jews. Moreover, Cyrenius came himself into Judea which was now added to the province of Syria, to take an account of their substance and to dispose of Archelaus's money; (*Antiq* XVIII 1:1)

Third century A.D. Church historian Eusebius quotes the same passage from a copy of *Antiquities* that is at least 500 years older.

> Quirinius, a member of the senate who had filled the minor offices and passed through them all to become consul and in other ways was a man

of great distinction, arrived with a few officials in Syria. He had been sent by by Caesar to be a supreme judge of the nation and to assess the value of their property. (Eusebius *History* Book 1:5)

Eusebius confirms that Josephus' Cyrenius and Luke's Quirinius refer to the same governor of Syria, with variant spellings on the name (or perhaps a transcription error). Quirinius was also Roman consul in 12 B.C.

In light of these narratives from Josephus, and according to the Book of Luke's direct account of the birth of Jesus, it must be concluded that the date of Jesus' birth was in the spring of A.D. 6 (though A.D. 7 would probably be acceptable). This would be after Archelaus was banished as king of Judea and after Augustus appointed the Equestrian Coponius as Judean prefect and ordered him to take a census.

The Problems in Luke

Accepting an A.D. 6 birth date, however, presents several problems. If Jesus was indeed born in the spring of A.D. 6, then John the Baptist would have been born six months earlier in the fall of A.D. 5. That would have made for at least an eight-year gap between the Angel Gabriel appearing to John's father Zacharias and John's own conception, since the Angel appeared to Zacharias during the reign of Herod the Great. Eight years is a long time for poor Zacharias to have remained mute!

Also, if John the Baptist was born in the fall of A.D. 5, when he started his ministry in A.D. 28 he would have been a very youthful 23 years of age–arguably not a realistic age to be taken seriously as a holy man in those times.

A spring A.D. 6 birth date for Jesus presents another problem. For Jesus to have started his Ministry when he was 30, as Luke says he does, and to have been born in the spring of A.D. 6, as Luke says he was, Jesus would have to have started his Ministry in A.D. 36. Since, as shall be seen, Joseph Caiaphas was removed as High Priest in A.D. 36 at the very latest, Jesus' entire Ministry would have lasted only a few months at the most. The Book of John documents that Jesus' ministry lasted for more than three years and so is in direct conflict to this. An A.D. 7 birth year for Jesus is untenable for the same reasons.

Therefore, the Book of Luke has obvious internal conflicts concerning the birth of Jesus that cannot be reconciled. From one set of data, a strong argument for a birth year of 3 B.C. can be made. From another, a birth year of A.D. 6 can be derived—although that is difficult to support for several reasons.

Some have argued that the supposed A.D. 6 census described in Luke actually refers to an earlier Roman census. Josephus does, in fact, report that in 3 B.C. Sabinus and Quintilius Varus took account of the "effects" of Herod (*Antiq* XVII 9:5) and reported their findings back to Augustus. However, a census–or an actual counting of the people–in Judea was not mentioned. Likewise, some have speculated that in 12 B.C., when Saturninus was president of Syria, a census was taken in the East and that this was the New Testament census referred to in Luke. Possibly, yes, but Josephus does not mention it, nor does any other ancient source.

It is in this state of confusion that the Book of Luke will be temporarily set aside and the Book of Matthew considered.

The Gospel of Matthew

The Book of Matthew gives facts on Jesus' birth that almost seem too detailed not to be true. Who could imagine a bright star in the sky heralding the birth of the Messiah–even in the most creative of Christian minds? Or the slaughter of innocent babies in Bethlehem as the infuriated Herod the Great had his soldiers search the village for the infant Messiah?

> [2:1]Now when Jesus was born in Bethlehem of Judaea in the days of Herod the king, behold, Wise-men from the east came to Jerusalem, saying, [2:2]Where is he that is born King of the Jews? for we saw his star in the east and are come to worship him. [2:3]And when Herod the king heard it, he was troubled and all Jerusalem with him. [2:4]And gathering together all the chief priests and scribes of the people, he inquired of them where the Christ should be born. [2:5]And they said unto him, In Bethlehem of Judaea: for thus it is written through the prophet,

^{2:6}And thou Bethlehem, land of Judah,
Art in no wise least among the princes of Judah:
For out of thee shall come forth a governor,
Who shall be shepherd of my people Israel.

^{2:7}Then Herod privily called the Wise-men and learned of them exactly what time the star appeared. ^{2:8}And he sent them to Bethlehem and said, Go and search out exactly concerning the young child; and when ye have found *him*, bring me word, that I also may come and worship him. ^{2:9}And they, having heard the king, went their way; and lo, the star which they saw in the east, went before them, till it came and stood over where the young child was. ^{2:10}And when they saw the star, they rejoiced with exceeding great joy. ^{2:11}And they came into the house and saw the young child with Mary his mother; and they fell down and worshipped him; and opening their treasures they offered unto him gifts, gold and frankincense and myrrh. ^{2:12}And being warned *of God* in a dream that they should not return to Herod, they departed into their own country another way.

^{2:13}Now when they were departed, behold, an angel of the Lord appeareth to Joseph in a dream, saying, Arise and take the young child and his mother and flee into Egypt and be thou there until I tell thee: for Herod will seek the young child to destroy him. ^{2:14}And he arose and took the young child and his mother by night and departed into Egypt; ^{2:15}and was there until the death of Herod: that it might be fulfilled which was spoken by the Lord through the prophet, saying, Out of Egypt did I call my son.

^{2:16}Then Herod, when he saw that he was mocked of the Wise-men, was exceeding wroth and sent forth and slew all the male children that were in Bethlehem and in all the borders thereof, from two years old and under, according to the time which he had exactly learned of the Wise-men. ^{2:17}Then was fulfilled that which was spoken through Jeremiah the prophet, saying,

^{2:18}A voice was heard in Ramah,
Weeping and great mourning,
Rachel weeping for her children;
And she would not be comforted, because they are not.

^{2:19}But when Herod was dead, behold, an angel of the Lord appeareth in a dream to Joseph in Egypt, saying, ^{2:20}Arise and take the young child and his mother and go into the land of Israel: for they are dead that sought the young child's life. ^{2:21}And he arose and took the young child and his mother and came into the land of Israel. ^{2:22}But when he heard that Archelaus was reigning over Judaea in the room of his father Herod, he was afraid to go thither; and being warned *of God* in a dream,

he withdrew into the parts of Galilee, ^{2:23}and came and dwelt in a city called Nazareth; that it might be fulfilled which was spoken through the prophets, that he should be called a Nazarene. (Mt)

In considering these passages, just as in the Book of Luke, the Herod question must be considered. "Herod" in ancient literature at times referred to several different kings of the Herodian line and not necessarily to Herod the Great himself. In the Acts of the Apostles, for instance, "Herod the King" actually refers to King Agrippa I, who was the grandson of Herod the Great (Acts 12:1-25). However, Matthew avoids this confusion by referring directly to Archelaus (Mt 2:22). Previously, in discussing the Book of Luke, the possibility was entertained that Luke's reference to "Herod" might have actually been to Archelaus, Herod's son. But the Book of Matthew is very clear on this; the "Herod" referred to is, without question, Herod the Great.

The Book of Matthew relates that King Herod (Herod the Great) sent the wise men to seek out the Christ child and to return when the child had been found. These wise men did, indeed, find Jesus, but they decided not to report back to Herod, knowing that Herod would likely kill the baby. Within only a few weeks, Herod probably realized that the three wise men were not going to return. Herod then acted with a vengeance and ordered the executions of all babies in and around Bethlehem "from two years old and under, according to the time which he had exactly learned of the Wise-men." Herod was a paranoid man and it can be reasonably assumed that he included a generous range of birth dates for those babies to be slaughtered.

With this scenario and knowing that the death of Herod the Great occurred in the fall of 4 B.C., Jesus had to have been born at the latest by the fall of 4 B.C. and possibly quite a bit earlier. But this date range is inconsistent with both sets of facts in Luke.

Also, in order to take the Book of Matthew seriously the infanticide story must be accepted as true. How likely is it, given what is known about Herod the Great? Infanticide committed on Herod the Great's orders is not documented in any of Josephus' writings, a historian who at times is excruciatingly detailed in the story of Herod's life. In other ancient sources, Herod the Great is mentioned only in passing, with no account given of infanticide. Does this mean that the slaughter of the infants did not occur?

The Infanticide Cover-Up

From previous chapters, we know that infanticide is totally within character for Herod if he thought his power was threatened. But Herod the Great ordering the slaughter of even a single infant should have been horrific enough to make the pages of Josephus.

Remember, however, that Josephus drew almost all of his source material from the now-lost works of Nicolaus of Damascus. Nicolaus was a friend and counselor to the king. Thus, Nicolaus could hardly be considered an objective historian of the Herodian era. Some might considered Nicolaus more apologist than scholar in this regard.

It is very possible that the slaughter of dozens–if not hundreds–of infants was so inexcusably evil that not even the resourceful Nicolaus could figure out a way to present it in a good light. Nicolaus perhaps realized that his most politic solution was to ignore the atrocity completely.

Josephus at times questions the integrity of the historian Nicolaus of Damascus. Josephus relates an incident when Herod the Great ordered his men to rob the Jerusalem tomb of David and Solomon by night. In the tomb, Herod's men found a large sum of silver and gold. Near the end of the heist, however, an explosion occurred deep within the tunnels, killing a slave. Herod became fearful and quickly extricated his men from the tomb. He sealed it back up and erected a monument in the front of it to appease the spirit of David.

And even Nicolaus his historiographer makes mention of this monument built by Herod, though he does not mention his going down into the sepulcher, as knowing that action to be of ill repute; and many other things he treats of in the same manner in his Book; for he wrote in Herod's lifetime and under his reign and so as to please him and as a servant to him, touching upon nothing but what tended to his glory and openly excusing many of his notorious crimes and very diligently concealing them. And as he was desirous to put handsome colors on the death of Mariamne and her sons which were barbarous actions in the king, he tells falsehoods about the incontinence of Mariamne and the treacherous designs of his sons upon him; and thus he proceeded in his whole work, making a pompous encomium upon what just actions he had done, but earnestly apologizing for his unjust ones. (*Antiq* XVI 7:1)

So, too, the slaughter of the infants might have been conveniently ignored by Nicolaus. For this reason, Josephus, who wrote almost a century after the infanticide incident, was simply not aware of it.

Would the Book of Matthew have been a legitimate source for Josephus? When Josephus was compiling his *Antiquities* which were published in A.D. 93, Christianity was still considered very much a cult religion. Josephus would not have taken any Christian manuscripts seriously even if he knew about them. Josephus clearly disapproved of all Messiah figures and various religious sects that had sprung up in the Jewish nation in the turbulent times prior to the Jewish revolt. Christianity would have been no exception to this. Josephus' famous "Testimonium Flavianum," as has already been discussed, was probably erroneously transcribed by later Christian copyists.

It must be remembered, too, that Herod the Great was the great grandfather of King Agrippa II, who was a benefactor and friend of Josephus'. Even if he was aware of Herod's infanticide, Josephus would have known that it would have reflected badly on his friend Agrippa II, and he might have left it out for that reason.

Eusebius

Besides the Books of Luke and Matthew, early Church historian Eusebius hundreds of years later also writes with some confidence about the birth year of Jesus.

It was the forty-second year of Augustus' reign and the twenty-eighth after the subjugation of Egypt and the deaths of Antony and

Cleopatra...at the time of the first registration, while Quirinius was governor of Syria..(Eusebius History I:5)

Calculations based on this information gives us a birth year for Jesus of 2 B.C. This is assuming that the death of Antony and Cleopatra occurred in early 30 B.C., and Augustus' (Octavian's) reign began after the assassination of Julius Caesar in early 44 B.C. This calculation, however, doesn't fit at all with Quirinius' known term of office from A.D. 6-12.

At this point no more direct information about the birth of Jesus is to be found in either the New Testament or any other of the ancient sources. But two indirect paths wait to be explored and one lies in the Book of John.

The Clue in John

Nothing specific is written about the birth of Jesus in the Book of John. The fourth Gospel does, however, indicate Jesus' approximate age at an identifiable time during Jesus' Ministry. This occurred during the feast of the Tabernacles just before the Passover of Jesus' crucifixion.

In the months leading up to what would prove to be his final Passover, Jesus preached frequently in the Second Temple.

[7:1]And after these things Jesus walked in Galilee: for he would not walk in Judaea, because the Jews sought to kill him. [7:2]Now the feast of the Jews, the feast of tabernacles, was at hand. [7:3]His brethren therefore said unto him, Depart hence and go into Judaea, that thy disciples also may behold thy works which thou doest. [7:4]For no man doeth anything in secret and himself seeketh to be known openly. If thou doest these things, manifest thyself to the world. (Jn)

[8:57]The Jews therefore said unto him, Thou art not yet fifty years old and hast thou seen Abraham? [8:58]Jesus said unto them, Verily, verily, I say unto you, Before Abraham was born, I am. [8:59]They took up stones therefore to cast at him: but Jesus hid himself and went out of the temple. (Jn)

At the Second Temple for the feast of the Tabernacles in the year before his final Passover, Jesus' relative youth was used against him by a group of nay-sayers who had been listening to him preach. The confrontational Jews observed that Jesus was "not yet fifty" as if true holy men had to be at least that age. But what exactly did "not yet fifty" mean? Was Jesus 49 years of age at that time? Or 48? Or 47?

There is no known religious importance to a male Jew reaching the age of 50. But 50 is an important number in another religious context. The feast of the Pentecost occurs 50 days after the Passover–or one day after a week of weeks, or one day after seven times seven days. But accepting this passage at face value, Jesus in the year before his crucifixion was in his forties and probably in his late forties.

This information from the Book of John is unfortunately the last piece of evidence that can be squeezed out of the New Testament. A wide range of birth years can be postulated for Jesus, depending on which set of data is chosen. In this, the year of Jesus' crucifixion would be very helpful and that will be the focus for the remainder of this book.

But there is one last avenue open to us, however and that lies in the fields of astronomy and mathematics.

Halley's Comet–the Star of the East?

The Book of Matthew tells of a star in the eastern sky that marked Jesus' birth. It was a celestial object so brilliant and unusual that wise men came from Parthia into Judea to inquire if another son had been born to Herod the Great. Could that star have actually been a comet, and could it specifically have been Halley's Comet?

Halley's Comet has been making regular appearances in the skies of earth for thousands of years. Halley's Comet is actually a giant ice ball originating from well beyond the orbit of the outer planet Uranus. Thousands of similar comets make up what is called the Kuiper belt in those far reaches of the Solar System.

Pluto in fact is a member of this class of solar bodies and not a solid, rocky planet at all.

These comets collide with each other at times which causes some to drop into more irregular and eccentric orbits that swoop elliptically through the inner part of the solar system. As these errant comets approach the sun, gases boil off from the comet's icy substrate due to the sun's heat. The delicate pressure of the sunlight itself is strong enough to push back these inflamed gases from the comet's surface and give the comet its brilliant luminescent tail–sometimes thousands of miles long. When the comet moves away from the sun, the tail is misnamed for it will precede the path of the comet.

Halley's comet is the most notable of these giant and errant Kuiper belt ice balls. The comet has a rough 76-year period of orbit around the sun which is counter-directional to the orbits of the rest of the planets. It's period of orbit slightly varies due to the influence of the gravity from the planets the comet passes on its journey. Two thousand years ago, Halley's comet would have been a much brighter sight in the sky, as all periodic comets lose an estimated 10 percent of their ice mass in the course of each orbit around the sun.

Astronomers have calculated the probable dates of appearances of Halley's comet which have been correlated by contemporaneous writings and the markings on ancient coins. During ancient times Halley's Comet has been assumed to have been seen over China in May 240 B.C. and Armenia in August 87 B.C. In 12 B.C., Chinese astronomers tracked a Comet from August through October over their skies that was likely Halley's. Could this celestial appearance been the star of the East that was also seen in Judea and reported by the Book of Matthew?

If so, extrapolating forward this comet should have made an appeerence over the earth for an extended period of time sometime in A.D. 65. Perhaps the sighting would have started in late A.D. 64, or maybe slightly later and lasting into early A.D. 66. Without question, Halley's Comet would have been the most spectacular "star" seen in the night sky. Likely, it could have been seen for a good portion of the daytime as well. What do the ancient sources say?

Other Ancient Stars

Josephus mentions a brilliant "star" that was seen in the sky shortly before the outbreak of the Jewish revolt which began after the Passover celebration of A.D. 66.

> Thus were the miserable people persuaded by these deceivers and such as belied God himself; while they did not attend nor give credit to the signs that were so evident and did so plainly foretell their future desolation, but, like men infatuated, without either eyes to see or minds to consider, did not regard the denunciations that God made to them. Thus there was a star resembling a sword which stood over the city and a comet, that continued a whole year. Thus also before the Jews' rebellion ... (*Wars* VI 5:3)

This comet lasted for an entire year and Josephus is clear that it was seen before the Jewish revolt began. It is very reasonable to assume that this was Halley's Comet and was seen for much of A.D. 65.

The historian Publius Tacitus documented a comet that appeared in A.D. 64, late in the year.

> At the close of the year people talked much about prodigies, presaging impending evils. Never were lightning flashes more frequent and a comet too appeared, for which Nero always made propitiation with noble blood. (*Annuls* 15:47)

Suetonius notes the same event.

> A blazing star which is vulgarly supposed to portend destruction to kings and princes, appeared above the horizon several nights successively " (Sue *Nero* 36)

Suetonius states that because of it, Nero initiated action against the minor conspiracy of Gaius Piso which Tacitus clearly documents in A.D. 65.

The persecutions of the Christians began in late A.D. 64. Nero blamed the Christians for starting the catastrophic fires in Rome that had swept through the city in July of that year. Did the appearance of the great comet (according to Tacitus, at least) play a role in Nero's decision to turn against the Christians?

Comet Calculations

Tacitus tracked meticulously the secession of the yearly consuls of Rome and he likely worked from the official records in the Imperial library. The dates derived from Tacitus' *Annuls* are as certain as anything in ancient history.

Josephus states that the comet observed just prior to the Jewish revolt lasted an entire year. In this, Josephus must be believed, since Josephus was alive during those years and personally observed it. Could the comet seen in late A.D. 64 in Rome be the same one as Josephus recorded which could be seen into the early spring of A.D. 65? With a 76-year period of orbit, this would then roughly correlate to the 12 B.C. sighting of Halley's comet in China. Also to be considered is that the star of the East might have occurred some months before or after Jesus' birth. A springtime birth for Jesus has been established, so using Halley's Comet "data" Jesus might have been born in the spring of 12 B.C. or 11 B.C.

Luke Revisited

The Book of Luke gave two conflicting sets of data on the question of Jesus' birth. Certainly, Luke's passage stating that Jesus was born in A.D. 6, shortly after the call for a census went out from Emperor Augustus, is untenable. Experts have suggested that a census had been ordered years earlier by Augustus, but no records support that, nor was there any particular reason for the emperor to want one. In 12 B.C., Herod the Great was in power and had the full confidence of Augustus.

The Book of Luke also states that Jesus began his Ministry when he was 30 years of age. This has to be questioned as well.

But what if Jesus began his Ministry when he was 40 and not 30? Is it possible that Luke gathered some erroneous information when he was researching his planned Gospel, or that an early seminal copy of Luke was transcribed incorrectly? If Jesus were 40 years of age in A.D. 28, his birth year would have been 13 B.C. Add in a one year margin of error and Jesus' birth could well have been in the spring of A.D. 12, with Halley's Comet appearing six months later.

Interlude: Driven by the Protecting Star?

Linking Halley's Comet to the birth of Jesus gives rise to interesting speculations about Jesus himself. Just before Herod's slaughter of the newborn in Bethlehem and surrounding areas, how many families joined Joseph and Mary as they fled into Egypt to escape the threat of Herod's soldiers? The Bible is clear that Joseph and Mary came from Nazareth, but it can be postulated that Mary and Joseph traveled to Judea not to be counted in a census but for Mary's period of confinement and the anticipated birth of their first child. A first birth for a woman can be very difficult and dangerous. Mary's cousin Elisabeth had either just given birth, or was then in late pregnancy with John. Mary's extended family could have all been living in the town of Judah and Mary wanted their support.

Did Herod the Great cast a wider net than the New Testament suggests in his search for the Messiah? Judah was not far from Bethlehem. And how close were the executioners when Joseph and Mary managed to escape with the new-born baby Jesus? It must have been a harrowing flight, indeed. Many years were then spent in Egypt in hiding.

After the 4 B.C. death of Herod the Great, according to the Book of Matthew, Joseph and his family returned to Judea. Jesus was eight years of age then, having spent his crucial early years in Egypt as a refugee. Joseph might first have considered staying in the small town of Judah with Mary's family. But it soon became apparent that the Ethnarch Archelaus was every bit as cruel and evil as his father had been. Perhaps Archelaus was also vigilant in looking out for the Messiah child that had escaped his father. So Joseph moved his family away from Judea and back to Galilee and Nazareth–the city he had left with Mary eight years before. Herod Antipas ruled there now and had a much milder reputation. Antipas was also building a capital city for himself in Sepphoris, so Joseph, who was a carpenter by trade, could probably find plenty of work there. Joseph decided to settle in the town of Nazareth along with his wife Mary, his eldest son Jesus and his other children.

In A.D. 6, when Augustus removed Archelaus and called for a census, Joseph and Mary probably did indeed go to Bethlehem to register with the Romans. Was Mary pregnant with one of Joseph's other children at the time, and did she give birth in a manger in Bethlehem because there was no room in the inn? At that time, Jesus would have been 17 and likely have stayed in Nazareth to run the family business— if the Roman census edict allowed it. The son born to Mary in Bethlehem might have been James, who grew up to be James the Just and played an important role as one of the first leaders of the Christian Church in Jerusalem. The birth stories of Jesus and James might have been confused as the decades passed. If true, that would make James the Just 54 years of age at the time of his execution in A.D. 62.

Jesus had a rough time of it in his early life. Spending a good many years in Egypt in semi-seclusion, Jesus did not benefit from a Jewish social network of any consequence. In fact, Jesus never had the opportunity to learn to read or write (Jn 7:15).

When Joseph decided to settle in Nazareth, he then had some measure of social stability. But by that time, Jesus would have been far behind the other students of his age group–a very discouraging situation. Certainly, uncomfortable questions also lingered concerning Jesus' legitimacy. Life would have been very difficult for Joseph's family in Nazareth for that reason alone given the strict and unforgiving nature of Jewish society in those times. Additionally, with this devastating social stigma attached to Jesus, an advantageous marriage within the Jewish community was out of the question.

For those same reasons, a religious "track" was closed to Jesus. He had religious leanings, but was probably thwarted in his pursuit of them by the circumstances of his birth. As a young boy, did Jesus turn to the slightly odd but kindly men of the Essenic community for companionship and guidance? Perhaps so.

As the years passed and Jesus grew into his teens, he likely fell into the day-to-day routine of working as a carpenter. Later in life, with his younger brothers carrying the load of the family business, Jesus might himself have even joined the community of the Essenes while still working days in the carpentry shop. With the Essenes, prior social standing and literacy were of no concern.

Then lightning struck! Jesus' cousin John had disappeared years before into the wilderness in Perea to live the life of an ascetic–not an unusual life's decision in those days. But unexpectedly, John became famous in Judea and Galilee as "the Baptizer," and people were talking about John being a prophet and perhaps the fulfillment of scripture–the Messiah himself. Excited and hopeful, and just passed his fortieth birthday, Jesus left Nazareth in order to join his cousin John. Jesus did not know what to expect, but he perhaps believed that God had a special purpose for him. Soon Jesus had been baptized by John and was building his own Ministry.

Was Jesus surprised at how successful his Ministry became? Probably so. Soon he had gathered a large following and was preaching throughout the Jewish East.

Through the dramatic odyssey of Jesus and his later Ministry, it is tempting to speculate that the star of the East played a great role in his life. What would give any person the amazing confidence to challenge not only a vast empire, but a 2,000 year old religion? In Jesus' case, it may well have been the fiery and brilliant comet that marked his birth.

Chapter 13   The Ancient Window of Years

So Pilate, when he had tarried ten years in Judea, made haste to Rome
(*Antiq* XVIII 4:2)

It is clear from several ancient writings that Jesus' final Passover occurred during Pontius Pilate's tenure as the Judean prefect and under the Imperial reign of Roman Emperor Tiberius Caesar. Starting from this broad range of years, additional information provided by the ancient sources will be evaluated in turn to determine the year of Jesus' final Passover. It is unavoidable, however, that at certain points subjective conclusions will have to be made. Rest assured, great care will be taken to present evidence supporting these key assumptions–some arguments taking up several chapters.

Herod the Great and Emperor Tiberius

The year of Herod the Great's death is an important reference point for all of ancient history. In *Antiquities*, Flavius Josephus documented the observation of a lunar eclipse that occurred in the spring of the year of Herod's death (*Antiq* XVII 6:4; chapter 1). Mathematicians have calculated that year to be 4 B.C. Starting with that year as a base, specific dates for many other ancient events can be derived.

Concerning Emperor Tiberius, scholars accept with confidence his date of ascension to be the 14th of August, A.D. 14 which, of course, is also the date of the death of Emperor Augustus. Tiberius retained power through to his own death on the 17th of March, A.D. 37 (although some sources say the 16th).

These dates of Tiberius' reign are roughly confirmed by Josephus.

> So when Tiberius had at this time appointed Caius to be his successor, he outlived but a few days and then died, after he had held the government twenty-two years five months and three days. (*Antiq* XVIII 6:10)

From the New Testament, it is accepted that the crucifixion of Jesus occurred during the Passover. This major Jewish festival usually began in late March of the Roman Calendar, or mid-Nisan in the Jewish Calendar. As Tiberius assumed his powers after the Passover of A.D. 14 and died before the Passover of A.D. 37, the potential Passovers during Tiberius' reign when Jesus' crucifixion could have taken place would have been one of 22, inclusive of the years A.D. 15-36.

Pilate's Tenure

Jesus was crucified during the tenure of the Judean Prefect Pontius Pilate. Here again, Josephus is most helpful. Note that the term "prefect" was changed to "procurator" during the reign of Emperor Claudius (A.D. 41-54). As a side note, in the New Testament, the term "governor" is also used. All three Roman terms–governor, procurator and prefect–are interchangeable and indicate the same position of authority.

> (Tiberius) was now the third emperor; and he sent Valerius Gratus to be procurator of Judea and to succeed Annius Rufus. This man deprived Ananus of the high priesthood and appointed Ismael, the son of Phabi, to be high priest. He also deprived him in a little time and ordained Eleazar, the son of Ananus, who had been high priest before, to be high priest; which office, when he had held for a year, Gratus deprived him of it and gave the high priesthood to Simon, the son of Camithus; and when he had possessed that dignity no longer than a year, Joseph Caiaphas was made his successor. When Gratus had done those things, he went back to Rome, after he had tarried in Judea eleven years, when Pontius Pilate came as his successor. (*Antiq* XVIII 2:2)

In this marvelous and crucial excerpt from *Antiquities*, not only is the Prefect Pontius Pilate mentioned but also the High Priest Joseph Caiaphas and former High Priest Ananus–all of whom figure prominently in the Gospel accounts of Jesus' crucifixion. However, despite the wealth of information this passage provides, reasoned assumptions now must be made. The next few paragraphs should be read carefully and perhaps more than once, since the rest of the investigation is based upon them.

Taking some liberties with Josephus, it is assumed that the Prefect Valerius Gratus served out a little more than 11 years rather than a little less. It is also assumed that Tiberius, as was his nature, would have waited a respectful amount of time after Augustus' death in August of A.D. 14 before sending Gratus out to replace Annius Rufus. There is no evidence that Rufus was particularly eager to leave the East, and it can also be assumed that every day he was there he was making additional money in some corrupt fashion. From all this information, it can be concluded that the Prefect Gratus probably arrived at his new post in Caesarea in late A.D. 14.

It should be noted that both Rufus and Gratus had been generals under Varus and had played key roles in the quelling of the insurrections in the Jewish East in 3 B.C.

Emmaus was also burnt by Varus's order, after its inhabitants had deserted it, that he might avenge those that had there been destroyed. From thence he now marched to Jerusalem; whereupon those Jews whose camp lay there and who had besieged the Roman legion, not bearing the coming of this army, left the siege imperfect: but as to the Jerusalem Jews, when Varus reproached them bitterly for what had been done, they cleared themselves of the accusation and alleged that the conflux of the people was occasioned by the feast; that the war was not made with their approbation, but by the rashness of the strangers, while they were on the side of the Romans and besieged together with them, rather than having any inclination to besiege them. There also came beforehand to meet Varus, Joseph, the cousin-german of king Herod, as also Gratus and Rufus, who brought their soldiers along with them, together with those Romans who had been besieged; but Sabinus did not come into Varus's presence, but stole out of the city privately and went to the sea-side. (*Antiq* XVII 10:9).

Judean Rulers Augustus-Tiberius

Emperor	King-Prefect	High Priest
Augustus 42 B.C. - A.D. 14	Herod the Great 37-4 B.C.	
		Jozar bar Boethus 3 B.C. - A.D. 7
	Archelaus 4 B.C. - A.D. 6	
	Coponius A.D. 6-9	Ananus bar Seth A.D. 7-22
	Ambivius A.D. 9-12	
	Rufus A.D. 12-14	
Tiberius A.D. 14- A.D. 37	Gratus A.D. 14-26	
		Ishmael A.D. 23
		Eleazar A.D. 24
		Simon A.D. 25
	Pilate A.D. 26-37	Caiaphas A.D. 26-36
	Marcellus (Marullus) A.D. 37-41	Jonathan A.D. 36-37

Both Gratus and Varus had strong military backgrounds; they knew Judea well and could handle any sort of provincial trouble.

If the Judean Prefect Gratus served out 11 full years, as Josephus says he did, then Gratus would have returned to Rome sometime during his 12th year of service which would be either late A.D. 26 or early A.D. 27. With a perpetual current of unrest in Judea, Gratus would not likely have left Caesarea until Pilate was firmly in place and comfortable with assuming full control. Counting up those eleven years, Gratus' last Passover would be that of A.D. 26. Pilate's first Passover as prefect would be that of A.D. 27.

Pilate's Departure

When did Pontius Pilate leave the office of prefect?

> So Pilate, when he had tarried ten years in Judea, made haste to Rome and this in obedience to the orders of Vitellius which he durst not contradict; but before he could get to Rome Tiberius was dead. (*Antiq* XVIII 4:2)

This passage introduces General Lucius Vitellius who will play a central role in Jesus' final Passover. For now, it is sufficient to know that Vitellius was the president of Syria from A.D. 35-38. In this office, Vitellius was Pontius Pilate's immediate superior under Emperor Tiberius.

Tiberius died on March 16 or 17 of A.D. 37. As Pilate was removed from office shortly before the death of Tiberius, his termination had to have occurred in early A.D. 37. From this, it can be concluded that Pilate was in power for the Passover of A.D. 36, but definitely not in power for the Passover of A.D. 37. With Pilate's first Passover as prefect in A.D. 27, there is a 10 year interval when the crucifixion of Jesus could have occurred.

Ananus and Caiaphas

The ancient sources are also clear that Joseph Caiaphas was the prosecuting High Priest when Jesus was arrested during his final

Passover. The Book of John states that Caiaphas' father-in-law Ananus was the first to interrogate Jesus after Jesus' arrest by the Temple guards. What were the years of power of both Ananus and his son-in-law Caiaphas in the High Priest position? Fortunately, Josephus tracks the succession of High Priests with some care.

> When Cyrenius had now disposed of Archelaus's money and when the taxings were come to a conclusion which were made in the thirty-seventh year of Caesar's victory over Antony at Actium, he deprived Joazar of the high priesthood which dignity had been conferred on him by the multitude and he appointed Ananus, the son of Seth, to be high priest (*Antiq* XVIII 2:1)

Cyrenius (Quirinius) was then the president of Syria. It was a powerful position and Cyrenius had authority over not only Syria but the Jewish lands to the south, even though those lands were technically ruled over by the sons of Herod. When Herod's son Archelaus was removed from power by Emperor Augustus in A.D. 6, it was Cyrenius who was sent to take account of Archelaus' property and money and see how best to administer the land. In fact, it might have been Cyrenius who, after considering the scope and complexity of Archelaus' territory, recommended to Augustus that a Roman prefect be sent to rule instead of a son of Herod the Great. Augustus agreed to this and appointed Coponius as the first Judean prefect.

Archelaus was removed as ethnarch by Emperor Augustus after serving nine full years in that position, plus some portion of a 10th. The record suggests that after Herod the Great's death in 4 B.C., Archelaus was considered to be the Judean king–even though it took nearly a year for Emperor Augustus to make up his mind and formally proclaim him such. So this is further evidence that it was in late A.D. 6 that Cyrenius started taking account of the affairs of the Herods in Samaria and Judea, completing the enrollment and taxation in A.D. 7.

Josephus references the defeat of Antony and Cleopatra's forces at the battle of Actium. Other Roman sources confirm that this event occurred in the fall of 31 B.C. Counting 37 years from that date would give us A.D. 7. Josephus writes that the High priest changeover was made after the taxation (enrollment) of Cyrenius. It would be reasonable that the taxations began in late A.D. 6 and ended in A.D. 7. Cyrenius would have allowed at least six months and possibly a year for all the people of the Jewish East to report and pay their taxes and for his agents to finish their assessment of the wealth and extent of Archelaus' empire.

During this period, Cyrenius familiarized himself with the politics of the East. In deciding on what was in the best interests of Rome, Cyrenius removed Archelaus' appointment as High Priest, Joazar, and replaced him with a young Simon Ananus — a fortunate day for Ananus!

Doing the calculations and assuming continuous service at the great Temple, the High Priest Joazar served for 10 Passovers before turning over the vestments to Simon Ananus bar Seth. From this, it can be assumed that Ananus' first Passover as Second Temple High Priest was probably for the Passover of A.D. 7.

Simon Ananus spent his early years in power assiduously cultivating his Roman superiors. With continued and unbroken support from the Caesars, Ananus would go on to build one of the great power dynasties in all of Jewish history–becoming a wealthy man in the process. This was the same Ananus who not only interrogated Jesus of Nazareth on Jesus' last day alive, but also briefly served as a leader of the Jewish revolt 30 years later in A.D. 68 (*Wars* IV 3:7).

Ananus served as High Priest until the Prefect Gratus was appointed by Tiberius to replace Rufus in A.D. 14. Previously, under Augustus, the Prefect Coponius was in power from A.D. 6-9 before being replaced by Marcus Ambivius. Ambivius served without incident from A.D. 9-12 until he was replaced by Annius Rufus–who was Augustus' last Judean prefect before he died.

> He (Tiberius) was now the third emperor; and he sent Valerius Gratus to be procurator of Judea and to succeed Annius Rufus. This man deprived Ananus of the high priesthood and appointed Ismael, the son of Phabi, to be high priest. He also deprived him in a little time and ordained

Eleazar, the son of Ananus, who had been high priest before, to be high priest; which office, when he had held for a year, Gratus deprived him of it and gave the high priesthood to Simon, the son of Camithus; and when he had possessed that dignity no longer than a year, Joseph Caiaphas was made his successor. When Gratus had done those things, he went back to Rome, after he had tarried in Judea eleven years, when Pontius Pilate came as his successor. (*Antiq* XVIII 2:2)

At some point, the Prefect Valerius Gratus removed High Priest Ananus and began to appoint different men to one-year terms as High Priest. Unfortunately, Josephus does not document exactly when Gratus started this new policy. Taking some liberties with the facts, it can be reasonably assumed that Ananus served as High Priest of the Second Temple from A.D. 7 through to the Passover of A.D. 22–an unbroken tenure of 15 years. Then Ismael, Eleazar (Ananus' son), and Simon were appointed to the High Priest's position for the Passovers of 23, 24 and A.D. 25, respectively–one-year terms each.

However, it is possible that Gratus replaced Ananus immediately upon arrival in Judea in A.D. 14 which would give Ananus a term of only seven years. Appreciating Ananus' subsequent power in Judea, however, this is less likely.

Which brings us to the infamous Joseph Caiaphas. If Caiaphas was not already Ananus' son-in-law at the time of his appointment to the High Priest's position, he soon would be. Caiaphas would also be Prefect Gratus' last choice for High Priest before he left office. Given the uncertainty over the tenure of Ananus, two scenarios for the term of office of Caiaphas can be made: either he was appointed in time to serve as the High Priest for the Passover of A.D. 26, or appointed earlier in time for the Passover of A.D. 19. So Caiaphas served from anywhere from 11 years to 18 years–taking years away from Ananus' term to arrive at the larger number for Caiaphas. However, more years for Ananus seems reasonable given Ananus' favor with the Romans and his subsequent importance even decades after he served.

The Prefect Gratus left the Jewish East with Joseph Caiaphas in the High Priest's position. In consideration of the constant turbulence in those territories, Gratus showed a great faith in

Caiaphas' ability to maintain the peace during the prefect changeover. An uneventful Passover of A.D. 27 would help the new Governor Pilate ease into his difficult administrative position. Of course, the real power behind Caiaphas was the former High Priest Ananus, who undoubtedly assured Gratus that Pilate would find the transition a smooth one.

Syrian President Lucius Vitellius removed Caiaphas in either A.D. 35 or A.D. 36.

> Besides which, he (Vitellius) also deprived Joseph, who was also called Caiaphas, of the high priesthood and appointed Jonathan the son of Ananus, the former high priest, to succeed him. After which, he took his journey back to Antioch. (*Antiq* XVIII 4:3)

The future of Lucius Vitellius would prove to be a bright one. Vitellius was to become a major behind-the-scenes power broker and adviser for three Roman emperors. In fact, Vitellius would be acting emperor for several months while Emperor Claudius was leading a military campaign in British Isles. His son, Aulus, would himself become emperor for a brief period in A.D. 69. But returning to Joseph Caiaphas, if Vitellius journeyed to Jerusalem and removed Caiaphas before the beginning of the Passover of A.D. 36, then the limiting year of Jesus' crucifixion would be the Passover of A.D. 35.

Conclusion

Using the duration of the reign of Tiberius as our initial parameter, the Passover of Jesus' crucifixion had to be in one of 22 years–those inclusive from A.D. 15 to A.D. 36. Using the tenure of the Prefect Pontius Pilate as a more limiting parameter, the Passover had to be in one of 10 years inclusive of A.D. 27-36. Considering the tenure of Joseph Caiaphas, the range of years is either unaffected, or limited to the years A.D. 27-35, depending on the year Caiaphas was removed from office by Vitellius. So we start off the investigation with a 9 or 10 year window within which Jesus' last Passover had to have occurred.

Chapter 14   The Ministry of John the Baptist

There came a man, sent from God, whose name was John. (Jn 1:6)

John the Baptist is a true religious icon. The popular image of John is likely not far off the mark–fire in his eyes, hair unshorn, wearing camel-hair skins and standing knee deep in a mighty flowing desert river. Under a blazing sun, his powerful voice booms out a message of salvation to the gathered crowd on the shore: Wash your sins away in the Jordan River and be reborn into God's kingdom!

John the Baptist's fame was widespread. Kings and Jewish priests feared his power over the common people. Decades after his violent death, John the Baptist still had his own cult following despite the increasing popularity of Jesus.

> [19:1] And it came to pass, that, while Apollos was at Corinth, Paul having passed through the upper country came to Ephesus and found certain disciples: [19:2] and he said unto them, Did ye receive the Holy Spirit when ye believed? And they *said* unto him, Nay, we did not so much as hear whether the Holy Spirit was *given.* [19:3] And he said, Into what then were ye baptized? And they said, Into John's baptism. (Acts)

But who was John really? Was he a simple religious hermit, who, after experiencing an epiphany in the desert, was driven to start a ministry based on his vision of the coming of God's kingdom? Or was John secretly a calculating zealot, fomenting revolution in the isolated wilds of Perea under the guise of religion?

Although John repeatedly denied that his objective was political (Jn1:25-7) and repeatedly denied that he was the Messiah, the Jerusalem Sanhedrin and the High Priesthood treated him with great caution. They knew that John's words could easily create sedition and rebellion amongst the Jews.

Jesus' Ministry didn't formally adopt John's water baptism ritual, though some Disciples of Jesus did practice it. Later, the Apostles modified the concept, arguing that it was better to be baptized in the Holy Spirit through the ceremony of communion than to be baptized by water. Certainly, it was convenient not to be tied to a natural water source for a gathering–only wine and bread was needed for communion.

John the Baptist's life is inextricably linked to the life of Jesus of Nazareth. What dates can be derived from John's story?

The Gospel of Mark

The Book of Mark has passages about John the Baptist and his teachings, but gives no clues as to dates.

> [1:2]Even as it is written in Isaiah the prophet, Behold, I send my messenger before thy face, Who shall prepare thy way. [1:3]The voice of one crying in the wilderness, Make ye ready the way of the Lord, Make his paths straight; [1:4]John came, who baptized in the wilderness and preached the baptism of repentance unto remission of sins. [1:5]And there went out unto him all the country of Judaea and all they of Jerusalem; And they were baptized of him in the river Jordan, confessing their sins. [1:6]And John was clothed with camel's hair and *had* a leathern girdle about his loins and did eat locusts and wild honey. [1:7]And he preached, saying, There cometh after me he that is mightier than I, the latchet of whose shoes I am not worthy to stoop down and unloose. [1:8]I baptized you in water; But he shall baptize you in the Holy Spirit. [1:9]And it came to pass in those days, that Jesus came from Nazareth of Galilee and was baptized of John in the Jordan. (Mk)

Note that in Mark, John the Baptist personally baptizes Jesus.

The Gospel of Matthew

In the Book of Matthew, as in Mark, there is no mention of specific dates for John's life or ministry.

> [3:1]And in those days cometh John the Baptist, preaching in the wilderness of Judaea, saying, [3:2]Repent ye; for the kingdom of heaven is at hand. [3:3]For this is he that was spoken of through Isaiah the prophet, saying,
> The voice of one crying in the wilderness,
> Make ye ready the way of the Lord,
> Make his paths straight.
> [3:4]Now John himself had his raiment of camel's hair and a leathern girdle about his loins; and his food was locusts and wild honey. [3:5]Then went out unto him Jerusalem and all Judaea and all the region round about the Jordan; [3:6]and they were baptized of him in the river Jordan, confessing their sins. (Mt)

It is also important to note that, in contrast to the Book of Mark, Matthew does not state that Jesus was baptized by John or any of John's disciples. A minor point is that Matthew doesn't mention Perea, only that John preached in the "wilderness" of Judea.

The Gospel of John

In John, as with Mark and Matthew, no early dates are given or alluded to, but John the Baptist himself is quoted as he debates with the Pharisees and later baptizes Jesus.

> [1:6]There came a man, sent from God, whose name was John. [1:7]The same came for witness, that he might bear witness of the light, that all might believe through him. [1:8]He was not the light, but *came* that he might bear witness of the light. [1:9]There was the true light, *even the light* which lighteth every man, coming into the world. [1:10]He was in the world and the world was made through him and the world knew him not. [1:11]He came unto his own and they that were his own received him not. [1:12]But as many as received him, to them gave he the right to become children of God, *even* to them that believe on his name: [1:13]who were born, not of

blood, nor of the will of the flesh, nor of the will of man, but of God. [1:14]And the Word became flesh and dwelt among us (and we beheld his glory, glory as of the only begotten from the Father), full of grace and truth. [1:15]John beareth witness of him and crieth, saying, This was he of whom I said, He that cometh after me is become before me: for he was before me. [1:16]For of his fulness we all received and grace for grace. [1:17]For the law was given through Moses; grace and truth came through Jesus Christ. [1:18]No man hath seen God at any time; the only begotten Son, who is in the bosom of the Father, he hath declared *him*. [1:19]And this is the witness of John, when the Jews sent unto him from Jerusalem priests and Levites to ask him, Who art thou? [1:20]And he confessed and denied not; and he confessed, I am not the Christ. [1:21]And they asked him, What then? Art thou Elijah? And he saith, I am not. Art thou the prophet? And he answered, No. [1:22]They said therefore unto him, Who art thou? that we may give an answer to them that sent us. What sayest thou of thyself? [1:23]He said, I am the voice of one crying in the wilderness, Make straight the way of the Lord, as said Isaiah the prophet. [1:24]And they had been sent from the Pharisees. [1:25]And they asked him and said unto him, Why then baptizest thou, if thou art not the Christ, neither Elijah, neither the prophet? [1:26]John answered them, saying, I baptize in water: in the midst of you standeth one whom ye know not, [1:27]*even* he that cometh after me, the latchet of whose shoe I am not worthy to unloose. [1:28]These things were done in Bethany beyond the Jordan, where John was baptizing. [1:29]On the morrow he seeth Jesus coming unto him and saith, Behold, the Lamb of God, that taketh away the sin of the world! [1:30]This is he of whom I said, After me cometh a man who is become before me: for he was before me. [1:31]And I knew him not; but that he should be made manifest to Israel, for this cause came I baptizing in water. [1:32]And John bare witness, saying, I have beheld the Spirit descending as a dove out of heaven; and it abode upon him. [1:33]And I knew him not: but he that sent me to baptize in water, he said unto me, Upon whomsoever thou shalt see the Spirit descending and abiding upon him, the same is he that baptizeth in the Holy Spirit. [1:34]And I have seen and have borne witness that this is the Son of God. (Jn)

The detail of this passage suggests that the author of the Book of John personally heard John the Baptist preach–an intriguing prospect.

The Gospel of Luke

In contrast to the other three Gospels, Luke goes into great detail about the birth of John, as we have seen in chapter 12. Later in Luke, we are given several more significant dates concerning the start of the ministry of John the Baptist.

3:1Now in the fifteenth year of the reign of Tiberius Caesar, Pontius Pilate being governor of Judaea and Herod being tetrarch of Galilee and his brother Philip tetrarch of the region of Ituraea and Trachonitis and Lysanias tetrarch of Abilene, 3:2in the highpriesthood of Annas and Caiaphas, the word of God came unto John the son of Zacharias in the wilderness. 3:3And he came into all the region round about the Jordan, preaching the baptism of repentance unto remission of sins; 3:4as it is written in the Book of the words of Isaiah the prophet, The voice of one crying in the wilderness, Make ye ready the way of the Lord, Make his paths straight. 3:5Every valley shall be filled and every mountain and hill shall be brought low; And the crooked shall become straight and the rough ways smooth; 3:6And all flesh shall see the salvation of God. 3:7He said therefore to the multitudes that went out to be baptized of him, Ye offspring of vipers, who warned you to flee from the wrath to come? 3:8Bring forth therefore fruits worthy of repentance and begin not to say within yourselves, We have Abraham to our father: for I say unto you, that God is able of these stones to raise up children unto Abraham. 3:9And even now the axe also lieth at the root of the trees: every tree therefore that bringeth not forth good fruit is hewn down and cast into the fire. 3:10And the multitudes asked him, saying, What then must we do? 3:11And he answered and said unto them, He that hath two coats, let him impart to him that hath none; and he that hath food, let him do likewise. 3:12And there came also publicans to be baptized and they said unto him, Teacher, what must we do? 3:13And he said unto them, Extort no more than that which is appointed you. 3:14And soldiers also asked him, saying and we, what must we do? And he said unto them, Extort from no man by violence, neither accuse *any one* wrongfully; and be content with your wages. 3:15And as the people were in expectation and all men reasoned in their hearts concerning John, whether haply he were the Christ; 3:16John answered, saying unto them all, I indeed baptize you with water; but there cometh he that is mightier than I, the latchet of whose shoes I am not worthy to unloose: he shall baptize you in the Holy Spirit and *in* fire: 3:17whose fan is in his hand, thoroughly to cleanse his threshing-floor and to gather the wheat into his garner; but the chaff he will burn up with unquenchable fire. ^{3:18}With many other exhortations therefore preached he good tidings unto the people; ^{3:19}but Herod the tetrarch, being reproved by him for Herodias his brother's wife and for all the evil things which Herod had done, ^{3:20}added this also to them all, that he shut up John in prison. ^{3:21}Now it came to pass, when all the people were baptized, that, Jesus also having been baptized and praying, the heaven was opened, ^{3:22}and the Holy Spirit descended in a bodily form, as a dove, upon him and a voice came out of heaven, Thou art my beloved Son; in thee I am well pleased. ^{3:23}And Jesus himself, when he began *to teach*, was about thirty years of age, being the son (as was supposed) of Joseph, the *son* of Heli, (Lk)

Luke provides us with a considerable amount of useful information. It will be digested in piecemeal fashion now, and referred to often in later chapters.

Unlike the other Gospels, specific dates are documented in the Book of Luke. A key passage bears repeating.

> Now in the fifteenth year of the reign of Tiberius Caesar, Pontius Pilate being governor of Judaea and Herod being tetrarch of Galilee and his brother Philip tetrarch of the region of Ituraea and Trachonitis and Lysanias tetrarch of Abilene, in the highpriesthood of Annas and Caiaphas, the word of God came unto John the son of Zacharias in the wilderness. (Lk 3:1)

Luke seems to mis-reference the High Priesthood of Ananus. Assuming that the 15th year of the reign of Tiberius was A.D. 28, Ananus would have been long past his official time of tenure. When Ananus was in power years earlier, Josephus Caiaphas was at least a novitiate Second Temple priest and likely a mere youth. Josephus, in fact, documents that three other High Priests held office between Ananus and Caiaphas (*Antiq* XVIII 2:2). However, Luke was probably referring to the tenure of Caiaphas, but with the assumption that Ananus was the real power behind him.

Tiberius became the emperor of Rome when Augustus died in August A.D. 14 which would have been the first Calendar year of his reign. The second calendar year would have started in

January, six months away. That would make the 15th year of Tiberius' reign the entire year of A.D. 28.

The Beginning

John the Baptist may have begun his ministry earlier than A.D. 28, but became famous outside of southern Perea in that year. Also, A.D. 28 is not necessarily the date that Jesus was actually baptized by John–Jesus could have been baptized much later. Indeed, in other Gospels, Jesus is not baptized by John at all.

An evaluation of the Book of Luke concludes that John the Baptist could not have baptized Jesus any earlier than A.D. 28. That leads to the conclusion that the earliest possible year for the Passover of Jesus' crucifixion was A.D. 28.

However, if A.D. 28 marked the Passover of the crucifixion, Jesus' Ministry lasted for at most three months. The Passover was a springtime festival celebrated in late March in the Julian Calendar. Logistically, this presents problems that are insurmountable. In that three-month period, not only did John the Baptist himself have to be arrested and executed, but Jesus had to have time to gather his disciples together and travel extensively with them throughout the Jewish lands. In those three months, Jesus had to spend time in Caesarea Philippi, Tyre, Sidon, Capernaum and Bethsaida–to say nothing of teaching in the Jerusalem Temple, working several miracles, and attending to various other activities. So while A.D. 28 is among the possible years for Jesus' crucifixion, it would contradict much of what is written in the Gospels about Jesus' Ministry and so is untenable.

From information provided in the Gospels on the life and ministry of John, the earliest possible year for Jesus' crucifixion is A.D. 28, with A.D. 29 being far more likely. The latest year for the crucifixion remains either A.D. 35 or A.D. 36.

The Execution of John the Baptist

The dates when John the Baptist was arrested by Herod Antipas and later executed are speculative. But it is clear from the

Gospels that certain events in the Ministry of Jesus took place before John was arrested; others occurred while John was in prison; and still others took place after his execution–the latter most notably being Jesus' own arrest and execution. It is unlikely that specific years can be derived about Jesus' Ministry from the story of John the Baptist, but a relative chronology can be constructed which will prove to be very useful.

The Gospel of John

In the Book of John, it is learned that Jesus' first Disciples were initially disciples of John the Baptist. After the baptism of Jesus, John encouraged these men to leave him and follow Jesus. Two men are mentioned; one is Andrew and the identity of the other is not clear. After talking with Jesus, Andrew was enthusiastic enough to later convince his brother Simon Peter to become a Disciple as well. All this, according to the Book of John, occurred in Perea, at John's wilderness encampment.

> $^{1:35}$Again on the morrow John was standing and two of his disciples; $^{1:36}$and he looked upon Jesus as he walked and saith, Behold, the Lamb of God! $^{1:37}$And the two disciples heard him speak and they followed Jesus. $^{1:38}$And Jesus turned and beheld them following and saith unto them, What seek ye? And they said unto him, Rabbi (which is to say, being interpreted, Teacher), where abideth thou? $^{1:39}$He saith unto them, Come and ye shall see. They came therefore and saw where he abode; and they abode with him that day: it was about the tenth hour. $^{1:40}$One of the two that heard John *speak* and followed him, was Andrew, Simon Peter's brother. $^{1:41}$He findeth first his own brother Simon and saith unto him, We have found the Messiah (which is, being interpreted, Christ). (Jn)

Also in the Book of John, before Jesus' first Passover at the Second Temple Temple in Jerusalem, Jesus traveled to Galilee, gathered more Disciples, performed his first miracle at Cana, and preached for a time. Then, later at the Passover celebration, Jesus challenged the moneychangers in the Temple. Learning of the incident, Nicodemus, a member of the Jerusalem Sanhedrin, became alarmed. He sought Jesus out in order to ask him questions and determine his intentions (Jn 3:1-2).

Also according to John, there was an overlapping period of time when both Jesus and John led rival religious factions. At one point, the two ministries were camped near each other along the shores of the same water source. Jesus' Disciples were baptizing new converts. John the Baptist was asked by his own disciples if he had given Jesus the authority to baptize–wasn't this new "sacrament" the sole domain of John's ministry?

> 3:22After these things came Jesus and his disciples into the land of Judea; and there he tarried with them and baptized. 3:23And John also was baptizing in Enon near to Salim, because there was much water there: and they came and were baptized. 3:24For John was not yet cast into prison. 3:25There arose therefore a questioning on the part of John's disciples with a Jew about purifying. 3:26And they came unto John and said to him, Rabbi, he that was with thee beyond the Jordan, to whom thou hast borne witness, behold, the same baptizeth and all men come to him. 3:27John answered and said, A man can receive nothing, except it have been given him from heaven. 3:28Ye yourselves bear me witness, that I said, I am not the Christ, but, that I am sent before him. 3:29He that hath the bride is the bridegroom: but the friend of the bridegroom, that standeth and heareth him, rejoiceth greatly because of the bridegroom's voice: this my joy therefore is made full. 3:30He must increase, but I must decrease. 3:31He that cometh from above is above all: he that is of the earth is of the earth and of the earth he speaketh: he that cometh from heaven is above all. 3:32What he hath seen and heard, of that he beareth witness; and no man receiveth his witness. 3:33He that hath received his witness hath set his seal to *this*, that God is true. 3:34For he whom God hath sent speaketh the words of God: for he giveth not the Spirit by measure. 3:35The Father loveth the Son and hath given all things into his hand. 3:36He that believeth on the Son hath eternal life; but he that obeyeth not the Son shall not see life, but the wrath of God abideth on him. (Jn).

According to the Book of John, after the first Passover in Jerusalem when Jesus challenged the moneychangers, John the Baptist had not yet been arrested. The Gospel also strongly implies that the Pharisees of Judea were willing to tolerate John the Baptist's presence, but that Jesus and his Ministry made them uneasy.

At any rate, after the "confrontation" with John's disciples, Jesus then retreated north into Galilee.

> 4:1When therefore the Lord knew that the Pharisees had heard that Jesus was making and baptizing more disciples than John 4:2(although Jesus himself baptized not, but his disciples), 4:3he left Judea and departed again into Galilee. (Jn)

Much later in his Ministry, after John's arrest and execution and shortly before Jesus' own crucifixion, Jesus returned to one of John's encampments, possibly Bethany Beyond the Jordan, where Jesus had been baptized.

> 10:40And he went away again beyond the Jordan into the place where John was at the first baptizing; and there be abode. 10:41And many came unto him; and they said, John indeed did no sign: but all things whatsoever John spake of this man were true. 10:42And many believed on him there. (Jn)

And that is the last direct reference to John the Baptist in the Book of John.

The Gospel of Mark

In Mark, contrary to the Book of John, Jesus is said to have found his first disciples, Andrew and Simon Peter, only after John the Baptist had been arrested and Jesus left Judea for Galilee.

> 1:14Now after John was delivered up, Jesus came into Galilee, preaching the gospel of God, 1:15and saying, The time is fulfilled and the kingdom of God is at hand: repent ye and believe in the gospel. 1:16And passing along by the sea of Galilee, he saw Simon and Andrew the brother of Simon casting a net in the sea; for they were fishers. 1:17And Jesus said unto them, Come ye after me and I will make you to become fishers of men. 1:18And straightway they left the nets and followed him. (Mk)

This is somewhat concerning and reflects poorly on the Book of John, for the author of the Book of Mark was supposedly John Mark, a disciple of Simon Peter himself!

At any rate, later a conflict arises between Jesus' Disciples and the Pharisees and John's disciples–the latter who, apparently, were still active even though John had been at least arrested and possibly already executed.

> 2:18And John's disciples and the Pharisees were fasting: and they come and say unto him, Why do John's disciples and the disciples of the Pharisees fast, but thy disciples fast not? (Mk)

Then comes famous story in Mark about how John the Baptist came to be arrested and subsequently executed. It is told in the context of the Tetrarch Herod Antipas becoming aware of Jesus and his reputed powers.

> 6:14And king Herod heard *thereof*; for his name had become known: and he said, John the Baptizer is risen from the dead and therefore do these powers work in him. 6:15But others said, It is Elijah. And others said, *It is a prophet, even* as one of the prophets. 6:16But Herod, when he heard *thereof*, said, John, whom I beheaded, he is risen. 6:17For Herod himself had sent forth and laid hold upon John and bound him in prison for the sake of Herodias, his brother Philip's wife; for he had married her. 6:18For John said unto Herod, It is not lawful for thee to have thy brother's wife. 6:19And Herodias set herself against him and desired to kill him; and she could not; 6:20for Herod feared John, knowing that he was a righteous and holy man and kept him safe. And when he heard him, he was much perplexed; and he heard him gladly. 6:21And when a convenient day was come, that Herod on his birthday made a supper to his lords and the high captains and the chief men of Galilee; 6:22and when the daughter of Herodias herself came in and danced, she pleased Herod and them that sat at meat with him; and the king said unto the damsel, Ask of me whatsoever thou wilt and I will give it thee. 6:23And he sware unto her, Whatsoever thou shalt ask of me, I will give it thee, unto the half of my kingdom. 6:24And she went out and said unto her mother, What shall I ask? And she said, The head of John the Baptizer. 6:25And she came in straightway with haste unto the king and asked, saying, I will that thou forthwith give me on a platter the head of John

the Baptist. $^{6:26}$ And the king was exceeding sorry; but for the sake of his oaths and of them that sat at meat, he would not reject her. $^{6:27}$ And straightway the king sent forth a soldier of his guard and commanded to bring his head: and he went and beheaded him in the prison, $^{6:28}$ and brought his head on a platter and gave it to the damsel; and the damsel gave it to her mother. $^{6:29}$ And when his disciples heard *thereof*, they came and took up his corpse and laid it in a tomb. (Mk)

This is a key passage that Josephus expands upon, and it will be referenced many more times. This narrative does not, however, in and of itself, suggest a date for the arrest or execution of John.

Following in the Book of Mark is another revealing passage.

$^{6:45}$ And straightway he constrained his disciples to enter into the boat and to go before *him* unto the other side to Bethsaida, while he himself sendeth the multitude away. $^{6:46}$ And after he had taken leave of them, he departed into the mountain to pray. $^{6:47}$ And when even was come, the boat was in the midst of the sea and he alone on the land. (Mk)

It is important to note that this action of Jesus occurs after the beheading of John the Baptist by Herod Antipas. Then, Jesus retreats with his Disciples to a "desert place." After the relocation, Jesus sends his Disciples to Bethsaida while he himself goes upon the "mountain" in order to pray.

During the later time that Jesus is in Caesarea Philippi, the Book of Mark provides further evidence that John the Baptist has been executed.

$^{8:27}$ And Jesus went forth and his disciples, into the villages of Caesarea Philippi: and on the way he asked his disciples, saying unto them, Who do men say that I am? $^{8:28}$ And they told him, saying, John the Baptist; and others, Elijah; but others, One of the prophets. (Mk)

It is reasonable to assume that Jesus would not supposed to be the spirit of John the Baptist if John was still living.

The Gospel of Matthew

In Matthew, no mention is made of when exactly Jesus began his ministry, but it does say that Jesus went to Galilee after John was "delivered up", i.e., after John was arrested by Herod Antipas.

4:12Now when he heard that John was delivered up, he withdrew into Galilee; 4:13and leaving Nazareth, he came and dwelt in Capernaum which is by the sea, in the borders of Zebulun and Naphtali: (Mt).

Note that the word "withdrew" is used, suggesting that Jesus was fearful of confrontation. Again, as in John and Mark, later the disciples of John challenge Jesus, apparently in Galilee.

Then come to him the disciples of John, saying, Why do we and the Pharisees fast oft, but thy disciples fast not? (Mt 9:14)

Later, John the Baptist, imprisoned by Herod Antipas, hears about the success of Jesus and sends a message to him.

11:1And it came to pass when Jesus had finished commanding his twelve disciples, he departed thence to teach and preach in their cities. 11:2Now when John heard in the prison the works of the Christ, he sent by his disciples 11:3and said unto him, Art thou he that cometh, or look we for another? 11:4And Jesus answered and said unto them, Go and tell John the things which ye hear and see: 11:5the blind receive their sight and the lame walk, the lepers are cleansed and the deaf hear and the dead are raised up and the poor have good tidings preached to them. 11:6And blessed is he, whosoever shall find no occasion of stumbling in me. (Mt)

Next, Matthew chronicles the execution of John the Baptist, in a passage very similar to that found in the Book of Mark.

14:1At that season Herod the tetrarch heard the report concerning Jesus, 14:2and said unto his servants, This is John the Baptist; he is risen from the dead; and therefore do these powers work in him. 14:3For Herod had laid hold on John and bound him and put him in prison for the sake of Herodias, his brother Philip's wife. 14:4For John said unto him, It is not lawful for thee to have her. ¹⁴:⁵And when he would have put him to death, he feared the multitude, because they counted him as a prophet. ¹⁴:⁶But when Herod's birthday came, the daughter of Herodias danced in the midst and pleased Herod. ¹⁴:⁷Whereupon he promised with an oath to give her whatsoever she should ask. ¹⁴:⁸And she, being put forward by her mother, saith, Give me here on a platter the head of John the Baptist. ¹⁴:⁹And the king was grieved; but for the sake of his oaths and of them that sat at meat with him, he commanded it to be given; ¹⁴:¹⁰and he sent and beheaded John in the prison. ¹⁴:¹¹And his head was brought on a platter and given to the damsel: and she brought it to her mother. ¹⁴:¹²And his disciples came and took up the corpse and buried him; and they went and told Jesus. (Mt)

In the Book of Matthew it is clear that after the beheading of John the Baptist, Jesus retreats to a "desert" place and then proceeds to other areas around the Gennesareth by way of a boat.

Now when Jesus heard it, he withdrew from thence in a boat, to a desert place apart: and when the multitudes heard thereof, they followed him on foot from the cities. And he came forth and saw a great multitude and he had compassion on them and healed their sick. And when even was come, the disciples came to him, saying, The place is desert and the time is already past; send the multitudes away, that they may go into the villages and buy themselves food. (Mt 14:13-15)

The movements of Jesus and his Disciples after John's execution are key points and they will be revisited later.

The Gospel of Luke

The baptism of Jesus is mentioned in Luke almost in passing. It is not clearly stated whether John himself was the baptizer, or if it was one of John's disciples. It is also not apparent if Jesus began his Ministry before or after Herod Antipas arrested John. In the Book of Luke, John the Baptist does talk about one who is mightier than he who was to come, but it is not clear if he was referring to Jesus or not.

John answered, saying unto them all, I indeed baptize you with water; but there cometh he that is mightier than I, the latchet of whose shoes I am not worthy to unloose: he shall baptize you in the Holy Spirit and *in* fire: (Lk 3:16)

Later, in Galilee Jesus is challenged by critics questioning the dedication of his Disciples. The disciples of John are mentioned, but John the Baptist himself is not, suggesting that at the time John was in prison.

> 5:33 And they said unto him, The disciples of John fast often and make supplications; likewise also the *disciples* of the Pharisees; but thine eat and drink. 5:34 And Jesus said unto them, Can ye make the sons of the bride-chamber fast, while the bridegroom is with them? (Lk)

As in Matthew, Luke relates the story of John's disciples, sent by John while he was in prison, to question Jesus–now in Galilee–about the source of his authority.

> 7:18 And the disciples of John told him of all these things. 7:19 And John calling unto him two of his disciples sent them to the Lord, saying, Art thou he that cometh, or look we for another? 7:20 And when the men were come unto him, they said, John the Baptist hath sent us unto thee, saying, Art thou he that cometh, or look we for another? 7:21 In that hour he cured many of diseases and plagues and evil spirits; and on many that were blind he bestowed sight. 7:22 And he answered and said unto them, Go and tell John the things which ye have seen and heard; the blind receive their sight, the lame walk, the lepers are cleansed and the deaf hear, the dead are raised up, the poor have good tidings preached to them. (Lk)

So even in Luke which is the only Gospel that tells us that Jesus and John were cousins–a very close relationship in Jewish families–, there is a clear disconnect between the two ministries and the hint of a rivalry.

Later in Luke, it is documented that Herod Antipas became interested in seeing Jesus, but, significantly this was after the tetrarch had already executed John. In response, Jesus moves to Bethsaida, a town very close to Lake Gennesareth.

^{9:7}Now Herod the tetrarch heard of all that was done: and he was much perplexed, because that it was said by some, that John was risen from the dead; ^{9:8}and by some, that Elijah had appeared; and by others, that one of the old prophets was risen again. ^{9:9}And Herod said, John I beheaded: but who is this, about whom I hear such things? And he sought to see him. ^{9:10}And the apostles, when they were returned, declared unto him what things they had done. And he took them and withdrew apart to a city called Bethsaida. (Lk)

These important points will be revisited later as well.

John the Baptist in Josephus

In Josephus' *Antiquities*, John the Baptist is discussed in a long, detailed passage. In his day, John the Baptist was far more well-known than was Jesus. Josephus confirms much of what is found in the Gospels concerning John, but also relates added facts that are fascinating and will prove to be of great consequence.

Now some of the Jews thought that the destruction of Herod's army came from God and that very justly, as a punishment of what he did against John, that was called the Baptist: for Herod slew him, who was a good man and commanded the Jews to exercise virtue, both as to righteousness towards one another and piety towards God and so to come to baptism; for that the washing [with water] would be acceptable to him, if they made use of it, not in order to the putting away [or the remission] of some sins [only], but for the purification of the body; supposing still that the soul was thoroughly purified beforehand by righteousness. Now when [many] others came in crowds about him, for they were very greatly moved [or pleased] by hearing his words, Herod, who feared lest the great influence John had over the people might put it into his power and inclination to raise a rebellion, (for they seemed ready to do any thing he should advise,) thought it best, by putting him to death, to prevent any mischief he might cause and not bring himself into difficulties, by sparing a man who might make him repent of it when it would be too late. Accordingly he was sent a prisoner, out of Herod's suspicious temper, to Macherus, the castle I before mentioned and was there put to death. Now the Jews had an opinion that the destruction of this army was sent as a punishment upon Herod and a mark of God's displeasure to him. (*Antiq* XVIII 5:2)

The Jews were upset over the marriage of Herodias to her uncle, the Tetrarch Herod Antipas, because it had taken place while Herodias' first husband–by whom she had a daughter–was still alive. Herodias had given her first husband a bill of divorce in Rome, but, according to Jewish law, women had no right to do so. John the Baptist and probably many others vehemently preached against her transgression and this infuriated Herodias. Also, the Jerusalem High Priesthood was likely very cool toward Herodias and Antipas' subsequent marriage to the woman for this reason, but would have remained silent on the matter. Antipas in his younger years, and more recently Herodias, had been favorites of the Caesars. The Temple High Priesthood knew their own authority came from Rome and would have been circumspect on such a delicate issue.

John the Baptist's attack against Herodias was also a "crypto" attack against Herod Antipas and the entire Roman Empire. Just as Herodias in God's eyes was an illegitimate wife, so, too, was Herod Antipas an illegitimate ruler–a puppet king propped up by the Romans. Worse, Antipas' bloodline was half-Arab and half-Samaritan Jew. In the minds of many Galilean and Judean Jews, Antipas had little inherent right to rule over them.

The Tetrarch Herod Antipas eventually had John arrested and later executed. The New Testament indicates that it was done at the request of Herodias, but Josephus does not agree. Rather, Josephus suggests that John was executed to prevent him from raising sedition within Antipas' Galilean army–an army that was preparing to battle neighboring Nabotea.

For at least a century, the Jews and the Arabs had maintained a longstanding feud. For the past few decades, however, there had been peace between the two countries. Not only had the stronger presence of Rome kept conflict to a minimum, but early in his reign the Tetrarch Herod Antipas had wisely married the daughter of the Arabian King Aretas IV of Nabotea. However Antipas had to divorce his Arabic wife, Pharaelis, in order to marry Herodias. This was a deadly insult to King Aretas.

Aretas and Antipas would eventually go to war. Whether the divorce was the dominant issue in the conflict is open to question. Land disputes between the two countries had roots not only in the reign of Herod the Great, but also 100 years before when the Asamoneans ruled the Jewish nation. But certainly, as long as Pharaelis was married happily to Herod Antipas, these were inconsequential issues.

At any rate, a great battle was fought between the Arabians (Naboteans) and the Roman auxiliaries united under Herod Antipas in his Galilean army. In the contest, Antipas was defeated decisively. The Jewish people, according to Josephus, ascribed this disaster to God's revenge for Antipas' beheading of the great prophet John the Baptist. In the key passage from *Antiquities* describing it, Herodias is not even mentioned.

Jesus and John the Baptist

The Gospels paint two very different and conflicting pictures of the relationship between the two men. Based mainly on the Book of Luke, it can be concluded that they could not have been closer. Jesus was not only John's blood cousin, but had been baptized by him and was encouraged by John to start his own Ministry.

But one can equally conclude that these religious leaders had essentially no relationship. From other Gospels, Jesus was not related to John the Baptist at all and was not even baptized by him. Indeed, Jesus might have started his own Ministry only after John's success, emulating many of the tenets of John's preachings as he did so. Further, Jesus might have begun his own "copycat" Ministry only after John's arrest, sensing opportunity in the religious vacuum created by John's imprisonment.

John the Baptist and the Chronology

Ancient references to John the Baptist reveal several valuable clues related to specific or relative dates. One is that John was imprisoned sometime after Herod Antipas married Herodias. John's term of imprisonment before his execution was likely counted in months–as John regularly communed with his disciples and had time to write and receive letters.

Another important fact is that only after John the Baptist's execution did the Tetrarch Herod Antipas became aware of Jesus. Herod then apparently made several unsuccessful attempts to meet Jesus over a period of time.

Herod did finally meet Jesus in Jerusalem on a Passover. At that time, Pontius Pilate presented the arrested Jesus to Herod for questioning. From the record, it cannot be determined whether Antipas had ill intent toward Jesus initially or not. Very possibly, Antipas was just curious to meet a holy man–someone who might be of use to him in predicting the future. But whatever Antipas' true intentions were, after John the Baptist's execution, Jesus assumed the worst and stayed out of Antipas' way.

Chapter 15   The Ministry of Jesus

> And the passover of the Jews was at hand and Jesus went up to
> Jerusalem. (Jn 2:13)

Through the tracking of the yearly Jewish festivals as documented in the New Testament, important information can be gained about the chronology of the Ministry of Jesus. The festivals were held at the Second Temple in Jerusalem and all Jews were encouraged to travel to Judea to attend. The celebrations were the social high points of the year, as Judaism provided for few other avenues of entertainment. The festivals were also important money-makers and supported the Temple and the High Priesthood in high style. Several priest families became extremely wealthy.

The most important of these festivals was the Passover. Jewish historian Flavius Josephus writes that more than three million pilgrims gathered in Jerusalem to celebrate the Passover of A.D. 66. Even if we accept that the real number was closer to 300,000, it is still an impressive one.

> And truly, while Cestius Gallus was president of the province of Syria,
> nobody durst do so much as send an embassage to him against Florus;
> but when he was come to Jerusalem, upon the approach of the feast of
> unleavened bread, the people came about him not fewer in number than
> three millions these besought him to commiserate the calamities of their
> nation and cried out upon Florus as the bane of their country. (*Wars* II
> 14:3)

In A.D. 66, people came from out of the countryside during the Passover expressly to petition Syrian President Gallus for relief from the cruelty of Procurator Florus. At the time, the Jewish East was only weeks away from complete rebellion. It can be expected that the attendance at that particular Passover would be higher than normal, but probably not in the millions — Jerusalem having an estimated population of 50,000.

We have investigated Josephus' use of very large numbers and generally have concluded that dividing a Josephus "mega" number by 10 will produce a quantity closer to the truth. But in the case of the Passover of A.D. 64, Josephus produces evidence that confirms the A.D. 66 number — unless there a problem with the word "thousand" itself.

> So these high priests, upon the coming of that feast which is called the Passover, when they slay their sacrifices, from the ninth hour till the eleventh, but so that a company not less than ten belong to every sacrifice, (for it is not lawful for them to feast singly by themselves,) and many of us are twenty in a company, found the number of sacrifices was two hundred and fifty-six thousand five hundred; which, upon the allowance of no more than ten that feast together, amounts to two millions seven hundred thousand and two hundred persons that were pure and holy; for as to those that have the leprosy, or the gonorrhea, or women that have their monthly courses, or such as are otherwise polluted, it is not lawful for them to be partakers of this sacrifice; nor indeed for any foreigners neither, who come hither to worship. (*Wars* VI 9:3)

The Passover, by all accounts, was one of the most attended events in all of the ancient world. This was due in no small part to the magnificence of the Second Temple. Many experts rank the Jerusalem Temple complex equal to any of the accepted Seven Wonders of the Ancient World. The reason given as to why it isn't on most lists is usually that the Temple existed in finished form for only about 30 years–being destroyed to its foundations in A.D. 70 by the Romans.

The Second Temple

The Second Temple was also known as Herod's Temple, or the great Temple. The Temple complex was built in the northern part of Jerusalem upon a large walled plateau. A virtual city unto itself, the ethereal white and gold inner Sanctuary building appeared, from the surrounding hills of Judea, to float over the rest of Jerusalem.

King Solomon had constructed the original Jerusalem Temple roughly 900 years before the times of Jesus, and it had suffered through many conquests by foreign invaders over the intervening centuries. Most recently, the Temple been rebuilt to a lavish degree by Herod the Great. This monumental project was begun in 20 B.C. with the foundation work completed by 10 B.C. Even 40 years later, the complex had not been finished.

The rectangular walls of the Temple plateau were made of huge white ashlar blocks cut from local quarries and faced with the traditional Herodian borders. Cloisters 40 feet high were constructed on top of these walls, made of columns cut from a single stone and roofed with ornately carved cedar. The outer colonnade was blocked in, to give a solid face to the outside. From the upper city to the west, the height of the outer walls to include the cloister was about 140 feet. On the other side of the Temple complex to the east plunged the Kidron Valley. It was here, at the southeast corner of the Temple's walls, where, in more ancient times, people adjudged by the priests to be sacrilegious were thrown to their deaths.

The perimeter of the plateau in total was almost a mile which enclosed a area of about 35 acres. The complex had a tiled outer courtyard of about 20 acres. The jewel of the complex was an elevated inner area, set apart from the outer courtyard by 60 foot walls and covering an area of 15 acres. Again, tall cloisters covered the perimeter of this area with the outer columns blocked in to show a solid face and limit access. The inner courtyard was also designed to serve as the fortress of last resort in times of war.

Set upon a special courtyard within these walls and with access limited further, was the gold-faced Temple building, wherein God was thought to dwell. A large, elevated bronze altar stood in front of the Sanctuary building. A fire was always kept burning under the alter and this was where sacrifices to the Jewish God were performed. The four-square alter was large enough to accommodate perhaps a score of sacrifices simultaneously.

The outer courtyard was open to all who cared to trek up the broad stone stairways built into the west and south walls. The walled inner courtyard, however, had restricted access–only purified Jewish men and women could enter. The male supplicants usually were required to wear white linen garb in order to pass through the courtyard's massive and ornate bronze gates. Women had their own entrance and were restricted only to certain areas.

Out of the north outer wall of the Second Temple jutted a four-towered fortress called the tower–or castle–of Antonia. Rebuilt by Herod the Great, it was renamed for Herod's friend Marc Antony, former co-ruler of the Roman Empire. Antonia was where the Roman garrison stayed and military supplies were kept. It was well-accepted that if there was to be trouble in Jerusalem during a festival, it would likely start nearby in the open Temple courtyard. In Antonia, the Roman soldiers were close by.

Jesus of Nazareth routinely preached in the 20-acre outer courtyard in the last few months before his crucifixion. Jesus' favorite spot was called Solomon's Portico along the Temple's eastern wall and probably just opposite to the inner courtyard's main gate. When Jesus was dying on the cross at Golgotha, most of his Galilean Disciples gathered at Solomon's Portico in confusion, praying for divine intervention and fearful of their own fate at the hands of the Romans.

The Major Festivals

The Jewish festivals are prominently mentioned in the New Testament and they are also described by Josephus and Philo. Unlike the Greeks and Romans, the Jews had no time for sports, plays, musical concerts, or gladiatorial contests; in fact, these pagan entertainments were considered an abomination. Jewish life centered around God, family, and the remembrance and celebration of great events in Jewish history. Many different festivals were celebrated throughout the year.

> In the next place, he (God) does not permit those who desire to perform sacrifices in their own houses to do so, but he orders all men to rise up, even from the furthest boundaries of the earth and to come to this temple, by which command he is at the same time testing their dispositions most severely; for he who was not about to offer sacrifice in a pure and holy spirit would never endure to quit his country and his friends and relations and emigrate into a distant land, but would be likely, being under the influence of a more powerful attraction than that towards piety, to continue attached to the society of his most intimate friends and relations as portions of himself, to which he was most closely attached.
> And the most evident proof of this may be found in the events which actually took place. For innumerable companies of men from a countless variety of cities, some by land and some by sea, from east and from west, from the north and from the south, came to the temple at every festival, as if to some common refuge and safe asylum from the troubles of this most busy and painful life, seeking to find tranquillity and to procure a remission of and respite from those cares by which from their earliest infancy they had been hampered and weighed down and so, by getting breath as it were, to pass a brief time in cheerful festivities, being filled with good hopes and enjoying the leisure of that most important and necessary vacation which consists in forming a friendship with those hitherto unknown, but now initiated by boldness and a desire to honour God and forming a combination of actions and a union of dispositions so as to join in sacrifices and libations to the most complete confirmation of mutual good will. (Philo *Special Laws* 68-70)

The Passover was one of three major annual events during the Jewish Calendar year. The other two were the Pentecost and the the feast of the Tabernacles.

The Passover

The Passover was celebrated in Nisan, a Jewish month that roughly corresponds to late March and early April in the Julian Calendar (chapter 1). A key consideration for the Jewish priests was that the Passover occurred after the end of the growing season. An integral part of the Passover celebration was "first fruits" day, when supplicants were to bring in produce just harvested and tithe it to the Temple. If the Passover occurred too early in the year, there would be scant offerings. So the Jewish astrologers paid close attention as to when the Vernal Equinox would occur and set the Calendar accordingly.

The Passover celebration commemorates the release of the Hebrew slaves by the Egyptian pharaoh which occurred an estimated 1,000 years before the times of Jesus. Note in the following passages that Nisan is described as being the first month in the Jewish Calendar, thus making the first day of Nisan the Jewish New Year as well.

> But when God had signified, that with one plague he would compel the Egyptians to let Hebrews go, he commanded Moses to tell the people that they should have a sacrifice ready and they should prepare themselves on the tenth day of the month Xanthicus, against the fourteenth, (which month is called by the Egyptians Pharmuth, Nisan by the Hebrews; but the Macedonians call it Xanthicus,) and that he should carry the Hebrews with all they had. Accordingly, he having got the Hebrews ready for their departure and having sorted the people into tribes, he kept them together in one place: but when the fourteenth day was come and all were ready to depart they offered the sacrifice and purified their houses with the blood, using bunches of hyssop for that purpose; and when they had supped, they burnt the remainder of the flesh, as just ready to depart. Whence it is that we do still offer this sacrifice in like manner to this day and call this festival Pascha which signifies the feast of the passover; because on that day God passed us over and sent the plague upon the Egyptians; for the destruction of the first-born came upon the Egyptians that night, so that many of the Egyptians who lived near the king's palace, persuaded Pharaoh to let the Hebrews go. Accordingly he called for Moses and bid them be gone; as supposing, that if once the Hebrews were gone out of the country, Egypt should be freed from its miseries. They also honored the Hebrews with gifts; some, in order to get them to depart quickly and others on account of their neighborhood and the friendship they had with them. (*Antiq* II 14:6)

> In the month of Xanthicus which is by us called Nisan and is the beginning of our year, on the fourteenth day of the lunar month, when the sun is in Aries, (for in this month it was that we were delivered from bondage under the Egyptians,) the law ordained that we should every year slay that sacrifice which I before told you we slew when we came out of Egypt and which was called the Passover; and so we do celebrate this passover in companies, leaving nothing of what we sacrifice till the

day following. The feast of unleavened bread succeeds that of the passover and falls on the fifteenth day of the month and continues seven days, wherein they feed on unleavened bread; on every one of which days two bulls are killed and one ram and seven lambs. Now these lambs are entirely burnt, besides the kid of the goats which is added to all the rest, for sins; for it is intended as a feast for the priest on every one of those days. But on the second day of unleavened bread which is the sixteenth day of the month, they first partake of the fruits of the earth, for before that day they do not touch them. And while they suppose it proper to honor God, from whom they obtain this plentiful provision, in the first place, they offer the first-fruits of their barley and that in the manner following: They take a handful of the ears and dry them, then beat them small and purge the barley from the bran; they then bring one tenth deal to the altar, to God; and, casting one handful of it upon the fire, they leave the rest for the use of the priest. And after this it is that they may publicly or privately reap their harvest. They also at this participation of the first-fruits of the earth, sacrifice a lamb, as a burnt-offering to God. (*Antiq* III 10:5)

And as the feast of unleavened bread was at hand, in the first month which, according to the Macedonians, is called Xanthicus, but according to us Nisan, all the people ran together out of the villages to the city and celebrated the festival, having purified themselves, with their wives and children, according to the law of their country; and they offered the sacrifice which was called the Passover, on the fourteenth day of the same month and feasted seven days and spared for no cost, but offered whole burnt-offerings to God and performed sacrifices of thanksgiving, because God had led them again to the land of their fathers and to the laws thereto belonging and had rendered the mind of the king of Persia favorable to them. (*Antiq* XI 4:8)

The Paschal feast of the Passover was celebrated on the 14th day of Nisan, with the feast of the unleavened bread being celebrated on the following seven days from the 15th through the 21st days of Nisan.

The Feast of the Pentecost

The feast of the Pentecost was celebrated 50 days after the Passover, or one day after seven-times-seven days from the Passover. Seven was a significant and mystical number for the Jews. Just as the seventh day of the week was a day of rest and every seventh year the land rested (Sabbatical year), seven weeks after the the end of the Passover a day was dedicated to God. At this Feast, like the Passover, there was much sacrificing and tithing.

Now when that feast which was observed after seven weeks and which the Jews called Pentecost, (i. e. the 50th day,) was at hand, its name being taken from the number of the days [after the passover], (*Wars* II 3:1)

When a week of weeks has passed over after this sacrifice, (which weeks contain forty and nine days,) on the fiftieth day which is Pentecost, but is called by the Hebrews Asartha which signifies Pentecost, they bring to God a loaf, made of wheat flour, of two tenth deals, with leaven; and for sacrifices they bring two lambs; and when they have only presented them to God, they are made ready for supper for the priests; nor is it permitted to leave any thing of them till the day following. They also slay three bullocks for a burnt-offering and two rams; and fourteen lambs, with two kids of the goats, for sins; nor is there anyone of the festivals but in it they offer burnt-offerings; they also allow themselves to rest on every one of them. Accordingly, the law prescribes in them all what kinds they are to sacrifice and how they are to rest entirely and must slay sacrifices, in order to feast upon them. (*Antiq* III 10:6)

After Jesus was crucified on the 16th of Nisan, a certain number of disciples stayed in Jerusalem until the Pentecost, as described in Acts.

And when the day of Pentecost was now come, they were all together in one place. (Acts 2:1)

Feast of the Tabernacles

The feast of the Tabernacles occurred in the fall, when winter was approaching. To remind the Jews of their nomadic origins, tents would be pitched in the courtyard of the great Temple, one for each of the ancient tribes, and many sacrifices were offered. The seventh month of the Jewish calender (Tisri) roughly corresponds to October.

But on the seventh month which the Macedonians call Hyperberetaeus, they make an addition to those already mentioned and sacrifice a bull, a ram and seven lambs and a kid of the goats, for sins. On the tenth day of the same lunar month, they fast till the evening; and this day they sacrifice a bull and two rams and seven lambs and a kid of the goats, for sins. And, besides these, they bring two kids of the goats; the one of which is sent alive out of the limits of the camp into the wilderness for the scapegoat and to be an expiation for the sins of the whole multitude; but the other is brought into a place of great cleanness, within the limits of the camp and is there burnt, with its skin, without any sort of cleansing. With this goat was burnt a bull, not brought by the people, but by the high priest, at his own charges; which, when it was slain, he brought of the blood into the holy place, together with the blood of the kid of the goats and sprinkled the ceiling with his finger seven times, as also its pavement and again as often toward the most holy place and about the golden altar: he also at last brings it into the open court and sprinkles it about the great altar. Besides this, they set the extremities and the kidneys and the fat, with the lobe of the liver, upon the altar. The high priest likewise presents a ram to God as a burnt-offering. Upon the fifteenth day of the same month, when the season of the year is changing for winter, the law enjoins us to pitch tabernacles in every one of our houses, so that we preserve ourselves from the cold of that time of the year; as also that when we should arrive at our own country and come to that city which we should have then for our metropolis, because of the temple therein to be built and keep a festival for eight days and offer burnt-offerings and sacrifice thank-offerings, that we should then carry in our hands a branch of myrtle and willow and a bough of the palm-tree, with the addition of the pome citron: That the burnt-offering on the first of those days was to be a sacrifice of thirteen bulls and fourteen lambs and fifteen rams, with the addition of a kid of the goats, as an expiation for sins; and on the following days the same number of lambs and of rams, with the kids of the goats; but abating one of the bulls every day till they amounted to seven only. On the eighth day all work was laid aside and then, as we said before, they sacrificed to God a bullock, a ram and seven lambs, with a kid of the goats, for an expiation of sins. And this is the accustomed solemnity of the Hebrews, when they pitch their tabernacles. (*Antiq* III 9:2-4)

Feast of the Dedication

The feast of the Dedication was a minor celebration in Jesus' time, taking place in December. It memorializes an earlier heroic event when the great Jewish leader Judas Maccabeus reclaimed Jerusalem from the Syrian Greeks and the Samaritans in 161 B.C.

The Jerusalem Temple then had fallen into neglect and Judas spent much time and money having it restored. The Greek Syrians had likely altered it substantially to function as a Greek bathhouse and exercise arena. When the renovation and repair was finished, Judas put on a feast. The feast of the Dedication is now associated with the modern-day Jewish celebration of Hanukkah.

> Now Judas celebrated the festival of the restoration of the sacrifices of the temple for eight days and omitted no sort of pleasures thereon; but he feasted them upon very rich and splendid sacrifices; and he honored God and delighted them by hymns and psalms. Nay, they were so very glad at the revival of their customs, when, after a long time of intermission, they unexpectedly had regained the freedom of their worship, that they made it a law for their posterity, that they should keep a festival, on account of the restoration of their temple worship, for eight days. And from that time to this we celebrate this festival and call it Lights. I suppose the reason was, because this liberty beyond our hopes appeared to us; and that thence was the name given to that festival. Judas also rebuilt the walls round about the city and reared towers of great height against the incursions of enemies and set guards therein. He also fortified the city Bethsura, that it might serve as a citadel against any distresses that might come from our enemies. (*Antiq* XII 7:7)

Besides these festivals, there were several other minor festivals held throughout the year for various special purposes. One example is the festival of Xylophory. There, supplicants were expected to bring firewood to the Temple to provide fuel for the eternally burning flame of the sacrificial altar–enough to last for the upcoming year. This festival was held during the full moon of the month of Ab (*Wars* II 17:6).

With this yearly Calendar progression of Jewish festivals in mind, let us now return to the New Testament and see how these celebrations meld in with the events of Jesus' Ministry.

Gospels of Matthew and Mark

In the Book of Matthew, only one Passover is documented–the one of Jesus' crucifixion (Mt 26 1-19). Therefore, either Jesus' Ministry lasted less than a year, or only one of Jesus' Passovers as a preacher–the final one–was deemed important enough by the author of Matthew to chronicle.

In Mark, the situation is similar. Only one Passover is documented–Jesus' last (Mk 14:1-13).

Gospel of Luke

In the Book of Luke, like Mark and Matthew, only the last Passover of Jesus is specifically mentioned. However, three chapters in rough sequence in Luke relate several Second Temple events. This "section" begins with Jesus casting out the Temple moneychangers and ends with Jesus' crucifixion. Significantly, nothing unequivocal in these passages suggest that all of these events occurred in sequence during a single Passover. Possibly, various Second Temple events that took place at different times over the years of Jesus' Ministry were grouped together in a this section.

A closer look at the progression of Temple events in the Book of Luke is revealing. In the 19th chapter:

> 19:45 And he entered into the temple and began to cast out them that sold, 19:46 saying unto them, It is written and my house shall be a house of prayer: but ye have made it a den of robbers. 19:47 And he was teaching daily in the temple. But the chief priests and the scribes and the principal men of the people sought to destroy him: 19:48 and they could not find what they might do; for the people all hung upon him, listening. (Lk)

Then, in the 21st chapter, Luke writes:

> 21:37 And every day he was teaching in the temple; and every night he went out and lodged in the mount that is called Olivet. 21:38 And all the people came early in the morning to him in the temple, to hear him. (Lk 21: 37-8)

Then Luke begins a new chapter, the 22nd.

^{22:1}Now the feast of unleavened bread drew nigh which is called the Passover. ^{22:2}And the chief priests and the scribes sought how they might put him to death; for they feared the people. (Lk 22:1-2)

Admittedly, it is probable that Jesus spent considerable time in the Temple teaching in the weeks and months leading up to the fateful Passover of his crucifixion; Luke's 21st and 22nd chapters could represent contiguous events. However, it is difficult to believe that Jesus would have caused such a problem with the moneychangers as described in the 19th chapter of Luke, without earning the hatred of the Temple priests. Would Jesus then have been tolerated in the Temple on subsequent days? More likely months, if not years, would have to pass before the priests would be convinced that Jesus was not a threat, or for the priests to have forgotten about the fracas entirely.

On the other hand, with several hundred thousand pilgrims in the Temple daily during the Passover and on the days leading up to it, perhaps the ruckus caused by Jesus was not as earthshaking as the Gospels suggest. The priests simply might not have cared that much or even known about a minor disturbance in the crowd where the perpetrators quickly disappeared. So it is not impossible that Jesus returned to teach day after day in the Temple despite the early-on trouble he had caused with the moneychangers.

But the Fourth Gospel presents a dramatically different picture of Jesus' Ministry.

Gospel of John

The Book of John indicates that during his Ministry Jesus was at the Second Temple on at least two separate Passovers, and he celebrated a third Passover outside of Judea.

Jesus' "first" Passover was celebrated in Jerusalem. This was after he had been baptized by John the Baptist, had collected his Disciples and after his first miracle in Cana. It was at this Passover where Jesus "cast out" the moneychangers.

^{2:13}And the passover of the Jews was at hand and Jesus went up to Jerusalem. ^{2:14}And he found in the temple those that sold oxen and sheep and doves and the changers of money sitting: ^{2:15}and he made a scourge of cords and cast all out of the temple, both the sheep and the oxen; and he poured out the changers' money and overthrew their tables; ^{2:16}and to them that sold the doves he said, Take these things hence; make not my Father's house a house of merchandise. ^{2:17}His disciples remembered that it was written, Zeal for thy house shall eat me up. ^{2:18}The Jews therefore answered and said unto him, What sign showest thou unto us, seeing that thou doest these things? ^{2:19}Jesus answered and said unto them, Destroy this temple and in three days I will raise it up. ^{2:20}The Jews therefore said, Forty and six years was this temple in building and wilt thou raise it up in three days? ^{2:21}But he spake of the temple of his body. ^{2:22}When therefore he was raised from the dead, his disciples remembered that he spake this; and they believed the scripture and the word which Jesus had said. ^{2:23}Now when he was in Jerusalem at the passover, during the feast, many believed on his name, beholding his signs which he did. ^{2:24}But Jesus did not trust himself unto them, for that he knew all men, ^{2:25}and because he needed not that any one should bear witness concerning man; for he himself knew what was in man. (Jn 2:13-25)

The second Passover of Jesus mentioned in the Book of John was not celebrated in the Jerusalem Temple at all, but in the mountains near the eastern shores of Lake Gennesareth (Sea of Tiberias).

^{6:1}After these things Jesus went away to the other side of the sea of Galilee which is *the sea* of Tiberias. ^{6:2}And a great multitude followed him, because they beheld the signs which he did on them that were sick. ^{6:3}And Jesus went up into the mountain and there he sat with his disciples. ^{6:4}Now the passover, the feast of the Jews, was at hand. ^{6:5}Jesus therefore lifting up his eyes and seeing that a great multitude cometh unto him, saith unto Philip, Whence are we to buy bread, that these may eat? (Jn 6:1-5)

The third Passover in John was the Passover of Jesus' crucifixion.

^{11:55}Now the passover of the Jews was at hand: and many went up to Jerusalem out of the country before the passover, to purify themselves. ^{11:56}They sought therefore for Jesus and spake one with another, as they stood in the temple, What think ye? That he will not come to the feast? ^{11:57}Now the chief priests and the Pharisees had given commandment, that, if any man knew where he was, he should show it, that they might take him. (Jn 11:55-57)

Thus John gives clear evidence that Jesus' Ministry lasted for at least the duration of three Passover celebrations.

Other Feasts in the Book of John

The Passover is also called a feast, and feasts are referenced several times in John. One was a private feast at the wedding at Cana which occurred before the first Passover. John also referred to a feast in Jerusalem that occurred after Jesus' first Passover as a preacher, but before the second Passover which Jesus observed in the hills surrounding Lake Gennesareth.

> After these things there was a feast of the Jews; and Jesus went up to Jerusalem. (Jn 5:1)

About this particular feast in Jerusalem John says little, except to relate the story about Jesus healing a cripple at the pools of Bethesda near the Sheep's Gate. This feast could have been a Passover, but no other details specific to a Passover are mentioned. It is just as likely to be either the feast of the Pentecost or the feast of the Tabernacles–both major celebrations. Possibly, too, it was a feast of a minor festival. For our purposes, it will be assumed that this feast was not a Passover.

A feast of the Tabernacles is also mentioned in the Book of John.

> ^{7:1}And after these things Jesus walked in Galilee: for he would not walk in Judaea, because the Jews sought to kill him. ^{7:2}Now the feast of the Jews, the feast of tabernacles, was at hand. ^{7:3}His brethren therefore said unto him, Depart hence and go into Judaea, that thy disciples also may behold thy works which thou doest. (Jn 7:1-3)

This feast occurred after the second Passover of Jesus' Ministry which was celebrated in the mountains near Lake Gennesareth. The feast of the Tabernacles would have been held in October, or mid-way between Jesus' Galilean Passover and Jesus' final Passover in Jerusalem, if we assume that the Book of John did not leave out any interim Passover celebrations.

Finally, another Temple feast is also mentioned in John.

> [10:22]And it was the feast of the dedication at Jerusalem: [10:23]it was winter; and Jesus was walking in the temple in Solomon's porch. [10:24]The Jews therefore came round about him and said unto him, How long dost thou hold us in suspense? If thou art the Christ, tell us plainly. (Jn 10:22-24)

Finding Jesus in the Second Temple in December celebrating this feast fits well. John's description of it is placed after the passage about Jesus at the feast of the Tabernacles in October and just before the upcoming spring feast of the Passover in early April of the next year–Jesus' last Passover. So according to the Book of John, Jesus was in Judea preaching at least intermittently for a seven-month period leading up to the Passover of his crucifixion.

Veracity of the Gospel of John

How much trust can we place in the Book of John? After all, in the other three Gospels only a single Passover is mentioned. Should this be enough to discount John's claim of three or more Passovers occurring during Jesus' ministry? Not necessarily. Remember that the three Synoptic Gospels could have worked from a single source document, or copied from each other.

The Book of John is the only Gospel where the author claims to be an eyewitness, giving it obviously greater weight if true. Indeed, many events occur in John that are found in no other Gospel. Also in the Book of John, the Temple events during Jesus' Ministry are well-delineated, taking place at their proper intervals over three years, to include the Feast of the Dedication and the Feast of the Tabernacles. This is lacking in the Synoptic

Gospels of Matthew and Mark where all of Jesus' Temple events take place at his final Passover. In the Book of Luke, it is suggested–but not clearly so–that Jesus was at the Temple for more than a single Passover.

Eusebius, working from older Christian sources now lost, states the reason why John the Evangelist was compelled to write his own Gospel.

> The three Gospels already written were in general circulation and copies had come into John's hands. He welcomed them, we are told and confirmed their accuracy, but remarked that the narrative only lacked the story of what Christ had done first of all at the beginning of His mission. (Eus *History* III:24)

Weighing the evidence, it will be assumed that the Book of John is the most accurate on this issue. Jesus' Ministry took place at least over three years and not just one, as the Synoptic Gospels suggest.

The Chronology So Far

From previous chapters, it has been concluded that Jesus was crucified on the Passover in one of nine consecutive years, from A.D. 28 to A.D. 36. If the time line in the Book of John is correct, it must be accepted that Jesus was ministering for at least two Passovers before the final one of his crucifixion. The first of these Passovers was celebrated at the Jerusalem Temple, and the second celebrated in the mountains close to the eastern shores of Lake Gennesareth.

This pushes up the earliest possible year for Jesus' final Passover by two years. With these new conclusions, the earliest year for the crucifixion can now confidently be set at A.D. 30, with the latest year remaining at either A.D. 35 or A.D. 36. Our nine-year window has been narrowed to seven years.

For additional clues, we must now temporarily leave the New Testament and return to the works of the Roman historians–Tacitus, Suetonius and Dio–as well as continuing to rely heavily on Flavius Josephus.

Chapter 16   Herodias

Herodias took upon her to confound the laws of our country and divorced herself from her husband while he was alive and was married to Herod [Antipas], her husband's brother by the father's side, he was tetrarch of Galilee (*Antiq* XVIII 5:4)

Herodias grew up in the glittering Imperial court of Rome during the late Augustan period. This was later termed Rome's golden age. She knew all of the famous Romans of those times and, along with her immediate family, enjoyed the special protection of Livia, the wife of Augustus. Tall and slender, Herodias was reputed to be one of the most beautiful women of her time, just as her grandmother Mariamne I was considered to be a half-century earlier. For 100 years, the Jewish rulers of the Asamonean line had their pick of the most desirable of Jewesses for wives, and Herodias could have been the crowning result.

But the charmed life of Herodias would end after she moved to the Jewish East and married the Tetrarch Herod Antipas, her uncle. Like Helen of Troy, Herodias became the cause of a war between two mighty nations; and just as Queen Cleopatra of Egypt bewitched her paramour Marc Antony and caused his downfall, the vain and avaricious Herodias would ultimately lead the Tetrarch Herod Antipas into poverty and banishment.

But Herodias' darkest legacy is her role the beheading of the Jewish prophet John the Baptist, and she can be very reasonably linked to the crucifixion of Jesus of Nazareth. For these reasons Herodias is one of the most vilified women in history. Her true story, however, is not entirely an unsympathetic one.

The Importance of Herodias

Flavius Josephus devotes much of *Antiquities* to documenting the lives of the descendants of Herod the Great, especially the immediate family of Herodias. This is for good reason. Herodias' brother became King Agrippa I, who eventually would rule over Herod the Great's former domain. Agrippa's son, Agrippa II, would also gain great powers and be a force within Imperial Rome well beyond the A.D. 70 destruction of Jerusalem and the Second Temple. For our purposes, these stories of the progeny of Herod the Great bear close scrutiny, for in the details of their lives, time clues relating to Jesus' Ministry can be found.

The life of Herodias is especially crucial in this regard. Herodias and Herod Antipas had already been married well before Jesus was crucified. It is also known that by the time of Jesus' last Passover, John the Baptist had been executed by Herod Antipas upon the request of Herodias' daughter. Also, by the time of that fateful Passover, Herod Antipas' Galilean armies had been been defeated in battle by the forces of King Aretas IV of Nabotea. Accurate dates on any of these three events–or on events leading up to these events–would tremendously helpful.

A key initial determination will be the year in which the beautiful Herodias left Rome for Galilee with the intention of marrying her uncle Herod Antipas. This marriage set into action the critical chain of events that would culminate in the crucifixion of Jesus. The most important question is the obvious one: why did Herodias agree to the May-December marriage? Herod Antipas was 20 years her senior, after all. What advantage did she see in the union?

The Herod Family and Incest

Learning about the family of Herod the Great can be a daunting task at times. Herod the Great had 10 wives and many children—Josephus wrote only about the legitimate ones. To further obfuscate matters, the Herod family was fond of incestuous cross-generational marriages–usually between uncles and their nieces. Why? The Herods believed that in-family marriages would strengthen the bloodlines and protect them from outsiders. But even in those days there were suspicions that incest was somehow unnatural and ultimately self-destructive — so much so that Rome had a law against it.

In fact, in A.D. 49 Emperor Claudius had to have special permission from the Roman Senate in order to marry his niece Agrippina the Younger (*Annuls* 12:6). This embracing of incest as a means of enhancing the family line might have had some short-term benefits, but, according to Josephus, the Herod family itself died out completely within three generations. A large contributing factor could have been infertility caused by genetic inbreeding.

A minor but complicating factor in studying the family of Herod the Great was the Jewish tradition of giving the same name to different family members. Many in the Herod clan claimed the name of Aristobulos, Alexander, Herod, Agrippa, Mariamne, Salome, etc., so the reader is advised to play close attention.

Herodias' Early Life

Herodias was born in 8 B.C. and was the youngest of five children.

> ..and Aristobulus had Herod and Agrippa and Aristobulus, his sons, with Herodias and Mariamne, his daughters and all by Bernice, Salome's daughter. (*Wars* I 28:1)

Herodias' father was Prince Aristobulos, of Royal Asamonean blood and her paternal grandfather was Herod the Great. Herodias' paternal great-great grandfather was one of the last true independent kings of the Jews, John Hyrcanus II.

Herodias' mother was Bernice, a beautiful woman of Idumean descent and herself a niece of Herod the Great. Bernice's mother was Salome–Herod the Great's infamous scheming sister. Bernice's father was an Idumean aristocrat named Costobarus. Costobarus had been appointed the governor of Idumea by

Herod the Great, who had then gave Costobarus his own sister-Salome-to marry.

The Murderous Herod

Herodias inherited a bloody family legacy. Herod the Great executed her father Aristobulos and her uncle Alexander in 7 B.C. Earlier, in   29 B.C., Herod had executed her paternal grandmother Mariamne I. Herod also executed Mariamne's brother Aristobulos, Mariamne's grandfather John Hyrcanus (Hyrcanus II), and later Herodias' maternal grandfather, Costobarus. How could the knowledge of these acts not have effected the young Herodias?!

As horrific as these deeds of Herod were, they were not without rational purpose. Herod the Great was born without Jewish Royal pretensions, although he did boast a measure of Royal blood from his Arabian ancestors. Herod embraced the Asamoneans early in his reign because he needed their support to bolster his own legitimacy to the throne. In later years and more secure in the powers given him by Rome, Herod worked to eliminate many of those same Jewish Asamoneans–those who could conceivably become rivals for his kingdom. By that time, Herod had given up trying to be popular with the Jewish people. The Jewish people themselves considered the Asamoneans, and not the Arabic Herod family, as true Jewish Royalty. This fact rankled Herod until his dying day and partially explains many of his violent actions against those of his own bloodline.

Salome and Bernice

Herod's contrived executions against the Asamoneans were encouraged by Herodias' grandmother Salome, Herod's sister and a woman who also had no Royal Asamonean claim. Cold and calculating, Salome also arranged the marriage of her beautiful daughter Bernice to Herod the Great's popular Royal son Aristobulos. Her purpose was merely to have someone on the "inside" to inform her of his activities and intentions. From this union came Herodias and her siblings. Herodias' own mother was a spy against her father!

> ..for Salome was of a harsh temper and ill-natured to Mariamne's sons; nor would she suffer her own daughter, who was the wife of Aristobulus, one of those young men, to bear a good-will to her husband, but persuaded her to tell her if he said any thing to her in private and when any misunderstandings happened, as is common, she raised a great many suspicions out of it; by which means she learned all their concerns and made the damsel ill-natured to the young man. And in order to gratify her mother, she often said that the young men used to mention Mariamne when they were by themselves; and that they hated their father and were continually threatening, that if they had once got the kingdom, they would make Herod's sons by his other wives country schoolmasters, for that the present education which was given them and their diligence in learning, fitted them for such an employment. And as for the women, whenever they saw them adorned with their mother's clothes, they threatened, that instead of their present gaudy apparel, they should be clothed in sackcloth and confined so closely that they should not see the light of the sun. These stories were presently carried by Salome to the king..(*Antiq* XVI 7:3)

Bernice played a key role in Salome's plan to turn Herod the Great against his Royal sons–the sons who were very popular with the Jewish people. Did she fully appreciate what she was doing? Mercifully, Herodias was only an infant when her father Aristobulos was executed in 7 B.C. and had no memory of either him or his death.

Salome's divorce of Costobarus

When Herodias divorced Herod Philip of Rome, she knew it was against Jewish law. But her grandmother Salome had done the same thing to her husband Costobarus, so Herodias might have felt somewhat justified. Costobarus came from Idumea, where Herod the Great had set him up as a ruler.

Idumea then was roughly what is now the Negev Desert, running from the Mediterranean seacoast east to the western regions of Lake Asphaltitis. In the past, the nation of Idumea had been a part of Nabotea before revolting from it. Idumea later became a Jewish nation by forced conversion after being conquered by the Jewish armies of John Hyrcanus I in 125 B.C.

> Costobarus was an Idumean by birth and one of principal dignity among them and one whose ancestors had been priests to the Koze, whom the Idumeans had [formerly] esteemed as a god; but after Hyrcanus had made a change in their political government and made them receive the Jewish customs and law, Herod made Costobarus governor of Idumea and Gaza and gave him his sister Salome to wife; (*Antiq* XV 8:9)

But Salome eventually divorced Costobarus–illegally, in the eyes of the Jews.

> But some time afterward, when Salome happened to quarrel with Costobarus, she sent him a bill of divorce and dissolved her marriage with him, though this was not according to the Jewish laws; for with us it is lawful for a husband to do so; but a wife; if she departs from her husband, cannot of herself be married to another, unless her former husband put her away. (*Antiq* XV 7:10)

After being divorced by Salome, Costobarus was later slain by Herod the Great. Herod had learned that Costobarus had plotted with Queen Cleopatra of Egypt to turn the country of Idumea over to Egypt.

The Children of Aristobulos

Herodias and her siblings were important figures in their own right in the first century A.D. Jewish East. Herodias had three older brothers of note, but also an older sister named Mariamne about whom little is known.

Herodias' most famous older brother was Herod Agrippa, born in 9 B.C. Agrippa, after many adventures was to eventually regain Herod the Great's old kingdom under Emperors Caius and Claudius. He died at fifty-two years of age in A.D. 44.

First Generation of Prince Aristobulos

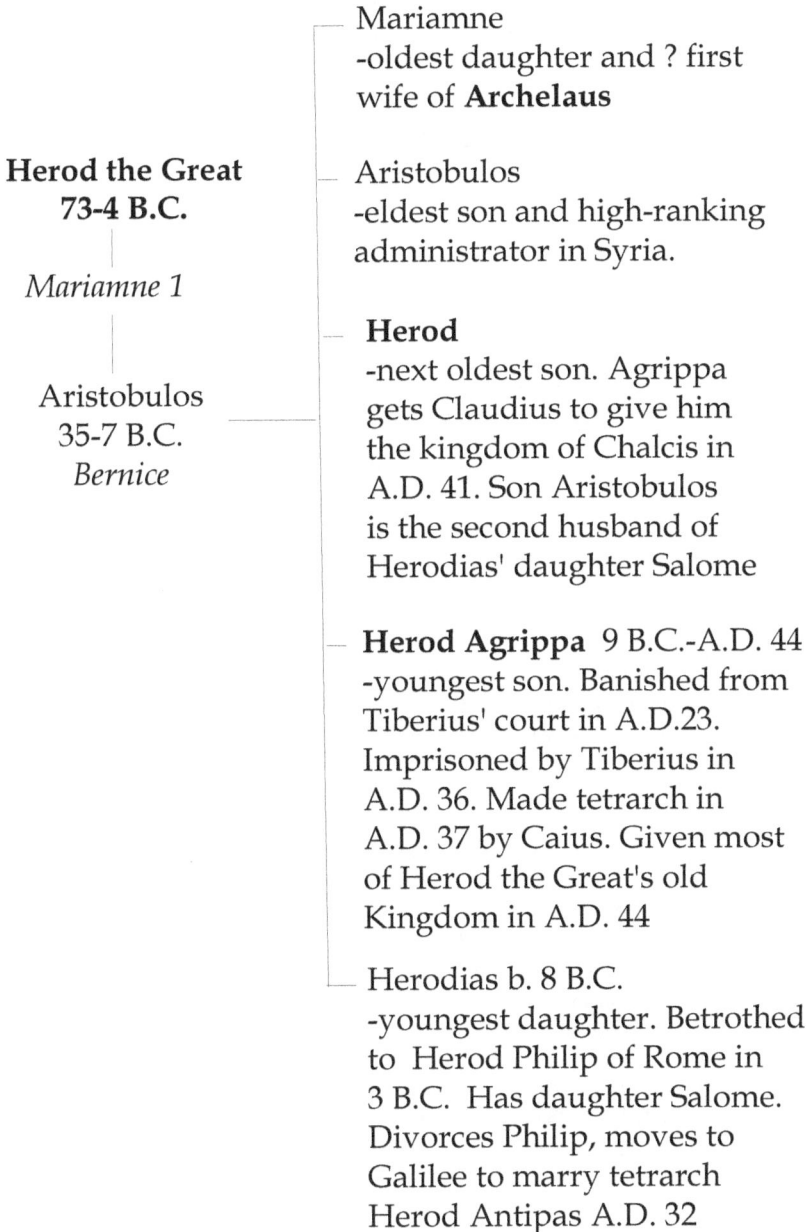

**Herod the Great
73-4 B.C.**

Mariamne 1

Aristobulos
35-7 B.C.
Bernice

Mariamne
-oldest daughter and ? first
wife of **Archelaus**

Aristobulos
-eldest son and high-ranking
administrator in Syria.

Herod
-next oldest son. Agrippa
gets Claudius to give him
the kingdom of Chalcis in
A.D. 41. Son Aristobulos
is the second husband of
Herodias' daughter Salome

Herod Agrippa 9 B.C.-A.D. 44
-youngest son. Banished from
Tiberius' court in A.D.23.
Imprisoned by Tiberius in
A.D. 36. Made tetrarch in
A.D. 37 by Caius. Given most
of Herod the Great's old
Kingdom in A.D. 44

Herodias b. 8 B.C.
-youngest daughter. Betrothed
to Herod Philip of Rome in
3 B.C. Has daughter Salome.
Divorces Philip, moves to
Galilee to marry tetrarch
Herod Antipas A.D. 32

Herodias' second older brother was Aristobulos, who was born at least three years earlier than Agrippa. Aristobulos proved to be an able administrator in the East under the Syrian legate Pomponius Flaccus and, in all probability, later under General Lucius Vitellius. When his brother Herod Agrippa rose to power under Emperor Caius and gained a kingdom, Aristobulos aided him and was given authority in Galilee. Aristobulos married Jotape, the daughter of the King of Emesa. Emesa was a small Arab kingdom that was near the city of Damascus, and might have included it.

Herod, Herodias' last older brother, was appointed the King of Chalcis by Emperor Claudius. After his brother King Agrippa I's death in A.D. 44, this King Herod also assumed control of the affairs of the Second Temple in Jerusalem and was responsible for the appointment of the High Priest. His son, Aristobulos, was the second husband of Herodias' daughter Salome.

Little is known about an older sister named Mariamne. She is thought to be the first wife of Archelaus, the son of Herod the Great who became an ethnarch in 4 B.C.

... Agrippa, was brought up with his other brethren, Herod and Aristobulus, for these were also the sons of the son of Herod the Great by Bernice; but Bernice was the daughter of Costobarus and of Salome, who was Herod's sister. Aristobulus left these infants when he was slain by his father, together with his brother Alexander, as we have already related. But when they were arrived at years of puberty, this Herod, the brother of Agrippa, married Mariamne, the daughter of Olympias, who was the daughter of Herod the king and of Joseph, the son of Joseph, who was brother to Herod the king and had by her a son, Aristobulus; but Aristobulus, the third brother of Agrippa, married Jotape, the daughter of Sampsigeramus, king of Emesa; they had a daughter who was deaf, whose name also was Jotape; and these hitherto were the children of the male line. But Herodias, their sister, was married to Herod [Philip], the son of Herod the Great, who was born of Mariamne, the daughter of Simon the high priest, who had a daughter, Salome; after whose birth Herodias took upon her to confound the laws of our country and divorced herself from her husband while he was alive and was married to Herod [Antipas], her husband's brother by the father's side, he was tetrarch of Galilee; but her daughter Salome was married to

Philip, the son of Herod and tetrarch of Trachonitis; and as he died childless, Aristobulus, the son of Herod, the brother of Agrippa, married her; they had three sons, Herod, Agrippa and Aristobulus; (*Antiq* XVIII 5:4)

In the last years of his life before his death in 4 B.C., Herod the Great took a special interest in the children of his executed sons Alexander and Aristobulos. Perhaps, as was the case after he executed his own wife Mariamne I, Herod realized he had made a horrific mistake in 7 B.C. and was trying to make amends.

Now Herod brought up his sons' children with great care; for Alexander had two sons by Glaphyra; and Aristobulus had three sons by Bernice, Salome's daughter and two daughters; and as his friends were once with him, he presented the children before them; and deploring the hard fortune of his own sons, he prayed that no such ill fortune would befall these who were their children, but that they might improve in virtue and obtain what they justly deserved and might make him amends for his care of their education. He also caused them to be betrothed against they should come to the proper age of marriage; the elder of Alexander's sons to Pheroras's daughter and Antipater's daughter to Aristobulus's eldest son. He also allotted one of Aristobulus's daughters to Antipater's son and Aristobulus's other daughter to Herod, a son of his own, who was born to him by the high priest's daughter; (*Antiq* XVII 1:2)

This "other daughter" that Josephus refers to in the last line of the preceding excerpt was Herodias. So Herodias, when she was no more than four years of age, was betrothed to the much older Herod Philip (of Rome), who was the son of Herod and Mariamne II, the daughter of the High Priest Simon.

Herod Philip of Rome

After Herod the Great executed his wife Mariamne (I) in 29 B.C., he fell in love with another Mariamne (II) and married her. Since she came from an unacceptably common background, Herod elevated her father to the Jerusalem High Priest's position before the official union took place. This Mariamne is referred to often as just "the High Priest's daughter."

He (Herod the Great) also fell in love again and married another wife, not suffering his reason to hinder him from living as he pleased. The occasion of this his marriage was as follows: There was one Simon, a citizen of Jerusalem, the son of one Boethus, a citizen of Alexandria and a priest of great note there; this man had a daughter, who was esteemed the most beautiful woman of that time; and when the people of Jerusalem began to speak much in her commendation, it happened that Herod was much affected with what was said of her; and when he saw the damsel, he was smitten with her beauty, yet did he entirely reject the thoughts of using his authority to abuse her, as believing, what was the truth, that by so doing he should be stigmatized for violence and tyranny; so he thought it best to take the damsel to wife. And while Simon was of a dignity too inferior to be allied to him, but still too considerable to be despised, he governed his inclinations after the most prudent manner, by augmenting the dignity of the family and making them more honorable; so he immediately deprived Jesus, the son of Phabet, of the high priesthood and conferred that dignity on Simon and so joined in affinity with him [by marrying his daughter]. (*Antiq* XV 9:3)

This Herod Philip, the son of Mariamne II and the grandson of the High Priest Simon, was older than Herod Antipas, the future tetrarch of Galilee, by probably a year or so. When Herodias was betrothed to Herod Philip, Herod Philip was perhaps in his early 20's. Herod the Great had high regard for Herod Philip's strength, character and fitness to rule. It didn't hurt that Herod Philip came from a long line of priests on his mother's side, and his grandfather served as High Priest of the Second Temple (although put in that position by Herod the Great himself). That pedigree would have given Philip instant credibility within the Jewish community at Rome, where Herod the Great himself likely had little. For these reasons, Herod the Great made Herod Philip second in the line of succession after his eldest son Antipater in one of his last wills.

as also his testament, wherein Antipater was appointed to be his successor; and that if Antipater should die first, his son [Herod Philip] by the high priest's daughter should succeed. (*Antiq* XVII 3:2)

So when Herodias was promised in marriage by Herod the Great to Herod Philip, it showed how highly Herod the Great favored the young child. Even at that young age–four at the most–Herodias must have had a certain charm and sparkle.

But Herod Philip's favored position with Herod the Great was to be short-lived. Mariamne II, Philip's mother, was indirectly implicated in a supposed plot to poison Herod. This paranoid episode of Herod's–one of many in his later years–occurred in either late 5 B.C. or early 4 B.C. when Herod was a diseased and dying man.

> The high priest's daughter also, who was the king's wife, was accused to have been conscious of all this and had resolved to conceal it; for which reason Herod divorced her and blotted her son out of his testament, wherein he had been mentioned as one that was to reign after him; and he took the high priesthood away from his father-in-law, Simeon the son of Boethus and appointed Matthias the son of Theophilus, who was born at Jerusalem, to be high priest in his room. (*Antiq* XVII 4:2)

Herod Philip and his mother fell from grace but at least they escaped with their lives and possibly a measure of their fortunes. Also, and somewhat curiously, Philip's betrothal to Herodias remained unaffected. However, Herod Philip's grandfather Simon was removed from the High Priest's position because of his daughter Mariamne's treachery.

Herodias also gained a stepfather in those early years. After the death of Aristobulos, Herod the Great arranged for Bernice to marry the brother of his first wife Doris, who was not of Royal blood (*Antiq* XVII 1:1). It is reasonable to assume that after Antipater's arrest and execution by Herod the Great in 4 B.C. that Doris also suffered a fall from grace. Bernice's marriage of convenience to Doris' brother could have been quietly set aside.

Life in Rome

After the death of Herod the Great, Bernice, with her family of five children, chose to live in Rome instead of Jerusalem. A factor might have been her second husband, the brother of Doris, who herself was the mother to Antipater. Perhaps in Rome, Bernice thought she could get away from the man who was likely forced upon her by the now-executed Antipater.

But this relocation was a choice that many other descendants of Herod the Great had made. Herod had been a cruel king and there were recurrent episodes of insurrection even after his death. In fact, 3 B.C. found Judea in frank rebellion over much of the countryside–a dangerous place for the "Royal" Herods.

But a greater factor was probably that Rome was simply a more cosmopolitan city than Jerusalem. During frequent visits to Rome when Herod the Great was living, the Herod family had likely acquired certain cultured and refined tastes that Jerusalem, with its stringent theocracy, could not satisfy. In Rome, too, Bernice and her family had the unequivocal support of Emperor Augustus and his wife Livia Drusilla (sometimes referred to as Julia Augustus after Augustus' death in A.D. 14), and they could enjoy the perks only available to those of the Royal court. For this reason, the relatives of Herod the Great and their servants probably made up a sizable community in Rome. The Herod family was respected, if not honored, as foreign Royalty by most Roman aristocrats.

Livia, the wife of Augustus and the mother of Tiberius, was probably especially aghast over Herod the Great's barbaric actions in the slaughter of his two sons in 7 B.C. The sons had spent years living in the Royal palaces and villas with Augustus and his family. For this reason, Livia became great friends with Bernice and offered her and her children comfort and a good life in Rome.

So from all accounts, the children of the slain Aristobulos grew up living privileged lives. Young Agrippa even ingratiated himself with Drusus, the son of the future Emperor Tiberius. As well as being close to Tiberius' mother Livia, the family was also looked after by Antonia, the honored widow of Drusus, Tiberius' brother. A more powerful circle of friends would be difficult to find.

At the time, Rome was the center of the world in every sense of the word, bustling with commerce, filled with important and talented people from all over the empire, and with great constructions everywhere–most faced with lustrous marble. Moreover, Roman society was a tolerant one where open debate was accepted if not encouraged and artisans, artists and philosophers flourished. In the architectural wonder of the Merchant Mart in the Roman Forum, exotic goods from the remotest parts of the empire were available for inspection and purchase. High-arched aqueducts brought in fresh water great distances from the surrounding hills, and a sophisticated underground sewer system drained the effluent of the city down to the Tiber River. Commonplace were beautiful fountains, pools, gardens and statuary. Roman aristocrats were able to attend special parties, plays, or musical concerts almost every evening, and there were amusements and even spectacles available routinely to the commonest of citizens.

The Greek geographer Strabo writes of Rome at a time when Herodias would have been in her 20's.

The Greek cities are thought to have flourished mainly on account of the felicitous choice made by their founders, in regard to the beauty and strength of their sites, their proximity to some haven and the fineness of the country. But the Roman prudence was more particularly employed on matters which have received but little attention from the Greeks--- such as paving their roads, constructing aqueducts and sewers. In fact they have paved the roads, cut through hills and filled up valleys, so that the merchandise may be conveyed by carriage from the ports. The sewers, arched over with hewn stones, are large enough in parts for actual hay wagons to pass through, while so plentiful is the supply of water from the aqueducts, that rivers may be said to flow through the city and the sewers and almost every house is furnished with water pipes and copious fountains.

We may remark that the ancients [of Republican times] bestowed little attention upon the beautifying of Rome. But their successors and especially those of our own day, have at the same time embellished the city with numerous and splendid objects. Pompey, the Divine Caesar [i.e. Julius Caesar] and Augustus, with his children, friends, wife and sister have surpassed all others in their zeal and munificence in these decorations. The greater number of these may be seen in the Campus Martius which to the beauties of nature adds those of art. The size of the plain is remarkable, allowing chariot races and the equestrian sports without hindrance and multitudes [here] exercise themselves with ball games, in the Circus and on the wrestling grounds. The structures that surround [the Campus], the greensward covered with herbage all the year around, the summit of the hills beyond the Tiber, extending from its banks with panoramic effect, present a spectacle which the eye abandons with regret.

Near to this plain is another surrounded with columns, sacred groves, three theaters, an amphitheater and superb temples, each close to the other and so splendid that it would seem idle to describe the rest of the city after it. ..(Strabo *Geography* V.iii)

While Bernice and her children had the option of a luxurious life in Jerusalem, Rome would have been a more logical choice for them. In fact, Jerusalem, with its strict adherence to Jewish law, its overbearing priesthood, and ingrained anti-Herodian bias, was probably never a serious consideration–even before Herod the Great's death in 4 B.C.

With all these advantages, it becomes even more of a puzzle as to why the thoroughly Romanized Herodias–now in her 30's– would divorce her husband and move away from Rome to the rough-and-tumble East with a daughter barely into puberty. The quote from Josephus in the chapter epigraph is accurate indeed– Herodias' action was "confounding" in the extreme!

Chapter 17   The Sons of Herod the Great

..for (Augustus) received these sons of Herod with all humanity and gave Herod leave to give his, kingdom to which of his sons he pleased; (*Antiq* XV 10:1)

Tetrarch Herod Antipas ordered John the Baptist to be executed and could have saved Jesus of Nazareth from crucifixion if he so chose. Despite this dark legacy, however, Herod Antipas, like his wife Queen Herodias, is not an entirely unsympathetic character. In fact, in a certain narrow light, Antipas can be viewed as a tragic figure in a true Shakespearean sense.

The youngest son of Herod the Great had been a respected ruler moving serenely into old age. He had ruled his difficult domain capably if not wisely for close to three decades. Then, suddenly, a younger woman entered his life–Herodias! Though Antipas had known his niece Herodias since she had been born, under the extraordinary circumstances of the times he made her a marriage proposal. Herodias accepted and abandoned her previous life and husband in Rome, joining Antipas in his Tiberian palace by the shores of Lake Gennesareth.

Antipas and Herodias were then married despite the muted objections of the Temple hierarchy. The priests' concern was that Herodias had been Antipas' brother's wife. The brother–Herod Philip of Rome–was still alive and so the marriage was against Jewish law. But the response from the Jewish people was not muted at all-the people were vociferous and hateful in their criticism.

As a result of the marriage, Antipas not only suffered the scorn of his subjects, but later became involved in a disastrous war with a neighboring kingdom. Worse, Antipas' long-contained ambition was inflamed by the avaricious Herodias. This resulted in both Antipas and Herodias being banished to a remote and cold part of the empire. There, the couple finished out their lives in disgrace and relative poverty.

Herod Antipas is a central figure in the life and Ministry of Jesus of Nazareth. He can be best understood in the context of his family, where he was only one of several sons of Herod the Great–all of whom contended with each other in the hopes of gaining their father's kingdom.

Antipas, Archelaus and Herod Philip

Herod Antipas was the youngest of seven Royal sons of Herod the Great. Herod likely had innumerable additional illegitimate offspring, but little is known about them. Herod Antipas was born either in 26 B.C. or close to it. Then, Herod the Great was firmly in power and so Antipas enjoyed the benefits of a full Royal pedigree.

Herod Antipas' mother was a Samaritan Jewess named Malthace, one of Herod the Great's nine wives. Malthace had an earlier son by Herod named Archelaus, and Herod had another son named Herod Philip by a different wife, Cleopatra of Jerusalem. These three sons grew up together, were educated at Rome together, and later Herod the Great's kingdom was divided between them to rule.

> One of his wives also was of the Samaritan nation, whose sons were Antipas and Archelaus... Archelaus and Antipas were brought up with a certain private man at Rome. Herod had also to wife Cleopatra of Jerusalem and by her he had his sons Herod and Philip; which last was also brought up at Rome. (*Antiq* XVII 1:3)

This Herod Philip should not be confused with the first husband of Herodias, also called Herod Philip, who was the son of Mariamne II, the High Priest's daughter. This future Tetrarch Herod Philip also had a brother Herod, of which little is known.

Although these young men–boys, actually–were treated Royally in Rome and given first-rate educations, they were technically hostages of the empire. Rome used this "hostage" system with many of the rulers of her client kingdoms. Through the centuries it had served the empire well. Benevolently interred in Rome, the sons of provincial kings could become familiar with Roman culture and learn the Latin language. The logic was that so educated these princes would then be far less likely to revolt against Rome should they later gain power in their native countries. Also, if a provincial king happened to be killed through enemy action, revolt, or mishap, Rome had a safe and ready supply of "replacement" kings of the proper bloodline. More darkly, should any of these puppet provincial kings ever turn upon Rome, their children could be used against them as actual blood hostages.

Rome wisely arranged to have hostages even with those nations and empires through which she had alliances, such as Parthia.

> Between the Parthians and ourselves there was an ancient friendship, founded on a state alliance and we ought to support allies who were our rivals in strength and yet yielded to us out of respect. Kings' sons were given as hostages, in order that when Parthia was tired of home rule, it might fall back on the emperor and the Senate and receive from them a better sovereign, familiar with Roman habits. (*Annuls* 12:10)

Apparently, this system was a one-way street. There is no record of Rome giving hostages of its own to, for instance, the Parthian Empire.

Aristobulos and Alexander

Archelaus, Herod Philip and Antipas were not the first sons of Herod to enjoy the Augustan Royal court. They were preceded a decade earlier by two older half-brothers of Asamonean blood, Aristobulos and Alexander. These two men were the sons of Herod the Great and Mariamne I, the granddaughter of the former King Hyrcanus II. One of these sons, Aristobulos, would later be the father of Herodias, Herod Antipas' future wife.

When were Alexander and Aristobulos born? Herod the Great had a great passion for their mother Mariamne I, a tall and youthful beauty with irresistible regal airs. Early in his reign and anxious to secure a Royal heir, Herod married Mariamne in 37 B.C. even while his army was laying siege to the city of Jerusalem. It is very probable that the eldest, Alexander, would have been born in 36 B.C. and Aristobulos a year later in 35 B.C.

Herod the Great was short of stature and probably not a handsome man. If he had been, his biographer and flatterer Nicolaus of Damascus surely would have remarked upon it. On the other hand, Mariamne I was the beautiful granddaughter of an Asamonean king and considered the unchallenged prize of the Jewish nation. Mariamne probably had to be talked into this marriage of convenience by her grandfather, the genial and practical ex-King Hyrcanus II. Mariamne, as with the other Royals and most of the Jewish nation, never accepted Herod's legitimacy to rule. She likely never fully accepted him as her husband, either. Mariamne's coolness toward Herod did not diminish through time and familiarity. But despite her callous demeanor, Herod loved her passionately.

Herod's natural sister, Salome, hated Mariamne. She schemed against Herod's wife, hoping to turn Herod against her. Eventually, Herod succumbed and had the beautiful Mariamne executed in 29 B.C. He immediately regretted this vile and rash act and it haunted him to his dying day.

Five years later, in 24 B.C., Herod sent his two now-motherless sons, Aristobulos and Alexander, to Rome for study and military training. The boys were now 11 and 12, respectively. Herod also had a third and younger son by Mariamne I. Josephus writes that this son died in Rome, but his age and the circumstances of his death are not recorded.

Emperor Augustus did not have to force Herod into giving up his two Royal sons as hostages. At the time, there was a great famine in the Jewish lands, and Herod suspected that an insurrection against him was more likely than not.

When Herod was engaged in such matters and when he had already re-edified Sebaste, [Samaria,] he resolved to send his sons Alexander and Aristobulus to Rome, to enjoy the company of Caesar; who, when they came thither, lodged at the house of Pollio, who was very fond of Herod's friendship; and they had leave to lodge in Caesar's own palace, for he received these sons of Herod with all humanity and gave Herod leave to give his, kingdom to which of his sons he pleased; (*Antiq* XV 10:1)

This passage mentions the name of Pollio, a man who housed Aristobulos and Alexander in Rome. It is quite likely that Pollio also housed Antipas, Archelaus and Herod Philip (the son of Cleopatra of Jerusalem), when these sons, too, were later sent to Rome. Augustus also gave the power of succession to Herod the Great which proved to be a deadly mistake.

In 19 B.C., after the sons of Herod had spent five years in the Royal court, Augustus released them back into Herod's care. Alexander was then 17 and Aristobulos 16. In Judea, the Royal sons were wildly popular. The Jewish people hailed them as future kings. Unfortunately, this public adulation proved to be the beginning of the Royal sons' downfall. Herod's sister Salome and his brother Phasaelus, both of common birth, became insanely jealous of their Royal nephews, just as they had been a decade earlier of their sister-in-law Mariamne I. Over the next 12 years they and others consistently plotted and railed against Aristobulos and Alexander. Eventually Herod the Great, a weak man in that respect, began to believe in the existence of these plots and schemes. Finally, in 7 B.C. Herod had his two Royal sons executed–along with 300 of his sons' most loyal supporters.

At the time, Alexander was 30 and Aristobulos was 29. Both men had young families; Aristobulos had five children with the youngest, Herodias, not yet a year old. As for the young Herod Antipas, these executions, as grisly as they were, worked to his advantage. Antipas, Herod's youngest son, was then 19 years old and a favorite of Salome and Phasaelus–perhaps because he was so malleable. With their deaths, Antipas moved up two notches in the line of Royal succession.

Antipater, the son of Doris

Antipater was Herod's oldest son. His mother, however, was Doris, a woman of common blood. Worse, Antipater was born before 40 B.C. which was before Herod the Great had been declared king of the East by Octavian and Antony. Accordingly, Antipater had no natural Royal standing.

Herod had benevolently banished Doris and Antipater from his court for this reason. But both were welcomed back years later when Herod began suspecting that his Royal sons Aristobulos and Alexander were becoming treasonous. The older Antipater was then groomed as a rival to the princes and Herod eventually made him his sole heir. Antipater, for his part, was very pleased with this change of affairs, for he now stood a good chance of becoming a king.

Near the end of the General Marcus Agrippa's tenure as president of Syria, about 15 B.C., Herod the Great brought Antipater to Rome. Then 28 years old, Antipater lived there for a time and became popular with his Roman benefactors and learned Roman ways. Antipater worked hard to erase the memories of his half-brothers Alexander and Aristobulos from the minds of the Roman people and the Royal court of Augustus. The Royal princes, now in the East and both with families, had made their own mark in Rome during the years 24-19 B.C.

Herod the Great showed unusual deference to Antipater on many issues and Antipater became a close adviser to his father. But despite this, Antipater still feared his two brothers. The Royal sons of Herod were tall, good-looking, and very popular with the Jewish people. Antipater joined his aunt Salome and uncle Phasaelus in plotting against Aristobulos and Alexander, even as he spent time in Rome. Antipater also married into the Asamonean Royal family; one of his wives was the daughter of defeated King Antigonus. In 7 B.C., all of the plotting had its desired effect on Herod and he found reason to execute his Royal sons. Antipater became the indisputable first heir to Herod's kingdom.

But Antipater soon grew tired of waiting for Herod to die and began his own plotting–against his father. Herod eventually unmasked the calumny and had his eldest son executed just days before his own death in 4 B.C.

Herod Philip, the son of Mariamne II

Yet another son of Herod the Great, also called Philip, was an integral part of the Herod clan. Later, he would become the first husband of Herodias. Herod Philip's mother was named Mariamne, but she was the second of Herod's wives to be called so. Mariamne II was the beautiful daughter of a priest called Simon, who was himself the son of an important Alexandrian Priest named Boethus. Herod the Great intentionally appointed Simon High Priest of the Jerusalem Temple in order to elevate Mariamne II's station and thus justify him marrying her. The marriage probably occurred around 25 B.C. with their son Herod Philip born later that year. Shortly afterward, Aristobulos and Alexander were sent off to Rome for education (*Antiq* XV 10:1), perhaps at her request.

Also in the mix at this time were other wives. Malthace was the mother of Herod Antipas and Archelaus. Cleopatra of Jerusalem also had her place in the Royal household, as the mother of Herod Philip, later the tetrarch. Herod the Great's Royal court in those years was surely a crowded one, and very early the seeds were sown for palace jealousy and intrigue.

Herod the Great had great regard for the son of Mariamne II, Herod Philip. At one point, Herod designated the Philip to be second in the line of Royal succession after his oldest son, Antipater. Philip was probably older than Herod Antipas, but likely by only a year or so. Inasmuch as the Herod Philip gained no Royal power in his lifetime, the writer Josephus, reflecting his source Nicolaus of Damascus, spends little time on him. In all likelihood, Herod Philip, the son of Mariamne II, was reared along with Archelaus, Antipas and Herod Philip first in Judea and then later in Rome when the whole passel was sent there for education and military training.

The Sons of Herod in Rome

This early Augustan period was later considered the golden age of the Roman Empire. Emperor Augustus, a wise and farsighted man, ruled with little challenge to his authority. Roman military might was unquestioned and as a result there was generally peace throughout the empire.

As the Roman coffers swelled from tax revenue, Emperor Augustus undertook marvelous building projects in Rome and all over the empire. Herod the Great, taking a cue from Augustus, began his own building projects with borrowed Roman designers and engineers. These constructions would, in fact, prove to eclipse the most ambitious of Augustus', although in the process Herod nearly bankrupted his domain.

From 15 B.C. to 7 B.C., it is entirely possible that at times all seven sons of Herod the Great were living in Rome. If they weren't actually living together (in Pollio's house, perhaps), they certainly were in close proximity to each other; they were foreigners of a similar feather, after all.

In Rome, these young men would have known the same people, gone to the same social gatherings, and been attended to by the same group of slaves and freedmen. They likely commingled on a daily basis with the high and mighty of the Royal Augustan court, forming valuable friendships that they hoped would serve them well in the future. Romans seeking advantage in the East would likewise have cultivated these sons of Herod the Great.

So while Herod the Great had grown up in the harsh and demanding world of Idumea and fought alongside his father Antipater, his sons were thoroughly Romanized and lived a life of luxury. These young men faced little overt hostility or challenges as they grew into manhood.

It is interesting to speculate on the dynamic between the seven brothers living together in Rome. Were they boon companions while they enjoyed the wonders of the greatest city in the world, or were they even then competing against each other–bitter rivals for their father's love, approbation and power? And what did these young men really think of their famous and powerful father Herod the Great? Herod's dark and suspicious nature surely must have been apparent to them at a young age. Their father had executed the Mariamne I, as well as several of their Asamonean relatives before most of them were born. Did Herod the Great manage to justify those barbarous acts to his children? Did he even bother to try?!

Certainly all the sons feared their father. But, as they played in Rome, could they also see the dark clouds forming on their own horizons? In murderous fact, before Herod the Great died in 4 B.C., he would have found reason to execute three of those seven sons.

Herod Antipas Gains a Kingdom

Herod Antipas was a favorite of Herod the Great, due in no small measure to the support Antipas had from Herod's sister Salome. Salome had the ear of her brother Herod and was the source for much of the doubt and suspicion that gripped Herod during his reign. Did Salome respect Antipas for his capabilities, or see in Antipas a young man whom she could control?

Growing up as the youngest son in the Royal Augustan court and the Royal court of Herod, Antipas was forced to learn early the art of diplomacy. Antipas was undoubtedly well used to bowing and scrapping before his older brothers. However, in 4 B.C., after Aristobolos and Alexander had been executed and Antipater disgraced and in jail, Herod the Great thought his youngest son, Antipas, competent enough–and old enough–to name as his sole heir (*Antiq* XVII 6:1). Assuming a birth year of 26 B.C., Antipas would have been 22 years of age then. Unfortunately for Antipas, Herod the Great later revised that will only days before his death. In it, Herod split up his kingdom and gave Antipas only a portion of it–Galilee and Perea. Upon Herod's death and the reading of the will, Antipas protested to Augustus. But after a hearing in Rome in 3 B.C., the emperor decided to enforce the final version.

Antipas' new territory had brought in a quarter of Herod's revenues–200 talents yearly; hence the term "tetrarchy" was applied to his realm. A talent is a measure of weight, generally taken to be 33 kilograms. With these funds, although considerable, Antipas had to maintain the infrastructure of the country and pay the military as well. And how much of this money was paid to Rome as tax and tribute is unknown.

Herod Philip, Antipas' older half-brother by Cleopatra of Jerusalem, received territory that lay north of Lake Gennesareth and east of the Jordan River–fertile lands which accounted for another quarter of Herod's revenue. Archelaus, Antipas' older full brother, received the lion's share of Herod's domain, gaining control over Idumea, Judea and Samaria and with it the prize city of Jerusalem. Those territories had accounted for half of Herod's income; hence the term "ethnarchy" is sometimes used to describe it.

> When Caesar had heard these pleadings, he dissolved the assembly; but a few days afterwards he appointed Archelaus, not indeed to be king of the whole country, but ethnarch of the one half of that which had been subject to Herod and promised to give him the royal dignity hereafter, if he governed his part virtuously. But as for the other half, he divided it into two parts and gave it to two other of Herod's sons, to Philip and to Antipas, that Antipas who disputed with Archelaus for the whole kingdom. Now to him it was that Peres and Galilee paid their tribute which amounted annually to two hundred talents, while Batanea, with Trachonitis, as well as Auranitis, with a certain part of what was called the *House of Zenodorus*, paid the tribute of one hundred talents to Philip; but Idumea and Judea and the country of Samaria paid tribute to Archelaus, but had now a fourth part of that tribute taken off by the order of Caesar, who decreed them that mitigation, because they did not join in this revolt with the rest of the multitude. There were also certain of the cities which paid tribute to Archelaus: Strato's Tower and Sebaste, with Joppa and Jerusalem; for as to Gaza and Gadara and Hippos, they were Grecian cities which Caesar separated from his government and added them to the province of Syria. Now the tribute-money that came to Archelaus every year from his own dominions amounted to six hundred talents. (*Antiq* XVII 11:4).

Banishment of Archelaus

Archelaus had the largest kingdom, but he also had the roughest time of it, having to deal with sedition on an almost constant basis. Pent-up anger and fury against Rome, previously held in check by the merciless rule of Herod the Great, exploded into rebellion upon Herod's death. As a result, Archelaus, as gentle a soul as he might have been previously, hardened into a brutal ruler much like his father.

Archelaus' ethnarchy lasted almost ten years before it was taken away by Augustus. Certainly, the Jews grew to hate Archelaus as much as they did Herod the Great. Apart from his brutality, a minor factor might have been the ethnarch's marriage to his brother's wife which Herod Antipas was to emulate years later. This would have been a sacrilegious act and unpopular.

> Moreover, he (Archelaus) transgressed the law of our fathers and married Glaphyra, the daughter of Archelaus, who had been the wife of his brother Alexander which Alexander had three children by her, while it was a thing detestable among the Jews to marry the brother's wife. (*Antiq* XVII 13:1)

This Alexander was the brother of Aristobulos, the father of Herodias, both of whom Herod had executed in 7 B.C.

It should be noted that the first wife of Archelaus, before Glaphyra, might well have been Mariamne, the oldest daughter of Aristobulos and Bernice and the older sister to Herodias.

> I cannot also but think it worthy to be recorded what dream Glaphyra, the daughter of Archelaus, king of Cappadocia, had, who had at first been wife to Alexander, who was the brother of Archelaus, concerning whom we have been discoursing. This Alexander was the son of Herod the king, by whom he was put to death, as we have already related. This Glaphyra was married, after his death, to Juba, king of Libya; and, after his death, was returned home and lived a widow with her father. Then it was that Archelaus, the ethnarch, saw her and fell so deeply in love with her, that he divorced Mariamne, who was then his wife and married her. (*Wars* II 7:4)

Josephus suggests that Archelaus treated his brothers very severely to the point where both joined in a petition to have him removed.

> But in the tenth year of Archelaus's government, both his brethren and the principal men of Judea and Samaria, not being able to bear his barbarous and tyrannical usage of them, accused him before Caesar and that especially because they knew he had broken the commands of Caesar which obliged him to behave himself with moderation among them. (*Antiq* XVII 13:2)

In A.D. 6, a delegation of principal men from Judea and Samaria, along with Herod Antipas and Herod Philip, traveled to Rome to present their case against Archelaus. Roman historian Dio, in a rare mention of the Herod family, agrees.

> Herod of Palestine, who was accused by his brothers of some wrongdoing or other, was banished beyond the Alps and a portion of the domain was confiscated to the state. (Dio 55: 27-6)

Lacking even his own brothers' support, Archelaus' crimes were probably indisputably heinous.

Herod Antipas and Philip might have had hopes of dividing Archelaus' ethnarchy between them, but Emperor Augustus had other ideas. He decided to place Judea and Samaria under direct Roman control.

Herod Antipas and Herod Philip were undoubtedly disappointed over the loss of a major part of Herod the Great's old kingdom, but these young men knew enough not to complain. Both stayed in power and secure in their kingdoms for 30 years after Archelaus' removal–and without serious challenge from either Rome or the people they ruled.

Antipas' Reign

Antipas ruled Galilee and Perea from 4 B.C. to A.D. 39. Soon after gaining the tetrarchy, Antipas married an Arabian princess named Pharaelis, daughter of King Aretas IV of the neighboring kingdom of Nabotea. It was a wise alliance. The marriage put to rest several issues of contention that had existed between King Aretas IV and Herod the Great.

Josephus affirms that King Aretas IV had no intrinsic love for the Herod family. In 3 B.C., Roman General Varus needed auxiliary forces in order to battle the insurrections that arose after the death of Herod the Great.

> Aretas also, the king of Arabia Petrea, out of his hatred to Herod and in order to purchase the favor of the Romans, sent him no small assistance, (*Antiq* XVII 10:9)

However, Varus soon was forced to disband this particular army because its Arab members were difficult to control and destroyed many Jewish towns unnecessarily in their zeal.

Facing no real outside enemies, Herod Antipas turned his attention toward building the infrastructure of his own country. He first undertook several construction projects in Sepphoris. The Judean cities of Jericho and Jerusalem both had Royal palaces of Herod the Great, so either city could rightfully claim to be the capital of Herod's domain. Now, with the Jewish East fragmented and Jerusalem under control of a Roman prefect, Herod Antipas wanted a capital city of his own in Galilee. The city of Sepphoris was located on the top of a southern Galilee hill and held a commanding position overlooking the broad northern Beth She'an plain. This fertile area spread from the Mediterranean seaport city of Ptolemais to the west, to the vast sunken basin of Lake Gennesareth in the east.

In later years, Antipas created a new city on the western shores of Lake Gennesareth that he named Tiberias in honor of then-Emperor Tiberius. There, Antipas built a sumptuous palace. In time, Tiberias replaced Sepphoris as the capital of Galilee.

The Nature of Antipas

Why did Herod the Great change his will in his last days and give Herod Antipas a quarter of his kingdom instead of all of it? Did Herod finally realize that Antipas was a weak man and not up to the task of dealing with the perpetually seditious Jews that were common to Judea and Jerusalem at that time? Herod Antipas had little military experience when growing up in Rome. Certainly, Antipas' later succumbing to the charms of Herodias so completely might indicate a certain lack of self-confidence.

Herod Antipas was also a superstitious man, but most people were in those days. Astrologers and seers were probably always close at hand to the tetrarch. It is doubtful that Antipas ever made a significant decision without their input.

While not a devout Jew, Antipas respected Jewish ritual to a degree and was very interested in Jewish cults and religious ascetics. While living in Macherus when John the Baptist was a prisoner there, Antipas talked with him on more than one occasion, according to the New Testament (Mk 6:20). Antipas probably had a philosophic side as much as any of his brothers. That might be what caused Emperor Tiberius to be such a strong supporter of him later, for Tiberius' hobby was the study of philosophy.

Indeed, Antipas was a Rome-educated man which was a rarity in the East and that gave him a measure of civility that Herod the Great could never have approached. Antipas probably also made regular trips back to Rome to enjoy the culture there and seek out the friends of his youth. Caesarea, on the east coast of the Mediterranean Sea, was a thoroughly Romanized city and not far from Galilee. Attracted by the plays, musical concerts and the hippodrome competitions that Caesarea had to offer, Herod Antipas probably visited there frequently as well.

Considering his length of tenure, it can also be inferred that Herod Antipas was a practical and tolerant individual, fair in his judgments and actions toward his people. Antipas fully realized that he served only at the pleasure of the Roman emperor and he would have taken to heart the disastrous example set by his brother Archelaus. Antipas would also have learned from the executions of his brothers Aristobulos, Alexander, and Antipater that it was ambition–perceived or otherwise–that had earned them their deaths.

It can be concluded that after a failed attempt to obtain the entire kingdom of Herod the Great when he was 23, Herod

Antipas quietly accepted his fate and settled down to enjoy life as the Roman puppet ruler of Galilee and Perea. For over 30 years, Antipas ruled his domain without major incident. Indeed, Antipas might well have died respected and in power but for the beauty and allure of his niece Herodias.

Motives for a Marriage

The reasons for Herod Antipas divorcing Pharaelis and marrying Herodias are easily understood. When Herodias became his wife, Antipas was probably in his mid-fifties and had ruled his tetrarchy competently for decades. Did Antipas have a vague feeling of boredom and dissatisfaction as the years passed? Certainly, despite the best efforts of physicians, herbalists and magicians, Antipas had to have been feeling his age. Pharaelis, Antipas' Arabian wife for over a quarter century, was at the very least less attractive than she once had been. Worse, the Nabotean princess had given Antipas no son. That is itself was justification for divorce under Jewish law.

Then Herodias entered Antipas' life and love blossomed. Herodias was much younger than Antipas and a tall beauty of Royal blood. She exuded refinement and elegance and her Roman-bred imperious airs probably made her all the more desirable. But a simple affair was out of the question. Herodias wanted marriage. Antipas had no choice but to agree.

But what would Antipas do about his wife Pharaelis? And Herodias, too, already had her own husband to deal with– Antipas' Rome-based half-brother Herod Philip. Herodias' solution was to divorce her husband. This act was especially sacrilegious because Herodias already had a daughter by the man.

For Antipas, the solution proved to be easier. Pharaelis learned about Antipas' passion for Herodias and took the situation into her own hands. She fled to her father in Nabotea fearful for her life. Would Antipas have found a way to execute Pharaelis as his father Herod the Great executed Mariamne I? Pharaelis was not going to take any chances! The erstwhile queen fled Galilee, and soon she was safe in Nabotea with her father King Aretas. Antipas was now free to marry.

Antipas probably hoped that his subjects would respond to the Asamonean blood of Herodias. Antipas himself was a Samaritan Jew on his mother's side and his father was pure Arabian. Antipas might have had hopes of Herodias bearing him a son and Royal heir, thus further legitimizing himself to the Jewish people he ruled.

Herodias' Choice

It is easy to conjecture that the aging Antipas had several good reasons to bring the young and beautiful Herodias into Galilee and make her his queen. So the question now returns to Herodias. What had she to gain from the move? Herodias was in her late thirties when she made her decision–a time when most women are well settled in their ways. Why would a beautiful and wealthy woman like Herodias, used to the finest Rome had to offer and with a teenage daughter to raise, decide to divorce her husband of 25 years and move to the provincial East?

Was Herod Philip of Rome, Herodias' first husband, a major factor? He was only slightly older than Antipas and in his fifties. Did Herodias simply tire of him? Did Herod Philip have an incapacitating medical condition? Did he lose his money? Josephus, unfortunately, gives us no hints as to the answer to these questions. But even if we assume that Herod Philip was a dissolute and penniless profligate, a formal divorce action initiated by Herodias was an unusual way to deal with the situation.

So the mystery remains: why would Herodias want to leave Rome and descend into the turbulence of the East? Women who are beautiful, wealthy, and cultured do not usually leave famous cities without good reason. But Herodias did. Why?

The answer to that key question will be the subject of the next two chapters and from it an important date will be derived.

Chapter 18   Tiberius Caesar

Tiberius..was as pre-eminent in intelligence and acuteness as he was in good fortune, (Philo *Embassy* VI 33)

Under the consecutive reigns of Emperors Augustus and Tiberius, the Roman Empire held absolute sway over much of the known world for almost 70 years. It was during this period–from 31 B.C. to A.D. 37–that Herod the Great and his descendants dominated the Jewish lands under Roman franchise and both John the Baptist and Jesus of Nazareth lived out their lives and met their destinies.

The Roman Empire then spanned the territory from the Pillars of Heracles in the west to the Euphrates River in the east, and from the British Isles in the north to the Sahara Desert in the south. By most accounts, those 70 years were peaceful and prosperous ones for Rome and the empire– excepting for a lone and singular event. In A.D. 31, a conspiracy fomented by a treacherous general came very close to deposing Emperor Tiberius and ending the rule of the Caesars.

Tiberius put down the high-level sedition, but while Tiberius' power continued unabated, the idyllic and progressive atmosphere of the city of Rome disappeared. The "golden" city took years to recover as perhaps thousands of conspirators and suspects were either executed from proscription lists or had their assets seized in banishment. Tens of thousands more citizens voluntarily fled Rome for the safety of the countryside or foreign provinces. According to Tacitus, this was one of the darkest chapters in the history of Rome (*Annuls* 6: 7,19).

Through all of the violence of the proscriptions, the sanguine Tiberius stayed in Capri aloof and detached–only adding to the fear of the citizens. Was this a show of supreme confidence, or did the emperor continue to avoid Rome in anticipation of even more violence and treachery?

A major hypothesis of this investigation will be that it was the near-revolution against Tiberius in late A.D. 31 and the social dislocations that followed that caused Herodias to leave Rome for the East. Herodias' brothers, Agrippa and Aristobulos, also left the city at roughly the same time and probably for much the same reason. The eastern tetrarchs Herod Antipas and Herod Philip, who survived the Sejanus plot with powers intact, held out the promise of security for them. And if Herodias and her brothers suspected that Tiberius' grip on the empire was weakening, and that the Sejanus affair would be the first of many attempts on the throne, all the more reason to leave Rome. These children of Aristobulos might have had vague hopes of leading a breakaway Jewish nation after the fashion of the Maccabees of old.

Tiberius Caesar

Tiberius Caesar, the Roman emperor from A.D. 14 to early A.D. 37, was a shrewd and successful administrator of the empire. The Alexandrian Jewish historian and philosopher Philo Judaeus, who lived through Tiberius' reign in its entirety, had nothing but praise for the man.

> For Tiberius, who was a man of very profound prudence and the most able to all the men of his court at perceiving the hidden intentions of any man and who was as pre-eminent in intelligence and acuteness as he was in good fortune (Philo *Embassy* VI 33)

Suetonius gives a physical description of Tiberius.

> (Tiberius) was large and strong of frame and of a stature above the average; broad of shoulders and chest; well proportioned and symmetrical from head to foot. His left hand was the more nimble and

stronger and its joints were so powerful that he could bore through a fresh, sound apple with his finger and break the head of a boy, or even a young man, with a fillip. He was of fair complexion and wore his hair rather long at the back, so much so as even to cover the nape of his neck; which was apparently a family trait. His face was handsome, but would break out on a sudden with many pimples. His eyes were unusually large and, strange to say, had the power of seeing even at night and in the dark, but only for a short time when first opened after sleep; presently they grew dim-sighted again. He strode along with his neck stiff and bent forward, usually with a stern countenance and for the most part in silence, never or very rarely conversing with his companions and then speaking with great deliberation and with a kind of supple movement of his fingers... He enjoyed excellent health which was all but perfect during nearly the whole of his reign, although from the thirtieth year of his age he took care of it according to his own ideas, without the aid or advice of physicians. (Suetonius *Tiberius* LXVIII)

Suetonius paints a godlike picture of tiberius–a strong and intelligent man, second to none in those areas, who could also see in the dark! A fitting leader for then the most powerful empire on earth.

Tiberius was the son of Augustus' wife Livia (Julia) by a former marriage and not related by blood to Emperor Augustus. This, however, presented only a minor problem for succession. Tiberius enjoyed a successful military career and was respected throughout the empire as Augustus' most capable general. Augustus, recognizing Tiberius' talents, meticulously groomed him to rule the empire for more than a decade before Augustus' own death in A.D. 14. Tiberius' subsequent claim to absolute power was expected and unchallenged.

Early Life

Tiberius was born in 42 B.C. He was the son of Tiberius Nero, a general who served well under Julius Caesar. In the war and chaos that followed Caesar's assassination in 44 B.C., Tiberius Nero found himself at odds with Octavian (later Augustus), who ruled the western empire. Tiberius Nero found favor, however, with Marc Antony, who ruled the East, and so Nero moved his family to Greece to serve under him.

Over time, Augustus forgave Tiberius Nero for whatever had originally caused the rift and invited Nero to return to Rome with his family to serve in his staff. Nero submitted, but he paid a high price; Emperor Augustus had fallen in love with Nero's wife Livia Drusilla. Once in Rome, Nero was forced to divorce the beautiful woman so Augustus could marry her. Livia, illustrative of the place women had in those times, had no choice in the matter. She married Augustus in 38 B.C.

So, when young Tiberius was three years of age, his mother Livia married the co-emperor of the Roman Empire. Only days earlier, Livia had given birth to Tiberius' full brother Drusus, another son fathered by Tiberius Nero. Fortunately for the child Tiberius, he was adopted by Augustus as his own son, as was Drusus, and Livia had no children by the emperor.

Tiberius began his career as a Roman advocate and magistrate after a rigorous period of military training. Later, he was given charge over various military commands and legions. Over two decades, Octavian–now the "divine" Augustus–sent Tiberius on numerous military campaigns in Gaul, Germany, Ilyrium, Armenia and Parthia. Intelligent and methodical, Tiberius was successful in them all.

But Tiberius took little glory in his military victories and the blood of war. Years later as emperor, Tiberius wrote that that the best type of warfare was diplomacy.

> He, Tiberius, had himself been sent nine times by Augustus into Germany and had done more by policy than by arms. (*Annuls* 2:26)

Self-imposed Exile in Rhodes

By 6 B.C., Tiberius had been consul of Rome twice and had been voted a tribunal. But with his star on the ascendant, Tiberius abruptly retired from public life and moved to the island of Rhodes. There, for seven years he lived a simple life with his philosopher friends. Tiberius was to say later that the reason was because Emperor Augustus had adopted his two grandsons, Caius and Lucius, as his own sons. Though these men were younger and unproven, Augustus clearly favored them for succession. Knowing his place, Tiberius did not want to overshadow whatever accomplishments his younger stepbrothers might achieve.

But Herod the Great might have also played a role in Tiberius' retreat. Just a year before, in 7 B.C, Herod the Great had executed his two Royal sons Aristobulos and Alexander which sent minor shock waves throughout the empire. Tiberius was only a few years older than the two slain men and he knew both of them well from their years together in Rome, where the two Jewish princes lived at times in the Royal palace. Tiberius, a cultured man who enjoyed the study of philosophy, was undoubtedly revolted by the executions. The deaths of his Jewish friends might have set him to thinking about his standing with his own powerful stepfather.

Other reasons for Tiberius' self-exile have been postulated. One factor might have been the death of his full brother Drusus, with whom Tiberius was very close and had gone through several military campaigns with. Drusus' death occurred only thee years earlier in 9 B.C. Another reason might have been a desire to get away from the absolute control of Augustus, as well as from Tiberius' wife Julia. Six years before, Emperor Augustus forced Tiberius to divorce the woman he loved–and had a son by–in order to marry Augustus' own daughter, Julia. Julia was later to become an embarrassing profligate, if she hadn't become one already.

Tacitus sheds some light on this as he writes about the death of Julia which occurred shortly after Tiberius became emperor in A.D. 14– a death which Tiberius might have had a hand in.

That same year Julia ended her days. For her profligacy she had formerly been confined by her father Augustus in the island of Pandateria and then in the town of the Regini on the shores of the straits of Sicily. She had been the wife of Tiberius while Caius and Lucius Caesar were in their glory and had disdained him as an unequal match. This was Tiberius's special reason for retiring to Rhodes. (*Annuls* 1:53)

Whatever the reason, Tiberius' self-imposed exile to Rhodes in 6 B.C. clearly irked Augustus and his relationship with his step-son was never quite the same afterward.

Return from Exile

Two years later, one of Augustus' adopted sons, Lucius, died from a disease. Livia urged Augustus to order Tiberius to return from Rhodes. Augustus was aging and there was no question that Tiberius was by far the best suited for succession. Augustus reluctantly agreed to this, and Tiberius returned to the Royal court. It proved to be a fortuitous move on the part of Augustus. Soon afterward his other adopted son, Caius, died from a battle wound.

From A.D. 4 until Augustus' death 10 years later, Augustus allowed Tiberius to virtually rule the empire. Tiberius spearheaded several military campaigns in Gaul, Germany and other northern provinces–all successfully and earning him great honors. Tiberius' ascension to power in A.D. 14 upon Augustus' death was without contest or controversy.

Tiberius as Emperor

Tiberius had no interest in expanding the empire he inherited; he was satisfied to simply maintain what Augustus and the generals of two previous generations had gained. Administration of the empire was a huge job, but as with his military campaigns Tiberius managed it successfully. One of Tiberius' strong points was his aversion to armed conflict. Tiberius learned early in his military career that few wars brought any lasting benefit to the empire and he held to that belief throughout his reign.

> Nothing made Tiberius so uneasy as an apprehension of the disturbance of any settlement. He commissioned a centurion to tell the kings not to decide their dispute by arms. (*Annuls* 2:65)

Late in his reign, many foes of Rome looked upon Tiberius' aversion to war as a sign of weakness. Several former allies, in fact, became bold in their actions. One was the king of Parthia, as will be seen in later chapters.

But for most of Tiberius' years in power, there was peace. Later historians were disappointed in this lack of military excitement. Rome, after all, was built on wars and conquest, and true Roman heroes were all fighting men! As Tacitus laments:

> My labours are circumscribed and inglorious; peace wholly unbroken or but slightly disturbed, dismal misery in the capital, an emperor careless about the enlargement of the empire, such is my theme...I have to present in succession the merciless biddings of a tyrant, incessant prosecutions, faithless friendships, the ruin of innocence, the same causes issuing in the same results and I am everywhere confronted by a wearisome monotony in my subject matter. (*Annuls* 4:32,33)

For all his boring ways, Tiberius was an insightful and efficient administrator. He recognized the inherent criminality of most government officials, especially those Romans sent as governors to foreign lands. Tiberius knew that away from the center of power and the oversight of a higher authority, corruption inevitably ensued. Partially for this reason, once appointed Tiberius was loathe to remove any provincial governor. Since Tiberius considered most of them criminals anyway–or they soon would be, given the temptations of their office–why replace one criminal with another? The change, Tiberius reasoned, could only be for the worse as the new official gorged himself afresh upon the blood of the people.

Lucius Sejanus

Although Tiberius had a reputation as a shrewd and capable man, one member of his inner circle fooled him completely. General Lucius Sejanus viewed the aging Tiberius as a weak ruler and plotted against him, even as Tiberius trusted him completely and deferred to his counsel on many matters.

For over 10 years, Sejanus methodically and relentlessly put his seditious plans into action while feigning to be Tiberius' staunchest supporter. By the time Sejanus' cabal had been discovered, the plans of the conspiracy were almost complete: Tiberius' son Drusus had already been murdered, and Tiberius himself was marginalized and living far outside of Rome on the island of Capri. Additionally, General Sejanus had the loyalty of a significant number of the principal men of Rome as well as the command of the 5,000 man Praetorian guard. How did Tiberius ever come to let this happen–the emperor whom Philo admired as being so intelligent and insightful?

It appears that a trusting nature and loyalty to a fault was to blame. Years earlier, Sejanus had physically thrown himself upon Tiberius in order to save the emperor from falling rocks during a minor earthquake. Afterward, Tiberius displayed complete and unquestioning faith in the man. Through the subsequent years of his reign, an increasingly complacent Tiberius left much of the day-to-day running of the empire to General Sejanus. Indeed, it was the powerful Sejanus who was likely responsible for the appointment of Pontius Pilate as prefect of Judea in A.D. 26, as well as most of the other major appointments of Tiberius.

> Sejanus was so great a person by reason both of his excessive haughtiness and of his vast power, that, to put it briefly, he himself seemed to be the emperor and Tiberius a kind of island potentate, inasmuch as the latter spent his time on the island of Capreae. (Dio 58:5)

Lucius Sejanus was not born of nobility, but was of the lesser equestrian class, as was Pontius Pilate. Sejanus, through the guidance of an ambitious father, rose through the ranks to become the prefect of the Roman Praetorian guard in A.D. 15 under Tiberius. As the general of the Praetorians, Sejanus was in charge of protecting the city of Rome from outside invasion and internal rebellion. Sejanus was also an adviser in security matters to the Royal family.

> Born at Vulsinii, the son of Seius Strabo, a Roman knight, he (Sejanus) attached himself in his early youth to Caius Caesar, grandson of the Divine Augustus and the story went that he had sold his person to Apicius, a rich debauchee. Soon afterwards he won the heart of Tiberius so effactually by various artifices that the emperor, ever dark and mysterious towards others, was with Sejanus alone careless and

freespoken. It was not through his craft, for it was by this very weapon that he was overthrown; it was rather from heaven's wrath against Rome, to whose welfare his elevation and his fall were alike disastrous. He had a body which could endure hardships and a daring spirit. He was one who screened himself, while he was attacking others; he was as cringing as he was imperious; before the world he affected humility; in his heart he lusted after supremacy, for the sake of which he sometimes lavish and luxurious, but oftener energetic and watchful, qualities quite as mischievous when hypocritically assumed for the attainment of sovereignty. (Tacitus *Annuls* 4:1)

In A.D. 18 Tiberius approved Sejanus' plan to house all nine cohorts of the Praetorian guard at a single place close Rome's city walls. Previously, these cohorts were scattered close by in various nearby towns. Supposedly, this change was to ensure that the troops could be mobilized quickly in time of emergency. According to Tacitus, however, the true purpose of Sejanus was to insulate the soldiers from public opinion and to have a ready force to do his bidding should events demand it. This structure was called the Castra Praetorium and can be seen to this day in the city of Rome.

The Death of Tiberius' Son

Germanicus was the son of Drusus, Tiberius' brother. Augustus had made Tiberius adopt Germanicus as his son as a condition for succession. Germanicus was a successful general early in Tiberius' reign as the Germanic tribes were always a source of trouble. Later, Germanicus negotiated a truce with King Artabanus of Parthia over the status of Armenia, the buffer kingdom between the two empires. Shortly after this, Germanicus contracted an illness while on a sight-seeing trip in Egypt and died in A.D. 19.

Germanicus was popular with the Roman people and suspicions were hurled Tiberius' way, but nothing was proven. In retrospect, Sejanus might have played a role, but there was no evidence to support that. More likely, with the convenient death of the heir to the empire, Sejanus saw opportunity.

With Germanicus now out of the way, Sejanus knew that Tiberius' son, Drusus Julius Caesar, also known as Drusus II, was the man to eliminate. Sejanus accomplished that by using Drusus' own wife, Livilla (Livia), as a co-conspirator.

There were however obstacles to his (Sejanus') ambition in the imperial house with its many princes, a son in youthful manhood and grown-up grandsons. As it would be unsafe to sweep off such a number at once by violence, while craft would necessitate successive intervals in crime, he chose, on the whole, the stealthier way and to begin with Drusus, against whom he had the stimulus of a recent resentment. Drusus, who could not brook a rival and was somewhat irascible, had, in a casual dispute, raised his fist at Sejanus and, when he defended himself, had struck him in the face. On considering every plan Sejanus thought his easiest revenge was to turn his attention to Livia, Drusus' wife. She was a sister of Germanicus and though she was not handsome as a girl, she became a woman of surpassing beauty. Pretending an ardent passion for her, he seduced her and having won his first infamous triumph and assured that a woman after having parted with her virtue will hesitate at nothing, he lured her on to thoughts of marriage, of a share in sovereignty and of her husband's destruction. And she, the niece of Augustus, the daughter-in-law of Tiberius, the mother of children by Drusus, for a provincial paramour, foully disgraced herself, her ancestors and her descendants, giving up honour and a sure position for prospects as base as they were uncertain. (Tacitus *Annuls* 4:3)

In A.D. 22 Tiberius arranged for his son Drusus to be voted tribunitian powers, making him *de facto* second in command of the empire. Sejanus, sensing that he must strike soon or Tiberius would retire and cede the throne to Drusus, boldly started an affair with Lavilla, Drusus' own wife. Completely won over by Sejanus, Livilla conspired against her own husband.

So Drusus died under suspicious circumstances in A.D. 23, possibly poisoned by his own wife. Tiberius did not suspect foul play but the emperor was greatly affected by the death of his son. Subsequently, Tiberius banished all of Drusus' friends from the Royal court, for their mere presence brought back memories of his son that were painful. This was unfortunate for young Agrippa, the brother of Herodias and the future King Agrippa I, since he was one of Drusus' closest friends. It is possible that

Agrippa's other two brothers, Herod and Aristobulos, were also Drusus' friends and banned as well.

Tiberius in Capri

Sejanus, having gotten away with murdering Drusus, now focused his attention on the children of Germanicus–who would be next in line of succession. Sejanus first requested that Tiberius approve his marriage to Livilla, the former wife of Tiberius' late son Drusus and thus gaining him something of a Royal claim. Tiberius rejected that proposal, forcing Sejanus to turn to other methods to gain power.

> Sejanus ... made it his aim to induce Tiberius to live in some charming spot at a distance from Rome. In this he foresaw several advantages. Access to the emperor would be under his own control and letters, for the most part being conveyed by soldiers, would pass through his hands. Caesar too, who was already in the decline of life, would soon, when enervated by retirement, more readily transfer to him the functions of empire; envy towards himself would be lessened when there was an end to his crowded levies and the reality of power would be increased by the removal of its empty show. So he began to declaim against the laborious life of the capital, the bustling crowds and streaming multitudes, while he praised repose and solitude, with their freedom from vexations and misunderstandings and their special opportunities for the study of the highest questions. (*Annuls* 4:41)

Tiberius lived at various Royal palaces outside the Rome city walls for almost two years before deciding to live permanently on the island of Capri. Tacitus blames Tiberius' self-exile from Rome–the second in Tiberius' life–on the scheming of Sejanus. But even Tacitus admits that Tiberius stayed on Capri for six years after Sejanus' execution, theorizing that Tiberius had become ashamed of his appearance in his old age.

> (Tiberius)..had indeed a tall, singularly slender and stooping figure, a bald head, a face full of eruptions and covered here and there with plasters. (*Annuls* 4:57)

Although Tiberius' retreat worked to Sejanus' advantage, Tiberius might have had his own reasons. He perhaps was still devastated by the death of Drusus and wanted to get away from Rome and its incessant reminders of happier days with his son. Tiberius' mother Livia by all accounts was a demanding and overbearing woman–by going to Capri, he could isolate himself from her. Tiberius also consulted astrologers frequently and perhaps their consensus opinion was that the stars were aligned against him should he ever again pass through the Rome city gates. Or the reason for Tiberius' retreat could be as simple as him trying to rediscover the peace and solitude he had enjoyed when, as a younger man, he lived in isolation on the island of Rhodes.

> But he (Tiberius) so loathed the towns and colonies and, in short, every place on the mainland, that he buried himself in the island of Capreae which is separated by three miles of strait from the extreme point of the promontory of Sorrentum. The solitude of the place was, I believe, its chief attraction, for a harbourless sea surrounds it and even for a small vessel it has but few safe retreats, nor can any one land unknown to the sentries. Its air in winter is soft, as it is screened by a mountain which is a protection against cutting winds. In summer it catches the western breezes and the open sea round it renders it most delightful. It commanded too a prospect of the most lovely bay.... (*Annuls* 4:67)

Sejanus in Power

By A.D. 27, Tiberius was settled on Capri and enjoying his 12 Imperial villas scattered about the high-cliffed rocky island (*Annuls* 4:67). The emperor would move from villa to villa depending upon his mood, the time of year, and the astrological signs. Since there were no beaches on Capri it was an easily defended stronghold, and Tiberius felt secure. Also, 18 miles away to the north was Misenum which was the base for the western fleet.

On the downside, all of Tiberius' communications with Rome and far-flung legions of the empire were channeled through Sejanus' Praetorian headquarters in Rome. As a result of this communications "choke point," Sejanus was in virtual control of the empire. Sejanus could, if he so desired, alter both incoming messages to Tiberius and outgoing messages from Tiberius as he pleased. Unchecked at Rome and with the senate not questioning any of his orders, General Sejanus set about increasing his power and wealth through the usual corrupt practices of the day–all the while he fine-tuning his plans for revolution.

Sejanus knew that Tiberius would not name him as his successor. There was a good chance, however, that Sejanus would be named as regent to Tiberius' grandson Tiberius Gemellus, or his grandnephew Caius, upon the emperor's death. If that occurred, then Sejanus at his leisure as regent could easily arrange the killing of either or both of them. And if Tiberius named another to succeed him as emperor, Sejanus was fully prepared to strike against Rome with his Praetorian army.

As the years passed, Tiberius did in fact appoint Sejanus as his co-consul in A.D. 31. Usually, serving as co-consul with the emperor indicated Royal succession. Because of this, Sejanus had every reason to believe that with Tiberius' supposedly failing health, and with Caius and Tiberius Gemellus (Tiberius' grandson) too young to rule, he would be the next emperor–and soon. At the very least, Sejanus expected to be appointed regent which would be the worse for Caius and Gemellus.

The Plot Uncovered

But early in A.D. 31, Tiberius was alerted of the plans that Sejanus had in store for him. Antonia, the widow of Tiberius' long-dead brother Drusus, brought it to Tiberius' attention in a letter. Unfortunately, sections from Tacitus' *Annuls* that deal with the details of the conspiracy have been lost. Josephus, however, does devote a small section to the conspiracy, as does Dio.

> She (Antonia) had also been the greatest benefactress to Tiberius, when there was a very dangerous plot laid against him by Sejanus, a man who had been her husband's friend and wire had the greatest authority, because he was general of the army and when many members of the senate and many of the freed-men joined with him and the soldiery was

corrupted and the plot was come to a great height. Now Sejanus had certainly gained his point, had not Antonia's boldness been more wisely conducted than Sejanus's malice; for when she had discovered his designs against Tiberius, she wrote him an exact account of the whole and gave the letter to Pallas, the most faithful of her servants and sent him to Caprere to Tiberius, who, when he understood it, slew Sejanus and his confederates; so that Tiberius, who had her in great esteem before, now looked upon her with still greater respect and depended upon her in all things. (*Antiq* XVIII 6:6)

When he learned of the plot, Tiberius knew that he had left himself vulnerable. How much loyalty in Rome did Sejanus command? Being away from the capital city for nearly five years, Tiberius could only guess at his own level of support. If it came to civil war, General Sejanus controlled the Praetorians, the home guard and possibly the Imperial troops that Tiberius depended upon as his personal guard. Tiberius knew that he would command the loyalty of most the generals and their legions stationed outside Italy. But could these outlying forces be mobilized in time to save him?

Dio gives us a slightly different picture of the situation. Instead of being surprised by Antonia's letter, Tiberius had actually suspected it for a considerable amount of time. In fact, that was why Tiberius ordered Antonia and her grandson Caius to Capri to live in April of A.D. 31. For months, Tiberius maintained a special fleet of ships nearby Capri to evacuate him to a safe place should Sejanus unexpectedly strike.

But whenever and however he discovered the plot, the canny Tiberius knew well the soul of the Roman people. The spirit of Caesar held great sway over the Romans, and the confident Tiberius expected that they would never accept another ruler.

Death of Sejanus

On the beautiful island of Capri, Tiberius played cat-and-mouse fashion with the ambition of Sejanus and the fickleness of the Roman people until he thought the time was right to strike.

He (Tiberius) kept sending despatches of all kinds regarding himself both to Sejanus and to the senate, now saying that he was in a bad state of health and almost at the point of death and now that he was exceedingly well and would arrive in Rome directly. At one moment he would heartily praise Sejanus and again would as heartily denounce him; and, while honouring some of Sejanus' friends out of regard for him, he would be disgracing others. Thus Sejanus, filled in turn with extreme elation and extreme fear, was in constant suspense; for it never occurred to him, on the one hand, to be afraid and so attempt a revolution, inasmuch as he was still held in honour, nor, on the other hand, to be bold and attempt some desperate venture, inasmuch as he was frequently abased. So also with the people at large: they kept hearing alternately the most contradictory reports which came at brief intervals and so were unable either to regard Sejanus any longer with admiration or, on the other hand, to hold him in contempt, while as for Tiberius, they were kept guessing whether he was going to die or return to Rome; consequently they were in a continual state of doubt (Dio 58-6)

Tiberius then put into play a brilliant and twisted plan to get rid of Sejanus. It depended on the loyalty of another of his generals, Sertorius Macro. Tiberius sent Macro to Rome by night with two letters for the senate. In Rome, still before the light of day, Macro confided the plan to Memmius Regulus, the senate consul and Graecinius Laco, the commander of the Nightwatch brigade. The only unknown was the loyalty of the Praetorian guard that Sejanus had commanded for years.

In the morning outside the senate house, Macro encountered Sejanus, who was surprised at Macro's presence. Usually, Tiberius would inform Sejanus first of any important senate messages. But Macro calmed his fears and told him that Tiberius was to recommend Sejanus be voted tribunitian powers and that Tiberius had wanted it to be a surprise. Sejanus was pleased at the news, even excited. The honor would have made Sejanus officially the second most powerful man in the empire. The letter, however, actually was a list of Sejanus' crimes against Rome and ended with Tiberius ordering Sejanus' immediate arrest.

Sejanus entered the senate chamber with anticipation, while Macro stayed outside. Macro then confronted Sejanus' Praetorian soldiers and showed them his letter of authority from Tiberius. Macro promised them each a sum of money and ordered them all to their camp just outside the Collina gate. The Praetorians obeyed and left Sejanus to his fate.

By then, Laco had arrived with his own capable soldiers of the Nightwatch brigade. Macro positioned them around the senate building. Then entering the distinguished chamber, Macro hand delivered the letter from Tiberius to Regulus to be read. Macro did not stay for the reading–he left the senate house and hurried to the camp of the Praetorians. If any were so loyal to Sejanus to be inclined to revolt at the arrest of their former commander, Macro was prepared to deal severely with them (Dio 58:10-11).

Meanwhile, in the senate house the first letter was read. Initially, Tiberius had mixed in compliments with mild accusations in order to keep Sejanus off-guard. However, as the letter neared its end, the accusations were clear and damning. The final sentence was an Imperial order for Sejanus' arrest along with two of his key staff. The second letter was then quickly read aloud over the increasing din of the senate members. It relieved Sejanus of command of the Praetorians and appointed General Macro in his stead.

The senate knew what was good for them and followed Tiberius' orders without hesitation. The shattered Sejanus was roughly escorted out of the chamber by senate guards. Outside of the senate house Sejanus was set upon by an unusually well-informed mob of citizens.

> Thereupon one might have witnessed such a surpassing proof of human frailty as to prevent one's ever again being puffed up with conceit. For the man whom at dawn... they were wont to adore and worship with sacrifices as a god, they were now leading to execution. (Dio 58-11)

Sejanus was quickly killed by the mob and for three days his torn body lay in the public forum before being thrown in the Tiber River.

Rome after Sejanus' Execution

The execution of Sejanus occurred on October 17, A.D. 31. That date began the transformation of Rome from a bright, open and enlightened city into a place of darkness, fear, and suspicion. Proscription lists were set in place; Rome became a city where no one could be trusted and former friends became enemies. Death sentences for alleged conspirators were passed against honorable men from honorable families on the flimsiest of evidence–or on no evidence at all. This was a shocking change in a city that had known tranquility for more than half a century – ever since the end of the Second Civil War in 31 B.C.

> And this was the most dreadful feature of the age, that leading members of the Senate, some openly, some secretly employed themselves in the very lowest work of the informer. One could not distinguish between aliens and kinsfolk, between friends and strangers, or say what was quite recent, or what half-forgotten from lapse of time. People were incriminated for some casual remark in the forum or at the dinner-table, for every one was impatient to be the first to mark his victim, some to screen themselves, most from being, as it were, infected with the contagion of the malady...Many authors, I am well aware, have passed over the perils and punishments of a host of persons, sickened by the multiplicity of them, or fearing that what they had themselves found wearisome and saddening would be equally fatiguing to their readers. For myself, I have lighted on many facts worth knowing, though other writers have not recorded them. (*Annuls* 6:7)

Charges of conspiracy could be brought against anyone and by anyone – with most of these charges little questioned. More often than not, innocent people would be convicted and quickly executed. Their assets would be seized and split amongst Tiberius and their accusers. Sejanus had been so powerful for so long that most men of substance had dealt with him in one way or another. Now even harmless relationships were labeled seditious.

> Executions were now a stimulus to his fury and he (Tiberius) ordered the death of all who were lying in prison under accusation of complicity with Sejanus. There lay, singly or in heaps, the unnumbered dead, of every age and sex, the illustrious with the obscure. Kinsfolk and friends were not allowed to be near them, to weep over them, or even to gaze on them too long. Spies were set round them, who noted the sorrow of each mourner and followed the rotting corpses, till they were dragged to the Tiber, where, floating or driven on the bank, no one dared to burn or to

touch them. The force of terror had utterly extinguished the sense of human fellowship and, with the growth of cruelty, pity was thrust aside. (*Annuls* 6:19)

Even in A.D. 34, three years later, the political prosecutions had not run their course. As Tacitus writes:

"Rome (was).. a scene of ceaseless bloodshed." (*Annuls* 6:29)

The dark and vengeful nature of Tiberius is reflected in Josephus' assessment of him upon Tiberius' death.

...Tiberius had brought a vast number of miseries on the best families of the Romans, since he was easily inflamed with passion in all cases and was of such a temper as rendered his anger irrevocable, till he had executed the same, although he had taken a hatred against men without reason; for he was by nature fierce in all the sentences he gave and made death the penalty for the lightest offenses... (Antiq XVIII 6:10)

Tiberius and the Jews

There is scant evidence for any overt antisemitic leanings in Tiberius. Josephus says it succinctly:

Nor was he (Tiberias) in one way of acting with respect to the Jews and in another with respect to the rest of his subjects. (*Antiq* XVIII 6:5)

This is not surprising, as the sons of Herod the Great were welcomed into the Royal household of Augustus. But there were some incidents during Tiberius' reign that bear mentioning. Years before the Sejanus affair, in A.D. 19, the senate passed a measure that forced military conscription upon the Egyptian and Jewish communities in Italia.

There was a debate too about expelling the Egyptian and Jewish worship and a resolution of the Senate was passed that four thousand of the freedmen class who were infected with those superstitions and were of military age should be transported to the island of Sardinia, to quell the brigandage of the place, a cheap sacrifice should they die from the pestilential climate. The rest were to quit Italy, unless before a certain day they repudiated their impious rites. (*Annuls* 2:85)

(Tiberius)..abolished foreign cults, especially the Egyptian and the Jewish rites, compelling all who were addicted to such superstitions to burn their religious vestments and all their paraphernalia. Those of the Jews who were of military age he assigned to provinces of less healthy climate, ostensibly to serve in the army; the others of that same race or of similar beliefs he banished from the city, on pain of slavery for life if they did not obey. He banished the astrologers as well, but pardoned such as begged for indulgence and promised to give up their art. (Sue *Tiberius* 36)

Josephus relates a version of the same story. There, the senate act was precipitated by a single incident. A Roman woman, after being converted to Judaism by Jewish scoundrels, was defrauded out of a portion of her wealth.

There was a man who was a Jew, but had been driven away from his own country by an accusation laid against him for transgressing their laws and by the fear he was under of punishment for the same; but in all respects a wicked man. He, then living at Rome, professed to instruct men in the wisdom of the laws of Moses. He procured also three other men, entirely of the same character with himself, to be his partners. These men persuaded Fulvia, a woman of great dignity and one that had embraced the Jewish religion, to send purple and gold to the temple at Jerusalem; and when they had gotten them, they employed them for their own uses and spent the money themselves, on which account it was that they at first required it of her. Whereupon Tiberius, who had been informed of the thing by Saturninus, the husband of Fulvia, who desired inquiry might be made about it, ordered all the Jews to be banished out of Rome; at which time the consuls listed four thousand men out of them and sent them to the island Sardinia; but punished a greater number of them, who were unwilling to become soldiers, on account of keeping the laws of their forefathers. Thus were these Jews banished out of the city by the wickedness of four men. (*Antiq* XVIII 3:5)

The total Jewish community in Rome probably numbered no more than 20,000 at the time. Certainly, the banishment of 4,000 Jews out of that number was substantial, but from Tacitus it is learned that the number included a significant portion of Egyptians as well. The fact that the Roman Senate acted so harshly over what appears to be an isolated act of fraud shows a definite bias against the Jews, if indeed that was the sole reason.

These two parallel stories in Josephus and Tacitus are interesting for another reason. Going by relative placement alone in Book XVIII of *Antiquities*, the banishment of the 4,000 Jews took place after the execution of Sejanus in late A.D. 31 and after the crucifixion of Jesus. But from Tacitus, the year is unequivocally A.D. 19 according to Roman consul-years. This would be more than 10 years earlier than Josephus suggests. In this matter, Tacitus, who presumably had access to the actual senatorial records of Rome, will be deferred to. This is also evidence that events documented by Josephus in Book XVIII of *Antiquities* are not necessarily placed in the correct chronological order. The earlier year also suggests that the impetus for the banishment came from Sejanus and not Tiberius.

At any rate, apart from this instance of involuntary conscription, Tiberius by most measures was tolerant of the Jews and other religions. Philo Judaeus so noted in his *Embassy to Caius*, wherein he petitioned the new Emperor Caius–later called Caligula–to remove a statue Caius had ordered placed the Jewish Temple in Alexandria:

> Tiberius is not desirous that any of our laws or customs shall be destroyed. And if you yourself say that he is, show us either some command from him, or some letter, or something of the kind, that we, who have been sent to you as ambassadors, may cease to trouble you and may address our supplications to your master. (Philo *Embassy* 301)

Interestingly, Philo, the Jewish historian who lived at same time as Tiberius, made no mention of Tiberius' conscription measure of 19 B.C. Either Tiberius wasn't as supportive of it, as Josephus suggests, or it was really Sejanus who was behind it. Possibly, Philo just thought it best not to bring the subject up to Caius.

Proclamation of A.D. 32

In A.D. 32, after the conspiracy of Sejanus had been unmasked, Tiberius issued a proclamation to the effect that the religious practices of the Jews and other religions of a peaceful nature were to be respected. Apparently he had been made aware of the abuses of Sejanus toward the Jews and, possibly, specifically those abuses of the Judean Prefect Pontius Pilate.

> Therefore, all people in every country, even if they were not naturally well inclined towards the Jewish nation, took great care not to violate or attack any of the Jewish customs of laws. And in the reign of Tiberius things went on in the same manner, although at that time things in Italy were thrown into a great deal of confusion when Sejanus was preparing to make his attempt against our nation; for he knew immediately after his death that the accusations which had been brought against the Jews who were dwelling in Rome were false calumnies, inventions of Sejanus, who was desirous to destroy our nation which he knew alone, or above all others, was likely to oppose his unholy counsels and actions in defence of the emperor, who was in great danger of being attacked, in violation of all treaties and of all honesty. And he sent commands to all the governors of provinces in every country to comfort those of our nation in their respective cities, as the punishment intended to be inflicted was not meant to be inflicted upon all, but only on the guilty; and they were but few. And he ordered them to change none of the existing customs, but to look upon them as pledges, since the men were peaceful in their dispositions and natural characters and their laws trained them and disposed them to quiet and stability. (Philo *Embassy* 159-161)

On its face, this proclamation was good news for the Jews of Rome. But did this edict really make Rome a less dangerous place for those of the Herod family? Remember, few Jews thought of the Herod family as legitimate Jewish aristocracy; they were thought of far more as Romans collaborators than as real Jews.

It is also possible that Tiberius issued his edict of A.D. 32 after Herodias, Agrippa and Aristobulos had already left Rome. Did Tiberius know of their departure and issued the proclamation partially to look out for their safety? The emperor knew very well all of the children of Bernice and was friends with their father.

The Herod Family after Sejanus' Execution

Now for the important question: How did Herodias fare in this uncertain period after the conspiracy of Sejanus was discovered? Was this the event that drove her away from Rome as well as her brothers Aristobulos and Agrippa? Did Antonia, who alerted Tiberius to the conspiracy, also alert Herodias and the rest of her family of the sedition–and possible revolution–that was brewing? If so, Herodias could have left before the execution of Sejanus.

Certainly, well before the Sejanus affair, however, the situation in Rome was not what it once was for Herodias. Emperor Tiberius, a friend and supporter, had abandoned Rome for Capri in A.D. 27. Herodias' mother, Bernice, had died earlier in A.D. 25. For decades, Tiberius' mother Livia favored the surviving family members of the executed Prince Aristobulos. But in A.D. 29, Livia had died. Earlier in A.D. 31, Antonia had been ordered away from Rome by Tiberias. Also a confounding factor was her brother Herod Agrippa. He owed substantial amounts of money to creditors in Rome.

Each of these considerations alone could conceivably have caused Herodias to leave, but remember that Herodias was apparently rich and secure. Her personal safety and that of her immediate family was never in jeopardy. That changed after the proscriptions.

Herodias at the time was married to Herod Philip. How did the Sejanus affair effect Herod Philip? Was it possible that Philip had dealings with Sejanus–dealings that alarmed Herodias to the point where she felt the need to leave Rome?

Herodias had a daughter to look after as well and the young girl was just entering a marriageable age. With Roman society effectively shattered and most foreigners fleeing, what future was there in Rome for the great-granddaughter of Herod the Great?

Tacitus also reports, that in A.D. 32, people burdened by excessive interest charges on their loans took advantage of the mayhem to stage their own "mini" revolt. Herod Philip, Herodias' husband, was the Herod family patriarch in Rome.

How much of the Herod family fortune had he managed to acquire? Herod Philip of Rome could have been an integral part of the moneyed class that lent out sums at high levels of interest and was subsequently ruined.

> Meanwhile a powerful host of accusers fell with sudden fury on the class which systematically increased its wealth by usury in defiance of a law passed by Caesar the Dictator defining the terms of lending money and of holding estates in Italy, a law long obsolete because the public good is sacrificed to private interest...Hence followed a scarcity of money, a great shock being given to all credit, the current coin too, in consequence of the conviction of so many persons and the sale of their property, being locked up in the imperial treasury or the public exchequer. (*Annuls* 6:16-17)

Thus, beginning with the rapid unraveling of Sejanus' own mini-empire in late A.D. 31 and continuing for years afterward, the city of Rome took on a dark and unfriendly cast. Even if Herodias and Herod Philip weren't caught up personally in the intrigue of Sejanus or ruined in the credit crunch that followed, Rome was still an unpredictable and dangerous place to be.

Conclusion

If it is assumed that Herodias left Rome in haste after the conspiracy of Sejanus was unmasked. For our purposes, this means that Herod Antipas had to have married Herodias after October A.D. 31.

How long did Herodias suffer in Rome after Sejanus' execution? A factor might have been the weather. October was late in the year and a trip to the East might have been very risky with winter approaching. But in the following spring of A.D. 32, it would have been a different story.

It is also reasonable to speculate that Herod Antipas made a trip to Capri early in A.D. 32 to meet with Tiberius in order to reaffirm his support. Such a journey by Antipas is not documented, but it is not crucial to the hypothesis in any case. It is also possible that Antipas and Herodias may have had a smoldering love relationship for years, whether consummated or not. Antipas, in fact, might have given Herodias an open invitation to come to East to be his wife should she so desire. The conspiracy of Sejanus might have caused her to act.

Previously, the years of Jesus' crucifixion were narrowed down to the years from A.D. 30-36. An immutable fact from the Gospels is that Jesus of Nazareth was crucified after the death of John the Baptist, who was imprisoned by Antipas after John criticized his marriage to Herodias. It will now be assumed that the marriage took place in the early spring of A.D. 32, shortly after Herodias arrived in Galilee. Accepting this, the possible Passovers of the crucifixion have been narrowed to A.D. 32-36, a span of five years.

Admittedly, however, some generous assumptions concerning Herodias and her reasons for leaving Rome have been made. What other supporting evidence can be found in the ancient records? For that, we will now turn to the story of Herod Agrippa, Herodias' brother.

Chapter 19   Agrippa the Great

Agrippa was by nature magnanimous and generous...(Antiq XVIII 6:1)

The odyssey of Agrippa as he wandered with his young family through the eastern Roman Empire in the early first century A.D. is a compelling tale. As the grandson of Herod the Great, Agrippa was born into wealth and power, but then fell into the depths of relative poverty—even being imprisoned by Tiberius for a short time. Never losing faith in his destiny, however, Agrippa triumphed over all adversity and was eventually crowned a king.

Josephus tells Agrippa's story in detail for the moral lessons to be learned. Significantly for us, Agrippa's life intertwines with Herodias' at several points. Time clues in the story of Agrippa will help validate the hypothesis that Herodias wed Herod Antipas in the spring of A.D. 32.

In A.D. 37, Agrippa was crowned king over a portion of the Jewish East by Emperor Caius. After four years, he gained control over the rest of it–appointed by Emperor Claudius. King Agrippa was popular in the Imperial court. Even while ruling the East, Agrippa spent much of his time in Rome playing key roles in Roman policy decisions and looking out for the interests of the scattered Jewish populations within the empire.

Of note is that Flavius Josephus almost certainly saw Agrippa I in person and possibly met him as well. The Jewish King died in A.D. 44 when Josephus was seven years of age. Josephus later became great friends with his son, Agrippa II.

Early Years with Augustus

Herod Agrippa was born in A.D. 9 and was a year older than his sister Herodias. Agrippa was named after General Marcus Agrippa, who was the guiding force and strategist behind Emperor Augustus. Agrippa was reared along with his siblings by his mother, Bernice, first in Jerusalem — possibly Jericho — and later, after the death of Herod the Great, in Rome under Royal Augustan tutelage. Agrippa might have had some dim memory of his father, Prince Aristobulos, who was executed by his grandfather Herod the Great in 7 B.C. when Agrippa was about two years of age. Before his own death, Herod the Great doted on the children of Prince Aristobulos, perhaps out of guilt.

Moving from the East to Rome, both Agrippa and Herodias lived privileged lives in the opulent Royal court during the golden age of the Roman Empire. Emperor Augustus, his wife Livia, and others of the Roman aristocracy, were probably extraordinarily kind to this family. The executed Royal sons of Herod, Alexander and Aristobulos, had spent five years in Rome growing up and living with Livia and Augustus in their palaces and villas. Emperor Augustus and the Royal family knew Herod's sons better than they knew Herod himself. Livia Augusta, the mother of Tiberius, was especially aghast at the murderous actions of Herod the Great. It may well have been Livia who most strongly encouraged Bernice to live in Rome even before Herod the Great's death.

Tiberius and Banishment

Over time, the rule of the empire passed seamlessly from Augustus to Tiberius, and the children of Bernice grew into adulthood still enjoying Royal favor. These were good years for Bernice and her family. Agrippa was known as an affable and generous man. Politically astute, he early-on made himself a boon companion to Tiberius' son Drusus, even though he was four years younger than Drusus. Agrippa's older brothers Herod and Aristobulos–closer in age to Drusus–were likely companions to him as well. Agrippa was also especially close to the Royal matron Antonia, who was to play a crucial role in his life years later. Antonia was the widow of   Drusus the Great, the full brother of Tiberius.

In A.D. 23 Agrippa's life took a turn for the worse. At that time, General Lucius Sejanus poisoned Tiberius' son, Drusus, aided by Drusus' own wife, Livilla. Tiberius suspected no foul play, but the emperor was so overcome by Drusus' death that Agrippa and Drusus' other friends were banned from the Royal court. Tiberius did not want to be reminded of his departed son.

This was a shocking development for Agrippa. Not only was his friend Drusus gone, but he had lost his Royal privileges and Royal access.

> A little before the death of Herod the king, Agrippa lived at Rome, and was generally brought up and conversed with Drusus, the emperor Tiberius's son, and contracted a friendship with Antonia, the wife of Drusus the Great, who had his mother Bernice in great esteem, and was very desirous of advancing her son. Now as Agrippa was by nature magnanimous and generous in the presents he made, while his mother was alive, this inclination of his mind did not appear, that he might be able to avoid her anger for such his extravagance; but when Bernice was dead, and he was left to his own conduct, he spent a great deal extravagantly in his daily way of living, and a great deal in the immoderate presents he made, and those chiefly among Caesar's freed-men, in order to gain their assistance, insomuch that he was, in a little time, reduced to poverty, and could not live at Rome any longer. Tiberius also forbade the friends of his deceased son to come into his sight, because on seeing them he should be put in mind of his son, and his grief would thereby be revived. (*Antiq* XVIII 6:1)

Things went from bad to worse for Agrippa when his mother Bernice died in A.D. 25. Without her restraint, Agrippa became free with his money. When that was gone, he took to borrowing large sums. He soon owed money to a great many people. How much Herodias and her husband Herod Philip–and others in the Herod clan–lent Agrippa was not known, but it was probably substantial.

Another negative for Agrippa was that by A.D. 27 Tiberius had left Rome completely. Though the banished Agrippa was not part of the Royal court, many of his friends likely were. They would have naturally followed Tiberius to the island of Capri–or at least to Campania that lay across the straits of Sorrentum. For these years of Tiberius' self-exile, cities in this region probably teemed with Royal petitioners or hangers-on who did not have enough stature or money to live on Capri itself.

Worse, Tiberius' mother Livia died in Rome two years later in A.D. 29. A great friend of Agrippa's late mother, Bernice, she might have also financially supported and protected Agrippa from his creditors when few other people did.

Then, in late A.D. 31, the conspiracy of General Sejanus was exposed and the city of Rome was turned upside down. The blood of aristocrats flowed as Tiberius meted out revenge upon those suspected of complicity. Though Agrippa was not directly involved in the conspiracy, times were bad for most everyone in the ruling class. Proscriptions lists were savagely enforced and virtually anyone could make an accusation. Many were able to bring enemies or creditors to trial and death with little hard evidence. Most of the Roman elite prudently left the city for their country estates in order to wait out the storm. The political uncertainty might have been a major factor in finally forcing Agrippa to leave Rome as well — as it might have been for his sister Herodias and brother Aristobulos.

Aristobulos

At this point, Aristobulos, the older brother of Herodias and Agrippa, should be brought into the story. Josephus does not relate many details about him. Aristobulos is referred to only tangentially in the storyline of Agrippa, Herodias, and Herod Antipas, since he never gained Royal stature himself. But it is important to note that Aristobulos was in the East at the same time as his two younger siblings. Was this coincidence, or did Herodias and Agrippa follow the lead of their older brother?

When Pomponius Flaccus became the president (governor) of Syria in A.D. 32, Aristobulos was one his principal magistrates. Did Flaccus, having little experience in the East, bring

Aristobulos with him from Rome to be his adviser on Jewish affairs? Antioch vied with Alexandria in Egypt as being the second-largest city in the Roman Empire. Being relatively close to the Jewish lands, Antioch likely had a large Jewish population. It is also possible that Aristobulos already in Antioch serving in the prior administration of Syrian President Aelius Lamia.

The president of Syria had authority over both of the Herod tetrarchies and also over the prefecture of Judea and Samaria. If Aristobulos was one of Flaccus' high-ranking officials–which by all indications he was–Aristobulos would be in an extremely powerful position. In fact, that in itself might have been a large factor in Herodias making the drastic decision to divorce Herod Philip and leave Rome. In Galilee, Herodias knew that, no matter what happened between her and Herod Antipas, she would have the protection of an older brother who lived not far away. It might also have influenced Agrippa's decision to leave Rome with his own young family. Even though Agrippa was not on good terms with any of his siblings, Agrippa knew that they were all Herods and would never abandon him if he were in a truly difficult situation.

Another influence on Agrippa's move to the East might have been urging of his wife, Cypros. She was a cousin to Herodias, and the two women were likely very close–as cousins frequently are. Cypros might have thought that Herodias, perhaps then already the queen of Galilee, would give her family an measure of security when and if they left Rome.

How many other members of the Herod clan left Rome during this time? Josephus focuses on the children of Bernice for most of them attained Royal status, but there might have been many others. So while Josephus suggests Agrippa left purely for monetary reasons, his decision was probably based on several other factors.

At any rate, at some point in time, Agrippa–then in his late thirties–gathered together his family and whatever entourage he could afford and left Rome for Jerusalem. By the time of the move East, Agrippa and Cypros had at least two small children to care for, and possibly three.

Jerusalem

Cypros was the granddaughter of Herod the Great and Mariamne I, and also the granddaughter of Phasaelus, Herod the Great's brother. Cypros by all accounts was a loyal and patient woman, putting up bravely with her husband's various predicaments and financial woes as she tried to keep the family together.

At the time of their move East, Cypros had two children by Agrippa–a son, also named Agrippa, born in A.D. 27, and a daughter, Bernice, born in A.D. 28. If Agrippa and his family traveled to the East in A.D. 32, the younger Agrippa would have been five years old, and Bernice four years of age–both barely of traveling age.

Agrippa and Cypros had a second son named Drusus. All that is known is that he died when he was a child. That Josephus doesn't go into details suggests that Drusus was the first-born son and died in Rome.

Agrippa and his entourage arrived first in Judea with the intent to live there permanently. How large his contingent was is open to speculation, but probably at least 10 staff and guards traveled with the family. Josephus gives us few details, but writes that there Agrippa found no sanctuary from his creditors. Faced with the same problems he had in Rome, Agrippa and his young family left Judea–perhaps not even getting to Jerusalem–and traveled south into the harsh desert country of Idumea. Whether or not Pontius Pilate hounded Agrippa for his Royal debts is unknown, but all Roman prefects had absolute authority to collect all personal debts–Royal or otherwise. If, indeed, Agrippa found protection in Idumea from his creditors, that would argue against Pilate's involvement, since Idumea was under Pilate's control as well.

Idumea

The family roots of Agrippa and Cypros ran deep in Idumea as it was the birthplace of Herod the Great. Today it is part of the

Negev desert. Herod the Great had ruled over Idumea by Roman proxy when he was alive, but Agrippa's great-great-grandfather had been a true independent Arab king there. The Jewish King Hyrcanus I would not invade Idumea for another generation (125 B.C.).

In the times of Jesus, Idumea supported a much larger population than the Negev does today. Rainfall certainly was more plentiful then, and freshwater springs might have existed in various places that have since dried up. In Idumea, Agrippa found himself an honored guest and protected from creditors. The ancient Herod family palace–Malatha–was made available for him and his family.

But compared to Jerusalem, and certainly compared to Rome, Idumea was a very rugged and rural place. Agrippa initially didn't care so long as he wasn't bothered by creditors. Soon, however, as the hopelessness of his situation became starkly apparent, Agrippa slipped into a suicidal depression.

> For these reasons he (Agrippa) went away from Rome, and sailed to Judea, but in evil circumstances, being dejected with the loss of that money which he once had, and because he had not wherewithal to pay his creditors, who were many in number, and such as gave him no room for escaping them. Whereupon he knew not what to do; so, for shame of his present condition, he retired to a certain tower, at Malatha, in Idumea, and had thoughts of killing himself; but his wife Cypros perceived his intentions, and tried all sorts of methods to divert him from his taking such a course; so she sent a letter to his sister Herodias, who was now the wife of Herod the tetrarch, and let her know Agrippa's present design, and what necessity it was which drove him thereto, and desired her, as a kinswoman of his, to give him her help, and to engage her husband to do the same, since she saw how she alleviated these her husband's troubles all she could, although she had not the like wealth to do it withal. (*Antiq* XVIII 6:2)

How long would it have taken for the proud Agrippa to become profoundly depressed over his situation in Idumea? Probably not long at all. So it can be reasonably speculated that within six months of arriving in Judea, Cypros found herself in Idumea writing a letter to her cousin Herodias appealing for help.

Sanctuary with Herodias

The marriage of Herodias and Antipas probably occurred in the spring of A.D. 32. Josephus himself does not mention the actual wedding ceremony and feast. With all the controversy surrounding Herodias' divorce and the frantic flight of Antipas' ex-wife Pharaelis–to say nothing of the fury of Antipas' now-former father-in-law King Aretas IV of Nabotea–the wedding celebration was probably small and private. Perhaps not even Agrippa and his wife Cypros would have been invited even if they were in the East at that time, and even if Agrippa had been on good terms with Antipas–which apparently he was not.

Though Agrippa was in dire straits and suicidally depressed he refused to turn for help to his uncle Herod Antipas, or to his uncle Herod Philip, or to his brother Aristobulos in Syria. Why not? Did he owe money to them and perhaps a substantial amount of it?

After a time Agrippa's wife Cypros in a letter appealed directly to Herodias for help. Fortunately for Cypros, Herodias had great sympathy and affection for her cousin and her children. Herodias then pleaded with her husband Herod Antipas to take in Agrippa and his family. Antipas agreed, perhaps reluctantly and against his better judgment. He welcomed Agrippa to Tiberias and gave him a position within his administration.

> So they (Herodias and Antipas) sent for him (Agrippa), and allotted him Tiberias for his habitation, and appointed him some income of money for his maintenance, and made him a magistrate of that city, by way of honor to him. Yet did not Herod long continue in that resolution of supporting him, though even that support was not sufficient for him; for as once they were at a feast at Tyre, and in their cups, and reproaches were cast upon one another, Agrippa thought that was not to be borne, while Herod hit him in the teeth with his poverty, and with his owing his necessary food to him. So he went to Flaccus, one that had been consul, and had been a very great friend to him at Rome formerly, and was now president of Syria. (*Antiq* XVIII 6:2)

After a period of time living in Tiberias with Herod Antipas and Herodias–Josephus writes it was "not long"–the natural arrogance of Agrippa combined with the influence of wine ("in their cups") led Agrippa into a confrontation with Antipas.

Josephus suggests that Agrippa left Galilee voluntarily because Antipas had hurt his pride. However, it is more probable that Agrippa was forced out and Josephus shaded the truth in order not to offend King Agrippa II. How long did Agrippa stay in Tiberias as a magistrate? Probably less than a year.

It is important to note that in the section in Josephus' *Antiquities* concerning Agrippa's stay with Herodias and Antipas, there is no mention of Herod Antipas' Galilean armies battling those of King Aretas of Nabotea, or even a hint of preparations for war. Those actions, apparently, were off in the future.

Luckily for Agrippa, after making himself unwelcome in Galilee, he had one last friend to appeal to. Pomponius Flaccus had been recently appointed the president of Syria in by Tiberius and was now most powerful man in the East. Formerly, Flaccus had been a drinking companion of Tiberius' and might have downed a drought or two with Agrippa as well (Sue *Tiberius* XLII). Agrippa contacted Flaccus and was given a position as a magistrate in Antioch, and so Agrippa left Galilee and sailed north into Syria with his family.

Agrippa knew, of course, that his brother Aristobulos held a high position with Flaccus. The two brothers were at odds with one another; Aristobulos was perhaps one of Agrippa's creditors. But Agrippa had few other options. Aristobulos, possibly for the sake of the steadfast Cypros and her children, smiled through gritted teeth and welcomed Agrippa into the ranks of the power elite in Antioch.

A Meeting in Rome

The date of Flaccus' appointment as president of Syria is important, for only after that date could Agrippa have left Galilee.

At the end of the year the death of Aelius Lamia, who, after being at last released from the farce of governing Syria, had become city-prefect, was celebrated with the honours of a censor's funeral. He was a man of illustrious descent, and in a hale old age; and the fact of the province having been withheld gained him additional esteem. Subsequently, on the death of Flaccus Pomponius, propraetor of Syria, a letter from the emperor was read, in which he complained that all the best men who were fit to command armies declined the service, and that he was thus necessarily driven to intreaties, by which some of the ex-consuls might be prevailed on to take provinces. (*Annuls* 6:27)

Aelius Lamia had been the governor of Syria previous to Flaccus' appointment. He had gained the position in A.D. 22. Tacitus labels Lamia's tenure a "farce" because Lamia never moved to Antioch to take control of the country. Possibly, Tiberius' purpose in the appointment was to allow Lamia to collect revenue from Syria in order to fund his retirement. Times were peaceful then and Tiberius knew that subordinates in Syria could easily administer the province. Lamia died in A.D. 33, but not before also serving as Rome city prefect for a short while. Lamia attained the position as city prefect just after the death of Lucius Piso–which occurred in A.D. 32. Piso apparently served in that position with great distinction.

About the same time Lucius Piso, the pontiff, died a natural death, a rare incident in so high a rank. Never had he by choice proposed a servile motion...But his chief glory rested on the wonderful tact with which as city-prefect he handled an authority, recently made perpetual and all the more galling to men unaccustomed to obey it. (*Annuls* 6:10)

According to Suetonius, however, Lucius Piso was appointed as city prefect the same time that Pomponius Flaccus was assumed his post as president of Syria.

Later, when emperor and at the very time that he was busy correcting the public morals, he spent a night and two whole days feasting and drinking with Pomponius Flaccus and Lucius Piso, immediately afterward making the one governor of the province of Syria and the other prefect of the city, and even declaring in their commissions that they were the most agreeable of friends, who could always be counted on. (Sue *Tiberius* XLII)

Suetonius is at odds with Dio on this point.

> When Piso, a city prefect, died, he (Tiberius) honoured him with a public funeral, a distinction that he also granted to others. In his stead he chose Lucius Lamia, whom he had long since assigned to Syria, but was detaining in Rome. (Dio 58 19:5)

It is here that Suetonius might be mistaken, thus resolving the conundrum. Suetonius writes that Flaccus and Piso were drinking with Tiberius, and afterward Flaccus was made the president of Syria, and Piso the prefect of Rome. But Dio states that Lamia had replaced Piso as prefect of Rome after Piso had died. Presuming that Flaccus replaced Lamia as president of Syria and there were no significant time gaps, this is not likely.

It is reasonable to assume that it was Lamia, not Piso, who was the third person in the room drinking with Tiberius and Flaccus when fates of Syria and Rome were being decided. In that scenario, Piso would have recently died in office as the prefect of Rome. At that time Rome needed a replacement prefect, and it would have been a perfect position for the aging Lamia with which to end his public service career. Syria, too, would benefit by gaining a vigorous and efficient new president.

This hypothesis is tangentially supported by Tacitus, who suggests that Lucius Piso had served as the prefect of Rome for a substantial number of years. Tacitus also writes that Piso did his job as prefect so well that Tiberius had given him a perpetual appointment to the position.

Remember, too, that the late A.D. 20s to the early A.D. 30s, Sejanus was at his most powerful. He likely had purposefully encouraged Tiberius to keep Lamia from physically taking his post in Syria. With eyes on the throne, the last thing Sejanus wanted was a powerful partisan of Tiberius in the East controlling four Roman Legions. Pontius Pilate was definitely a Sejanus appointee, and, without the president of Syria physically in Antioch, Pilate would have been the senior military official in the East. Should a third Roman Civil War have commenced after Sejanus seized power, Pilate would have been expected to hold the Tetrarchs Herod Antipas and Herod Philip–both strong partisans of Tiberius–in check.

In fact, under this scenario it can be further speculated that possibly the death of Lucius Piso was, in fact, a forced suicide. Tiberius might have had evidence that Piso was part of the Sejanus conspiracy. Since Piso served as the prefect of Rome, that was quite likely the case. As Piso came from an honored family, Tiberius allowed him a measure of dignity in his death.

So the meeting of Tiberius, Lamia, and Flaccus was far more than a drinking bout. In the wake of the proscriptions and the possible secret execution of Lucius Piso, power was being shuffled about. Flaccus was being given Syria, and Lamia, who never really did govern Syria, was given authority over Rome. At that time, General Sertorius Macro controlled the Praetorian guard and would work with Lamia to keep Rome peaceful through to the end of the proscriptions.

In conclusion, this passage strongly suggests that Pomponius Flaccus was president of Syria beginning in early A.D. 32. Therefore, it was only after that time when Agrippa could have appealed to Flaccus for help.

Agrippa and the Tetrarch Herod Philip

Curiously, in all of Josephus' narratives on the adventures of Agrippa, the Tetrarch Herod Philip is not mentioned. Where was the brother of Herod Antipas–the ruler of Antipas' neighboring kingdom of the Trachonitis, the Batanea, and the Gaulonitis–during all this drama? Surely, Herod Agrippa would have appealed to his other uncle for support before he traveled the goodly distance north with his family to live in Syria. In fact, Philip's kingdom adjoined Antipas' and was an easy sail away across Lake Gennesareth from Tiberias. Herod Philip was Cypros' uncle as well, and Cypros apparently was on good terms with everyone in her family. It was documented that bad blood existed between Herod Agrippa and his oldest brother Aristobulos, so a retreat into Syria had to be a bitter pill for the battered Agrippa to swallow–to be taken only if all else failed.

Why did Herod Agrippa bypass his other uncle, Herod Philip, in favor of Pomponius Flaccus when Herod Antipas made it clear he was to leave as soon as possible? By all accounts, Herod Philip was a shy, retiring man. Even if Agrippa owed him a large sum of money, turning away a desperate Agrippa with a young family would not seem in character for Philip.

The probable answer is as simple as it is straightforward. At the time Agrippa was exploring options outside of Tiberias, the Tetrarch Herod Philip had already died. In fact, it is possible that the verbal fight that Agrippa and Antipas had was caused by the recent death of the tetrarch. After Philip's death, Emperor Tiberius, instead of giving the tetrarchy over to Herod Antipas, had placed Philip's kingdom under Flaccus' temporary stewardship. Did Agrippa make a disparaging remark to Antipas speculating on Tiberius' real opinion of him?!

This also suggests another motivation for Agrippa to find a haven within Flaccus' administration. Agrippa might have had a faint hope of somehow gaining the tetrarchy that Philip had so recently left behind–an opportunity to rule! Toward that end, Agrippa decided that it would be to his advantage to establish a credible administrative record within the government of Syria, thus impressing both Emperor Tiberius and President Flaccus in the process. As Herod Philip died in early A.D. 34., under this scenario Herod Agrippa likely made his move to Syria in early A.D. 34 or later.

Banished from Syria

It wasn't long before Agrippa ran into troubles in Syria.

> Hereupon Flaccus received him kindly, and he lived with him. Flaccus had also with him there Aristobulus, who was indeed Agrippa's brother, but was at variance with him; yet did not their enmity to one another hinder the friendship of Flaccus to them both, but still they were honorably treated by him. However, Aristobulus did not abate of his ill-will to Agrippa, till at length he brought him into ill terms with Flaccus; the occasion of bringing on which estrangement was this: The Damascens were at difference with the Sidonians about their limits, and when Flaccus was about to hear the cause between them, they

understood that Agrippa had a mighty influence upon him; so they desired that he would be of their side, and for that favor promised him a great deal of money; so he was zealous in assisting the Damascens as far as he was able. Now Aristobulus had gotten intelligence of this promise of money to him, and accused him to Flaccus of the same; and when, upon a thorough examination of the matter, it appeared plainly so to be, he rejected Agrippa out of the number of his friends. So he was reduced to the utmost necessity..(*Antiq* XVIII 6-3)

Agrippa was caught taking bribes in an important provincial land dispute. Worse, Agrippa was accused by his own brother Aristobulos. In this passage, Josephus tends to cast a shadow upon Aristobulos more so than Agrippa, but this could be another example of Josephus' pro-Agrippa bias at work. At any rate, an investigation by Flaccus into the affair soon followed. Flaccus found him guilty and the ill-starred Agrippa found himself ostracized in Antioch.

In shame, Agrippa and his family traveled to the port city of Ptolemais (Accra), where they scrambled to get enough money together to sail back to Italy. Even Idumea might not be a safe haven for Agrippa now! Neither Flaccus, the president of Syria, nor the Tetrarch Herod Antipas, nor even Judean Prefect Pontius Pilate, could be counted on for protection. The doors of the East were rapidly closing on Agrippa and his ambition.

Anthedon and Arrest

Agrippa, freshly supplied with money, then traveled with his wife and family north to Anthedon–a large seaport city near Syria. There, Agrippa secured a ship with the intent of taking his family and their servants back to Italy. But by now, the word was out that Agrippa was in Anthedon and was fair game for debt collectors. Agrippa had lost the support of his powerful sister Queen Herodias in Galilee, his brother Aristobulos, and President Flaccus in Syria. Also, being far away from Idumea, there were no "rough cousins" to come Agrippa's rescue to prevent his arrest.

The Roman prefect of the region, Herennius Capito, saw opportunity and prevented Agrippa from leaving Anthedon. Capito demanded that Agrippa repay the 300,000 in silver drachmas that Agrippa owed to the treasury of Caesar. For surety, Capito impounded Agrippa's vessel in the harbor and kept him and his family captives upon it.

This action was well within Capito's authority. Prefects throughout the provinces were expected to collect any Royal debt if possible. At the very least, Capito could throw Agrippa into debtor's prison which was something that President Flaccus, and Herod Antipas, perhaps, would not have minded at all. Capito, in fact, might have been alerted to Agrippa's situation and presence by one or both of them.

Escape to Egypt

Agrippa, with his family and belongings already loaded on board the ship, decided upon a bold course of action. That night Agrippa ordered the captain to cut the ropes imprisoning his ship. Under cover of darkness, the hired sailors quietly rowed the vessel out of the harbor. In the open sea, the ship hoisted sail and sailed away in the night. In a few days, the ship reached Alexandria in Egypt.

Now in civilized Alexandria with his wife and children, Agrippa remained there for some months–perhaps as long as a year. Alexandria boasted a large Jewish community. Eventually Agrippa approached Alexander the alabarch, who was the brother of the historian Philo Judaeus. Agrippa asked Alexander for money to complete his journey to Italy. Alexander had no small measure of power in the Alexandrian Jewish community and was wealthy. His title allowed him to settle Jewish disputes under the authority of Rome.

Alexander the alabarch knew of Agrippa's spendthrift ways and refused him personally the money, but did agree to lend it to his wife Cypros upon her good reputation. This done, Cypros and Agrippa came to an understanding; Cypros would travel to Judea with their children and a portion of the money while

Agrippa would take his chances and proceed on alone to Campania in Italy in hopes of meeting with Tiberius.

Why did Agrippa want to meet with Tiberius?

Looking ahead on our time line, Herod Antipas had a disastrous battle with King Aretas IV of Nabotea in the early fall of A.D. 35. We will see that Agrippa in fact left Alexandria for Campania in the early spring of A.D. 36. It is very possible that Agrippa had some information on the conflict that he thought Tiberius needed to know. Remember, too, that Herod Philip's kingdom had been vacant for close to two years — another plum territory that Agrippa coveted. With Antipas' star falling, it was high time for Agrippa to make a final effort to reestablish a relationship with the powerful emperor!

Cypros, having moved her young family for the fourth time in three years, was angry and tired and wanted to take their chances back in Jerusalem. By that time, Cypros had another daughter to worry about — Mariamne was not yet two years old, having been born in A.D. 34. In Jerusalem, the sons and daughters of Hyrcanus II always had a place to stay at the Asamonean Royal palace which was just west of the Second Temple.

Also looking ahead on our time line, Herodias would be in Jerusalem for the Passover of A.D. 36. The two cousins likely exchanged letters frequently. In fact, it could have been Herodias who suggested Cypros abandon her husband and come back to Jerusalem with her children. Herodias was planning on being there for the Passover and would help in get Cypros settled in the Royal palace.

(Agrippa)..sailed to Alexandria, where he desired Alexander the alabarch to lend him two hundred thousand drachmae; but he said he would not lend it to him, but would not refuse it to Cypros, as greatly astonished at her affection to her husband, and at the other instances of her virtue; so she undertook to repay it. Accordingly, Alexander paid them five talents at Alexandria, and promised to pay them the rest of that sum at Dicearchia [Puteoli]; and this he did out of the fear he was in that Agrippa would soon spend it. So this Cypros set her husband free, and dismissed him to go on with his navigation to Italy, while she and her children departed for Judea. (*Antiq* XVIII 6:3)

Return to Italia

At this point, Josephus obligingly provides a solid date in the Agrippa saga which we have already alluded to. The future king traveled from Alexandria in Egypt to Campania early in the spring of A.D. 36, as Tiberius died in March of A.D. 37.

> ..but Agrippa, the son of Aristobulus, went up to Rome, a year before the death of Tiberius, in order to treat of some affairs with the emperor, if he might be permitted so to do. (*Antiq* XVIII 5:3)

Pomponius Flaccus, the president of Syria, died in office in late A.D. 34, as will be established. From this, it can be deduced that Agrippa's adventures in Ptolemais, Anthedon and Egypt lasted well over a year after his ouster from Antioch by Flaccus.

At any rate, according to Josephus, March of A.D. 36 found Agrippa in the Italian mainland city of Puteoli. Presumably, Cypros and her children were traveling from Alexandria to Jerusalem to settle into their new home–possibly in time to celebrate the Passover of A.D. 36.

Puteoli was a city located on the bay of Sorrentum conveniently across from the Isle of Capri, where Tiberius and his court lived. In Puteoli, Agrippa boldly wrote a letter to Tiberius requesting an audience.

Surprisingly, Tiberius responded promptly and with favor. He cordially invited Agrippa to come and visit him on the beautiful island. Agrippa was overjoyed at the quick response he received. Tiberius was a famous procrastinator and would routinely keep ostensibly important emissaries waiting for months before seeing them. Agrippa lost no time in sailing the short distance over the straits to Capri from Campania.

On the rocky island, things went well for Agrippa. He soon found himself a favorite in Tiberius' court once again. It had been more than 12 years since the death of Drusus and Tiberius' previous banishment of him.

Tiberius' unexpectedly warm reception of the once-shunned Agrippa might have been due to more than just rekindled memories and Tiberius' acceptance of his son's Drusus' death. It was early A.D. 36, and the new president of Syria, Lucius Vitellius, had just finished defeating the Parthian forces in Armenia with a mercenary army. The canny Tiberius was fully aware that Agrippa had recently spent several years in the East and at least a year in Syria itself. It is probable that Tiberius wanted to question Agrippa closely on details of the military and political situation there.

Also, Tiberius might have wanted information about the Tetrarch Herod Antipas. During the year that Agrippa and his family were in Alexandria, Antipas' Galilean army had been destroyed by King Aretas IV of Nabotea. Perhaps Agrippa mentioned both military situations in his letter to the emperor, knowing that it would pique Tiberius' interest. To be fair, perhaps Agrippa did, in fact, possess valuable information about those military engagements that would have been useful to Tiberius and his generals. At the very least, Tiberius–a practical man to his core–knew that Agrippa–smart and observant–would be a good and trustworthy source of information. And so the banishment was lifted.

Now safely in Capri and back in Royal favor, all appeared to be going well for Agrippa. But soon a letter from the Prefect Herennius Capito arrived for the emperor, describing to Tiberius how Agrippa had dishonorably escaped Capito's authority by stealing away by night in an impounded sailing vessel. Capito also undoubtedly reminded Tiberius of the debt Agrippa owed to the Caesars.

In his old age, Tiberius had developed an unpredictable hair-trigger temper. He became angry at Agrippa for his lack of disclosure. Perhaps Agrippa had even lied to him in his letter. It might have been worse for Agrippa, but Antonia intervened. Antonia was Tiberius' widowed sister-in-law, the granddaughter of Marc Antony, and a person whom Tiberius trusted implicitly.

Antonia, famous for her beauty and discretion.. (Plu *Lives: Antony and Cleopatra*)

Antonia personally paid all of Agrippa's debts, and Agrippa was again safe–for a time, at least.

While enjoying life in the Royal court in Capri, Agrippa cultivated the friendship of 24 year-old Caius Caesar, who was the son of Germanicus and later known as Emperor Caligula. Tiberius also had Agrippa, who was a learned and erudite man for all his faults, appointed as the educator of his own young grandson and heir-apparent, Tiberius Gemellus.

This tranquil and happy time for Agrippa lasted only through the summer of A.D. 36. During the last six months of his reign, Tiberius had Agrippa locked in chains for supposedly treasonous statements. When Tiberius died and Caius became emperor, Agrippa was released and was given a kingdom—a story to be told later.

Conclusion

Several of Herod the Great's Royal grandchildren left the city of Rome and returned to the Jewish East at about the same time in A.D. 32. The probable reason was to avoid being caught up in the political maelstrom in Rome that developed following the Sejanus conspiracy.

Agrippa's interactions—or lack thereof— with certain key people associated with known dates supports our pivotal hypothesis that Herodias married Antipas in the spring of A.D. 32. Important are that Pomponius Flaccus served as Syrian president from A.D. 32 to late A.D. 34., that Tetrarch Herod Philip died in early A.D. 34, and that Herod Agrippa, after a period of reconciliation with Tiberius, was thrown into a political prison by the emperor in October of A.D. 36.

Chapter 20   The Tetrarch Herod Philip

(Philip) ..showed himself a person of moderation and quietness in the conduct of his life and government; (*Antiq* XVIII 4:6)

The Tetrarch Herod Philip was Herod Antipas' half-brother and like Antipas was given a quarter of Herod the Great's old kingdom to rule after Herod's death. Philip had a retiring nature and a reputation for even-handedness which made him very popular in a kingdom where Jews constituted a minority. The year of Philip's death is one of the few solid dates that the historian Josephus documents.

Philip's exact date of birth is not recorded, but it can be speculated that Philip was born no earlier than 31 B.C. Philip had a full brother named Herod, who is mentioned once by Josephus and never referred to again. Philip's mother was Cleopatra of Jerusalem.

Kingdom Divided

After the death of Herod the Great in 4 B.C., Herod's last will was immediately put in force. Philip received the Trachonitis, Batanea, the Auranitis, and Paneas–which had been a part of the House of Zenodorus–and other territories (most significantly the Gaulonitis). This land was located east of the Jordan River and north and east of Lake Gennesareth.   Philip's territories accounted for a quarter of Herod the Great's revenue.

While Philip was satisfied with his share, his brother Herod Antipas made it known that he was contesting the will. Upon the urging of Syrian President Varus, Philip went to Rome as well to argue his rights before Augustus. Apparently, General Varus was impressed with the character and capabilities of Herod Philip.

> Philip also was come hither out of Syria, by the persuasion of Varus, with this principal intention to assist his brother [Archelaus]; for Varus was his great friend: but still so, that if there should any change happen in the form of government, (which Varus suspected there would,) and if any distribution should be made on account of the number that desired the liberty of living by their own laws, that he might not be disappointed, but might have his share in it. (*Antiq* XVII 11:1)

After hearing from all the Royal brothers and interested parties, Augustus' decision was to affirm the last will of Herod the Great.

The Tetrarch Herod Philip was to rule his lush and fertile land without major incident for over three decades, as Herod Antipas would rule his.

Philip's Kingdom

Herod Philip's mother was from Judea, whom Josephus refers to as Cleopatra of Jerusalem. The Jews traditionally look to the mother when determining "Jewishness," so Philip had inherent standing within the Judean and Galilean Jewish communities, whereas Herod Antipas and Archelaus–both born of the Samaritan Malthace–did not.

The Jews of Samaria and the Jews of Galilee and Judea practiced a separate form of Judaism. As well as living in their own separate countries, they also had their own variant interpretation of the Torah and their own sets of rituals. Each also had their own great Temple. The Samaritans' Temple was located at Sebaste and had been sumptuously rebuilt by Herod the Great at the same time he had rebuilt the Second Temple in Jerusalem. Both countries also had their own governing Sanhedrin councils.

Much of the population of Philip's territory was of Arabic and Syrian Greek stock, however, with a healthy percentage of

Parthians and Armenians. Jews were in the minority. In fact, most of Philip's territories had historically never been a part of ancient Judah or Israel at all, but were given to Herod the Great to rule by Emperor Augustus in 20 B.C. Then, the Trachonites were an especially troublesome nation for Rome. Many of the Trachonites were professional robbers and bandits–criminal gangs that the Syrian President Varro found impossible to control. Frustrated at Varro's lack of success, Augustus gave the country over to Herod the Great, thinking he could do a better job. Herod, in fact, proved to be a brutally efficient ruler of the Trachonitis and established order quickly (*Antiq* XV 13:1).

Despite the patchwork history and troublesome mix of ethnicities in his tetrarchy, Philip was known as a good and just ruler. He would settle disputes promptly and was not known for taking unreasonable bribes. Whereas most of the other sons of Herod made frequent trips to Rome, Philip seldom traveled outside his tetrarchy–apparently well satisfied with his life in the lush upper Jordan River valley.

> He (Philip) had showed himself a person of moderation and quietness in the conduct of his life and government; he constantly lived in that country which was subject to him; he used to make his progress with a few chosen friends; his tribunal also, on which he sat in judgment, followed him in his progress; and when any one met him who wanted his assistance, he made no delay, but had his tribunal set down immediately, wheresoever he happened to be, and sat down upon it, and heard his complaint: he there ordered the guilty that were convicted to be punished, and absolved those that had been accused unjustly. (*Antiq* XVIII 4:6)

Philip built a capital city near the headwaters of the Jordan River in Paneas, 25 miles north of Lake Gennesareth. This city was named Caesarea Philippi, and it was one of the most pleasant places in the ancient world. Today, it is called Banias, located in the forests and fields to the south of Mount Hebron.

Several temples–ancient even in Philip's time–had been built close to a mysterious and beautiful south-facing water cave at the base of Mount Hebron. The pure water flowed out to form one of headwaters of the Jordan River. Philip made great use of this resource in his flagship city of Caesarea Philippi–constructing scattered gardens and pools throughout.

Herod Philip also improved the city now known as Bethsaida, mentioned in the bible, which was built on a large hill overlooking the north shore of Lake Gennesareth. Philip called the city Julias, after Augustus' wife and the mother of Tiberius.

Herod Philip divided his time between Caesarea Philippi and Julias. During the winter, Lake Gennesareth, more than 500 feet below sea level, was usually a warm, pleasant place to be. In the heat of the summer, Caesarea Philippi, with its forests and constantly flowing waters, was Philip's home. One of the coolest places in the Jewish East, the mountains around Caesarea Philippi would commonly have snow well into the summer.

Philip and Antipas

With few hard facts to build on, reasonable speculation must be employed. What was the relationship between Herod Antipas and Herod Philip? What role did Philip play in Herod's controversial marriage to Herodias and the later defeat of Antipas' army by King Aretas IV?

If the dispute over Herod the Great's will in 3 B.C. had driven the two brothers apart, they had no choice but to work together seven years later when threatened by their older brother Archelaus. Then, they successfully petitioned Emperor Augustus to remove Archelaus as the ruler of Judea and Samaria. From that point on, the bothers likely realized more than ever that in order to survive in a modern Roman world, they had to work together, support each other, and keep their people contented–or at least keep their subjects from complaining to Caesar.

Both Antipas and Philip engaged in incestuous marriages late in life. Shortly after Antipas wed Herodias, Philip wed Salome, Herodias' young daughter. It was the second marriage for Antipas, but the first known marriage for Philip. What did Philip think about Antipas' marriage to Herodias, and Antipas' cruel dismissal of his first wife Pharaelis, the princess from Nabotea? Philip was probably against it for the simple reason that it reopened old wounds that had festered for decades between the Arabians and the Herod family. In the event of a war between King Aretas of Nabotea, Pharaelis' father, and Herod Antipas, Philip would be obligated to take his brother's side. With a much larger Arab population in his territories, Philip would be then put in a difficult situation. Conversely with a smaller Jewish population, the actual "illegality" of the marriage of Herodias to Antipas would have been a minor concern.

Herod the Great had encouraged incestuous marriages within his family. This tradition was continued long after Herod's own death. It was thought to keep the family strong through the generations, and the bloodline pure. In fact, a Herod marrying outside the family was rare unless such a union–as in Antipas' case–held some political advantage.

Antipas and Tiberius

When the conspiracy of Sejanus was unmasked and the proscriptions began in late A.D. 31, the Roman world was rocked to its foundations and the atmosphere became thick with fear and uncertainty. The Jewish lands would have been no exception to this. Antipas was a consummate politician if nothing else. It can be reasonably speculated that after the fall of Sejanus Antipas made a personal trip to Capri in order to pledge his loyalty before Tiberius.

Whether or not Tiberius received Antipas in Capri is open to question. Tiberius refused to see many others from Rome who sought to pledge their loyalty to him after the death of Sejanus.

> When, now, he learned that Sejanus was dead, he rejoiced, as was natural, but he would not receive the embassy that was sent to congratulate him, though many members of the senate and many of the knights and the populace had been sent out, as before. Indeed, he even rebuffed the consul Regulus, who had always been devoted to his interests and had come in response to the emperor's own command, in order to ensure the safety of his journey to the city. (Dio 58:13)

But Antipas was a personal friend, so Tiberius might have viewed Antipas' visit as a refreshing change from the usual aristocrats and petitioners from Rome. However, if Antipas was refused an audience in Capri with Tiberius, or the audience was delayed for whatever reason, that only gave him more time to spend in Rome with Herodias.

Immediately after the crushing of the conspiracy, hard winter had set in and travel upon the Mediterranean would have been dangerous. During the winter, most ships of commerce and transport usually laid up in their home ports to wait for the spring and better weather. So it would have been the spring of A.D. 32 when the different foreign emissaries came to Capri seeking to pledge their loyalty. Antipas would have been no exception, but it is also possible that Antipas would have braved the unpredictable fall weather to be the first to offer Tiberius aid and succor after the Sejanus affair. Antipas' half-brother, however, the Tetrarch Herod Philip, probably did not make the trip.

In early A.D. 32, Philip was perhaps 62 years old and five years older than Antipas. It is documented that Philip resisted travel outside his kingdom for any reason. Furthermore, Philip might have been too sick to travel. The tetrarch died less than two years later, and possibly even in A.D. 32 Philip was beginning to feel the effects of whatever finally caused his death. In fact, in anticipation of his death, Herod Philip had time to construct a monument to himself near the city of Julias. This suggests that Herod Philip suffered from a chronic illness that even in ancient times was recognized as fatal.

At this point, a key section from Josephus bears reviewing.

> About this time Aretas (the king of Arabia Petres) and Herod had a quarrel on the account following: Herod the tetrarch had, married the daughter of Aretas, and had lived with her a great while; but when he was once at Rome, he lodged with Herod, who was his brother indeed, but not by the same mother; for this Herod was the son of the high priest Sireoh's daughter. However, he fell in love with Herodias, this last Herod's wife, who was the daughter of Aristobulus their brother, and the sister of Agrippa the Great. This man ventured to talk to her about a marriage between them; which address, when she admitted, an

agreement was made for her to change her habitation, and come to him as soon as he should return from Rome: one article of this marriage also was this, that he should divorce Aretas's daughter. So Antipus, when he had made this agreement, sailed to Rome; but when he had done there the business he went about, and was returned again, his wife having discovered the agreement he had made with Herodias, and having learned it before he had notice of her knowledge of the whole design, she desired him to send her to Macherus which is a place in the borders of the dominions of Aretas and Herod, without informing him of any of her intentions. Accordingly Herod sent her thither, as thinking his wife had not perceived any thing; now she had sent a good while before to Macherus which was subject to her father and so all things necessary for her journey were made ready for her by the general of Aretas's army; and by that means she soon came into Arabia, under the conduct of the several generals, who carried her from one to another successively; and she soon came to her father, and told him of Herod's intentions. So Aretas made this the first occasion of his enmity between him and Herod, who had also some quarrel with him about their limits at the country of Gamalitis. So they raised armies on both sides, and prepared for war, and sent their generals to fight instead of themselves; and when they had joined battle, all Herod's army was destroyed by the treachery of some fugitives, who, though they were of the tetrarchy of Philip, joined with Aretas's army.. (*Antiq* XVIII 5:1)

While not central to the chronology, it will be postulated that Antipas finalized his plans with the beautiful Herodias sometime during his trip to Capri in early A.D. 32., or possibly late A.D. 31.

Interlude: Antipas' Trip to Capri

With a large contingent, perhaps 80 men, Antipas would have sailed from Caesarea to Alexandria in Egypt, and then on to Italy. Assuming good weather, his contingent would have sailed around what is now Sicily. Likely he would have bypassed Capri at first, to sail further north to land at Ostia and spend time in Rome. There, Antipas could rest and consult with other family members. Herod Philip, the son of Mariamne II and the grandson of Simon–the former Jerusalem High Priest–had grown up with Antipas and was now the leader of the Herod clan in Rome. If Herod Philip was Antipas' host, the hostess would have been Herod Philip's beautiful wife–Herodias!

It is not hard to imagine how relieved the Herods of the second and third generation must have been to see the powerful Antipas among them. Rome was then in turmoil in the aftermath of the Sejanus affair. Innocent people were being executed and even long-time neighbors held new and deadly suspicions against each other. Roman aristocrats after the fall of Sejanus probably had little time for the Herod family with all their demands and Herodian faux-Royal pretensions.

Thus, Antipas would have been a welcome figure in the Herod "colony" in Rome. During the short time he was there, Antipas probably held open court frequently with the family members, listening to their horror stories of the conspiracy and the proscriptions that followed, and doing what he could to make things better. Antipas might have even extended an open invitation to his relatives to live in the East if they so wished–a return to the homeland.

Then, Herodias probably saw in Antipas a way out of a dangerous and unpredictable situation. For this reason, it is an easy case to make that Herodias was the aggressor in the relationship. But what was Antipas to do? The aging tetrarch could not help but be smitten by the much younger beauty. For Herodias, love probably didn't play much of a role in her pursuit of Antipas. Antipas was a reassuring rock of stability and his kingdom in the East–as provincial as it was–was a way to escape the danger in Rome.

Antipas' subsequent visit to Capri went well. Tiberius reaffirmed Antipas and by proxy Herod Philip in their tetrarchies. It can be speculated that Tiberius discussed with Antipas his vision for the future of the Roman Empire. Tiberius perhaps talked about appointing Pomponius Flaccus as president of Syria and retiring Lamia to govern Rome. Antipas then might have put in a good word for his nephew Aristobulos, Herodias' brother, as a good candidate to aid Flaccus in Antioch.

After his success with Tiberius, Herod Antipas then left Capri and returned to Rome to stay with Herodias and Herod Philip (of Rome) for a time more. The excited, rejuvenated Antipas now made secret plans and promises with his new love, Herodias.

Herodias agreed to divorce her husband and come to live in Galilee with Antipas. Her daughter Salome would come with her. This would be the start of a grand new life for both of them!

Thus Antipas returned to Galilee a happy man. He had been reaffirmed in his kingdom by his old friend Tiberius and had captured the love of a beautiful, younger woman as well.

Pharaelis and the Path to War

But Antipas' Arabian Princess wife Pharaelis surely noticed the difference in him when he returned to Tiberias. Soon, she discovered the plans that Antipas and Herodias had made and fled Galilee in panic—first to Macherus in southern Perea and then on to her father's kingdom of Nabotea.

Pharaelis' fears were understandable. Antipas' father, Herod the Great, had killed his own beautiful wife Mariamne I as well as several of his own sons and relatives. Murder was, in fact, part of the Herod legacy. Would Antipas do the same to be rid of her? In Pharaelis' mind, she shouldn't take the chance!

Pharaelis' sudden disappearance was a pleasant and convenient surprise for Antipas. His first wife was now out of the way and he could send for Herodias. Antipas likely gave little consideration to the possibility of repercussions from King Aretas, Pharaelis' father. By challenging Antipas, Aretas would be challenging Rome herself, and that would be suicide–even for a nation as large as Nabotea.

Herodias in Rome received the good news from Antipas, and soon had divorced her own husband without apparent incident. Within a few weeks, Herodias had set her affairs in order and was traveling to the East along with her attendants and her daughter Salome.

Herod Philip and Herodias

Perhaps the strongest case for assuming that Philip did not accompany Antipas to Rome is that Antipas' romance with Herodias had progressed as far and as quickly as it did. Philip would surely have been the voice of reason to Antipas had he been in Rome to observe the couple. Philip might have even talked to Herodias alone and warned her of the problems she would cause if she forced herself on Antipas.

It is also possible that by the time Philip became aware of the situation between Herodias and Antipas, Antipas had already been weeks back in Galilee and a terrified Pharaelis had already fled to her father in Petra.

When Philip did learn of it, he was probably not pleased at the complications that Herodias was bringing to both tetarchies. Later, when it became general knowledge, the common Jews were solidly against Herodias' divorce and remarriage. They expressed their disapproval with varying levels of intensity. The ascetic preacher John the Baptist, who was gaining more and more fame in the wilds of Perea, was also critical of the marriage of Antipas and Herodias. The High Priesthood in Jerusalem as well was not supportive of Antipas, but they remained judiciously silent.

While Philip was initially against Antipas' planned marriage, he likely softened his stance when he met Herodias. She turned on her charms and Philip was probably quickly won over, as most men were. In fact, less than a year later–and probably within months–Philip would marry Herodias' daughter.

Gamala and the Gamalitis

If it weren't for the respect and fear King Aretas IV had for Rome, his Nabotean armies would have quickly invaded Perea and Galilee, meting out revenge on Antipas for his insult to Aretas' daughter. The tetrarchy of Herod Philip would have been targeted as well.

But in lieu of all-out war, King Aretas apparently began a cat-and-mouse game with Antipas. He first moved a token force of troops into a disputed territory between Perea and Nabotea–a northern territory that Josephus calls the Gamalitis. But where was this territory exactly? It is a logical assumption that the land was close to the city of Gamala which Josephus refers to many times and was the site of an important stronghold in the Jewish revolt of A.D. 66. Logically, if the location of Gamala can be found, then the Gamalitis should be surrounding it. If the Gamalitis was close to Herod Philip's territory, all the more reason for Philip to play the peacemaker.

Gamala was rediscovered in 1967 and is, in fact, close to the southern boundaries of Herod Philip's kingdom. It lies a few miles due east of Bethsaida–an ancient city just off the north shore of Lake Gennesareth. Bethsaida is within the territory of Herod Philip.

Aretas' claim to the Gamalitis is easy to understand, because the boundaries of Nabotea are directly to the east, and the land is fertile and productive. But if Herod Antipas claimed land in that area, it would have to be as a part of Perea, making Perea extend to the north much further than has generally been recognized. Perea would then have to meander around the cities and territories of the Decapolis–almost reaching the city of Gamala.

The Decapolis was a group of at least 10 ancient cities and their surrounding land with large Syrian Greek populations. All had a Hellenic history and enjoyed a semi-independent status under Rome. These cities and territories made up much of the eastern shoreline and environs of Lake Gennesareth. General Pompey had formed the Decapolis in 63 B.C. Recognizing the large Greek population of the cities, Pompey sought to avoid their having to live under the Jewish theocracy that then ruled the rest of the area.

Scythopolis was the largest city of the Decapolis. Located 20 miles south of Lake Gennesareth, it was the only Decapolis city west of the Jordan River. The others, according to Pliny the Elder were: Damascus, Opoton, Philadelphia (present-day Amman, Jordan), Raphana, Gadara, Hippondion (Sussita, or Hippus), Pella, Galasa and Canatha (Pliny the Elder *Natural History* 5:16:74). Other ancient sources included the cities of Dion and Jerash. Hippus is the only city known to be near the eastern shores of the Gennesareth, but there were probably more; sources suggest that as many as ten additional cities were in this general area and under Decapolis control.

But in spite of all the trouble just taken in defining the location of the Gamalitis, the battle between Antipas and Aretas very likely occurred nowhere near it. There were many cities and areas of contention that lay between Nabotea and the Jewish lands that were claimed by both Antipas and Aretas, and not just the Gamalitis. These conflicts went back at least to the early first century B.C., when King Alexander Jannaeus conquered several Arab cities that should have rightfully belonged to Nabotea. Josephus mentions a few of them when discussing Hyrcanus II's negotiations with Aretas III in about 64 B.C.

> Moreover, Hyrcanus promised him (Aretas), that when he had been brought thither, and had received his kingdom, he would restore that country, and those twelve cities which his father Alexander had taken from the Arabians which were these, Medaba, Naballo, Libias, Tharabasa, Agala, Athone, Zoar, Orone, Marissa, Rudda, Lussa, and Oruba. (*Antiq* XIV 1:4)

While Josephus emphasizes the Gamalitis as a bone of contention, the actual battle between Antipas and Aretas could have been over any of the above mentioned cities, or perhaps one not mentioned.

Marriage to Salome

Once in the East, Herodias arranged the marriage between her daughter Salome and the Tetrarch Herod Philip.

> But Herodias, their sister, was married to Herod [Philip], the son of Herod the Great, who was born of Mariamne, the daughter of Simon the high priest, who had a daughter, Salome; after whose birth Herodias took upon her to confound the laws of our country, and divorced herself from her husband while he was alive, and was married to Herod [Antipas], her husband's brother by the father's side, he was tetrarch of Galilee; but her daughter Salome was married to Philip, the son of Herod, and tetrarch of Trachonitis; and as he died childless, Aristobulus, the son of Herod, the brother of Agrippa, married her; they had three sons, Herod, Agrippa, and Aristobulus; (*Antiq* XVIII 5:4)

Salome was probably 14 or 15 when she was married to her great-uncle Philip. Josephus gives us an indirect indication of Salome's age later in *Antiquities*. In A.D. 53, King Agrippa II gave his sister Drusilla away in marriage to a "client" king of the Roman Empire. Drusilla's father, Agrippa I, had died in A.D. 44 and so could not perform that function. Females were considered of marriageable age after menarche, and available for betrothal even as a child. Drusilla was born in A.D. 38, and would have been 15 when betrothed.

The union between the young Salome and Herod Philip was advantageous to Herodias for several reasons. Herodias knew that Philip was old, sickly, and, like Herod Antipas, had no male heir. Perhaps enough time had passed in her marriage to Antipas that Herodias suspected that Antipas was incapable of fathering a child. If Salome married Herod Philip and successfully bore him a male heir, the succession of the tetrarchies–both Antipas' and Philip's–into Herodian hands would be assured. Even if Herod Philip proved unable to father a child but died with Salome as queen, it would be easier for Emperor Tiberius to meld Philip's tetrarchy in with Antipas', thus increasing Herodias' own power and influence. It was also possible–but not likely–that the young Salome herself might get a portion of Philip's territory to rule upon his death. Salome, after all, was a mere teenager, and Philip's territory was militarily important.

Another reason for the marriage of Salome to Philip might have been far more basic and uncomplicated. Salome perhaps had developed into a passionate woman–as Herodias might have been at her age–and it was simply time for her to marry. In Herodias' eye, few candidates in the provincial East were of the proper station and heritage to provide Salome with an acceptable match. Herod Philip was old and ailing, yes, but he was powerful, rich, and without an heir–why not have Salome marry him?

Salome, of course, had little choice in the matter; she would not dare disobey her mother in any case. Philip soon discovered, as Antipas had discovered before him, that resisting the desires of

Herodias and Salome was futile. So shortly after the marriage of Antipas and Herodias, perhaps in late A.D. 32, the wise and venerated Tetrarch Herod Philip found himself exchanging vows with the young and beautiful Salome, Herodias' daughter.

Both brothers now had new wives and life was good. Herodias had to be satisfied, having ties through marriage and her daughter to control one-half of Herod the Great's old kingdom. And both she and Salome were now queens!

Did marriage change Philip? Probably not in the way that Herodias would have liked. Philip likely remained the voice of moderation to Antipas, encouraging him not to respond aggressively to Aretas' continued threats and hostility. Philip might even have been mildly amused at the situation Antipas had gotten himself into–considering both John the Baptist and King Aretas of Nabotea as not much of a threat. As a further blow to Herodias, as the months passed it became apparent that Herod Philip, for whatever reason, would not be giving Salome a child. With none of her plans working out and Antipas' continued reluctance to engage King Aretas or silence the religious men who continued to excoriate her, Herodias would have seethed with impotent fury.

The Death of Herod Philip

It wouldn't be fair to say that Salome was the death of Philip, but according to the time line thus far constructed the beloved tetrarch lived for no more than a year and a half after exchanging marriage vows with his niece. However, with a much younger wife and still in the honeymoon period, a case can be made for Philip dying a happy man.

Josephus gives a date for the death of Herod Philip.

> About this time it was that Philip, Herod's brother, departed this life, in the twentieth year of the reign of Tiberius, after he had been tetrarch of Trachonitis and Gaulanitis, and of the nation of the Bataneans also, thirty-seven years. .. He died at Julias; and when he was carried to that monument which he had already erected for himself beforehand, he was buried with great pomp. His principality Tiberius took, (for he left no

sons behind him,) and added it to the province of Syria, but gave order that the tributes which arose from it should be collected, and laid up in his tetrarchy. (*Antiq* XVIII 4:6)

The 20th year of Tiberius' reign and the 37th year of Herod Philip's reign would have been A.D. 34.

When Herod Philip died, the moderating voice of Antipas' trusted brother was gone. Herodias, and perhaps Antipas' Galilean generals, could now make their arguments for war against Aretas and for silencing John the Baptist unopposed.

The Real Reason for War?

King Aretas' rattling his sword, however, may have been only a minor factor in Antipas engaging Nabotea in war. In fact, it might not have been a factor at all.

After Herod Philip's death in early A.D. 34, Tiberius decided not to turn Philip's tetrarchy over to Herod Antipas to rule. Instead, he gave the kingdom over to the president of Syria to administrate. In early A.D. 34, this would have been Pomponius Flaccus. Significantly, the domain of Philip was to be maintained separately with the monies from it accruing in a segregated account while Tiberius made up his mind about its final disposition. Herod Antipas had to be concerned that Tiberius did not automatically give it over to him. Herodias had to be furious over the snub. Less of a surprise was Tiberius' ignoring whatever threadbare claim that Philip's widow, Salome, had to Philip's rich tetrarchy.

What a cruel blow—Philip's territory had been ruled by the Herod family for more than half a century and now it was being taken away and turned into a *de facto* province of the empire–at least temporarily.

Why would Emperor Tiberius do this–especially to Herod Antipas, who was a personal friend and who, less than two years before, had made a special trip to Capri to pledge his loyalty? Did Tiberius sense something back then at their meeting that disturbed him? Did Tiberius later learn about Herodias and the controversial marriage and think the less of Antipas for it?

Herod Antipas, for his part, could not help but suspect that Tiberius had developed a waning faith in his judgment, his strength, and his ability to rule. Perhaps the whole system of Herodian proxy monarchs was losing credibility and usefulness as the eastern Roman Empire matured. Was Antipas fearful that Tiberius might take away his own kingdom at the first opportunity?!

As for Queen Herodias, she had to realize that if Antipas were to die, she had no assurance of any consideration by Tiberius, just as Tiberius gave no consideration to Salome after Philip's death. Would she lose all her power and wealth in the end? That was not why Herodias risked everything to come to the East!

Even though ill will between King Aretas and Antipas had been brewing for almost two years, the added sting of losing Philip's kingdom now gave Antipas an additional reason to fight. Without the moderating presence of Herod Philip, with Herodias' continuing exhortations, and perhaps Antipas' generals' recommending war, Antipas decided to act.

Another factor to be considered–which will be dealt with at length in later chapters–is the aggressive posturing of the Parthian Empire to the north. Nabotea lay just to the south of Parthia and together they made up the eastern boundary of the Roman Empire. It can be speculated that Herod Antipas might have had information that Aretas had an alliance with Parthia, and so decided to act unilaterally and preemptively against the Arabs. The intent was to prove to Emperor Tiberius that he could be a military man if given the chance, and so Antipas acted alone against the formidable enemy.

To be fair, there is little supporting evidence for a Parthian-Nabotean alliance. And the assumption that Antipas felt the need to prove himself as a capable warrior to Tiberius and so initiated the war is based on circumstantial evidence. Tiberius was loathe to have any conflicts with any of the empire's neighbors as well.

Antipas' Battle

It was at least mid-A.D. 34 before Antipas knew that Philip's territory was not going to be his. Assuming this, the battle with Aretas had to have occurred sometime after this. What other evidence supports this assumption?

One clue is that Antipas blamed the defeat of his army on betrayals from many men in Philip's territory who decided to join Aretas' army.

> ..all Herod's army was destroyed by the treachery of some fugitives, who, though they were of the tetrarchy of Philip, joined with Aretas's army (*Antiq* XVIII 5:1)

If the Tetrarch Herod Philip was alive at the time of the battle, he would have supported his brother unequivocally. Philip's loyal troops then would then be fighting on Antipas' side–and not be found joining Aretas' army as mercenaries. Josephus talks only of these "fugitives" from Philip's kingdom and makes no mention of Herod Philip himself, or Philip's standing army. It is a reasonable deduction that, at the time of the battle, Philip had already died. What had been formerly Herod Philip's army was now either disbanded or under the loose and careless control of Syrian President Flaccus. Philip's former soldiers left for Nabotea when presented with better opportunities by agents of Aretas.

Assuming this, another question arises. Why would Philip's former soldiers go over to the Naboteans to actively fight against the Galileans? But it must be remembered that most of the people of Philip's old kingdom were not Jews, but Syrian Greeks, Arabs, and people derived from other ethnic groups. Indeed, much of Philip's tetrarchy itself was never a part of any ancient Jewish kingdom at all. It would probably have not taken much of a promise from King Aretas–or money–for Philip's soldiers to join the Naboteans.

Another motive for the perceived treachery of Philip's soldiers is possible. Remember that Herodias was an unpopular figure throughout the Jewish lands. Whatever respect Antipas had earned through his decades as tetrarch was likely severely compromised by his marriage to her. Despite Herodias' royal Asamonean pedigree, devout Jews thought her to be the very image of evil and far more Roman than Jewish.

It is easy to imagine the suspicions of some people when Philip died so soon after what had to be a controversial marriage. Was poison suspected? Or even witchcraft?! Under this scenario, it is understandable that "fugitives" from Philip's old kingdom would have additional reason to fight for Nabotea and with little encouragement. Invitations for adventure from agents of Nabotea would have been received with at least interest by the sizable Arabic and Greek-Syrian population.

As for Salome, after the funeral ceremonies, likely the very sad and lonely young widow quietly retreated to her mother's palace in Tiberias to live, sensing her own unpopularity in Philip's former kingdom.

Conclusion

The Tetrarch Herod Philip was a moderating influence to Herod Antipas in the wake of public outcry against Antipas' marriage to Herodias. For this reason, Herod Philip indirectly protected John the Baptist and other critics from retaliation by Antipas as long as he was alive.

Since Philip died in early A.D. 34, and after the Passover of A.D. 33, John the Baptist could only have been arrested and executed after that time. According to the fourth Gospel, after John's arrest there were two Passovers observed by Jesus–one celebrated in the hills of the eastern Gennesareth, and Jesus' last in Jerusalem. That leaves us with two possibilities for the year of Jesus' final Passover – either A.D. 35 or A.D. 36.

Chapter 21   The Dance of Salome

..and when the daughter of Herodias herself came in and danced, she pleased Herod and them that sat at meat with him; (Mk 6:22)

Herodias' daughter is not given a name in the New Testament, but Josephus reveals it to be Salome. Then a lonely young widow and still a teenager, Salome's seductive dance before Herod Antipas and his generals led to the beheading of John the Baptist. Alas, if Salome had not danced, it is possible that John the Baptist might well have lived to a very old age, and the religion of Christianity as it is known today might never have come into being.

Who was this woman who played such a significant role in western history? Physically, Salome was probably tall and beautiful, much like her mother, Queen Herodias, and with the haughty allure possessed by most of the Royal Asamonean women. But within Salome also flowed the cruel and passionate blood of desert Idumean kings–she was the great granddaughter of Herod the Great, after all. An unknowable factor with Salome was the effect of two generations of genetic inbreeding. Did Salome possess an artistic brilliance that can often be found in such individuals? Or was she afflicted with the mental and emotional instability that is also common to the inbred?

Salome was the child of divorce, and, at an early age, her mother dragged her away from Rome where her father and friends were. Reluctantly relocated in the rustic and agrarian land of Galilee, she found herself thrust into the middle of a hostile situation with few social supports. In Galilee, Salome's mother Herodias became a target for the anti-Roman animosity of the day, with Salome absorbing much of the scorn as well. Salome's subsequent marriage to her great-uncle, the Tetrarch Herod Philip, further inflamed the Jews of the East. And when the aged Philip died less than two years after marrying Salome, how suspicious his subjects must have been of her! Salome performed her infamous dance in Macherus before her stepfather, Herod Antipas, barely a year after Philip's death. It was a dance that gained Salome a notoriety that will last as long as Christianity itself.

In partial defense of Salome, if Herodias had not suggested she ask Antipas for John the Baptist's head, Salome would surely have asked for something quite different–a portion of Antipas' kingdom, perhaps, or maybe something as simple as a glittering jewel. What a difference that would have made for history!

Antipas' Birthday Celebration

What facts can be gleaned from the accounts of the dance of Salome and the execution of John the Baptist, and how would this advance our developing chronology? Important passages in the Books of Mark and Matthew concerning Salome and John the Baptist will be repeated.

> [6:14]And king Herod heard *thereof*; for his name had become known: and he said, John the Baptizer is risen from the dead, and therefore do these powers work in him. [6:15]But others said, It is Elijah. And others said, *It is a prophet, even* as one of the prophets. [6:16]But Herod, when he heard *thereof*, said, John, whom I beheaded, he is risen. [6:17]For Herod himself had sent forth and laid hold upon John, and bound him in prison for the sake of Herodias, his brother Philip's wife; for he had married her. [6:18]For John said unto Herod, It is not lawful for thee to have thy brother's wife. [6:19]And Herodias set herself against him, and desired to kill him; and she could not; [6:20]for Herod feared John, knowing that he was a righteous and holy man, and kept him safe. And when he heard him, he was much perplexed; and he heard him gladly. [6:21]And when a convenient day was come, that Herod on his birthday made a supper to his lords, and the high captains, and the chief men of Galilee; [6:22]and when the daughter of Herodias herself came in and danced, she pleased

Herod and them that sat at meat with him; and the king said unto the damsel, Ask of me whatsoever thou wilt, and I will give it thee. 6:23And he sware unto her, Whatsoever thou shalt ask of me, I will give it thee, unto the half of my kingdom. 6:24And she went out, and said unto her mother, What shall I ask? And she said, The head of John the Baptizer. 6:25And she came in straightway with haste unto the king, and asked, saying, I will that thou forthwith give me on a platter the head of John the Baptist. 6:26And the king was exceeding sorry; but for the sake of his oaths, and of them that sat at meat, he would not reject her. 6:27And straightway the king sent forth a soldier of his guard, and commanded to bring his head: and he went and beheaded him in the prison, 6:28and brought his head on a platter, and gave it to the damsel; and the damsel gave it to her mother. 6:29And when his disciples heard *thereof*, they came and took up his corpse, and laid it in a tomb. (Mk)

14:1At that season Herod the tetrarch heard the report concerning Jesus, 14:2and said unto his servants, This is John the Baptist; he is risen from the dead; and therefore do these powers work in him. 14:3For Herod had laid hold on John, and bound him, and put him in prison for the sake of Herodias, his brother Philip's wife. 14:4For John said unto him, It is not lawful for thee to have her. 14:5And when he would have put him to death, he feared the multitude, because they counted him as a prophet. 14:6But when Herod's birthday came, the daughter of Herodias danced in the midst, and pleased Herod. 14:7Whereupon he promised with an oath to give her whatsoever she should ask. 14:8And she, being put forward by her mother, saith, Give me here on a platter the head of John the Baptist. 14:9And the king was grieved; but for the sake of his oaths, and of them that sat at meat with him, he commanded it to be given; 14:10and he sent and beheaded John in the prison. 14:11And his head was brought on a platter, and given to the damsel: and she brought it to her mother. 14:12And his disciples came, and took up the corpse, and buried him; and they went and told Jesus. (Mt)

Josephus identifies the prison of John the Baptist as being in the old Herodian fortress of Macherus. Macherus was located on top of a rocky mountain ridge that lay just to the east of briny Lake Asphaltitis in Perea.

Now when [many] others came in crowds about him, for they were very greatly moved [or pleased] by hearing his words, Herod, who feared lest the great influence John had over the people might put it into his power and inclination to raise a rebellion, (for they seemed ready to do any thing he should advise,) thought it best, by putting him to death, to prevent any mischief he might cause, and not bring himself into difficulties, by sparing a man who might make him repent of it when it would be too late. Accordingly he (John the Baptist) was sent a prisoner, out of Herod's suspicious temper, to Macherus, the castle I before mentioned, and was there put to death. Now the Jews had an opinion that the destruction of this army was sent as a punishment upon Herod, and a mark of God's displeasure to him. (*Antiq* XVIII 5:2)

Josephus does not mention Salome's dance which is one of the greatest stories in the Bible. It is possible that Josephus left it out on purpose, not wanting to offend King Agrippa II. Agrippa was a personal friend of Josephus' and Salome would have been Agrippa's cousin. For the same reason, Josephus might have not mentioned the hatred of Herodias as a cause for John the Baptist's arrest–Herodias was Agrippa II's aunt. But Josephus does bring in a factor not mentioned in either the Book of Mark or Matthew, that Herod Antipas feared for the sedition that John could cause within his army. But why would he be fearful of John the Baptist if the prophet kept to the wilds of Perea and stayed far away from Galilee?

Macherus

Macherus, along with Masada, was thought to be the best protected and fortified of all the Herodian strongholds outside of Jerusalem. Originally constructed by the Jewish King Alexander Jannaeus, it had later been meticulously rebuilt by Herod the Great. In Antipas' time, it had fallen into some disrepair, as peace with Nabotea had reigned for decades–at least until Antipas divorced Pharaelis.

(Macherus) was itself (situated) a very rocky hill, elevated to a very great height; which circumstance alone made it very hard to he subdued. It was also so contrived by nature, that it could not be easily ascended; for it is, as it were, ditched about with such valleys on all sides, and to such a depth, that the eye cannot reach their bottoms, and such as are not easily to be passed over, and even such as it is impossible to fill up with earth. For that valley which cuts it on the west extends to threescore furlongs, and did not end till it came to the lake Asphaltitis; on the same side it was also that Macherus had the tallest top of its hill elevated above the rest. But then for the valleys that lay on the north and south sides, although they be not so large as that already described, yet it is in like manner an impracticable thing to think of getting over them; and for the valley that lies on the east side, its depth is found to be no less than a hundred cubits. It extends as far as a mountain that lies over against Macherus, with which it is bounded.

Now when Alexander [Janneus], the king of the Jews, observed the nature of this place, he was the first who built a citadel here which afterwards was demolished by Gabinius, when he made war against Aristobulus. But when Herod came to be king, he thought the place to be worthy of the utmost regard, and of being built upon in the firmest manner, and this especially because it lay so near to Arabia; for it is seated in a convenient place on that account, and hath a prospect toward that country; he therefore surrounded a large space of ground with walls and towers, and built a city there, out of which city there was a way that led up to the very citadel itself on the top of the mountain; nay, more than this, he built a wall round that top of the hill, and erected towers at the corners, of a hundred and sixty cubits high; in the middle of which place he built a palace, after a magnificent manner, wherein were large and beautiful edifices. He also made a great many reservoirs for the reception of water, that there might be plenty of it ready for all uses, and those in the properest places that were afforded him there. (*Wars* VII 6:1-2)

Fire signals could be sent from Macherus to her sister fortress, Masada, on the other side of Lake Asphaltitis, and also to Herodium. Herodium lay to the northwest of Macherus and also across the Asphaltitis–but just five miles south of Jerusalem. From Herodium, signals could be easily relayed to Jerusalem, and from Jerusalem on to Jericho. These fortresses were the anchors of Herod the Great's southern command strategy.

However, in Herod Antipas' time Macherus had been transformed into a seldom-visited winter palace with a small permanent garrison and a minimal stockpile of provisions. It probably also served as the headquarters for Antipas' customs agents who monitored the flow of goods into Perea from Nabotea on the nearby King's Highway and taxed them accordingly.

Why Macherus?

The story of Antipas' birthday party is not told in Josephus, but the Jewish historian is unequivocal about John the Baptist being held prisoner in Macherus and executed there. Conversely, the Book of Mark tells about the party, but not the location of it. Mark and Matthew both suggest that the execution was carried out swiftly and the head of John presented to Salome and Herodias during the same celebration. The logical conclusion is that Antipas' birthday celebration was, in fact, held in Macherus.

While Macherus was a pleasant enough winter-time palace, it was situated an out-of-the-way location in the southernmost part of Perea. The city of Tiberias in Galilee, being below sea level and on the shores of Lake Gennesareth, was also very enjoyable in winter and under normal circumstances Antipas and his court would be there. But in this case, the circumstances were not normal at all. It is probable that Antipas was in Macherus with his generals in order to train and prepare his army for war with Nabotea.

This conclusion leads to another question: why prepare for war at Macherus in the very southern part of Perea when Josephus earlier suggested that Aretas had his troops occupying a disputed area of the Gamalitis which was 80 miles to the north? One possible answer could be that there was more than one area of dispute; the more important one was closer to Macherus and not mentioned by Josephus. In his writings, Josephus documents many cities of contention over the years between the Jews and the Naboteans along the southern boundaries of the two countries (*Antiq* XIV 1:4).

However, it is also very possible that Antipas was using the excuse of Gamalitis to mount a more ambitious military campaign, perhaps an outright invasion of Nabotea. If so, southern Perea and Macherus would be the natural staging area for his armies; Macherus was Antipas' closest fortress to Petra, the rich capital city of Nabotea and home base to King Aretas IV. If Petra was captured, Antipas and his generals knew that the rest of the nation of Nabotea would likely fall quickly.

An interesting speculation to be sure, but how probable would that have been? No evidence exists that Emperor Tiberius or the Syrian President Flaccus approved of any such military action. Tiberius, in fact, disapproved strongly of wars of any sort in the provinces, no matter the reasons for them. So aggressive actions against Aretas by Antipas were politically risky and Antipas had to know that. But King Aretas had sworn blood vengeance against Herod Antipas on many occasions. The Arabian King stated that he would not rest until he had killed the son of Herod. Words like that from a sovereign were tantamount to an act of war in those days.

Antipas also might have felt that the Herods had a historical right to rule Nabotea anyway. Antipas' father, Herod the Great, had actually did rule Nabotea for a brief time under Antony. In years past, it had been the stated intention of Octavian to permanently give the land over to Herod the Great were it not for the opportunistic actions of King Aretas' father.

> But still Caesar was offended with Aretas, that he had taken upon himself the government, without his consent first obtained, for he had determined to bestow Arabia upon Herod; (*Antiq* XVI 10:9)

A factor for Antipas might have also been the aggressive actions of King Artabanus of the Parthian Empire. To the north in Armenia, Artabanus was threatening the Roman-controlled country in no uncertain terms. Parthia and Nabotea were neighbors and Antipas might have justifiably concluded that Aretas was in league with Artabanus. With the Naboteans and the Parthians united, it would be advantageous to stop Aretas as early as possible. What a time to prove himself to Tiberius, and in the process gain the late Tetrarch Herod Philip's kingdom!

Nothing suggests that the Judean Prefect Pontius Pilate and Syrian Governor Pomponius Flaccus contributed anything to Antipas' war efforts. Either they rejected Aretas as a threat when petitioned by Antipas for support, or Antipas kept them out of the military operation on purpose. Was Antipas expecting an easy victory and did not wish to share the glory?

Evidence that Antipas was planning a major campaign is suggested later in *Antiquities*. In A.D. 39, a conflict arose between Herod Antipas and King Agrippa I. During the course of it, Agrippa revealed to Emperor Caius that Antipas had enough arms in his stores for, according to Josephus, 70,000 men–far above what was likely needed to simply defend his borders.

> Now Caius saluted Herod, for he first met with him, and then looked upon the letters which Agrippa had sent him, and which were written in order to accuse Herod; wherein he accused him, that he had been in confederacy with Sejanus against Tiberius's and that he was now confederate with Artabanus, the king of Parthia, in opposition to the government of Caius; as a demonstration of which he alleged, that he had armor sufficient for seventy thousand men ready in his armory. Caius was moved at this information, and asked Herod whether what was said about the armor was true; and when he confessed there was such armor there, for he could not deny the same, the truth of it being too notorious, (*Antiq* XVIII 7:2)

Caius was not pleased by this, and it did not bode well for Antipas. Certainly, there is no other evidence to suggest Antipas ever considered turning on Rome in favor of Parthia, or that he earlier supported the conspiracy of Sejanus. Very possibly, Antipas might have been stockpiling arms thinking that the Roman Empire would break apart upon Tiberius' death, with the East going to the strongest and best-prepared ruler. But the massive weapons store could also simply have been leftover from Antipas' abortive plan years earlier to invade Nabotea and reclaim old Herodian territory.

The Sabbatical Year

Assuming that Tiberius didn't send Antipas on a "secret" war to eliminate Aretas as an ally of Parthian King Artabanus in A.D. 35, Antipas likely made his decision to invade Nabotea sometime in mid A.D. 34. This would be after Herod Philip's death and Tiberius' subsequent decision to give Philip's tetrarchy to Syria. Aretas had been provoking Antipas for two years over his divorce of his daughter. Perhaps in a previous communication, Tiberius had given Antipas license to go to war against Aretas.

Assuming the decision was made in mid A.D. 34, from a military standpoint it would have made sense for Antipas to attack Nabotea immediately, within months, perhaps, in order to catch Aretas off-guard. But the actual battle took place 18 months later.

The delay could have been for religious reasons. The fall of A.D. 33 marked the beginning of the Jewish Sabbatic year, a religious period when the land and the people rested, and no offensive wars could be fought. Just as the seventh day of the Jewish calendar week was known as the Sabbath and was a day of rest, every seven years was a Sabbatic year and considered holy. As Julius Caesar noted in one of his decrees:

> "Caius Caesar, imperator the second time, hath ordained, That all the country of the Jews, excepting Joppa, do pay a tribute yearly for the city Jerusalem, excepting the seventh which they call the sabbatical year, because thereon they neither receive the fruits of their trees, nor do they sow their land; (*Antiq* XIV 10:6)

To sustain themselves over the Sabbatical year, the Jewish people saved a part of their produce from each of the preceding six years.

> And Moses commanded them, "At the end of every seven years, at the set time in the year of release, at the Feast of Booths, when all Israel comes to appear before the LORD your God at the place that he will choose, you shall read this law before all Israel in their hearing. Assemble the people, men, women, and little ones, and the sojourner within your towns, that they may hear and learn to fear the LORD your God, and be careful to do all the words of this law."
> (Deut. 31:10-12)

Feast of the Booths is the same as the feast of the Tabernacles, an October event. During a Sabbatic year, while it was forbidden to mount an offensive military campaign, the Jews could fight to defend themselves.

Placement of these Sabbatical years can be determined by reading Josephus. In *Antiquities*, Herod the Great first married Mariamne in the spring of 37 B.C. and then prepared in earnest for the siege-conquest of Jerusalem with his forces (*Antiq* XIV 16:1).

> Now the three bulwarks were easily erected, because so many hands were continually at work upon it; for it was summer time, and there was nothing to hinder them in raising their works ...They also erected new works when the former were ruined, and making mines underground, they met each other, and fought there; and making use of brutish courage rather than of prudent valor, they persisted in this war to the very last; and this they did while a mighty army lay round about them, and while they were distressed by famine and the want of necessaries, for this happened to be a Sabbatic year. (*Antiq* XIV 16:2)

Note that Herod built his bulwarks in the summer, and the main walls of the city largely capitulated at least several weeks or possibly months later. From this, it can be assumed that Jerusalem fell in the fall of 37 B.C. Josephus states that this happened during a Sabbatical year, and that in the final stages of the siege the Jewish defenders were famished. If the Sabbatical year began in the fall during the siege, then these soldiers would hardly be famished, because supplies would have been laid up in preparation. But if the Sabbatical year had started in the fall of the previous year, and the previous year's harvest had not been a particularly good one, the Jews certainly might be feeling the effects of food deprivation under a prolonged siege situation.

Josephus gives us more clues.

> At this time Herod, now he had got Jerusalem under his power, carried off all the royal ornaments, and spoiled the wealthy men of what they had gotten; and when, by these means, he had heaped together a great quantity of silver and gold, he gave it all to Antony, and his friends that were about him. He also slew forty-five of the principal men of Antigonus's party, and set guards at the gates of the city, that nothing might be carried out together with their dead bodies. They also searched the dead, and whatsoever was found, either of silver or gold, or other treasure, it was carried to the king; nor was there any end of the miseries he brought upon them; and this distress was in part occasioned by the covetousness of the prince regent, who was still in want of more, and in

part by the Sabbatic year which was still going on, and forced the country to lie still uncultivated, since we are forbidden to sow our land in that year. (*Antiq* XV 1:2)

Given all the problems Herod Antipas had with the religious leaders over his marriage to Herodias, it is unlikely that he would commit his Jewish army to fight any time during the Sabbatic year. The morale of Antipas' army was low enough as it was, so it would be doubtful that any of Antipas' soldiers really cared to fight for the honor of Herodias, their supposed queen. Characterizing Nabotea as an imminent threat to Perea was also a difficult sell to the troops. A greater carrot would have been the untold riches of Petra–which was on a major trading route to the far East. The soldiers could look forward to much plunder–a great motivator for fighting men of any era! But even so, religious law had to be obeyed and the invasion was put off.

That Antipas delayed his action for the Sabbatical year also supports the supposition that he was the aggressor. If Aretas had actually invaded Perea or Galilee, the Sabbatic year would not be an issue. Under circumstances of invasion, Jewish warriors were permitted to defend themselves and their country.

With these assumptions, Antipas could have started his campaign as early as the fall of A.D. 34, when the Sabbatical year had ended. But remember that even if the seeds were sown immediately, it would be still months before the first harvest would have been possible. Then would come the summer of A.D. 35, certainly a hot, uncomfortable time of year in Nabotea. Antipas, too, might have felt nervous about the invasion and grasped at any reason to delay it — he had little experience in war.

Based upon these reasons, it is postulated that Antipas moved back his invasion plans to the fall of A.D. 35, and that was when the battle was fought.

The Arrest of John the Baptist

Another important question is when Antipas arrested John the Baptist. John the Baptist was likely imprisoned for months before his actual beheading. While imprisoned, John's disciples were allowed to see him frequently, and John the Baptist himself was sending out letters and receiving them. In fact, Herod Antipas probably treated John the Baptist quite well.

The Book of Mark suggests that Antipas was very respectful of Jewish holy men–and true holy men of any stripe. Antipas would have arrested John the Baptist only when he had no other options. While John was loosely imprisoned in Macherus, Antipas visited and talked with him, and listened to his preachings, even as he prepared for war.

> Herod feared John, knowing that he was a righteous and holy man, and kept him safe. And when he heard him, he was much perplexed; and he heard him gladly.(Mk 6:21)

With this inherent respect, what made Antipas risk the wrath of God and–against his own instincts–have John arrested in the first place?

The Gospels lay much of the blame on Herodias' desire for revenge for all of John the Baptist's invectives against her over the years. Josephus, however, does not mention Herodias at all. According to Josephus, Antipas was fearful of the large crowds John was gathering and the possibility of sedition arising from them. The truth probably lies somewhere in between, but it should be noted that, if our postulated time line is accurate, Herodias had been Herod Antipas' wife for more than two years before Antipas finally had the prophet arrested. This would tend to support Josephus' interpretation where Herodias was a non-factor.

Other scenarios should be considered. Was it possible that John the Baptist was arrested in late A.D. 32, shortly after the marriage of Antipas and Herodias? Probably not. Remember that John kept to the wilds of Perea, far out of the way of the major population centers of Judea and Galilee. Antipas was also a seasoned ruler and knew his people well. Arresting the popular John would mean trouble no matter what the reason or circumstance. Antipas, an unusually tolerant man for those times, probably thought that the critical voice of John and others would fade over time as people lost interest and found something else to complain about. Indeed, the original furor over Herodias might well have been subsiding when his brother Philip died and Antipas failed to gain Philip's domain. Then, reassessing his own situation, and perhaps suspecting a liaison between Artabanus and Aretas, Antipas decided on a full-scale war with Nabotea — perhaps with encouragement from Tiberius.

In the months following his decision, Antipas built up his army through conscription and the hiring of mercenaries, and moved men and supplies from Galilee into southern Perea. The refurbishing and fortification of Macherus likely took many months to accomplish. Macherus was only a few miles southeast of the delta valley where the Jordan River emptied into Lake Asphaltitis. John the Baptist had his main camp at a place called Bethany Beyond the Jordan which was not far away. At the time, John was tremendously popular and the camp had grown into a settlement with perhaps hundreds or even thousands of permanent residents. Certainly, scores of pilgrims visited the camp daily to hear John preach and undergo John's trademark baptismal ritual.

When Antipas started massing his troops in southern Perea, his intentions were obvious. Religious critics from all over Judea, Galilee and Perea doubtlessly took aim at Herodias and Antipas with renewed vigor. John the Baptist was probably just one of many such critics, but unfortunately for John his base was far too close to the troops for Antipas to ignore him. What before had been a remote part of Perea was now near the center of a major military operation. Herod Antipas, as tolerant as he was of John the Baptist before, simply could not risk the sedition that John could potentially cause within his army.

So John was arrested and imprisoned in an empty cistern in the nearby fortress-palace of Macherus. Antipas gave instructions that the prophet was to be treated well and John was allowed visitors. The Book of Mark implies that Antipas sought council from the holy man and talked with him on more than one occasion. Perhaps John the Baptist was even allowed to walk about the lower city of Macherus under guard. After the war, it was quite likely that Antipas planned on releasing John to his freedom. In fact, Antipas might have personally promised John as much.

The Dance of Salome and the Death of a Prophet

In early A.D. 35, in the midst of preparing for war and far away from his idyllic palace in Tiberias, Antipas observed a birthday. Perhaps it was a significant one that would have merited attention even under ordinary circumstances. The date of Antipas' birth is speculative, but a reasonable assumption is that Antipas was born in 26 B.C. In A.D. 35, Antipas would be 60–a milestone year by any measure and certainly one worthy of high celebration.

Other reasons place this celebration in early A.D. 35. The Book of Mark states that with Antipas were "his lords, and the high captains, and the chief men of Galilee." But conspicuously absent from this birthday party was Herod Philip–Antipas' own brother. But by early A.D. 35, Herod Philip had died.

It has been postulated that Herodias' teenage daughter Salome married the Tetrarch Herod Philip shortly after arriving in Tiberias in the summer of A.D. 32. Salome was suddenly transformed from a young teenager into a powerful queen. However, at Antipas' birthday party, Salome dances seductively and wantonly in front of Antipas and his generals. This vulgar behavior hardly befitted someone in her Royal position. However, in early A.D. 35, Philip was not only dead, but had been entombed for over a year. With the mourning period for Philip officially over, the widowed Salome's drunken and unrestrained dance becomes a little less outrageous–and perhaps even understandable.

The A.D. 35 birthday party was only Antipas' second without Philip. Surely, Antipas missed his older brother tremendously, especially with such dangerous times ahead. Would Herodias, realizing this, strive to make this particular birthday celebration of Antipas' as special as possible?

Interlude: Herodias' Surprise

Now comes speculation of a more extreme nature. Herodias would have been acutely aware of Antipas' increasing sadness over many developments. Antipas was nearing 60 and feeling his own mortality with his advancing years. He was soon to face a formidable foe in Aretas and for the first time in his life his older brother Herod Philip would not be by his side. Pontius Pilate was not supporting him against Aretas, nor was Pomponius Flaccus. Herod Antipas was indeed on his own as much as he had ever been. And how much did the continuing unpopularity of Herodias with the common people continued to weigh upon him?

Depressed and moody, Antipas might have been spending most of his time in Macherus just to get out of Tiberias and be alone with his thoughts. It is a surety that Antipas let his generals oversee most of the preparations for war. In periods of self-doubt, perhaps during sleepless nights, did Antipas seek out counsel from John the Baptist, his famous prisoner, who was held only meters away in an empty cistern? The Book of Mark suggests that he did.

Herodias' daughter Salome was similarly in a bad way. Not only had she lost a husband in Herod Philip, but Emperor Tiberius had denied her Philip's kingdom–Salome had naively expected to inherit it. Was Salome forced out of her palace in Caesarea Philippi and back to Tiberias to live with her mother? Perhaps so. And whom would Salome marry now?! Herodias, in Tiberias with her widowed daughter, would be painfully aware of Salome's loneliness and depression.

Herodias came from Rome, where extravagant parties were commonplace for the wealthy and priviledged. She might have decided that a grand birthday celebration was just the thing to bolster the spirits of both Salome and Antipas. It is possible that Herodias, Salome, and their entourage, along with some of the principal men of Galilee, made a special trip south into Perea for just that reason. In fact, Antipas' Macherus birthday celebration might have been–as much as was possible–a surprise to the tetrarch.

Herodias had probably had never been to Macherus before. When she arrived at the mountain city after the four-day journey, how did she feel knowing that one of her chief tormentors, John the Baptist, was held prisoner close by? For over two years, she had tried to persuade Antipas to kill the man, but Antipas had refused even to have him arrested. After her arrival in Macherus, Herodias might have been additionally annoyed to discover that John the Baptist had been given the freedom to move about parts of the city at times, and was allowed visitors within his large cistern cell. Was he a prisoner or an honored guest?! When she arrived at Macherus, did the disciples of John who attended upon him look at Herodias with arrogance and scorn? How that must have grated on the proud woman!

The party itself was a tremendous success, with the military men happy to have the company of the female attendants Herodias and Salome had brought with them. The tension of the impending war was temporarily broken, and the wine flowed freely as the night wore on. Salome, too, was enjoying the attention she was receiving. When her mother was out of the room, she felt especially free, and the drunken military men, sensing her loneliness, urged her on to perform for them.

So the young widow Salome danced recklessly and provocatively in front of her stepfather and his generals. Antipas, intoxicated and with his depression lifting, was smitten by her. The radiant Salome was a younger copy of his love Herodias! After the dance, the overwhelmed and drunken Antipas promised Salome anything she wanted–even up to half his kingdom.

Salome, flushed with wine, the excitement of the occasion, the physical exhaustion of the dance, and the promise of wealth, breathlessly left the room. She quickly found Herodias and asked her what she should request from Antipas, for Salome probably never did anything without the approval of her mother. When Herodias heard of Antipas' promise, she sensed opportunity.

Herodias realized by then that Antipas had no intention of executing the hated John the Baptist.

So Salome was told what to ask for, and she obediently brought her mother's demand back to Antipas at the banquet table. Antipas was surprised–and even shocked–at Salome's request, as were those in attendance. Likely there was silence for several seconds as all eyes focused on Antipas. The head of John the Baptist! But Antipas realized he had no choice but to obey. Antipas had made the promise to Salome in front of his generals and he could not now back away from it.

John the Baptist was held in an empty cistern and during the evening could probably hear the music from the birthday celebration. Late in the dark night, the guards came into John's cell for the purpose of carrying out the order. John, in his last minutes of life, would have been stunned when he realized what his fate was to be. This was not what Antipas had promised! The execution was swiftly and efficiently carried out and head of John was presented to Salome and Herodias.

How dark a sentence should Herodias receive for her role in this affair? Given the circumstances, an even darker accusation could easily be made: that Herodias planned the surprise party only after learning that John was imprisoned in Macherus. Did she make the arduous trip to the remote desert outpost with the determined goal of somehow eliminating John the Baptist once and for all? And to that end, could it have been Herodias herself, and not the drunken revelers, who suggested to Salome that she dance for Antipas? Salome, after all, did nothing without her mother's approval! Was Antipas somehow maneuvered into promising Salome anything she desired, and so giving Herodias her chance to kill the hated John?

Or would that be an unfair speculation?!

Chapter 22   The Retreat of Jesus

^{6:1}After these things Jesus went away to the other side of the sea of Galilee which is *the sea* of Tiberias. (Jn)

From the previous chapters, we have determined that the death of the Tetrarch Herod Philip occurred in early A.D. 34. As for John the Baptist, he was likely arrested in mid-to-late A.D. 34. John's execution was some months later, in early A.D. 35 during Herod Antipas' 60th birthday celebration and before the Passover of that year. How do these newly derived dates correlate with the Ministry of Jesus?

The Gospel of John

In the Book of John, Jesus' ministry lasted for at least three Passovers. John the Baptist was alive and free after Jesus' first Passover which was the Passover where Jesus confronted the moneychangers. As John the Baptist was imprisoned at least before Jesus' second Passover, and possibly dead, the Book of John supports a date of A.D. 34 for Jesus' first Passover, and A.D. 36 for Jesus' third and final Passover.

The Gospel of Mark

According to Mark, after the beheading of John the Baptist by Antipas, Jesus retreats with his Disciples to a "desert place," where later 5,000 followers are miraculously fed from only a few loaves of bread. Afterward, Jesus has his Disciples get on a boat and instructs them to cross over to Bethsaida, while he "departed" into the mountains to pray.

> And straightway he constrained his disciples to enter into the boat, and to go before him unto the other side to Bethsaida, while he himself sendeth the multitude away. And after he had taken leave of them, he departed into the mountain to pray. (Mk 6:45-46)

All the "desert places" by Lake Gennesareth, then as now, are near its eastern shores. The village of Bethsaida is two kilometers away from the north shore of Lake Gennesareth and just to the east of the Jordan River. Bethsaida–also called Julias–was a city that the Tetrarch Herod Philip had reconstructed to serve as the place of his winter palace.

The Gospel of Luke

The Book of Luke also documents similar movements of Jesus after John the Baptist's execution.

> And Herod said, John I beheaded: but who is this, about whom I hear such things? And he sought to see him. And the apostles, when they were returned, declared unto him what things they had done. And he took them, and withdrew apart to a city called Bethsaida. (Lk 9:9-10)

The Gospel of Matthew

In the Book of Matthew, a passage also discusses the retreat of Jesus.

> 14:9 And the king was grieved; but for the sake of his oaths, and of them that sat at meat with him, he commanded it to be given; 14:10 and he sent and beheaded John in the prison. 14:11 And his head was brought on a platter, and given to the damsel: and she brought it to her mother. 14:12 And his disciples came, and took up the corpse, and buried him; and they went and told Jesus.
> 14:13 Now when Jesus heard it, he withdrew from thence in a boat, to a desert place apart: and when the multitudes heard thereof, they followed

him on foot from the cities. ^{14:14}And he came forth, and saw a great multitude, and he had compassion on them, and healed their sick. ^{14:15}And when even was come, the disciples came to him, saying, The place is desert, and the time is already past; send the multitudes away, that they may go into the villages, and buy themselves food. ^{14:16}But Jesus said unto them, They have no need to go away; give ye them to eat. ^{14:17}And they say unto him, We have here but five loaves, and two fishes. ^{14:18}And he said, Bring them hither to me. ^{14:19}And he commanded the multitudes to sit down on the grass; and he took the five loaves, and the two fishes, and looking up to heaven, he blessed, and brake and gave the loaves to the disciples, and the disciples to the multitudes. ^{14:20}And they all ate, and were filled: and they took up that which remained over of the broken pieces, twelve baskets full. ^{14:21}And they that did eat were about five thousand men, besides women and children. (Mt)

A specific city is not mentioned, but it is clear that after the beheading of John, Jesus retreats to a "desert" place–the eastern Gennesareth area–and then shortly thereafter the miracle of feeding the 5,000 occurs.

Sanctuary

The territories to where Jesus retreats after John's imprisonment and execution were either under the rule of the Decapolis, or, as was the case with Bethsaida, within the tetrarchy of Herod Philip. Later in the Book of Mark, after visiting Bethsaida, Jesus also travels to Tyre and Sidon. Though not a part of the Decapolis, these cities, too, enjoyed an independent status–and most importantly were not under the control of Herod Antipas (Mk 7:31).

Herod Antipas, educated in the cosmopolitan city of Rome, had previously been a fairly tolerant ruler. Now, the tetrarch was preparing in deadly earnest for a dangerous military excursion into Nabotea. If Jesus and his Disciples were surprised when John the Baptist was arrested by Antipas, they were absolutely stunned when the prophet was executed. The Jews thought John was the very voice of God–a prophet on the same order of an

Isaiah or Joel. Had Antipas gone mad like his father Herod the Great? Who would Antipas kill next?!

It can be speculated that, after learning of John the Baptist's death, Jesus, in a controlled panic, sought sanctuary in a place out of Antipas' grasp. Free from the threat of Antipas, there Jesus could rest and pray and wait for divine guidance as to his next move. Where could he find safety? Jesus went to the eastern regions of Lake Gennesareth and the city of Bethsaida. The Greek-Syrian Decapolis league controlled the eastern Gennesareth, so Jesus was naturally safe there. But what about Bethsaida–Herod Philip's city? Herod Philip was Antipas' brother after all. Surely, if Antipas wanted, Philip would have Jesus and his Disciples arrested!

But remember by that time Herod Philip was no longer alive. It would have been only after Philip's death that Bethsaida and the northeastern Gennesareth area could provide a safe haven for Jesus and his Disciples. The western half of the Gennesareth, of course, was controlled by Herod Antipas and remained a place of potential danger. In fact, Jesus took to traveling to the western sections of Lake Gennesareth by boat, so that he could easily escape from danger to the other side of the lake if need be.

Tiberius gave control of Philip's tetrarchy upon Philip's death to the president of Syria, who then was Pomponius Flaccus–and not to Antipas. Flaccus also controlled the cities and territories of the Decapolis. The Syrian president would have little reason to hunt Jesus down for the purpose of turning him over to Antipas and would have been even less interested in allowing Antipas' men to enter his territory for the same purpose. Religious squabbles were adjudicated by the Sanhedrin and Rome paid little attention to them.

The Book of John Revisited

It has been concluded that John the Baptist was executed in early A.D. 35 and before the Passover of that year. This precipitated the retreat of Jesus from not only Judea but Galilee as well. The Book of John, however, does not mention specifically the movement of Jesus after the execution of John, as the three Synoptic Gospels do. The Book of John does refer, though, to the miracle of the feeding of the 5,000 which provides a link to the events in the other Gospels.

> [6:1]After these things Jesus went away to the other side of the sea of Galilee which is *the sea* of Tiberias. [6:2]And a great multitude followed him, because they beheld the signs which he did on them that were sick. [6:3]And Jesus went up into the mountain, and there he sat with his disciples. [6:4]Now the passover, the feast of the Jews, was at hand. [6:5]Jesus therefore lifting up his eyes, and seeing that a great multitude cometh unto him, saith unto Philip, Whence are we to buy bread, that these may eat? (Jn)

Note that the feeding of the 5,000 occurred approximately the same time as the Passover Jesus celebrated in Galilee which has been determined to be a year before Jesus' final Passover in Jerusalem. From the Book of Matthew, it is clear that the feeding of the 5,000 occurred after John's beheading. Melding these events together, it can reasonably be assumed that this Galilean Passover occurred after the execution of John the Baptist in A.D. 35.

Conclusion

The arrest of John the Baptist occurred after the death of Herod Philip and after the Passover of A.D. 34–probably in late A.D. 34. Salome's dance and John the Baptist's execution occurred in early A.D. 35 and before the Passover of that year. It can be reasonably concluded that the Passover of A.D. 35 was celebrated by Jesus in the hills east of Lake Gennesareth. Concerning the battle between Antipas and King Aretas, the actual campaign into Nabotea, initiated by Antipas, would have been in the early fall of A.D. 35.

The evidence is pointing toward a final Passover year of A.D. 36, but there are still more factors to consider.

Chapter 23   Pontius Pilate

And Pilate said unto the chief priests and the multitudes, I find no   fault in this man. (Lk 23:4)

Pontius Pilate served as the prefect of Judea under Emperor Tiberius for the years A.D. 26-37. Pilate had the "power of Caesar," which meant he could sentence men to death if he so decided. Pilate was also responsible for tax collections in his territory and served as the senior Roman military officer in the Jewish East, with an auxiliary force of soldiers under his command.

Pilate had more power than most prefects in the empire simply because Tiberius never bothered to appoint a functional president of Syria, Pilate's natural superior, for most of his tenure. The elder General Aelius Lamia was the supposed legate of Syria, but he spent all his time in Italy. Lamia was replaced by General Lucius Vitellius only in A.D. 35. It is thought that Pilate, during his early years as prefect of Judea, reported directly to Rome's Praetorian guard general and erstwhile conspirator Lucius Sejanus.

Pontius Pilate held the power as prefect in the East for almost 11 years and is infamous for condemning Jesus of Nazareth to crucifixion. The New Testament portrays Pilate as Jesus' reluctant executioner. This, however, might have not have been completely accurate.

Jewish Historian Philo Judaeus was a contemporary of Pontius Pilate. He writes:

(Pilate) was.. of a very inflexible disposition, and very merciless as well as very obstinate.. at all times a man of most ferocious passions," (Philo *Embassy* 301, 303)

(Pilate was known for his)...corruption, and his acts of insolence, and his rapine, and his habit of insulting people, and his cruelty, and his continual murders of people untried and uncondemned, and his never ending, and gratuitous, and most grievous inhumanity..(Ibid 302)

This is a considerable condemnation, especially since Philo had no Christian bias and quite possibly had met Pilate personally. Philo's invective against Pilate stands in contrast to his frank admiration for Emperor Tiberius.

Tiberius..was as pre-eminent in intelligence and acuteness as he was in good fortune, (Philo *Embassy* VI 33)

Certainly Pilate was a corrupt man by today's standards, but in the ancient Roman foreign service graft and bribery were an accepted way of provincial administration. Corruption of even the most honest and well-intentioned of prefects was inevitable; the only question was the degree of compromise. Cruelty was also the expected norm, for a prefect had to be brutal and preemptive when it came to matters of potential insurrection–in fact, the survival of the empire demanded it.

Profits from criminal activity were an expected revenue source and pursued openly. In fact, most high Roman officials in the provinces became wealthy during their years of public service. At times, a loyal Roman bureaucrat of limited means would be given a plum position simply in order to support his retirement with minimal effort.

In contrast to Philo, according to the Gospels Pilate was reluctant to condemn Jesus, even showing a sensitive and philosophic side during the "trial" of the Nazarene. If Pilate was the bloodthirsty brute that Philo describes, then why should he care? Or was Pilate feigning a reluctance to convict Jesus just to irritate the arrogant High Priesthood?

Apart from the New Testament and Philo, Pilate is also mentioned in the works of Tacitus and Josephus. Tacitus makes only a brief reference to Pilate in a passage about the early Christians, as was discussed earlier. Flavius Josephus, however, mentions Pontius Pilate several times.

The Appointment of Pilate

Pontius Pilate was appointed governor of Judea and Samaria, which included Jerusalem, in A.D. 26. Pilate's first Passover as prefect was in A.D. 27. Pilate served in his high post for a little more than 10 years, until he was removed by Syrian President Lucius Vitellius a few months–perhaps only weeks–before the Passover of A.D. 37.

At the time of Pilate's appointment in A.D. 26, Emperor Tiberius had decided, perhaps encouraged by Sejanus, to retire from Rome completely and live on the island of Capri. During this introspective period, Tiberius had unwisely left much of the running of the empire to Sejanus, who, sensing opportunity, was quietly appointing men loyal to him to positions of power. Pilate could well have been Sejanus' choice for prefect; in fact, Pilate might possibly have been an unproscripted Sejanus co-conspirator.

Little is known about Pilate's earlier life except he had been one of Tiberius' lieutenants in the Imperial guard–possibly on his personal staff–and was of the equestrian class, a rank just below that of the senators. Equestrians were used extensively for foreign service and were considered trustworthy enough for the handling of public money.

> ...the equestrian order, as it was styled, ..(was)..esteemed by the citizens equal in dignity and wealth with the senators, because out of them the senators were themselves chosen; (*Antiq* XIX 1:1)

Pilate had the standard military training of the day given to all those serving close to the emperor and those selected for duty in troublesome provinces. He was also a married man, according to the Book of Matthew. In Matthew, when Jesus was brought before him for judgment, Pilate's wife had a bad dream the night previously and warned Pilate not to harm this "righteous" man (Mt 27:19).

Josephus and Philo present several stories about the Prefect Pontius Pilate to consider. Both concern Pilate's challenging of the religious beliefs of the Jews.

Caesar's Effigies

Flavius Josephus wrote *Antiquities* about fifty years after Philo wrote *Embassy to Caius*.

> But now Pilate, the procurator of Judea, removed the army from Cesarea to Jerusalem, to take their winter quarters there, in order to abolish the Jewish laws. So he introduced Caesar's effigies which were upon the ensigns, and brought them into the city; whereas our law forbids us the very making of images; on which account the former procurators were wont to make their entry into the city with such ensigns as had not those ornaments. Pilate was the first who brought those images to Jerusalem, and set them up there; which was done without the knowledge of the people, because it was done in the night time; but as soon as they knew it, they came in multitudes to Cesarea, and interceded with Pilate many days that he would remove the images; and when he would not grant their requests, because it would tend to the injury of Caesar, while yet they persevered in their request, on the sixth day he ordered his soldiers to have their weapons privately, while he came and sat upon his judgment-seat which seat was so prepared in the open place of the city, that it concealed the army that lay ready to oppress them; and when the Jews petitioned him again, he gave a signal to the soldiers to encompass them routed, and threatened that their punishment should be no less than immediate death, unless they would leave off disturbing him, and go their ways home. But they threw themselves upon the ground, and laid their necks bare, and said they would take their death very willingly, rather than the wisdom of their laws should be transgressed; upon which Pilate was deeply affected with their firm resolution to keep their laws inviolable, and presently commanded the images to be carried back from Jerusalem to Cesarea. (*Antiq* XVIII 3:1)

The same incident was described in *Wars* which was written by Josephus 15 years earlier.

> Now Pilate, who was sent as procurator into Judea by Tiberius, sent by night those images of Caesar that are called ensigns into Jerusalem. This

excited a very among great tumult among the Jews when it was day; for those that were near them were astonished at the sight of them, as indications that their laws were trodden under foot; for those laws do not permit any sort of image to be brought into the city. Nay, besides the indignation which the citizens had themselves at this procedure, a vast number of people came running out of the country. These came zealously to Pilate to Cesarea, and besought him to carry those ensigns out of Jerusalem, and to preserve them their ancient laws inviolable; but upon Pilate's denial of their request, they fell down prostrate upon the ground, and continued immovable in that posture for five days and as many nights.

On the next day Pilate sat upon his tribunal, in the open market-place, and called to him the multitude, as desirous to give them an answer; and then gave a signal to the soldiers, that they should all by agreement at once encompass the Jews with their weapons; so the band of soldiers stood round about the Jews in three ranks. The Jews were under the utmost consternation at that unexpected sight. Pilate also said to them that they should be cut in pieces, unless they would admit of Caesar's images, and gave intimation to the soldiers to draw their naked swords. Hereupon the Jews, as it were at one signal, fell down in vast numbers together, and exposed their necks bare, and cried out that they were sooner ready to be slain, than that their law should be transgressed. Hereupon Pilate was greatly surprised at their prodigious superstition, and gave order that the ensigns should be presently carried out of Jerusalem. (*Wars* II 9:2-3)

In Eusebius' *History*, the first paragraph of the *Wars'* selection concerning the Roman ensigns is translated from a copy more than 500 years older than today's generally accepted reference copy.

> As procurator of Judaea Tiberius sent Pilate, who during the night, secretly and under cover, conveyed to Jerusalem the images of Caesar known as signa. When day dawned this put the Jews into a frenzy; for those who were near were amazed at the sight which meant that their laws had been trampled on–they do not permit any portrait-image to be set up in the city, (Eusebius *History* Book II–*Wars* II 9:2)

In this narrative, the troops of Pilate's legion bring effigies (small statues) of Caesar into the city of Jerusalem as a part of their military regalia. These effigies were probably set upon posts and were carried in the front of the legion when on the march and then set on display at the entrance to whatever camp the legion had constructed.

The Jews thought any artificial representation of a natural living form to be a challenge to the perfection of God and so was sacrilegious. The Jews were desperately alarmed at this desecration and went in "multitudes" to Caesarea to petition for the removal of these ensigns. Pilate initially threatened to kill them all, but then seeing their readiness to die for their beliefs thought the better of it. Pilate then orders the effigies removed from Jerusalem and sent back to Caesarea.

Note here the mention of the "judgment seat." This was a special chair, probably large and ornately decorated, that would accompany Pilate wherever he went. It was a symbol of his office and of Roman power. If there was a conflict that needed adjudication, the chair would be set up, Pilate would sit upon it, and a trial would commence. This would likely have been the same "tribunal" chair that Pilate brought to Jerusalem and used for the trial of Jesus years later.

It is also worth noting that in the effigy incident the principal men of Jerusalem did not write directly to either Emperor Tiberius or to the Syrian president to complain about Pilate. Instead, thousands of Jews traveled to Caesarea in an organized protest to Pilate himself, risking his wrath and their own executions. Pilate, however, wisely backed down, not wishing to slay any Jews over such a matter. This would indicate that the effigy affair occurred relatively early in Pilate's tenure, when Pilate was perhaps less confident in his position.

There were probably several more instances–albeit less dramatic–wherein Pilate slyly or overtly challenged the religious beliefs of what he and most Romans thought was a peculiar and troublesome nation of people. It can be speculated that the effigies brought into Jerusalem by the Roman soldiers was perhaps the first major incident that Pilate intentionally orchestrated to provoke the Jews. Josephus tells us that Pilate's goal was to "abolish the Jewish laws"–suggesting Pilate was fresh in his position and did not fully appreciate the nature of the Jewish culture or the obstinacy of the Jewish people.

Gold Shields

Pilate proceeded to rule over Judea in the usual corrupt manner of the times for many years. It can be assumed that Pilate bled the country as much as possible for his own monetary benefit, as well as irritating the people with minor malicious actions whenever possible. Another episode soon arose where Pilate again transgressed the laws of the Jewish nation, this time documented by Philo in *Embassy to Caius*-one of Philo's last works.

"Pilate was one of the emperor's lieutenants, having been appointed governor of Judaea. He, not more with the object of doing honour to Tiberius than with that of vexing the multitude, dedicated some gilt shields in the palace of Herod, in the holy city; which had no form nor any other forbidden thing represented on them except some necessary inscription which mentioned these two facts, the name of the person who had placed them there, and the person in whose honour they were so placed there. But when the multitude heard what had been done, and when the circumstance became notorious, then the people, putting forward the four sons of the king, who were in no respect inferior to the kings themselves, in fortune or in rank, and his other descendants, and those magistrates who were among them at the time, entreated him to alter and to rectify the innovation which he had committed in respect of the shields; and not to make any alteration in their national customs which had hitherto been preserved without any interruption, without being in the least degree changed by any king of emperor. "But when he steadfastly refused this petition (for he was a man of a very inflexible disposition, and very merciless as well as very obstinate), they cried out: 'Do not cause a sedition; do not make war upon us; do not destroy the peace which exists. The honour of the emperor is not identical with dishonour to the ancient laws; let it not be to you a pretence for heaping insult on our nation. Tiberius is not desirous that any of our laws or customs shall be destroyed. And if you yourself say that he is, show us either some command from him, or some letter, or something of the kind, that we, who have been sent to you as ambassadors, may cease to trouble you, and may address our supplications to your master.' "But this last sentence exasperated him in the greatest possible degree, as he feared least they might in reality go on an embassy to the emperor, and might impeach him with respect to other particulars of his government, in respect of his corruption, and his acts of insolence, and his rapine, and his habit of insulting people, and his cruelty, and his continual murders of people untried and uncondemned, and his never ending, and gratuitous, and most grievous inhumanity. Therefore, being exceedingly angry, and being at all times a man of most ferocious passions, he was in great perplexity, neither venturing to take down what he had once set up, nor wishing to do any thing which could be acceptable to his subjects, and at the same time being sufficiently acquainted with the firmness of Tiberius on these points. And those who were in power in our nation, seeing this, and perceiving that he was inclined to change his mind as to what he had done, but that he was not willing to be thought to do so, wrote a most supplicatory letter to Tiberius. And he, when he had read it, what did he say of Pilate, and what threats did he utter against him! But it is beside our purpose at present to relate to you how very angry he was, although he was not very liable to sudden anger; since the facts speak for themselves; for immediately, without putting any thing off till the next day, he wrote a letter, reproaching and reviling him in the most bitter manner for his act of unprecedented audacity and wickedness, and commanding him immediately to take down the shields and to convey them away from the metropolis of Judaea to Caesarea, on the sea which had been named Caesarea Augusta, after his grandfather, in order that they might be set up in the temple of Augustus. And accordingly, they were set up in that edifice. And in this way he provided for two matters: both for the honour due to the emperor, and for the preservation of the ancient customs of the city. (Philo, *Embassy*, 299-305)

Herod the Great in about 25 B.C. had built a walled 15-acre palace complex in the upper city of Jerusalem with three towers, two apartments, and lavishly detailed grounds and gardens. The different Roman prefects or procurators would stay there when on business in the city. Pilate placed several golden battle shields in one of the palace buildings. On these shields were inscriptions which included the names of those to whom the shields were dedicated and the names of those who had ordered the shields made.

The principal men of Jerusalem, however, asked Pilate to remove them, since even the writing of the names of men in the holy city was against Jewish law. But Pilate refused. The principal men then threatened to petition Tiberius directly to have them removed, but Pilate still did not back down.

True to their word, a letter was sent from the principal Jews to Tiberius. According to Philo, Tiberius became very angry when he read it and immediately sent a letter to Pilate. He ordered that the shields be removed from Herod's palace and sent to Caesarea to be set up in the temple of Augustus—a politic solution to a thorny problem.

Pilate instigated the incident well after the effigy affair. Why this conclusion? In the gilt shields incident, the principal men of Jerusalem now knew the nature of Pilate and realized that a personal plea to the prefect would not work. Their only option was to petition Tiberius directly for relief.

The Aqueduct

In *Antiquities*, Josephus relates another story about Pontius Pilate. This time, the prefect sought to build a 30-mile long freshwater aqueduct to serve Jerusalem. To fund the hugely expensive project, Pilate planned on using the Corban, or the holy money, that was stored in the inner Sanctuary building of the Second Temple complex. This store of sanctified money which was given by pilgrims to the priests of the Second Temple, was to be used only for religious purposes. The Jerusalem Jews when they found out about it protested vociferously. Pilate eventually had to abandon the aqueduct project, but not before he had his soldiers pommeled to death many of the more virulent demonstrators that had gathered to protest in Jerusalem.

> But Pilate undertook to bring a current of water to Jerusalem, and did it with the sacred money, and derived the origin of the stream from the distance of two hundred furlongs. However, the Jews were not pleased with what had been done about this water; and many ten thousands of the people got together, and made a clamor against him, and insisted that he should leave off that design. Some of them also used reproaches, and abused the man, as crowds of such people usually do. So he habited a great number of his soldiers in their habit, who carried daggers under their garments, and sent them to a place where they might surround them. So he bid the Jews himself go away; but they boldly casting reproaches upon him, he gave the soldiers that signal which had been beforehand agreed on; who laid upon them much greater blows than Pilate had commanded them, and equally punished those that were tumultuous, and those that were not; nor did they spare them in the least: and since the people were unarmed, and were caught by men prepared for what they were about, there were a great number of them

slain by this means, and others of them ran away wounded. And thus an end was put to this sedition. (*Antiq* XVIII 3:2)

In *Wars*, the same story is told slightly differently.

> After this he raised another disturbance, by expending that sacred treasure which is called Corban upon aqueducts, whereby he brought water from the distance of four hundred furlongs. At this the multitude had indignation; and when Pilate was come to Jerusalem, they came about his tribunal, and made a clamor at it. Now when he was apprized aforehand of this disturbance, he mixed his own soldiers in their armor with the multitude, and ordered them to conceal themselves under the habits of private men, and not indeed to use their swords, but with their staves to beat those that made the clamor. He then gave the signal from his tribunal [to do as he had bidden them]. Now the Jews were so sadly beaten, that many of them perished by the stripes they received, and many of them perished as trodden to death by themselves; by which means the multitude was astonished at the calamity of those that were slain, and held their peace. (*Wars* II 9:4)

For comparison, reproduced is the same *Wars* selection, translated from Eusebius' older reference copy.

> After this he (Pilate) stirred up further trouble by expending the sacred treasure known as Corban on an aqueduct thirty-five miles long. This roused the populace to fury, and when Pilate visited Jerusalem they surrounded the tribunal and shouted him down. But he had foreseen this disturbance, and had made the soldiers mix with the mob, wearing civilian clothing over their armour, and with orders not to draw their swords but to use clubs on the obstreperous. He now gave the signal from the tribunal and the Jews were cudgelled, so that many died from the blows, and many as they fled were trampled to death by their friends. The fate of those who perished horrified the crowd into silence. (Eusebius *History* Book II 6- *Wars* II 9:4)

In this selection, Pilate again assumes his position of authority on his tribunal chair. This time, however, he is in Jerusalem. It is probable that Pilate set the chair up in the same area, Gabbatha, where Jesus was to face trial. Gabbatha was a public area just outside the walls of the old Herod palace–where Pilate stayed when he was in Jerusalem.

Also of interest, note that in *Wars*, the distance of the aqueduct is 400 furlongs, while in *Antiquities* the distance is 200 furlongs. In the Eusebius copy, the distance has been conveniently translated into standard distances–35 miles. Given accepted distances for the mile and 700 feet for the length of a furlong, Eusebius translates the length of the aqueduct to be 250 furlongs–approximately the average of the two distances given in *Antiquities* and *Wars*.

With his aqueduct project, it can be seen that Pilate has changed somewhat from his former confrontational self, despite the ultimately bad outcome. No longer is Pilate a malicious challenger of the Jewish faith but a public official working for Jerusalem civic improvements. What could be more beneficial for Jerusalem than added supplies of fresh water?

No one at the time could argue that Jerusalem didn't need a better water supply. The existing Gihon spring and cistern system had a limited capacity, and the city population was growing. Pilate himself lived in Caesarea, a beautiful city that already had two aqueducts bringing in fresh water from miles away. The Caesarea aqueduct system had been built by Herod the Great 50 years before, and had been crucial in transforming Caesarea from a dusty port town into a cosmopolitan city. Pilate knew similar system could likewise benefit Jerusalem, making it a cleaner and more livable place for the Jews. But why did Pilate, by all accounts a cruel and merciless administrator, care one way or another?

Pilate Reinvented

One explanation is that Pilate thought up the plan after the conspiracy of Lucius Sejanus was exposed and Sejanus himself executed. Sejanus was no friend of the Jews and as long as Sejanus was in power, Pilate, too, paid scant attention to Jewish concerns and well-being. After the unexpected removal of Sejanus in late A.D. 31, Pilate might have been fearful of losing his position–and possibly his life–in the proscriptions that followed. But to Pilate's relief, although hundreds if not thousands of citizens in Rome were condemned as conspirators and executed, none of the governors or prefects were impugned. Pilate retained his position–and his life.

But clearly Pilate had been Sejanus' man and Pilate might have realized that his exoneration was more indicative of Tiberius' conciliatory nature rather than Tiberius' belief in Pilate's innocence. It is also possible that, as postulated in the case of the Tetrarch Herod Antipas, Pilate had traveled to Capri personally to profess his loyalty to the emperor after Sejanus' execution. Tiberius was impressed enough with the gesture to keep him on.

A passage from Philo, previously quoted in the chapter on Tiberius, will be repeated.

> Therefore, all people in every country, even if they were not naturally well inclined towards the Jewish nation, took great care not to violate or attack any of the Jewish customs of laws. And in the reign of Tiberius things went on in the same manner, although at that time things in Italy were thrown into a great deal of confusion when Sejanus was preparing to make his attempt against our nation; for he knew immediately after his death that the accusations which had been brought against the Jews who were dwelling in Rome were false calumnies, inventions of Sejanus, who was desirous to destroy our nation which he knew alone, or above all others, was likely to oppose his unholy counsels and actions in defence of the emperor, who was in great danger of being attacked, in violation of all treaties and of all honesty. And he sent commands to all the governors of provinces in every country to comfort those of our nation in their respective cities, as the punishment intended to be inflicted was not meant to be inflicted upon all, but only on the guilty; and they were but few. And he ordered them to change none of the existing customs, but to look upon them as pledges, since the men were peaceful in their dispositions and natural characters, and their laws trained them and disposed them to quiet and stability. (Philo *Embassy* 159-161)

Tiberius' edict in A.D. 32 instructing the governors in all the provinces to respect the rights and religions of their peace-loving peoples–the Jews in particular–was likely aimed at Pilate. How many letters protesting one or another of Pilate's actions against the Jews then existed in the Royal archive in Rome? Two thousand years later, at least two are known. How many more petitions were not deemed important enough for Philo,

Josephus, or the authors of the New Testament Books to document?!

Without Sejanus to excuse or cover-up Pilate's behavior, and with Tiberius scrutinizing all of his provincial governors after the conspiracy, how close was Tiberius to removing Pilate? Tiberius likely at least cast a cool eye across the sea at Pilate, but in the end he was willing to give Pilate the proverbial "one last chance."

At any rate, Pilate escaped the Sejanus proscriptions with his power and position intact, and with the presumed tepid support of Tiberius. An intelligent man who probably had further political ambitions, Pilate reconsidered his position on the Jews , and perhaps attempted to "reinvent" himself in the mold of a concerned public official.

By A.D. 32, after six years in the East, Pilate had become quite rich through bribes, kickbacks, and other criminal schemes. In all likelihood, Ananus and the High Priesthood were funneling money directly to Pilate one way or another with the tacit understanding that he not interfere with their lucrative Temple operation. Merchants moving goods through Caesarea would likewise give Pilate monetary consideration for expeditious and favorable treatment. Perhaps Pilate got a cut in organized criminal enterprises in Judea as well; later Judean prefects certainly did. At the time of Sejanus' execution, Pilate was probably just beginning to feel comfortable in the Jewish East. Pilate was understanding how the game was played — he liked it and was profiting by it.

But after Sejanus was gone, circumstances changed considerably. Pilate had to feel politically vulnerable. It was not Sejanus but Tiberius whom Pilate now had to impress. Tiberius had issued a proclamation protecting the Jews' right to exist and practice their religion. Pilate knew he had many black marks against him in the Royal archive from angry Jews. The aqueduct project was a to make amends and preserve his position

The Corban

The Corban was secured in the Temple Sanctuary building of
the of the Second Temple complex. It was watched over and
accounted for by a specially appointed priest. Josephus writes
that Pilate was planning on seizing the money with the intent to
use it to fund the expensive water project. That, however, might
not have been totally correct.

Pilate had to know that confiscating the Corban would mean
immediate violence if not outright war within Judea. But the
whole point of the aqueduct project was to engender goodwill
between Rome and the Jewish people. What sense would it make
to start the project off with an inexcusable action against the
Temple?

It can be speculated that Pilate actually had the tacit approval
of the powerful Jewish High Priesthood for the temporary use of
the money. Perhaps this was an "inside deal" that only Ananus,
Caiaphas, the Temple treasurer, and a few other select priests
would know about. In exchange for their contribution, Pilate
might have promised the priests the construction of a separate
aqueduct supplying freshwater to the high plateau of the Second
Temple and the tower of Antonia. Another dedicated branch
might have been planned to serve the Jerusalem upper city
residential neighborhood of the High Priesthood.

Was this a proper use of the Corban? Ananus might have
thought so. It was, after all, to be used for the ultimate glory of
God's own house. The High Priest might have had great plans to
beautify the 35-acre Second Temple courtyards with the added
water supply. Pools could be constructed and additional ritual
baths set in place around the outside of the Temple. Subterranean
sewers as well could be put in place in order to take the effluent
away from the Temple complex. The sacrificing of animals had
to be an extraordinarily messy business; an efficient sewer
system could help mitigate that problem. Ananus also knew that
from the added revenues from water use fees the Corban would
be replaced in time.

But perhaps the zealots, when they inadvertently heard of the plan, dismissed the positive aspects of it and took the opportunity to inflame the common people with lies and innuendo. Pilate was going to steal the Corban! There was never to be a water project! It was a plot against the Jews! The priests, surprised at the public outcry, would have quickly withdrawn their support for Pilate's plan.

For these reasons, the aqueduct incident likely occurred after the death of Sejanus. Assuming that Pilate conceived of the project after Sejanus was executed in late A.D. 31, and that it took time for the Roman engineers to make the initial rough cost estimates and come up with a design, a date of late A.D. 33 or early A.D. 34 for the aqueduct "rebellion" is not unreasonable.

It can be certain, however, that Tiberius, or at least the president of Syria Pomponius Flaccus, knew about the violent deaths that had occurred as a result of the aqueduct incident and strongly disapproved of it. Very possibly, Tiberius reprimanded Pilate privately through a letter, coming ever closer to removing the equestrian from office. But the one incident that did result in the removal of Pilate in A.D. 37–the slaying of hundreds of Samaritan Jews–occurred after the crucifixion of Jesus.

Conclusion

In this chapter, we have found that nothing documented about the Judean Prefect Pontius Pilate that is at odds with an A.D. 36 crucifixion year. But there is one last obstacle. If Caiaphas was removed as High Priest in A.D. 35, as Josephus apparently suggests, then A.D. 36 as the year of Jesus' final Passover would be untenable. But was that really the case? To that end, and to bring our quest to a conclusion, there is one last character in the crucifixion drama that needs to be studied.

Chapter 24   Syrian President Lucius Vitellius

> Lucius (Vitellius) attained the consulate and then was made governor of Syria...Later he held, with the emperor Claudius, two more regular consulships and the censorship. He also bore the charge of the empire while Claudius was away on his expedition to Britain. He was an honest and active man... (Suetonius *Vitellius* 2)

Lucius Vitellius had a comfortable life in Capri as a minor confidante of Emperor Tiberius when, in late A.D. 31, the conspiracy of Sejanus was unmasked. In the proscriptions that followed, Tiberius purged suspected traitors from his administration with a vengeance. To replace them, Tiberius brought in people like Vitellius–men whose qualifications for office were slight, but whose loyalty was unquestioned. Indeed, if Lucius Vitellius had been an ambitious man, he would have years before abandoned the aging Tiberius to throw his lot in with the rising star of the dynamic and charismatic Sejanus. It was to Tiberius' great good fortune–and Rome's–that Vitellius did not.

Born in 5 B.C., Lucius Vitellius was the youngest of four sons. His father, Publius, was a Roman equestrian who had served honorably as the steward of Emperor Augustus' considerable store of private property. It was perhaps from his father that Vitellius learned the art of Royal subservience. That politic skill served Vitellius well under three Roman emperors and brought him to the heights of power. In fact, the son of Lucius Vitellius, Aulus, was emperor of Rome for a brief eight-month period–this after the chaos that followed Emperor Nero's forced suicide in A.D. 68. Lucius Vitellius, however, did not live to see his son reign as emperor, dying in A.D. 51.

The Family of Vitellius

Suetonius reports uncertainty concerning the Vitellian forebears (Sue *Vitellius* 1, 2-1). Some sources have the family coming from honored stock, others state they arose from commoners–borderline criminals and strumpets, no less. But there was no controversy concerning the patriarch Publius. He was a loyal aid that the Augustus trusted implicitly and rose to a position of great power as Augustus gained the empire. Publius had three other sons besides Lucius — Aulus, Publius, and Quintus.

Aulus achieved the rank of Senate co-consul along with Domitian, the father of the future emperor Nero. Aulus was given over to luxurious living and feasting, but was apparently a commendable public servant. He died as consul in A.D. 32. Aulus' death was suspicious, as it occurred during the early proscriptions of Sejanus. From an honored family, he might have killed himself to preserve the family name. But Lucius' older brother, Publius, was definitely kinked to Sejanus. Publius committed suicide in prison as a suspected conspirator in late A.D. 31. The third other son, Quintus, achieved the rank of senator, but Tiberius stripped him of that honor–along with several other senators–for not being worthy of it (Ibid 2-2).

Assignment in Asia

Lucius Vitellius was given great responsibility by Tiberius after the Sejanus conspiracy — the treachery of Publius and possibly Aulus notwithstanding. In high office, Vitellius' capabilities as an administrator and political strategist soon became apparent. Within two years, Lucius was appointed to the top of the Roman bureaucratic hierarchy, becoming Senate co-consul in A.D. 34 at the age of 38.

At that time, the Parthian Empire was beginning to make threatening moves in Armenia, perceiving Tiberius to be weak and the eastern Roman Empire ripe for the taking. Interestingly, King Artabanus of Parthia had been a great admirer of

Germanicus, with whom he had forged an alliance 15 years before. Artabanus suspected Tiberius of killing Germanicus and hated him for it.

To help plan countermeasures, Tiberius turned to Lucius Vitellius. In A.D. 35, Vitellius was elevated from consul and appointed to the second most powerful post in the Roman Empire–the governorship of Syria. Vitellius would assume command of Syria's four Roman legions in Antioch. He replaced Pomponius Flaccus, who had died in office in late A.D. 34. To be fair, Vitellius was not Tiberius' first choice–several other candidates refused the office when offered.

This situation Tiberius faced in Asia was a difficult one. In A.D. 34, Artabanus had put his son Arsaces on the throne of Armenia, effectively seizing control of a country which historically had been a Roman client kingdom. Furthermore, Artabanus was making public comments that all of the eastern Mediterranean should be Parthian by historic right. Tiberius had little choice; Artabanus had to be neutralized by any means possible. A negotiated peace was always preferable, but if it took the instigation of a Parthian revolution–or, barring that, an outright Roman invasion of the empire–General Lucius Vitellius would have Tiberius' full backing.

The uncertainty in Asia reverberated south into the Jewish lands. Did the Tetrarch Herod Antipas look northward and, seeing the Parthian aggression, start making plans to preserve his own kingdom if Rome was defeated by Artabanus and his sons? Did Antipas fear that Artabanus had allied Parthia with Nabotea and his new nemesis, King Aretas IV?

Certainly, Jewish zealots saw the hand of God at work as the Roman stranglehold on the East was apparently weakening. Did this herald the creation of a new Jewish nation–or even coming of the Messiah?!

Armenia

The kingdom of Armenia was a rough and mountainous country, lying just to the north and east of Syria. A century before, the Roman General Gnaeus Pompey had set up Armenia as a "buffer" kingdom between the Roman and Parthian empires. The Euphrates River was the official boundary between the empires, but the large mountainous country of Armenia where the Euphrates originated was located to the north of both of them. South of the Black Sea, Armenia included much of present-day eastern Turkey.

> (Armenia) had been of old an unsettled country from the character of its people and from its geographical position, bordering, as it does, to a great extent on our provinces and stretching far away to Media. It lies between two most mighty empires, and is very often at strife with them, hating Rome and jealous of Parthia. (*Annuls* 2:56)

Politically, Armenia was dominated by several tribes, each with its own chieftain and each with variable levels of allegiance to the recognized Armenian king. The Armenians were known for their expertise in horsemanship–as would be expected in a mountainous country. In war, the Armenian cavalry was especially effective.

The Parthian Empire

The Parthian Empire stretched from the Euphrates River eastward more than 1,000 miles to India, and from the Caspian Sea in the north 700 miles southward to the Persian Gulf and the Arabian Sea. The western territories of Parthia bordered Syria for 100 miles, and, directly south of Syria, bordered the Arabic country of Nabotea for an additional 250 miles. The Parthian Empire itself was made up of a score or so of separate states ruled over by wealthy aristocratic families. The ancient Parthian Empire had been considerably larger at one time and it had included much of Asia Minor now under the control of Rome.

While the Parthian king led his own army and lived in luxury in the capital city of Seleucia, in reality he served at the pleasure of the Parthian nobles. These nobles were the leaders of wealthy families that controlled the economic lifeblood of the Parthian Empire. The nobles also had their own large standing armies and owned vast amounts of land. When Artabanus made his aggressive intentions known, some of these nobles thought that he had overstepped his authority. The last thing most nobles wanted, especially those who lived in the western states, was a war with the Roman Empire. Many of these nobles had, in fact, grown rich trading with the eastern Roman provinces and client kingdoms.

The Rise of Artabanus

Phraates IV had ruled the Parthian empire unchallenged for 35 years. In 37 B.C., his father, Orodes II, voluntarily relinquished the throne in favor of his son. Seizing the moment, and perhaps in emulation of neighboring King Herod the Great, who might have been guilty of patricide, the ruthless Phraates immediately put his father to death and killed all of his brothers and their families as well. In those violent times, the surest way to retain power was to eliminate all possible rivals.

After the death of Phraates IV in 2 B.C., the Parthian nobles requested Rome to supply them with king of the proper lineage. Emperor Augustus chose Vonones, the son of Phraates IV, from the Roman stable of provincial Royal hostages. Augustus sent Vonones to the East with a Roman force to ensure his acceptance. Vonones did, in fact, attain control of Parthia for a time, but soon found himself having to fight off rivals. Vonones with his Romanized ways was increasingly unacceptable to many of the Parthian nobles and minor kings. One of these was young King Artabanus of Media. A empire-wide war soon followed. Despite an initial impressive victory, Vonones was ultimately defeated by Artabanus' revolutionary army. After only a few years in power, he was forced to retreat north into Armenia with the remnants of his force. So Vonones found himself a king with an army, but with no country to rule!

Vonones then asked Emperor Augustus to be given Armenia as a consolation prize. While Augustus leaned toward granting his request, Vonones had little support from the Armenian chieftains. Augustus had no choice but to deny Vonones' request, leaving the would-be king and his army stranded in the East (*Antiq* XVIII 2:4). In Parthia, after more years of unsettled leadership, the nobles finally offered King Artabanus of Media the Royal throne in A.D. 10 which he accepted. Artabanus was no friend of Rome, openly asserting that all of Asia Minor belonged rightfully to the Parthians. But, with the formidable Augustus in power, this was a hollow threat.

In A.D. 14, Tiberius succeeded to the throne after the death of Augustus. One of Tiberius' first actions was to address the potential problem of Parthia. Tiberius realized that a strong king in Armenia sympathetic to Rome would be the best way to keep the ambitions of Parthia and Artabanus in check. In A.D. 17, Tiberius sent his adopted son Germanicus (actually his nephew) to the East and gave him broad discretionary powers to deal with the matter.

Surprisingly, Germanicus managed a peaceful settlement and became friends with King Artabanus in the process. Artabanus agreed to accept a man called Artaxias to be the King of Armenia, but only if Rome guaranteed that Vonones, who was still rattling around Armenia with his army, would leave the East and never return. Germanicus agreed, and the pact was made. Vonones–the king without a country–moved on to Cilicia, where he died in A.D. 19.

Armenia in A.D. 35

In A.D. 35, 20 years later, the situation had changed. King Artabanus now saw weakness in the Rome Empire where before there had been only strength. Tiberius was viewed as a man barely clinging to power–an aging and reclusive emperor who trembled in Capri and was fearful of even visiting his own capital city. The near-revolution of Sejanus three years before had confirmed to Artabanus, and many in the ancient world, that the Caesar family was like a large, rotten oak tree–outwardly strong but decayed and rotting on the inside. Only a slight wind would be needed to topple it! Old ambitions were reawakened, and with strong sons clamoring for their own glory, Artabanus decided it was again time to challenge Rome. He had never liked Tiberius anyway, suspecting him of murdering his friend Germanicus.

Opportunity presented itself in late A.D. 34 when King Artaxias of Armenia died. With no clear replacement coming from Rome, Artabanus boldly placed his eldest son Arsaces on the throne and moved Parthian troops into Armenia to ensure Arsaces' acceptance. It was a bold, bloodless takeover of Armenia and a *de facto* act of war against the Roman Empire. Adding insult to injury, King Artabanus was vocal and open about his desire to gain control of the old empire of Alexander the Great. Solidly-Romanized Syria would be conquered according the Artabanus' stated plan, as well as Ionia and the entire Greek peninsula.

In the consulship of Caius Cestius and Marcus Servilius (A.D.35), some Parthian nobles came to Rome without the knowledge of their king Artabanus. Dread of Germanicus had made that prince faithful to the Romans and just to his people, but he subsequently changed this behaviour for insolence towards us and tyranny to his subjects. He was elated by the wars which he had successfully waged against the surrounding nations, while he disdained the aged and, as he thought, unwarlike Tiberius, eagerly coveting Armenia, over which, on the death of Artaxias, he placed Arsaces, his eldest son. He further added insult, and sent envoys to reclaim the treasures left by Vonones in Syria and Cilicia. Then too he insisted on the ancient boundaries of Persia and Macedonia, and intimated, with a vainglorious threat, that he meant to seize on the country possessed by Cyrus and afterwards by Alexander. The chief adviser of the Parthians in sending the secret embassy was Sinnaces, a man of distinguished family and corresponding wealth. Next in influence was Abdus, an eunuch, a class which, far from being despised among barbarians, actually possesses power. These, with some other nobles whom they admitted to their counsels, as there was not a single Arsacid whom they could put on the throne, most of the family having been murdered by Artabanus or being under age, demanded that Phraates, son of king Phraates, should be sent from Rome. "Only a name," they said, "and an authority were wanted; only, in fact, that, with Caesar's consent, a scion of the house of Arsaces should show himself on the banks of the Euphrates."

This suited the wishes of Tiberius. He provided Phraates with what he needed for assuming his father's sovereignty, while he clung to his purpose of regulating foreign affairs by a crafty policy and keeping war at a distance. Artabanus meanwhile, hearing of the treacherous arrangement, was one moment perplexed by apprehension, the next fired with a longing for revenge. With barbarians, indecision is a slave's weakness; prompt action king-like. But now expediency prevailed, and he invited Abdus, under the guise of friendship, to a banquet, and disabled him by a lingering poison; Sinnaces he put off by pretexts and presents, and also by various employments. Phraates meanwhile, on arriving in Syria, where he threw off the Roman fashions to which for so many years he had been accustomed, and adapted himself to Parthian habits, unable to endure the customs of his country, was carried off by an illness. Still, Tiberius did not relinquish his purpose. He chose Tiridates, of the same stock as Artabanus, to be his rival, and the Iberian Mithridates to be the instrument of recovering Armenia, having reconciled him to his brother Pharasmanes, who held the throne of that country. He then intrusted the whole of his eastern policy to Lucius Vitellius. (*Annuls* 6:31,32)

Early in the year A.D. 35 a delegation of Parthian nobles appeared before Tiberius and asked him for the release of Phraates, the son of a former king of Parthia. These wealthy nobles were fearful of the growing ambition of King Artabanus and they did not want war with the Roman Empire; they preferred a controlled revolution and a new Parthian king instead.

Tiberius' Initial Response

Emperor Tiberius did not enjoy war, but faced with Parthia's naked aggression, he knew that he had no choice but to act. The best and easiest solution for Rome would be if Artabanus was deposed through internal revolution. So Tiberius agreed to the plan of the Parthian nobles, pledged Roman support, and sent the Roman hostage Phraates to Syria along with a large military force. Phraates was one of the four sons of Phraates IV–ruler of the Parthian Empire from 37-2 B.C. Phraates, technically a hostage, had been reared in the Roman Royal court for just such an eventuality–just as Vonones had been decades before.

Once Phraates was in the East, however, complications developed. King Artabanus learned of the plot and poisoned two of the main conspirators. Then the would-be King Phraates died within weeks of his arrival in Syria. Was Phraates, too, poisoned by agents of Artabanus? Possibly so, although Tacitus does not suggest it.

Tiberius moved quickly on the news, replacing the late Phraates with the much younger Tiridates III, another Royal Parthian hostage. Tiridates shared a bloodline with Artabanus, as well as being a grandson of Phraates IV. As such, he was a second-generation Roman hostage, whereas Phraates had been first generation.

Tiberius also readied other plans. With the Parthian revolution now compromised, and Artabanus' aggressive plans apparent, Tiberius had to prepare his Roman legions for a possible invasion of Parthia–no small task for a military softened by years of peace.

The Death of Flaccus

Late in A.D. 34 the governor of Syria, Pomponius Flaccus, died in office. There are few details regarding his death. Considering that Syria was on the verge of war, was Flaccus poisoned by agents of Artabanus, as was the case with Phraates? Artabanus' intent could well have been to throw the Roman East into as much disarray as possible as a prelude to invasion.

> Subsequently, on the death of Flaccus Pomponius, propraetor of Syria, a letter from the emperor was read, in which he complained that all the best men who were fit to command armies declined the service...(*Annuls* 6:27)

Tacitus states that Lucius Vitellius was not Tiberius' first choice for the post. More qualified men had turned Tiberius down apparently realizing what a difficult task lay ahead. Certainly, Tiberius took a gamble appointing Vitellius, since Vitellius had only the standard military training of the day and no battlefield experience. But that was a natural consequence of peace. Tiberius' stable of generals had had little opportunity to hone their war skills in a major campaign–Tiberius himself by far was the most experienced and successful general of the lot!

Tiberius had no choice–Vitellius, a man he trusted implicitly, would be sent to the East.

Concerning Armenia itself, Tiberius knew he would have to have the full support of all the minor kingdoms surrounding that territory. To this end, Tiberius arranged for a peace between two warring Royal brothers in Iberia, a country that abutted Armenia on the west. This included the payment of a substantial amount of money. These brothers proved to be the key leaders in the mercenary army that eventually re-took Armenia.

Vitellius in Syria

After the arrival of Tiridates and Vitellius in Antioch in A.D. 35, Tacitus continues with his narrative.

Of the petty chiefs Mithridates was the first to persuade Pharasmanes to aid his enterprise by stratagem and force, and agents of corruption were found who tempted the servants of Arsaces into crime by a quantity of gold. At the same instant the Iberians burst into Armenia with a huge host, and captured the city of Artaxata. Artabanus, on hearing this, made his son Orodes the instrument of vengeance. He gave him the Parthian army and despatched men to hire auxiliaries. Pharasmanes, on the other hand, allied himself with the Albanians, and procured aid from the Sarmatae, whose highest chiefs took bribes from both sides, after the fashion of their countrymen, and engaged themselves in conflicting interests. But the Iberians, who were masters of the various positions, suddenly poured the Sarmatae into Armenia by the Caspian route. Meanwhile those who were coming up to the support of the Parthians were easily kept back, all other approaches having been closed by the enemy except one, between the sea and the mountains on the Albanian frontier which summer rendered difficult, as there the shallows are flooded by the force of the Etesian gales. The south wind in winter rolls back the waves, and when the sea is driven back upon itself, the shallows along the coast, are exposed.

Meantime, while Orodes was without an ally, Pharasmanes, now strengthened by reinforcements, challenged him to battle, taunted him on his refusal, rode up to his camp and harassed his foraging parties. He often hemmed him in with his picquets in the fashion of a blockade, till the Parthians, who were unused to such insults, gathered round the king and demanded battle. Their sole strength was in cavalry; Pharasmanes was also powerful in infantry, for the Iberians and Albanians, inhabiting as they did a densely wooded country, were more inured to hardship and endurance. They claim to have been descended from the Thessalians, at the period when Jason, after the departure of Medea and the children born of her, returned subsequently to the empty palace of Aeetes, and the vacant kingdom of Colchi. They have many traditions connected with his name and with the oracle of Phrixus. No one among them would think of sacrificing a ram, the animal supposed to have conveyed Phrixus, whether it was really a ram or the figure-head of a ship. Both sides having been drawn up in battle array, the Parthian leader expatiated on the empire of the East, and the renown of the Arsacids, in contrast to the despicable Iberian chief with his hireling soldiery. Pharasmanes reminded his people that they had been free from Parthian domination, and that the grander their aims, the more glory they would win if victorious, the more disgrace and peril they would incur if they turned their backs. He pointed, as he spoke, to his own menacing array, and to the Median bands with their golden embroidery; warriors, as he said, on one side, spoil on the other.

Among the Sarmatae the general's voice was not alone to be heard. They encouraged one another not to begin the battle with volleys of arrows; they must, they said, anticipate attack by a hand to hand charge. Then followed every variety of conflict. The Parthians, accustomed to pursue or fly with equal science, deployed their squadrons, and sought scope for their missiles. The Sarmatae, throwing aside their bows which at a shorter range are effective, rushed on with pikes and swords. Sometimes, as in a cavalry-action, there would be alternate advances and retreats, then, again, close fighting, in which, breast to breast, with the clash of arms, they repulsed the foe or were themselves repulsed. And now the Albanians and Iberians seized, and hurled the Parthians from their steeds, and embarrassed their enemy with a double attack, pressed as they were by the cavalry on the heights and by the nearer blows of the infantry. Meanwhile Pharasmanes and Orodes, who, as they cheered on the brave and supported the wavering, were conspicuous to all, and so recognised each other, rushed to the combat with a shout, with javelins, and galloping chargers, Pharasmanes with the greater impetuosity, for he pierced his enemy's helmet at a stroke. But he could not repeat the blow, as he was hurried onwards by his horse, and the wounded man was protected by the bravest of his guards. A rumour that he was slain which was believed by mistake, struck panic into the Parthians, and they yielded the victory. Vitellius had assembled his legions and, by starting a report that he meant to invade Mesopotamia, raised an alarm of war with Rome. Armenia was then abandoned, and the fortunes of Artabanus were overthrown, Vitellius persuading his subjects to forsake a king who was a tyrant in peace, and Artabanus very soon marched with the whole strength of his kingdom, intent on vengeance. The Iberians from their knowledge of the country fought at an advantage. Still Artabanus did not retreat till ruinously unsuccessful in war.

And so Sinnaces, whose enmity to the prince I have already mentioned, drew into actual revolt his father Abdageses and others, who had been secretly in his counsel, and were now after their continued disasters more eager to fight. By degrees, many flocked to him who, having been kept in subjection by fear rather than by goodwill, took courage as soon as they found leaders. Artabanus had now no resources but in some foreigners who guarded his person, men exiled from their own homes, who had no perception of honour, or any scruple about a base act, mere hireling instruments of crime. With these attendants he hastened his flight into the remote country on the borders of Scythia, in the hope of aid, as he was connected by marriage alliances with the Hyrcanians and Carmanians. Meantime the Parthians, he thought, indulgent as they are to an absent prince, though restless under his presence, might turn to a better mind. (*Annuls* 33-37)

In the spring of A.D. 35, Vitellius gave the surrounding kingdoms tacit authorization to invade Armenia as an allied force. The chieftains loved a good fight anyway, so this initial battle against "King" Arsaces and his forces probably occurred only months after Vitellius arrived in Antioch. Using mountain mercenaries was also a brilliant move by Vitellius — though likely suggested by the canny Tiberius. Rome's heavy infantry was invincible in siege situations and on flat plains, but the force lacked skilled horsemen and thus would be vulnerable in the mountainous terrain of Armenia. On the other hand, the forces of Albania, Iberia and the other mercenary kingdoms all boasted a strong cavalry.

The combined barbarian armies of Iberia (where two warring brothers, Mithridates and Pharasmanes, had made peace for the campaign), Albania, Sarmatae, and other kingdoms, poured into Armenia from the northwest to fight. It was a successful action, with the forces of Arsaces taken by surprise. The capital city of Artaxata was captured and a large portion of Armenian nation capitulated. It was a stunning success for Vitellius and was accomplished without any involvement of any Roman troops.

Parthia Strikes Back

This unexpected defeat incensed Artabanus, who was keeping his distance in Seleucia, intentionally giving his son autonomy. King Artabanus had, however, been closely monitoring Vitellius' Roman legions, assuming that they would be the real power in the final assault on Artaxata. With the unexpected defeat of his son by a collection of barbarian horsemen, an angry Artabanus dispatched another of his sons, Orodes, into Armenia to avenge Arsaces–who had probably been killed in the action. But eventually, in a second great battle in the fall of A.D. 35, Parthia was defeated by the allied army once again.

Artabanus Deposed

These defeats triggered a revolution within Parthia and Artabanus was, in fact, deposed after a quarter century in power. Along with his remaining loyalists, Artabanus fled to the remote northern Parthian country of Scythia where he found refuge with his wife's family.

The restoration of Armenia to Roman control and the apparent overthrow of the Parthian King Artabanus were spectacular triumphs for General Lucius Vitellius. He had been governor of Syria for less than a year, yet already his delicate mission was largely accomplished. Mithridates, a petty chief who was the brother of King Pharasmanes of Iberia, now replaced Arsaces as the king of Armenia. The way was now clear for Tiridates III to stake his claim to the throne under the sponsorship of Rome. Through it all, not a single Roman soldier had died in battle. Vitellius knew that Tiberius would be very pleased, indeed.

This dramatic sequence of events marked the end of the northern war "season" in the late fall of A.D. 35.

Reverberations in the Jewish East

At the time Vitellius was directing the army of the mercenaries against Artabanus in Armenia, Herod Antipas battled King

Aretas of Nabotea. In this, Antipas' armies were soundly defeated–destroyed, in fact, according to Josephus. Was Antipas encouraged in his aggression by the unexpected success of Vitellius to the north? Did Antipas possibly have evidence that Aretas, whose country shared a long border with Parthia, was in league with Artabanus against Rome? Whatever the motivation, Antipas' military adventure was just as disastrous as Vitellius' was successful.

Jesus was preaching in the Temple regularly by at least October A.D. 35 during the feast of the Tabernacles. It would make sense that the defeat of Antipas' army occurred before that time. Antipas afterward presumably returned to Galilee to lick his wounds. Jesus, likely fearful of Antipas' return, at the same time decided to leave Galilee and the Decapolis for Judea. The Jewish population had to be very angry over Antipas' military blunder and the deaths of thousands of Jewish soldiers, as well as Antipas' beheading earlier in A.D. 35 of John the Baptist.

With Antipas' star falling with the common people, and Judea itself in mild political disarray, Jesus returned to Bethany, his Judean base, and the Jerusalem Second Temple, in time for the fall Feast of the Tabernacles of A.D. 35.

Wars in A.D. 36

Tacitus continues with the events of A.D. 36, but he unfortunately does not mention either Antipas or Aretas.

> Vitellius, as soon as Artabanus had fled and his people were inclined to have a new king, urged Tiridates to seize the advantage thus offered, and then led the main strength of the legions and the allies to the banks of the Euphrates. While they were sacrificing, the one, after Roman custom, offering a swine, a ram and a bull; the other, a horse which he had duly prepared as a propitiation to the river-god, they were informed by the neighbouring inhabitants that the Euphrates, without any violent rains, was of itself rising to an immense height, and that the white foam was curling into circles like a diadem, an omen of a prosperous passage. Some explained it with more subtlety, of a successful commencement to the enterprise which, however, would not be lasting, on the ground, that though a confident trust might be placed in prognostics given in the

earth or in the heavens, the fluctuating character of rivers exhibited omens which vanished the same moment. A bridge of boats having been constructed and the army having crossed, the first to enter the camp was Ornospades, with several thousand cavalry. Formerly an exile, he had rendered conspicuous aid to Tiberius in the completion of the Dalmatic war, and had for this been rewarded with Roman citizenship. Subsequently, he had again sought the friendship of his king, by whom he had been raised to high honour, and appointed governor of the plains which, being surrounded by the waters of those famous rivers, the Euphrates and Tigris, have received the name of Mesopotamia. Soon afterwards, Sinnaces reinforced the army, and Abdageses, the mainstay of the party, came with the royal treasure and what belonged to the crown. Vitellius thought it enough to have displayed the arms of Rome, and he then bade Tiridates remember his grandfather Phraates, and his foster-father Caesar, and all that was glorious in both of them, while the nobles were to show obedience to their king, and respect for us, each maintaining his honour and his loyalty. This done, he returned with the legions to Syria.

I have related in sequence the events of two summer-campaigns, as a relief to the reader's mind from our miseries at home. Though three years had elapsed since the destruction of Sejanus, neither time, intreaties, nor sated gratification, all which have a soothing effect on others, softened Tiberius, or kept him from punishing doubtful or forgotten offenses as most flagrant and recent crimes. (*Annuls* 6:37-38)

In A.D. 36, with the revolution against Artabanus well underway, Vitellius suggested that Tiridates immediately press his advantage. While the only real cities that Tiridates could claim unequivocally were those founded by the Macedonian Greeks in western Parthia, there was no reason to think that the other cities would not fall into line. The Euphrates River celebration by Tiridates, the Roman legions, and the Parthian nobles who supported Tiridates as king, probably took place in the early summer of A.D. 36 while the river was flooding from mountain runoff. But the celebration turned out to be premature.

Tiridates meanwhile, with the consent of the Parthians, received the submission of Nicephorium, Anthemusias and the other cities which having been founded by Macedonians, claim Greek names, also of the Parthian towns Halus and Artemita. There was a rivalry of joy among the inhabitants who detested Artabanus, bred as he had been among the Scythians, for his cruelty, and hoped to find in Tiridates a kindly spirit from his Roman training...Seleucia now celebrated the arrival of

Tiridates with all the honours paid to princes of old and all which modern times, with a more copious inventiveness, have devised. Reproaches were at the same time heaped on Artabanus, as an Arsacid indeed on his mother's side, but as in all else degenerate. Tiridates gave the government of Seleucia to the people. Soon afterwards, as he was deliberating on what day he should inaugurate his reign, he received letters from Phraates and Hiero, who held two very powerful provinces, imploring a brief delay. It was thought best to wait for men of such commanding influence, and meanwhile Ctesiphon, the seat of empire, was their chosen destination. But as they postponed their coming from day to day, the Surena, in the presence of an approving throng, crowned Tiridates, according to the national usage, with the royal diadem.

And now had he instantly made his way to the heart of the country and to its other tribes, the reluctance of those who wavered, would have been overpowered, and all to a man would have yielded. By besieging a fortress into which Artabanus had conveyed his treasure and his concubines, he gave them time to disown their compact. Phraates and Hiero, with others who had not united in celebrating the day fixed for the coronation, some from fear, some out of jealousy of Abdageses, who then ruled the court and the new king, transferred their allegiance to Artabanus. They found him in Hyrcania, covered with filth and procuring sustenance with his bow. He was at first alarmed under the impression that treachery was intended, but when they pledged their honour that they had come to restore to him his dominion, his spirit revived, and he asked what the sudden change meant. Hiero then spoke insultingly of the boyish years of Tiridates, hinting that the throne was not held by an Arsacid, but that a mere empty name was enjoyed by a feeble creature bred in foreign effeminacy, while the actual power was in the house of Abdageses.

An experienced king, Artabanus knew that men do not necessarily feign hatred because they are false in friendship. He delayed only while he was raising auxiliaries in Scythia, and then pushed on in haste, thus anticipating the plots of enemies and the fickleness of friends. Wishing to attract popular sympathy, he did not even cast off his miserable garb. He stooped to wiles and to entreaties, to anything indeed by which he might allure the wavering and confirm the willing. He was now approaching the neighbourhood of Seleucia with a large force, while Tiridates, dismayed by the rumour. and then by the king's presence in person, was divided in mind, and doubted whether he should march against him or prolong the war by delay. Those who wished for battle with its prompt decision argued that ill-arrayed levies fatigued by a long march could not even in heart be thoroughly united in obedience, traitors and enemies as they had lately been, to the prince whom now again they were supporting. Abdageses, however, advised a retreat into Mesopotamia. There, with a river in their front, they might in the interval summon to their aid the Armenians and Elymaeans and other nations in their rear, and then, reinforced by allies and troops which would be sent by the Roman general, they might try the fortune of war. This advice prevailed, for Abdageses had the chief influence and Tiridates was a coward in the face of danger. But their retreat resembled a flight. The Arabs made a beginning, and then the rest went to their homes or to the camp of Artabanus, till Tiridates returned to Syria with a few followers and thus relieved all from the disgrace of desertion. (*Annuls* 6:41-44)

In the summer of A.D. 36, Tiridates' initial plan was to march through Parthia and secure the loyalties of the nobles and principal men in that country, ending up in the Royal palace at Seleucia amid thousands of adoring and cheering subjects. But Tiridates, lustful for the gold and concubines of Artabanus, decided to first lay siege to a fortress where the exiled king had hidden away both. As the months passed and the pointless siege continued, a few key supporting nobles of Parthia grew suspicious. Was Tiridates purposefully avoiding the more difficult cities and the diplomacy necessary to win them over? Was he that obsessed with gold and women? Many other Parthian nobles also resented Tiridates' for other reasons–chiefly his inexperience and dependence on Rome–and so purposefully delayed their formal affirmation of him as their king. Over the months, this dissatisfaction grew to the point where they abandoned Tiridates entirely and sought out Artabanus in Scythia. The nobles appealed to him to come out of exile and resume his authority over them, even though most of them had repudiated Artabanus earlier. Artabanus, of course, was agreeable and formed a large army quickly.

The youthful Tiridates then became fearful. He had little battlefield experience and was loathe to face the legendary Artabanus in open combat on Parthian soil even when supported by several Roman legions and battle-hardened Armenian and Iberian allies. Tiridates retreated into Syria with his army, foregoing any hopes of wintering in Seleucia. So at the end of the campaign season of A.D. 36, Tiridates had secured the loyalty of only a portion of Parthia, and his claim on the Parthian Empire was threadbare and slipping.

From the standpoint of Vitellius and Rome, it was not the best way to end a year that had started off with such promise. But at least Syria and Armenia were secure, and Artabanus, while the head of an another army and still ostensibly the Parthian king, had abandoned his previous ambition.

On the negative side, while Rome and many Parthian nobles still supported Tiridates III as the legitimate king of Parthia, Tiridates had shown an unkingly reluctance to engage the armies of Artabanus, and his avaricious and lustful nature was showing itself in disturbing ways. Was Tiridates even fit to rule the vast empire?!

On this note of uncertainty, Tacitus concludes his account of Roman military actions in the East in A.D. 36.

Chapter 25   Vitellius to Jerusalem

> But Vitellius came into Judea, and went up to Jerusalem; it was at the time of that festival which is called the Passover (*Antiq* XV 11:4)

Like the Roman historian Tacitus, Jewish historian Flavius Josephus also writes about Syrian President Lucius Vitellius' military adventures of A.D. 35-37. According to Josephus, however, in the midst of helping mastermind revolutions in both Armenia and Parthia, Vitellius managed not one but two trips to Jerusalem–trips that Tacitus' *Annuls* ignores completely.

Tacitus also fails to document the late A.D. 35 battle between Herod Antipas' Galilean army and King Aretas' Naboteans, even though Josephus reports it was a major action. This is somewhat curious because, according to Josephus, Emperor Tiberius ordered Vitellius to invade Nabotea because of it. In fact, Vitellius had two legions in position to do just that when Tiberius died.

Vitellius' First Visit

The year of Lucius Vitellius' first visit to Jerusalem is crucially important. At that Passover, Vitellius removed Joseph Caiaphas as High Priest. This would then mark the last year possible for the crucifixion of Jesus.

> But Vitellius came into Judea, and went up to Jerusalem; it was at the time of that festival which is called the Passover. Vitellius was there magnificently received, and released the inhabitants of Jerusalem from all the taxes upon the fruits that were bought and sold, and gave them leave to have the care of the high priest's vestments, with all their ornaments, and to have them under the custody of the priests in the

temple which power they used to have formerly, although at this time they were laid up in the tower of Antonia, the citadel so called, and that on the occasion following: There was one of the [high] priests, named Hyrcanus; and as there were many of that name, he was the first of them; this man built a tower near the temple, and when he had so done, he generally dwelt in it, and had these vestments with him, because it was lawful for him alone to put them on, and he had them there reposited when he went down into the city, and took his ordinary garments; the same things were continued to be done by his sons, and by their sons after them. But when Herod came to be king, he rebuilt this tower which was very conveniently situated, in a magnificent manner; and because he was a friend to Antonius, he called it by the name of Antonia. And as he found these vestments lying there, he retained them in the same place, as believing, that while he had them in his custody, the people would make no innovations against him. The like to what Herod did was done by his son Archelaus, who was made king after him; after whom the Romans, when they entered on the government, took possession of these vestments of the high priest, and had them reposited in a stone-chamber, under the seal of the priests, and of the keepers of the temple, the captain of the guard lighting a lamp there every day; and seven days before a festival they were delivered to them by the captain of the guard, when the high priest having purified them, and made use of them, laid them up again in the same chamber where they had been laid up before, and this the very next day after the feast was over. This was the practice at the three yearly festivals, and on the fast day; but Vitellius put those garments into our own power, as in the days of our forefathers, and ordered the captain of the guard not to trouble himself to inquire where they were laid, or when they were to be used; and this he did as an act of kindness, to oblige the nation to him. Besides which, he also deprived Joseph, who was also called Caiaphas, of the high priesthood, and appointed Jonathan the son of Ananus, the former high priest, to succeed him. After which, he took his journey back to Antioch. (*Antiq* XVIII 4:3)

These vestments king Herod kept in that place; and after his death they were under the power of the Romans, until the time of Tiberius Caesar; under whose reign Vitellius, the president of Syria, when he once came to Jerusalem, and had been most magnificently received by the multitude, he had a mind to make them some requital for the kindness they had shewn him; so, upon their petition to have those holy vestments in their own power, he wrote about them to Tiberius Caesar, who granted his request: and this their power over the sacerdotal vestments continued with the Jews till the death of king Agrippa; (*Antiq* XV 11:4)

At first read, Josephus' narration on Vitellius' visit to Jerusalem suggests that it came early in his first year as Syrian president in A.D. 35. This would mean that the Passover of A.D. 35 would be the Passover when Jesus was crucified. But is this a correct interpretation of the passage?

The Parthian Threat

At this point, a review of the significant events leading up to Vitellius' appointment as president of Syria is in order. In late in A.D. 34, King Artabanus of Parthia bloodlessly took over Armenia by placing his own son on the throne as king. At that time, Artabanus was also openly threatening war against Rome. Many Parthian nobles did want war and instead plotted revolution against Artabanus. To that end, they enlisted the support of Roman Emperor Tiberius. Tiberius agreed to release a hostage to serve as a replacement king, and supply a supporting military force. Phraates, the son of former Parthian king, was selected, and quickly was dispatched to Syria.

But Phraates died shortly after arriving. Worse, Syrian President Flaccus unexpectedly died about that same time. Tiberius then chose Parthian Royal Tiridates, who was a generation younger than Phraates, to take his place. Lucius Vitellius was selected as President of Syria almost by default. So in the early months of A.D. 35, Vitellius and Tiridates likely sailed together to Syria with a large force of Roman soldiers in order retake Armenia and effect a revolution in Parthia.

For all these important events that occurred in the first part of A.D. 35, how likely is it that Vitellius had time for a side trip to Jerusalem to attend the Passover which occurred late in March? And even if Vitellius did have the time, with Parthia threatening war, why would he bother?

Chronology of Josephus

But, through story placement, Josephus does suggest that Vitellius visited Jerusalem first before moving on to Antioch. But

Josephus himself later writes that, at the end of his first visit to Jerusalem, Vitellius "..took his journey back to Antioch" (*Antiq* XVIII 4:3). This implies that Vitellius had arrived at Antioch first before going to Jerusalem–an important distinction. Of course, Antioch could have been a regularly scheduled stop for any vessel sailing from Rhodes to Caesarea.

But there are other examples of narratives within Book XVIII of *Antiquities* that are definitely out of time sequence. Pilate's removal as prefect which occurred in late A.D. 36 at the very earliest, was placed before Vitellius' first visit to Jerusalem which happened, as shall be seen, in the spring of A.D. 36 at the very latest. Also, the banishment of 4,000 Egyptians and Jews from Rome to Sardinia occurred in A.D. 19, according to Tacitus (*Annuls* 2:85). In Josephus, the same story is placed after Jesus' final Passover which has been determined to be either A.D. 35 or A.D. 36 (*Antiq* XVIII 3:5)–a significant difference.

So relying on relative placement within Josephus for the dating of events is not foolproof. This is especially true for Book XVIII of *Antiquities* in which Josephus apparently did not rely on any single source.

Vitellius and the Passover of A.D. 36

For these reasons, it is most likely that Vitellius' first visit to Jerusalem was during the Passover of A.D. 36, after he had completed a year's successful military action in Armenia. This is not just based on logistical considerations, although that is a powerful stand-alone argument. Much circumstantial evidence supports the hypothesis as well.

During the first visit, Josephus portrays Vitellius as being in a good mood. As the Syrian president, he goes out of his way to please the Jewish people and demonstrate Roman magnanimity. Vitellius reduces taxes for the Jews and releases to the High Priest the holy Temple vestments, previously kept in a special room in the tower of Antonia under Roman lock and key. The Jews responded favorably, and Vitellius became a very popular figure.

But would Vitellius have been in a good mood in the spring of A.D. 35 when Parthia was an unknown quantity and Armenia was still under the control of Arsaces? At that time, the untested Tiridates had not yet ventured into Parthia in an attempt to gain the support of the nobles. Remember, too, that Vitellius knew he possibly might have to lead four Roman legions in an invasion of Parthia. By any measure, the spring of A.D. 35 was no time for a public relations trip to Jerusalem!

But moving one year ahead to the spring of A.D. 36, the situation was quite different. The Parthian army in Armenia had been defeated and Parthia itself was in a state of revolt. Tiridates was organizing the dissident elements within Parthia and there was every reason to think that Tiridates' complete control of Parthia was just a matter of months away. Armenia was back in Roman hands and Syria and the eastern Roman Empire were in a vastly more secure position. So if the Passover of A.D. 36 marked the first visit of Vitellius' to Jerusalem, Josephus' assertion that Vitellius was in an expansive and generous mood fits in well with what Tacitus describes.

Also to be noted is that, in the interval from the spring of A.D. 35 to A.D. 36, according to our time line Herod Antipas had his fateful battle with King Aretas IV, resulting in devastation for his Galilean army. If the Jerusalem Jews feared that King Aretas would aggressively move into Judea, they would have been especially happy to see Vitellius and his personal guard at the Passover festival in Jerusalem months later.

The Request of Tiberius

In the spring of A.D. 36, the Roman Empire in the East had stabilized considerably. Armenia was back under Roman control and King Artabanus of Parthia had ostensibly been deposed. But still it was odd that Vitellius would leave his legions in Syria and observe a religious festival in a country of marginal significance more than 100 miles to the south. Why did Vitellius do it? As with so many other questions, the answer is found in Josephus.

> So they raised armies on both sides, and prepared for war, and sent their generals to fight instead of themselves; and when they had joined battle, all Herod's army was destroyed by the treachery of some fugitives, who, though they were of the tetrarchy of Philip, joined with Aretas's army.. So Herod wrote about these affairs to Tiberius, who being very angry at the attempt made by Aretas, wrote to Vitellius to make war upon him, and either to take him alive, and bring him to him in bonds, or to kill him, and send him his head. This was the charge that Tiberius gave to the president of Syria. (*Antiq* XVIII 5:1)

Angered by the defeat that Herod Antipas had suffered at the hands of King Aretas of Nabotea, Tiberius wrote a letter to Vitellius and instructed him in no uncertain terms to engage and eliminate the Arab king. Whatever Tiberius' reasoning was, Vitellius knew that he dare not delay in carrying out the emperor's wishes. It can be postulated that Vitellius decided to personally travel to the Jewish lands as soon as it was practical in order to assess the situation. The spring of A.D. 36 presented Vitellius with just that opportunity.

Vitellius probably received the directive from Tiberius concerning Aretas in late A.D. 35, after Vitellius' own defeat of Orodes and with the Parthian revolt against Artabanus well underway. Vitellius, with Syria secure, would have felt safe in leaving Antioch in order to visit Jerusalem. He likely traveled with a token force of Roman soldiers as befitted his position—perhaps no more than a few centuries of men (a century is 10 tent groups; a tent group is composed of eight men). Vitellius knew that Pilate was well-supplied with auxiliary forces should they be needed.

In A.D. 36, Vitellius' intention in Judea was not war, but reconnaissance, assessment—and politics. Given the unstable situation with both Parthia and Nabotea, and the recent unexplained deaths of Phraates, Flaccus, and others, Vitellius likely kept his visit a secret as long as possible. The High Priesthood of the Second Temple might have been given only a few days notice of the visit by Judean prefect Pontius Pilate.

While in Jerusalem, Vitellius could meet with the generals he would eventually be commanding in the war against Nabotea. Preliminary plans for invasion could be made. Vitellius and his officers could also get a first-hand feel for the lay of the land and the temperament of the people.

To this end, Vitellius would have made sure that Herod Antipas would be in Jerusalem for the Passover of A.D. 36 as well—which Antipas was according to the Gospel of Luke. During the Passover, Vitellius could meet with Antipas and his generals and discuss strategic options and unemotionally dissect the reason for Antipas' recent defeat. Also, Pontius Pilate was a key man in the East, and Vitellius had not yet met with Pilate since his appointment.

Herod Antipas bore no great affection for Pontius Pilate and Pilate had given no aid to Antipas in Antipas' recent battle with Aretas. Did Antipas cite Pilate's lack of support as a factor in his defeat when he wrote to Tiberius informing him of the debacle? Over the years, there were continuing questions about Pilate's fitness to serve as prefect. In the same letter where Tiberius commanded Vitellius to avenge Antipas' defeat, Tiberius, in his anger, might have given blanket authority to Vitellius to remove Pilate for cause if circumstances warranted it.

Vitellius in Jerusalem

According to Josephus, Vitellius was treated "magnificently" in Jerusalem during the Passover of A.D. 36. This was likely not just because it was his due as the most powerful man in the Roman East. Vitellius' official host would have been Pontius Pilate, who had to have known that his own standing with Tiberius was in question. Perhaps Pilate suspected that his job rested on impressing Vitellius. For this reason, Pilate would have spared nothing in showing Vitellius a good time.

Originally, Herod Antipas had probably planned on spending the Passover of A.D. 36 quietly in his palace in Tiberias licking his wounds after his disastrous military defeat. On the command of Vitellius, however, Antipas was summoned to Jerusalem. In Jerusalem, Antipas, too, would have gone out of his way to make Vitellius' visit a pleasant and memorable one. After all, Vitellius was to be his avenging Angel against King Aretas.

Herodias' brother Aristobulos probably also accompanied Vitellius to Jerusalem. He had served well under Pomponius Flaccus, and, given the inexperience of Vitellius, Aristobulos would have been a trusted aide. Since he had Royal Jewish Asamonean blood and was the nephew of Galilean Tetrarch Herod Antipas, Aristobulos was probably the "point man" in Antioch concerning Jewish affairs and would have held great power. In fact, it may have been Aristobulos himself who boldly suggested that Vitellius attend the Passover in A.D. 36, confident that Artabanus was contained and knowing the importance the Jews placed on the festival. It also might have been Aristobulos who suggested to Vitellius certain conciliatory actions towards the Jews, such as releasing the holy vestments back to the control of the priesthood.

Vitellius and Caiaphas

If Vitellius removed Caiaphas as High Priest during the Passover of A.D. 36, does that mean Jesus had to be crucified during the Passover of A.D. 35? Not necessarily–and for the following reasons.

The High Priest position of the Second Temple had a great many duties during the celebration of the Passover. In fact, the Passover was the focal point of the entire preceding year. It would be unlikely that that Vitellius would have removed Caiaphas just before the start of this great celebration or even during it, unless the circumstances were extraordinary. On the advice of Pilate–and perhaps Aristobulos, Antipas, and even Ananus–Vitellius would have allowed Caiaphas to fulfill his duties during the Passover celebration itself. Most likely, Vitellius did not reveal his decision to remove Caiaphas until the very end of the Passover week and more probably just before he departed Jerusalem to return to Syria.

Remember, too, that it was early in the Passover week of A.D. 36 that Jesus was arrested, tried, and executed–in fact all of those events taking place on the second day of the feast of the Unleavened Bread. It can be postulated that Vitellius had not yet arrived. Under that scenario, Caiaphas could have received the shocking news of his dismissal only days after Jesus had been crucified.

Second trip to Jerusalem

Vitellius' second visit to Jerusalem was unmistakably during the Passover of A.D. 37, since Emperor Tiberius had died shortly before (March 17th, A.D. 37). Josephus opens the narrative in Book XVIII of *Antiquities* with Vitellius taking two legions out of Syria with the intent of avenging the recent defeat of Herod Antipas' Galilean army.

> So Vitellius prepared to make war with Aretas, having with him two legions of armed men; he also took with him all those of light armature, and of the horsemen which belonged to them, and were drawn out of those kingdoms which were under the Romans, and made haste for Petra, and came to Ptolemais. But as he was marching very busily, and leading his army through Judea, the principal men met him, and desired that he would not thus march through their land; for that the laws of their country would not permit them to overlook those images which were brought into it, of which there were a great many in their ensigns; so he was persuaded by what they said, and changed that resolution of his which he had before taken in this matter. Whereupon he ordered the army to march along the great plain, while he himself, with Herod the tetrarch and his friends, went up to Jerusalem to offer sacrifice to God, an ancient festival of the Jews being then just approaching; and when he had been there, and been honorably entertained by the multitude of the Jews, he made a stay there for three days, within which time he deprived Jonathan of the high priesthood, and gave it to his brother Theophilus. But when on the fourth day letters came to him which informed him of the death of Tiberius, he obliged the multitude to take an oath of fidelity to Caius; he also recalled his army, and made them every one go home, and take their winter quarters there, since, upon the devolution of the empire upon Caius, he had not the like authority of making this war which he had before. It was also reported, that when Aretas heard of the coming of Vitellius to fight him, he said, upon his consulting the diviners, that it was impossible that this army of Vitellius's could enter Petra; for that one of the rulers would die, either he that gave orders for the war, or he that was marching at the other's desire, in order to be subservient to his will, or else he against whom this army is prepared. So Vitellius truly retired to Antioch; (*Antiq* XVIII 5:3)

When Vitellius learned about the death of Tiberius and received no orders from the new Emperor Caius to initiate the war of revenge against Aretas, he needed no more encouragement. Vitellius promptly and with great relief abandoned the planned invasion.

The above narrative has many interesting aspects. It is a testament to Tiberius' wrath that Vitellius would even have considered leaving Syria with two full Roman legions–half the normal Antioch contingent–for the purpose of invading Nabotea. Tacitus states that Tiridates' claim to the throne of Parthia at that time was shaky at best. While outwardly deposed and on the run, former King Artabanus still had an active and growing army in Parthia and the renewed support of many important nobles.

In fact, in early A.D. 37 the former Roman hostage Tiridates had become a real question mark. Did Tiridates truly have the proper mettle to rule an empire? The young king seemed to avoid battle as he traveled through Parthia garnering the support of whatever nobles he could during the summer of A.D. 36. During that marginally successful campaign, Tiridates seemed more concerned with the pursuit of gold and a harem of women than with solidifying his position as the Parthian monarch. Almost shamefully, Tiridates decided to spent the winter in Syria instead of pursuing his original plan of taking Seleucia and wintering there.

For the usually cautious Vitellius, to move two Roman legions out of Syria during that crucial time can only mean one thing: he had unequivocal orders from Tiberius to do so. Evidence suggests that Vitellius himself did not think that the move was wise, for, as Josephus documents, when Tiberius died, and the new Emperor Caius gave no order for continuance, Vitellius quickly abandoned the Nabotean campaign. To Herod Antipas, Vitellius' decision had to be a crushing disappointment.

Return to the New Testament

That Vitellius removed Caiaphas during the same Passover at which Jesus was crucified is supported by the New Testament. It is well established that Caiaphas was the High Priest when Jesus was crucified. Mark, Matthew, and John all document that fact. But, interestingly, the Book of Luke suggests that months after the crucifixion, Joseph Caiaphas was not the High Priest any longer.

In the weeks after the crucifixion of Jesus, most of his Disciples remained in Jerusalem, praying for Jesus' return. Barring that, the Disciples were at least hoping to get some sort of sign from Jesus giving them direction on what to do next. These Disciples spent a lot of time in the Second Temple, probably on Solomon's portico which was located on the eastern cloisters of the Temple. Just across from the portico were the massive bronze gates and major entrance to the walled-off inner courtyards. Jesus liked to hold forth there to his Disciples and other gathered followers and interested pilgrims. After the crucifixion, the Disciples would also congregate and pray outside of Jerusalem on the Mount of Olives, a site where Jesus had promised to return with his Angels.

The Pentecost is a yearly celebration that occurs fifty days after the Passover. In A.D. 36, after the crucifixion of Jesus, it was during the day of the Pentecost that the miracle of the "tongues" occurred. The Holy Spirit entered into the disciples, and caused them to preach with inspiration and in many different languages. The story of this miracle takes up the entire second chapter of Acts of the Apostles.

In the third chapter of Acts, a story is told involving Jesus' Disciples John and Peter, both "unlearned and ignorant men" (Acts 4:13). They were entering the Second Temple through the gate that was named "Beautiful" when they saw a cripple begging for alms. Peter laid hands on the man and healed his affliction. The Temple priests observed the apparent miracle and were enraged. The two Disciples were arrested and held overnight as prisoners, probably in the in tower of Antonia. The next day, both John and Peter were questioned by members of the Jerusalem Sanhedrin.

$^{4:1}$And as they spake unto the people, the priests and the captain of the temple and the Sadducees came upon them, $^{4:2}$being sore troubled because they taught the people, and proclaimed in Jesus the resurrection from the dead. $^{4:3}$And they laid hands on them, and put them in ward unto the morrow: for it was now eventide. $^{4:4}$But many of them that heard the word believed; and the number of the men came to be about five thousand. $^{4:5}$And it came to pass on the morrow, that their rulers and elders and scribes were gathered together in Jerusalem; $^{4:6}$and Annas the high priest *was there*, and Caiaphas, and John, and Alexander, and as many as were of the kindred of the high priest. (Acts)

Note that Joseph Caiaphas is mentioned in this passage, but he is not referred to as the High Priest. Instead, the High Priest is called Annas which is a translational variant of Ananus, Caiaphas' father-in-law. However, if the "John" that is mentioned is the succeeding High Priest to Caiaphas, Jonathan, then that presents a problem.

The incident of Peter and John occurred only months after Jesus' crucifixion which likely took place during the Passover of A.D. 36. Caiaphas was the High Priest when Jesus was crucified, but only days later, he was removed by Syrian President Lucius Vitellius. Months later, and after the Pentecost, there was no reason to refer to Caiaphas as High Priest.

Speculating further, and taking liberties with Josephus, until a replacement could be decided upon, Ananus could have been temporarily serving in that capacity. Caiaphas' removal by Vitellius was certainly a surprise. Ananus, the Jewish elder and a leader of the High Priesthood, was unprepared to recommend a replacement immediately. Vitellius, understanding this, perhaps left it up to Ananus to decide who should take Caiaphas' place, and then left for Antioch with his staff and soldiers.

Ananus eventually appointed his own son Jonathan to the position, but only many weeks later. During the interim, Ananus unofficially assumed the High Priest's position which he had first held 30 years before and was serving in that capacity when Peter was arrested.

Year of the Passover

It is now concluded that Jesus died during the Passover year of A.D. 36. Returning to an earlier chapter, this adds another dimension regarding the birth year of Jesus. Recall that relying heavily on comet "data" and the Book of Matthew, it was determined that Jesus was likely born born in the spring of either 12 B.C. or 11 B.C.

Using that birth year range, in A.D. 36 Jesus would have been either 47 or 48 years old. This fits in well with the clue in the Book of John (Jn 8:57). There, at the Feast of the Tabernacles which was six months before his final Passover, Jesus was admonished for preaching with authority though being "not yet fifty."

A crucifixion year of A.D. 36 would also provide for an eight-year Ministry which is consistent with the Book of John's documented three-year Ministry and the assertion by John himself that there was much more substance to Jesus' Ministry than he wrote about.

> [21:24]This is the disciple that beareth witness of these things, and wrote these things: and we know that his witness is true. [21:25]And there are also many other things which Jesus did, the which if they should be written every one, I suppose that even the world itself would not contain the books that should be written. (Jn)

With the chronology of Christian events up to Jesus' crucifixion complete, many of Jesus' later actions can be placed in their proper context and with a greater understanding of them. John the Baptist was executed by Herod Antipas in the winter of early A.D. 35 in Perea which adjoins Judea. Jesus then became fearful for his own life, and retreated north out of Judea and beyond the reach of Antipas. For many months, Jesus' Ministry was purposefully based in the territories controlled by the Roman governor of Syria and not by Antipas. The Passover of A.D. 35 was celebrated in semi-seclusion by Jesus in the hills surrounding eastern shores of Lake Gennesareth–in Decapolis territory.

With Antipas' defeat by the Naboteans in the early fall of A.D. 35, political chaos ensued. This was especially the case in Jerusalem and Judea–being so close to the battlefield in northern Nabotea. Antipas returned to Galilee cowed and beaten. Jesus, thinking of his cousin John the Baptist, might have thought it best to avoid Antipas completely and leave the northern Jewish lands. With post-battle confusion reigning in Judea, Jesus felt it safe to return to Jerusalem and the Second Temple where he did, after all, have his supporters.

Jesus preached in and around Jerusalem in the six months leading up to the Passover of A.D. 36, with no apparent fears from the High Priesthood. Had a truce of sorts been brokered between Jesus and Caiaphas by a powerful "secret" disciple–Nicodemus, perhaps?

In late A.D. 35, Emperor Tiberius ordered the Syrian President Vitellius to move against King Aretas of Nabotea in revenge for Antipas' defeat. Vitellius then reluctantly arranged to visit Jerusalem for the Passover of A.D. 36 in order to assess the situation and confer with Pilate and Antipas. The High Priest Joseph Caiaphas learned of Vitellius' visit probably only a few days before his arrival in Jerusalem. To Caiaphas, Vitellius was an unknown quantity–and potentially dangerous.

Chapter 26   Interlude: The Summit Meeting

> So Herod wrote about these affairs to Tiberius, who being very angry at
> the attempt made by Aretas, wrote to Vitellius to make war upon him,
> and either to take him alive, and bring him to him in bonds, or to kill
> him, and send him his head. This was the charge that Tiberius gave to
> the president of Syria. (*Antiq* XVIII 5:1)

The Passover of A.D. 36 would have been significant even if
Jesus had managed to avoid arrest and escape crucifixion. There
were two new wars in the Roman East. In one of them, a major
battle had been fought only six months ago and less than 30
miles away from Jerusalem — and the Jews had lost. The other
was 120 miles away in Armenia. Adding to the uncertainty was
that the execution of John the Baptist. It happened only a year
previously was still fresh in the minds of the Jews.

Partially to quell these fears, the most powerful official in the
eastern empire, General Lucius Vitellius, planned to   visit
Jerusalem for the Passover. Vitellius was barely a year into his
tenure as Syrian president, and now he found himself having to
plan and manage a second war. In Judea, Vitellius wanted to
personally assess the situation in order to plan a counterstrike
against King Aretas of Nabotea. For that reason, the largest and
most holy city of the Jewish nation was about to become host to a
summit meeting involving General Lucius Vitellius, Judean
Prefect Pontius Pilate, Galilean Tetrarch Herod Antipas, and all
of their top generals.

What might have been the thoughts and concerns of these
important people and others as the Passover approached?

Pontius Pilate

Pontius Pilate was philosophical on the eve of the Passover of A.D. 36 over the impending arrival of General Lucius Vitellius. Emperor Tiberius was not happy that Antipas' army had been destroyed and held him responsible.

Tiberius had written to Pilate and expressed his disappointment over the way he had handled the situation. Tiberius stated that Pilate as the senior Roman military official in the area should have anticipated problems and mediated a peace between the feuding kings.

Pilate had to admit that Tiberius was correct. The prefect now regretted his arrogance in the matter, though he did enjoy Antipas' defeat. King Herod Antipas indeed!

But if Tiberius wanted to replace him, it would have been done already. Or was that to be the purpose of Vitellius' visit? Was Pilate's replacement already sailing with Vitellius from Ptolemais? But whatever the future might bring, Pilate had no option now but to treat Vitellius as Royalty and hope for the best. Already the tower of Phasaelus had been readied for the governor and his staff, and preparations for the daily feasts and a variety of entertainments and excursions were well under way.

Pilate had learned recently that Herod Antipas, too, was coming to Jerusalem to celebrate the Passover–and so soon after his defeat. What had the man written to Tiberius about him?! Probably nothing good. Still, Pilate was going to put Antipas and his entourage up in the tower of Mariamne for the Passover. The luxurious palace apartment called Caesareum would be used as a meeting place for all involved to discuss the important eastern issues of the Roman Empire.

Herod Antipas

Herod Antipas had every reason to be sullen and angry about the upcoming Passover of A.D. 36, but instead he looked forward to it. In Jerusalem, Antipas would finally meet with Vitellius and plan for revenge against Aretas. After his humiliating defeat last fall, Antipas had retreated north to the cool lakeside city of Tiberias in shame and bitterness — falling into a deep depression. In his darkest moments, Antipas had written angry letters to Tiberius blaming the defeat of his army on everything from the stars to mutiny to betrayal by Pilate–missives which Antipas now regretted. But Tiberius proved to be a great and understanding friend. Ignoring the issue of Antipas' competence, Tiberius promised to send Vitellius to avenge his defeat.

With that unexpectedly good news, Antipas' depression lifted. Within two weeks of the receipt of the Royal communication, Antipas received a letter from Vitellius himself who wrote that he was coming to Jerusalem for the Passover celebration. Vitellius wanted Antipas there, and was looking forward to renewing an old friendship. Vitellius told Antipas to bring his generals as well. Antipas had not planned on attending the Passover in Jerusalem, but now he would–and with pleasure.

Herodias

Herodias was looking forward to the trip and she made sure that Antipas and the entourage arrived early for the celebration. She was excited that Pilate had promised them the Mariamne tower to stay in, the most sumptuous of the three palace towers. Herodias had lost a bit of her pride and arrogance in her four years in the East. She knew that she had been the root cause of Antipas' disastrous recent military adventure. Antipas was in his sixties now, and at an age when a man should be comfortable and enjoying life. Instead, Antipas was rattling his saber and going to war like a man 30 years younger. While Antipas had talked about defending her honor, Herodias knew that Antipas wanted to prove himself to Tiberius and all of Rome. That his brother Philip's kingdom had not been given to him had hurt Antipas greatly.

Herodias was especially anxious to see her cousin Cypros. She would be coming to Jerusalem from Alexandria with her three children, and Herodias had promised to help her settle in. Cypros had been saddled with her obnoxious brother, Agrippa, for too long and it was high time to be free of him. Agrippa was going off to Capri on borrowed money in hopes of gaining Tiberius' good graces — the fool.

Her daughter Salome would come to Jerusalem as well. Still alone after the death of Herod Philip, Salome expressed excitement at seeing Cypros and helping to take care of her children. If Jerusalem didn't work out for her cousin, Cypros would always be welcome in Galilee.

Lucius Vitellius

Lucius Vitellius, as he rested in Caesarea before leaving for Jerusalem with his 80-man escort, considered what he could expect. Nabotea might well have to be invaded, and Vitellius did not want to be unprepared if that were the case. Nabotea was a dry, rocky, and mountainous country that did not play into the strengths of the Roman army. Auxiliaries with horsemen would have to secured and paid for.

The Jewish people, too, were a peculiar lot and prone to sudden sedition. Possibly, through negotiation the war could be averted entirely–although that was not probable. Tiberius wanted Aretas' head–a tough order to achieve peacefully.

According to Tiberius, Antipas had also accused Pilate of borderline treason. Tiberius expressed doubt to Vitellius about that accusation, but he wanted Vitellius to investigate the charge and take whatever action he deemed appropriate. Vitellius knew that many complaints against Pilate were on record in Rome but Tiberius tended to downplay their significance. Tiberius would say in defense of Pilate that the Jewish East was a difficult region to administer even in the best of times.

To that ends, Vitellius had with him a grandson of Herod the Great, Aristobulos. He had several ideas about how Vitellius could ingratiate himself with the Jewish people. Aristobulos was also the nephew of Herod Antipas, who would also be there.

Ananus

The High Priest Simon Ananus was disquieted over his son-in-law's zeal in capturing Jesus. Ananus knew that most of these country prophets usually self-destructed in one way or another — only rarely did the Sanhedrin have to intervene. Ananus had seen dozens come and go over the past 40 years. Eventually, the frauds were unmasked and either run off by the people they took advantage of or fade into obscurity as the people grow tired of them. In being aggressive against these "prophets" the Sanhedrin could only do itself harm.

Ananus had bluntly told Caiaphas as much on several occasions, but his son-in-law was not convinced. This, in itself, was a concern to Ananus. Perhaps it was time to think about a replacement. Caiaphas had been High Priest for over 10 years now and was clearly showing signs of strain.

Vitellius' upcoming visit to Jerusalem was another matter entirely and a complete surprise to Ananus. What secret orders did Vitellius have from Tiberius? Ananus knew that it was imperative that he meet early with the powerful Roman and determine Vitellius' true intentions. Ananus had already made arrangements with the Temple treasurer to have ready a large quantity of gold for the new president of Syria. Bribery was traditionally the best way to guarantee Roman support.

Joseph Caiaphas

Joseph Caiaphas was nervous and fearful as the Passover of A.D. 36 approached. Caiaphas served at the pleasure of Emperor Tiberius, General Lucius Vitellius, and, to a lesser degree, Pontius Pilate. That both Vitellius and Pilate were in Jerusalem for the Passover meant that any possible threat of violence had to be eliminated quickly and definitively.

Caiaphas had evidence this year that the Galilean Jesus and his followers–all part of John the Baptist's group–were massing and planning some sort of action. Only days before, Jesus had performed one of his "miracles" in the nearby town of Bethany.

He had brought a man back from the dead–one who had been entombed for three days, according to Caiaphas' spies. Not surprisingly, the resurrected man was a member of the Galilean's inner circle. Caiaphas would have been amused if the intent of the miracle were not so subversive. According to these same spies, thousands around Bethany were massing and proclaiming Jesus to be the Messiah.

Caiaphas now realized that he had been a fool to let the man preach at the Temple for so long. He thought he had been extending an olive branch to a disenfranchised group by doing so, but now their intent was clear.

And so with Vitellius on the way Caiaphas decided put out substantial reward money to anyone who could lead him to the Nazarene. There was simply no point in putting up with Jesus any longer – despite his Sanhedrin defenders.

Jesus of Nazareth

Jesus had been enjoying an unstated truce with the High Priesthood for months. His powerful supporters within the Sanhedrin had told him that he would be allowed to preach in the Temple if he did not inflame the people–the memory of John the Baptist was still fresh in their minds, after all. And Jesus was following the rules in that regard. But outside of Jerusalem, he had been taking chances. Jesus realized now that that might not have been wise.

First, there was the miracle with Lazarus. Then, the next day, Jesus fulfilled Old Testament prophecy by riding on the back of a young colt through the streets of Bethany–to the cheers of the small but enthusiastic crowd. Jesus expected the High Priesthood not to care as Bethany was well outside of Jerusalem, but only days later came the warrant for his arrest from Caiaphas.

It was an unexpected and confusing development. But soon, Jesus learned the real reason behind it. Syrian President Lucius Vitellius was on his way to Jerusalem for the Passover. Vitellius would be the highest ranking Roman to visit Jerusalem more than 50 years. Jesus knew that Caiaphas was not taking any chances–whatever truce that had been in effect was now abrogated. Jesus was a marked man if he stayed in Judea.

Was it time to again retreat to the Decapolis as he did last year upon the news of John's execution?

Jesus knew that Caiaphas and Ananus owed their positions to Rome. They would be ruthless in putting down any hint of sedition—hence the preemptive call for Jesus' arrest. With the impending arrival of Vitellius, Jesus knew a deadly and dark cloud was forming over him. The longer he remained in Jerusalem, the less chance he had of leaving the city alive!

This marks the end of **Year of the Passover**, *but the investigation continues in* **Fires of Rome** *with a detailed look at the Passover of A.D. 36, the subsequent journeys and adventures of the Apostles, the trials of Paul, Nero's persecution of the Christians, and the disastrous Jewish revolt of A.D. 66. Many of the biographies started in* **Year of the Passover** *will be brought to their conclusions.*

Author John Hagan is a medical physician, with a special interest in ancient history. Non-fiction works include *Year of the Passover, Fires of Rome,* and *The Essene Diet.*

Bibliography

The New Testament; American Standard Version 1901

The Works of Flavius Josephus; translated by William Whiston 1737

The Complete Works of Tacitus; translated by Alfred John Church and William Jackson Brodribb 1942

The Works of Philo Judaeus; translated by C.D. Yonge 1854

Eusebius: The History of the Church; translated by G.A. Williamson Penguin Classics 1965

Cassius Dio: History of Rome; Loeb Classical Library, 9 volumes, Greek texts and facing English translation: Harvard University Press, 1914-1927. Translation by Earnest Cary.

Suetonius: The Lives of the Twelve Caesars; translated by J. C. Rolfe 1914

Pliny the Elder: The Natural History; translation by John Bostock and H. T. Riley 1855

Index

www.ingramcontent.com/pod-product-compliance
Lightning Source LLC
Chambersburg PA
CBHW031228090426
42742CB00007B/121